MW00812691

"In this meticulously researched work of historical reimagining, Jefferson offers a Southern California leisure world of African American place-makers and community builders during the Jim Crow era. Seaside recreation, black-owned businesses, and a refusal to give up. What's here is new and important."
—Krista Comer, professor of English at Rice University and author of *Surfer Girls in the New World Order*

"From Bruce Beach in Manhattan Beach to Eureka Villa in the San Clarita Valley, Jefferson's book unearths a fascinating and forgotten—if not willfully obscured—history of African American leisure sites in the Golden State. This remarkable study broadens our understanding of black life, leisure, and struggles for integration in early twentieth century California, underlines the complex relationship between the promise of the American West and the realities of Jim Crow, and emphasizes the need to protect more diverse African American sites that have been heretofore underappreciated."
—Brent Leggs, executive director of the African American Cultural Heritage Action Fund, National Trust for Historic Preservation

"Jefferson's pathbreaking study places African American leisure at the heart of Los Angeles history, African American, urban, and suburban history, and the histories of recreation and Civil Rights, and reclaims their places of leisure, demonstrating why they matter to us all."
—Lawrence Culver, author of *The Frontier of Leisure: Southern California and the Shaping of Modern America*

"Alison Jefferson interrogates five sites of memory in Southern California to illuminate how African Americans challenged established racial hierarchies while occupying public spaces and sites of recreation. Jefferson's path-breaking scholarship reclaims these frontiers of leisure and reanimates their contested, hidden histories, locating Black Angelenos in their own pieces of the California Dream. Jefferson's account reveals how de facto Jim Crow operated openly in California—contrary to the Golden State's popular reputation as an Edenic place of equal opportunity and access."
—Anthea M. Hartig, director of the National Museum of American History

"Alison Jefferson's important and timely work creatively expands our understanding of the possibilities and limits of the California dream for Black Americans. Jefferson demonstrates how the desire and the struggle to enjoy the leisure opportunities of the region reveals much about how Black Angelenos confronted and struggled against racism that was a painful and resilient as that which they hoped to have left behind when they migrated west in search of the California dream."

—Lonnie G. Bunch III, founding director of the National Museum of African American History and Culture and author of *Call the Lost Dream Back: Essays on History, Race, and Museums*

LIVING THE CALIFORNIA DREAM

Living the California Dream

AFRICAN AMERICAN LEISURE SITES DURING THE JIM CROW ERA

Alison

Alison Rose Jefferson

August 29, 2022

UNIVERSITY OF NEBRASKA PRESS LINCOLN

Portions of this book originally appeared as "African American Leisure Space in Santa Monica: The Beach Sometimes Known as 'Inkwell,' 1900s–1960s" in *Southern California Quarterly* 91, no. 2 (2009): 155–89. Republished with permission of the University of California Press; permission conveyed through Copyright Clearance Center, Inc.

Library of Congress Cataloging-in-Publication Data
Names: Jefferson, Alison R., author.
Title: Living the California dream: African American leisure sites during the Jim Crow era / Alison Rose Jefferson.
Description: Lincoln: University of Nebraska Press, 2020 | Includes bibliographical references and index.
Identifiers: LCCN 2019015601
ISBN 9781496201300 (cloth: alk. paper)
ISBN 9781496219282 (epub)
ISBN 9781496219299 (mobi)
ISBN 9781496219305 (pdf)
Subjects: LCSH: African Americans—Recreation—California, Southern—History—20th century. | Leisure—Social aspects—California, Southern—History—20th century. | Resorts—Social aspects—California, Southern—History—20th century. | African American neighborhoods—California, Southern—History—20th century. | Discrimination in public accommodations—California, Southern—History—20th century. | African Americans—California, Southern—Social conditions—20th century. | California, Southern—Race relations—History—20th century.
Classification: LCC E185.93.C2 J44 2020 |
DDC 305.896/07307949—dc23
LC record available at https://lccn.loc.gov/2019015601

Set in Miller Text by Laura Ebbeka.
Designed by N. Putens.

This book is dedicated to my mother, Marcelyn Cobbs Jefferson (1927–95), and my father, Albert Watts Jefferson Sr. (1918–2009), and my other ancestors, all of whom provided the foundational support of my life's journey, this book, and more projects in the future.

CONTENTS

ACKNOWLEDGMENTS

I want to thank everyone who helped me over the years to uncover the stories that this book records. I am especially grateful to all my professors at the University of California, Santa Barbara (UCSB), and the University of Southern California (USC), who supported and guided me in the production of knowledge to write this manuscript and in my career.

This book would not have become a reality without the women and men, the survivors of the era of my study, telling me the stories of their lives and the lives of others who partook in the experiences and places I have documented. I thank them all for letting me interview them, or for sharing their networks of family and friends and their personal archives with me. I deeply appreciate the time and generosity of Halvor Miller, Esq., and his extended family, George Brown, Arthur and Elizabeth Lewis, Cristyne Lawson, the Ivan J. Houston family, Rick Blocker, Sonya Reese Greenland, Anne Bradford Luke, Harold Peace Jr., Liza Griffith Scruggs, and those who have passed on: the late LeRoy A. Beavers Sr., Anne Smith Cunningham, Navalette Tabor Bailey, and Walter L. Gordon Jr. in assisting me in unearthing and reclaiming these important lost and underrepresented stories to introduce to the academy and the public sphere. I also thank Sandra Seville-Jones and Jan Dennis, residents of the city of Manhattan Beach, for sharing their personal files with me, which held a treasure trove of useful materials, some of which I cite in this book.

Randy Bergstrom guided my doctoral graduate student career at UC Santa Barbara, for which I am deeply thankful. I am also appreciative of the influence that UCSB's Mary Hancock, Paul Spickard, George Lipsitz, Douglas H. Daniels, Patricia Cohen, and the late Clyde Woods (1957–2011) had on my thinking about the African American experience in Southern California and the West, American history generally, and on my professional career. Darcy Ritzau, the UCSB graduate advisor (for continuing students), was a very helpful administrator during my graduate doctoral student career. Kelly, Regents', and other UC Santa Barbara fellowships supported my dissertation research, which remains important to the present volume.

Public historian consulting work on the Angels Walk LA Central Avenue heritage trail project and the SurveyLA "Citywide Historic Context Statement, African American History of Los Angeles" contributed to sustaining me financially and to support the time I needed to complete the writing of this book. I received a Historical Society of Southern California (in conjunction with the Ahmanson Foundation) book publishing fund award which covered my book index cost.

I am forever thankful to Kenneth (Ken) Breisch, who was my advisor when I was a graduate student at USC working on earning my master of heritage conservation, for suggesting after reading a draft of my master's thesis that I should think about earning a doctorate in history or American studies. Research for that thesis project became parts of chapters in my UC Santa Barbara dissertation, and now this book. I am grateful to the late Kevin Starr (1940–2017), with whom I took a California history course in my first year as a graduate student and who served on my thesis committee at USC. In his class with Karin Kuebner as his teaching assistant, I did my first formal research and wrote my first paper about Southern California African American leisure sites. At that time, in encouraging me to produce that paper, Starr noted that my topic was something he and other California historians did not have knowledge of, and that the project had the beginnings of adding a new understanding of the African American experience and California history. I regret he is not here to see how that first paper has evolved into a book and my career has developed. Taking an American West seminar with William (Bill) Deverell at USC further heightened my awareness of the stories that needed to be told about the

African American experience and other marginalized groups to inform a more inclusive American history and collective identity.

I am grateful to Christopher David West, Jose M. Alamillo, and Lawrence Culver for reading early paper drafts that turned into essential parts of this book, as well as for their constructive feedback and encouragement. I am forever appreciative of both Josh Sides and Mary Ovnick at California State University, Northridge, who unknowingly prompted me to have a more serious internal dialogue about pursuing my doctorate when they invited me to participate in the Whitsett Graduate Seminar and contribute an article to the *Southern California Quarterly* journal. Many research and public libraries supported this work, and I am grateful to the professionals at these institutions who have helped me over the years. I thank artist Derrick Adams for graciously allowing his artwork to be used for the cover of this book.

Much appreciation goes to my editor at the University of Nebraska Press, Bridget Barry, who believed my manuscript could become a book. Working with her has been an extraordinarily rewarding experience. My thanks to the press's anonymous reviewers, whose instructive feedback helped to make the manuscript better.

LIVING THE CALIFORNIA DREAM

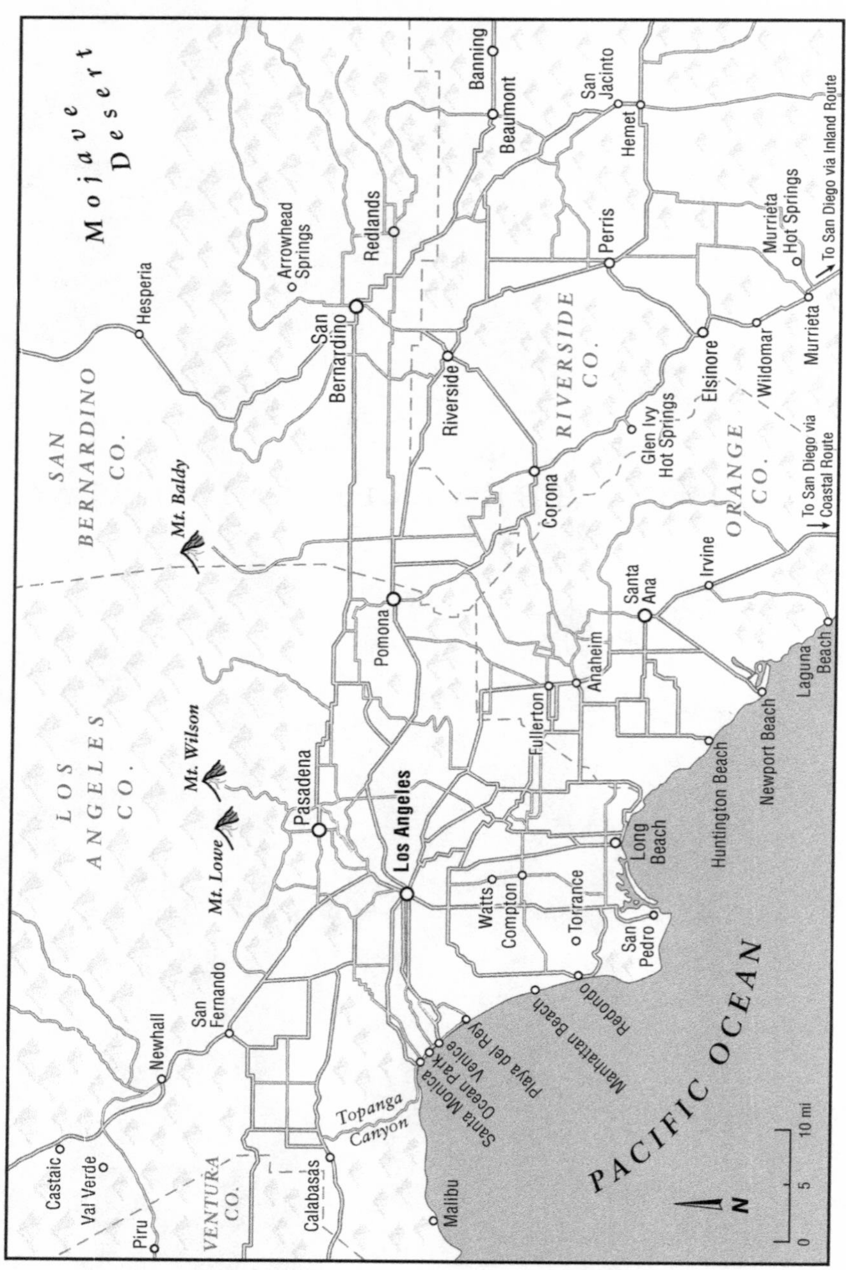

FIG. 1. African American leisure sites and Southern California before the freeway system existed. Map © Erin Greb Cartography.

Introduction

In a 1924 article for the *Messenger*—a national monthly magazine published in New York City that featured information about African American communities—Noah D. Thompson, an African American Los Angeles journalist, real estate entrepreneur, and civic activist and booster, remarked that the horn of plenty was a better design for California's state flag than the grizzly bear. He reasoned that this symbol better represented the place he called "the beautiful home of the setting sun, where flowers grow wild the year round" at the shoreline of the world's largest ocean, the Pacific, which "holds the key to the Western gate, of the Western Hemisphere." Homing in on conditions in Los Angeles at the time, Thompson asserted that many people from all over the world first arrived in the region to play, as tourists, including a few African Americans. He continued that, once all of them viewed the great opportunities California offered, many remained, or went home and later returned, "to work and grow rich in health, wealth and intellect." He cautioned those deciding to make their home in the city had to have a determination to succeed; otherwise they would find nothing but the wonderful climate, which was not sufficient for their sustainability in California. He described a partial list of data collected on the scope of African American work professions and businesses in Los Angeles. This study was prepared by the Commercial Council, an organization set up by African Americans to engage their group in moving to California. Calling out Los Angeles as one of the state's important cities, along with San Francisco and San Diego, Thompson remarked on the increasing opportunities for African Americans in varied industries, including agriculture, petroleum, and motion pictures, along with "unsurpassed school systems."[1]

In his estimation, California's future was going to grow beyond anyone's imagination, due to its strategic location for commerce and trade on the Pacific Rim, and African America could be a part of this growth. Thompson joined other black boosters and entrepreneurs of the era, such as Sidney P. Dones—who in 1924 was the president of the California Realty Board—in proclaiming that African Americans, in proportion to their means, had many opportunities to substantially "improve their condition through work and thrift" in the city and California, generally. They spread the word that investing in Los Angeles–area real estate had provided several African Americans with nice homes and income-producing properties. Through national and regional black media and various social networks, Dones, like Thompson, "broadcast[ed] to colored Americans everywhere, the opportunities, the welcome, the hope and cheer, which free California, its hills and valleys, its industries and commerce, its fruits and always shine, offer[ed] to the American Negro."[2]

The fond admiration for the region expressed in the booster rhetoric of Thompson, Dones, and others charmed and attracted African Americans to move and become new Angeleno residents, who invested in property and the California Dream lifestyle imaginary.[3] This book recaptures the experience and investment of African Americans in these California Dream lifestyle imaginary at several "frontier of leisure" destinations in Southern California during the Jim Crow era.[4] African Americans enjoyed these places and attempted to create communities and business projects in conjunction with the era's growing Southern California African American population. These sites have been obscured in Southern California and western U.S. history and public memory. This is the first academic study that includes these sites and their unrecognized voices to offer a better understanding of the past and challenges the cultural and social meaning of these places and the politics of space. The stories in this book recast the significance, meaning, and place of leisure by recognizing African American agency and action, giving a more complex understanding of the American experience in the West, where de facto racial discrimination existed in practice rather than legal prescription (Jim Crow de jure) in the postenslavement, modern capitalist era.

The memory of African American leisure destinations in Southern California communities remains a political issue for some that complicates defining a public past for citizens and their civic identity. The social meaning of these places and their histories is a powerful tool in developing a more inclusive definition of the collective past and civic identity that includes African Americans. My study demands and broadens reconsideration of how African Americans made California history by challenging racial hierarchies when they occupied recreational sites and public spaces at the core of the state's mid-twentieth-century identity. The stories I present in this work are of Southern California's largest and most popular, although not broadly remembered, African American leisure destinations, which were sites of pleasure, civil rights struggle and contestation, and economic development between the 1900s and the 1960s.

The stories of the making of these Los Angeles metropolitan leisure sites are what historian Victoria Wolcott identifies as documentation of the national mass movement to open recreational facilities and space to all Americans. These are the stories of African Americans of all socioeconomic classes—the "New Negro," who migrated out of the U.S. South to northern, midwestern, and far-western cities in the post–World War I decades to escape racial injustice, as well as migrants and soldiers arriving home from Europe after the Great War—who were more self-confident, and sometimes militant, in demanding their rights as citizens and consumers. In its recovery of early twentieth-century leisure and its subsequent memory, my study continues the expansion of analysis by historians who have moved beyond the "master narrative" of civil rights to include cultural and economic contestation as well as overtly political campaigns in order to rethink the struggle for public accommodations in the extended context of the long freedom rights struggle. There is some urgency to this research. Many stories about this contest are getting lost, along with the structures that housed various leisure experiences, because our society has neglected to recognize and document them. This lack of documentation, heritage conservation, and interpretation is especially true for the African American resort and destination experience. As critical as it is to understanding the larger historical struggle for freedom and equality, the documentation of these cultural landscapes is valuable in its own right, since it offers important information to historians and the general public and provides a fuller truth about the ethnic diversity of California.[5]

Even though in the twentieth century's later decades a broader wave of socially critical scholarship opened a path for more diverse and politically critical interpretations of history, there are still stories to be recorded, not only for our understanding of the historical West, but for the impact on Americans' historical consciousness of western places. This project contributes to the accumulating body of knowledge examining African American agency and the consideration of memory as a mechanism of power in race and resistance, while acknowledging the importance of the historical writings documenting the racial victimization, terror, violence, discrimination, and inequalities perpetrated against African Americans.[6]

In presenting the historic context of black Angeleno community formation and the development of Southern California leisure destinations from their early twentieth-century beginnings, two stories unfold. I elucidate the creative assertion of full social and civic membership and social and economic invention by African American leisure community agents. As the era's enterprise and construction have largely been erased, I examine the stories of the destination sites' evolution and heritage. Preserving the common and divergent patterns of many African American leisure retreats in California and across the United States is important for the public memory of these sites, as well as a proper understanding of them as places of commerce, social networks, community, identity, contestation, and civil rights struggle.

In each chapter, I investigate the ties of African American leisure-site promoters to the Los Angeles civic, social, and business development infrastructure in their community, and, where applicable, in the white community. When possible, I present the view of African American users about their experiences at these sites. I examine the regional social context in which the individual leisure sites arose and were negotiated through the twentieth century. These site-specific histories help recompose the historic geographic spread of the African American community in Los Angeles. I consider the racialized issues and prejudices that arose at the sites enjoyed by black Angelenos in the local communities where these leisure destinations were situated. I also consider the contested history of some of these leisure-site districts. The racialization and contestation pose another question for this study: What kind of boosterism and other rhetoric did the entrepreneurs embrace in promotion of themselves as proprietors and of their ventures, and how did black users define or embrace these discourses?

Black Angelenos' leisure destinations, particularly in beach areas, were also places where African Americans attempted to participate in the population expansion into outlying areas for future opportunities of new housing and commerce, and have been for the most part unrecorded until this study. These destinations, as Lawrence DeGraaf proposed in 1970, "generally had the dual aim of providing a 'more cultured and sophisticated recreation' and of being nuclei for black residential colonies." They were part of an assertive strategy in the collective use of places as a community development tool. The historical nexus of leisure and residence means this study is integral to understanding the racial geography of contemporary U.S. black citizens' endeavors to join the 1920s housing boom in Los Angeles and beyond, in suburban areas, where they were rejected. I look at how the remembrance of these leisure sites has evolved (or not evolved) in the layered public memory of Southern California and the American West.[7]

The leisure sites I examine are worthy of remembrance because of the radical vision and agency of those who tried to provide an opportunity for African Americans to transcend race-based limits and control their own destiny, as well as the similar vision and the agency of those African Americans who used these sites. Historian Paul A. Shackel observes that the histories of African Americans and other community of color groups are about struggle, racism, and tragedy. As many Americans continue to struggle with the commemoration of these histories, that of African American and other community of color groups is important, as it allows them to make a claim on public memory and cultural belonging. In the U.S. history uncovered in this book, the forgetting of African American history was constructed and resisted and has mattered politically. Southern California leisure sites were symbols of hope, and they had great significance in the context of the political, racial, and economic currents during the time of their existence. Although these places may not exist today in their initial form, they are sites of African American history and possess value for regional and national collective memory and identity. They show the depths of character and agency of the men and women who attempted, through their enjoyment of these sites, economic development and racial self-determination for themselves and future generations of all Americans.[8]

Excluding the experiences of African Americans and the social diversity of these Southern California leisure destinations inhibits the sense of civic identity that the collective history of a shared territory can convey. Neglecting a larger historical topic, as in the case of African American leisure sites, administers a double dose of erasure or loss. Recovery of memory has proven an important tactic in greater political inclusion and reclaiming of public presence of African Americans in recent times. Decisions about what is to be remembered and protected situate the narratives of cultural identity in the collective memory of and history about a place. I concur with historian John Hope Franklin that expanding our knowledge of various places and exploring historical experiences from multiple viewpoints makes history more interesting and tells a more accurate and more inclusive story about the United States and its citizens.[9]

The stories in this book broaden the intellectual traditions of the African American experience in the West and in California historiography and expands the scholarship exploring salient themes, interpretations, and text of western mythology, as well as the group representations, cultural production, and actors that have influenced historical writings on the western African American experience since the 1890s. Until the last few decades of the twentieth century, the intellectual traditions, major organizing themes, and core narrative structures of historians of the American West focused on Euro-Americans, mostly on heroic male conquest and migration across the continent from the Atlantic to the Pacific Ocean. These perspectives deemphasized, or excluded altogether, the multiethnic, multicultural nature of western U.S. history as well as the influence of the federal government, white privilege, and white supremacy on western development, and they neglected the urbanized West and twentieth-century western history.[10] Additionally, peoples of color were viewed as victims rather than as agents of historical change. Later, historians interpreted the history of the American West as a global narrative of many diverse peoples—most of whom have been overlooked—who conquered and inhabited the region. Historical studies of the African American West were scarce until the 1970s. With the victories of the modern civil rights movement and its failures emerged a heightened interest in and demand for more knowledge about the historical experiences of African Americans generally and opened employment opportunities for professional historians to pursue research to fulfill that demand.[11]

The historiographical change occurred when historians began to voice recognition of the urbanization occurring more or less simultaneously with the settlement of the West, and that the western African American experience needed to be viewed in this context before the 1940s. This recognition connected to the multiethnic and racial heritage of the West to reveal the interaction of black westerners with other communities of color. The growing acknowledgment of the African American past in the West joined historical analyses of race, class, gender, the environment, and cultural expression to become part of the study of what would eventually be called "New Western History" in the latter decades of the twentieth century.[12]

This refocusing in the 1970s wrought new topical directions that have informed my work, such as earlier histories of black communities, Garveyism, cultural production, and civic uprising by scholars Rudolph M. Lapp (1977), Emory J. Tolbert (1980), Albert S. Broussard (1993), Douglas H. Daniels (1980), Quintard Taylor (1994), Dolores McBroome (1993), Gretchen Lemke-Santengelo (1996), Gerald Horne (1995), Shirley Ann Wilson Moore (2000), Lawrence G. DeGraaf (1970 and 1975), Kevin Mulroy et al. (2001), and Robert O. Self (2003). Research themes included Marcus Garvey's Universal Negro Improvement Association's western region influence; early African American settlers in California in the 1850s to 1900s; black San Francisco from the 1880s to the 1950s; black communities in the East Bay and Oakland; women and worker experiences; West Coast jazz, R&B, and gospel music; as well as the 1965 Watts rebellion and other black Los Angeles twentieth-century community and group studies. Important research was conducted examining such cities as San Francisco,

Oakland, Richmond, and Los Angeles, California; Seattle, Washington; and Wichita, Kansas. Since the 1980s, scholars have explored multiple directions as they attempted to illuminate, reconstruct, and interpret the hidden African American experience in the West. These efforts set the stage for even more diverse and interdisciplinary research explorations by succeeding generations of scholars in rethinking the community formation and transformation of the multiethnic U.S. West.[13]

In 1998 Quintard Taylor published what is the reigning reinterpretation of the African American experience in the West. His "new interpretative historical survey" includes the black urban western experience from the late nineteenth century to 1990 and illuminates how African American westerners moved to integrate themselves into "both the larger social and political lives of their cities and the cultural and political life of the national African American community." Taylor joins other New Western History scholars in arguing that different communities of color suffered different levels of discrimination and prejudice and had different philosophies for solutions. This multiracial western distinctiveness presented social and historical differences that also created a different African American experience than in other regions of the United States, where enslavement and de jure Jim Crow predominated.[14]

Taylor contemplated—as many other scholars after him have also considered—whether the region has lived up to the western ideal as the place for the best chance for racial equality and equality of opportunity. These themes of hope, opportunity, and freedom are central in both African American and other U.S. western histories. He concluded that African American westerners learned the region was not the panacea of opportunity and racial justice they had hoped for, but they stayed and chose to pursue political and cultural struggle because there was no better place to go. Another idea he pondered was that California (and, more specifically, the city of Los Angeles) emerged as the center of African American life and politics on the Pacific slope; its influence grew through the twentieth century. In comprehending the African American West, one must understand the history of California and the city of Los Angeles. Our knowledge of these themes has resulted in the expansion of research offerings, to which this study contributes, regarding lifestyles, memory, and placemaking in the experience of African Americans and others in the U.S. West.[15]

Taylor, DeGraaf, and Mulroy prodded this New Western History further in a 2001 anthology of essays illustrating how many African Americans regarded the Golden State as tantamount to the greater freedom and economic opportunities they sought in the West, even after some of them experienced discrimination and disappointment. The dominant theme of the essays is the search for the American Dream in real and mythologized opportunities offered through the California Dream from the colonial period to the twentieth century. When American and Western ideals and mythologies are combined with California's romanticized Spanish and Mexican heritage, the region's beautiful landscape and its warm climate, reputation for tolerance and inclusiveness, and pioneering spirit, the fully developed California Dream emerges. As the volume's editors and contributors assert, for many in whichever ethnic or racial group, California was and still is the land of opportunity and the good life that historian Kevin Starr so eloquently describes in his American and California Dream multivolume series. This anthology adds understanding of aspects of African Americans' historical roles in California and the American West while at the same time revealing how much of this history has been ignored, as well as the research that still needs to be conducted to round out the view of African American Californians and westerners.[16]

One of the volume's essays, by historian and founding director of the Smithsonian National Museum of African American History and Culture, Lonnie G. Bunch III, examines the black boosterism of Jefferson L. Edmonds (1845–1914), the publisher of the early twentieth-century monthly news magazine the *Liberator*. An early leading proponent and propagandist of the California Dream for African Americans, Edmonds and other black boosters also painted an unvarnished and frank portrayal revealing both the challenges and opportunities they would find in Los Angeles. As Douglas Flamming (2005) notes, throughout the early twentieth century the editors, including Edmonds, of black newspapers and other publication in Los Angeles, with their booster rhetoric, masterfully "contrasted the idealized West and the racist West . . . [to create] a distinctly African American vision of the urban West, somewhere between an endorsement and an indictment." Edmonds's vision of the California Dream, as Bunch and other scholars assert, enticed African Americans' migration to the state during much of the twentieth century. Some of those persuaded by this vision became new residents of Los Angeles and leisure makers at the Southern California sites studied in this book.[17]

Other research has emerged since 2000 on the black Angeleno community's networks that attracted the waves of African American migrants in the twentieth century and that offer a view of the shapers of the Los Angeles environs and the leisure makers examined in this work. With extensive statistical analysis of African American households during the late nineteenth and early twentieth centuries, Marnie Campbell (2016) built on efforts by J. Max Bond (1936), to expand our knowledge of the founding black Angeleno urban community formation. Flamming (2005) and Josh Sides (2003) added scholarship on the African American migrant experiences of the middle and blue-collar classes before and after World War II. Even as some were able to attain the "California Dream" and the "Western Ideal," de facto racial inequality and structural racism still afflicted many African Americans.[18]

My work departs from and draws on these studies, which offer an understanding of the black western experience in the past, present, and future, within the context of African American history, western history, urban studies, and American history. Although none of these volumes cover much about the social and cultural history and traditions of the black Angeleno community, their class-based and institutional analysis offers a necessary preview and foundation for further examination of the rich social and cultural landscape. Informed by the ground covered in these volumes, my study builds on their work and adds needed illumination and interpretation to the social and cultural landscape.

Moving beyond these structural analyses, other studies have pointed out that essential elements of understanding the African American experience in the West lie in the particular areas of innovation and culture. Works have been published in the last twenty years on the music scene by Jacqueline Cogdell DjeDje and Eddie S. Meadows (1998); Clora Bryant, Buddy Collette et al. (1999); and R. J. Smith (2006). Publications by Donald Bogle (2005), Daniel Widener (2010), and Kellie Jones (2017) broaden our understanding of movie industry history and black agency in the mid- to late twentieth-century music and arts scene. Blake Allmendinger (2008) offers a noteworthy analysis of how African Americans have pictured their role in the West in various types of literature, cinema, and rap music during the nineteenth and twentieth centuries. Brenda Stevenson (2013) and Kelly Lytle Hernández (2017) present perspectives to reshape our understanding of race, ethnicity, gender, class, justice, and the history of immigration and incarceration in Los Angeles. The wide-ranging approach of original essays in the volume edited by Darnell Hunt and Ana-Christina Ramon (2010) expands our vision of black Angeleno life, and Bruce A. Glasrud and Cary D. Wintz (2012) edited an anthology of essays about the Harlem Renaissance in the West that reshapes our understanding of the national impact of this movement. The volume of original multidisciplinary essays edited by Herbert G. Ruffin II and Dwayne A. Mack (2018) explores the black urban western experience in a multicultural frontier from 1900 and illustrates parallels to and differences from that of the rest of African America and the West. My stories of leisure production, agency in economic development, and civil rights struggle is another new area of inquiry, adding new elucidation about how African Americans seized their California Dream to appropriate and shape their new environment in the Far West.[19]

Even with this growing body of scholarship over the last twenty years, there continues to be large areas of the African American past in the U.S. West that have not been fully documented or studied, especially in social and cultural history, including leisure culture and all aspects of the African American experience prior to the mid-twentieth century. The diversity of individual lives and institutions needs to be studied further and presented to the public by the scholarly community. Even with this caveat, the representative scholarly works I have discussed are repopulating U.S. history with previously excluded experiences and, in the process, demanding reframing of the very understanding of the subjects or agents of historical change who are central to the history of the United States.

Historical narratives provide the foundation for incorporation into the U.S. historical public memory, or what Pierre Nora calls *lieux de mémoire*, or "sites of memory." These are the material or nonmaterial memory heritage of sites, people, ideals, and events that resonate historically, intellectually, and emotionally and that are linked in the landscape of national consciousness. The history of memory is one aspect of the African American history of the U.S. West that, in analyzing the landscape of national consciousness, promises to reveal distinctive elements of community, place, self-understanding, and politics in asserting public remembrance.[20]

Responding to the demand to restore African Americans to the history of the U.S. West, scholars and community advocates have also focused on public programs, such as museum exhibitions; conferences; local, state, and national landmark designations; and other public programs. Public history research has increasingly recognized that scholarship does not automatically affect public awareness, and the construction of public memory has itself been a topic for close scholarly analysis and argument. These historiographical turns are important elements for the continued development of programming to infuse the black experience of the U.S. West and its diversity into the history of western states, of African Americans, and of the United States generally, as well as into the national consciousness.

As historian David Thelen asserts, historical public memory is constructed and "is not made in isolation but in conversations with others that occur in the context of community, broader politics, and social dynamics. . . . The struggle for possession and interpretation of memory is rooted in the conflict and interplay among social, political, and cultural interests and values in the present." Still with us today is the gap scholar Michael Frisch identified in 1990 (and that others have recognized since then) "between the content that amateur audiences associate with 'American History' and the content . . . presently taught in most graduate departments of history." As historians since the 1970s have rediscovered African American history in the western United States, they have also been attending to the renewed struggle to recognize that history in public. In the middle of the second decade of the twenty-first century, resistance to its recognition continues. Due to the fact that much of this history is about struggle, racism, and tragedy, some whites, who are in institutional capacities with tremendous influence on the dissemination of information, resist incorporating and commemorating the histories of African

Americans, other people of color, and other marginalized groups into the regional and national American narrative.[21]

The development of a more inclusive national consciousness and identity is a slow struggle. My work contributes both to the public dimension and to the professional practice of history. In the stories of this book I attempt to more broadly locate African American representation on the landscape in order to further integrate African Americans into the historical consciousness of California, the U.S. West, and the nation. Further, my study of the history and memory of African American leisure pushes the heritage conservation field to reconceive itself beyond architecture and to reevaluate whose experience gets featured, in determining what social activity is significant and how. The field has begun to do this in many ways, but it needs to go much further in recognizing and affirming more sites and landmarks important to the celebration of a more inclusive American experience and identity.

Just as the leisure and resort spaces in other parts of the United States were developed by African Americans during the Jim Crow era, in Southern California African American leisure spaces developed to promote the interests of the race and advance a complex mix of political perspectives supporting freedom, economic development, and emotional and physical rejuvenation. Unwilling to accept exclusion, black Angelenos, like their counterparts in other places, developed separate leisure spaces to oppose oppressive racial subjugation of the era and to promote a renewed sense of racial pride, cultural self-expression, economic independence, and progressive politics that were the embodiment of the "New Negro," who was determined to achieve a fuller participation in American society. The experiences and memories of these leisure spaces and destinations, as well as the attention they gained in public memory and newspapers of the era, offered African Americans new and broader visions of themselves, a new identity, and a new collective sense of freedom, contributing to cultural and intellectual efforts that defined the "New Negro." In Southern California, African Americans' ambitions and initiatives for leisure space also radically claimed, challenged, and promoted the region's identity in the consumption of leisure as a "lifestyle" that would spread across the country to develop a new suburban, middle-class culture.[22]

This book is composed of six chapters. Chapter 1 offers a brief historical context of the history of leisure and its significance in framing the changing U.S. culture from a producer to a consumer identity. Also explored are the U.S., California, and African American experience context in the aspirational discourse of the California Dream and Los Angeles community formation. The chapter also illuminates the distinctive elements, significance, and centrality of leisure in the twentieth century to the emerging California lifestyle ideal and its impact on the nation, as it intersected with African American leisure.

Chapters 2 through 6 unearth and analyze formation of the historical context of the development of specific Southern California geographic environments in which leisure resorts grew that included African American agents and consumers from the late 1800s into the twentieth century and the new millennium of the twenty-first century. At each of the sites discussed in these chapters, I illuminate the history of the development of leisure of a specific sort in the social, political, and economic particulars of the time and place.

Chapter 2 exhumes Bruce's Beach in Manhattan Beach, a coastal community in southwestern Los Angeles County. This was one of the earliest (1912 to 1920s) successful African American residential resort and leisure destinations. Eventual racial exclusionary measures aided by the destructive use of state power in 1925 eliminated residential and economic development, with attempts to erase the site's memory from history. Only through political assertion has a limited revival of the history of Bruce's Beach and its incorporation into the public record emerged in the first decades of the twenty-first century.

Chapter 3 elucidates Santa Monica's Bay Street beach near Pico Boulevard, sometimes controversially called the "Inkwell." Santa Monica formed as a suburban community to Los Angeles in the late 1880s for a leisure lifestyle residential community and recreation space. A small African American community staked a place in this enclave. African American regional residents and Los Angeles entrepreneurs attempting leisure space service business expansion for blacks were challenged by various racial exclusionary measures inhibiting residential expansion and economic development. Nonetheless African American citizens' public beach usage and a small local residential community persisted. The local African American community's persistence has mattered in the reclamation of place and memory in twenty-first-century heritage conservation efforts and public history programming that have been initiated by public officials and citizen groups.

Chapter 4 explores Lake Elsinore in Riverside County, a somewhat successful residential and leisure destination for the general population and African Americans even in its marginality between the 1910s and the 1960s. This was one of the farthest inland of the African American leisure spaces that developed. The vagaries of the lake conditions and changing leisure taste over the years impacted African American entrepreneurs' resort business opportunities and success. The African American presence has been left out of local history narratives and landmark designation programming. This omission of African American experiences from the heritage conservation programming obstructs our understanding of the full, shared history of the agents and their impact and contributions to the development of the Lake Elsinore community and the Southern California region.

Chapter 5 unearths the history of the Parkridge Country Club (1927–29) in Corona, Riverside County. This was a private club and leisure space development originally built for a whites-only constituency. A group of very ambitious African American businessmen purchased the site to operate as an interracial space of recreation and an attempt at black community suburbanization. The local white citizens strongly contested this new venture in the Corona community. The African American businessmen's efforts to make it a success have been left out of local history narratives, and there have been no local attempts to revive or incorporate the history into the local community's public record, thereby limiting our understanding of the Corona community's historical actors and development.

Chapter 6 excavates the history of Eureka Villa (later known as Val Verde) in the Santa Clarita Valley area of Los Angeles County, initially an African American and Euro-American resort community development project begun in the mid-1920s. Other land development projects are also illuminated that were in direct competition with Eureka Villa for African American leisure makers' patronage and dollars. Public money contributed to the development of a park and swimming pool, and multiple marketing efforts by Val Verde boosters helped sustain interest of African American consumers' leisure usage of the hidden canyon area until the crumbling of the racial apartheid era in the 1960s. By 2015 the Val Verde community had been recast as one of the last rural areas remaining with affordable housing in the Santa Clarita Valley area, with limited public memory of the African American heritage.

Finally, the conclusion considers where memory of these Southern California leisure sites discussed stands in the middle of the second decade of the twenty-first century. I reflect on what the effect of reclaiming and reinserting these African American communities can mean to the regional community understanding of its history, and how memory work demonstrates continuities with (and departures from) the assertion of leisure early in the twentieth century. I offer programming ideas to engage the broader community with African American heritage, which could be part of larger efforts to memorialize the collective history of cities where these leisure destinations are located.

This work adds the historic African American cultural landscape to the narrative and collective memory of the heritage of the region, by giving voice to places where these people were present, prospered in the past, and contributed to the growth and character of the local community, the state, and the nation. These stories recast the understanding of leisure in the struggle against racial oppression in a still longer and broader freedom rights struggle and civil rights movement, and of the African American community's intellectual and spatial composition in Southern California and the U.S. West. The stories of the people in the pages that follow recast our understanding of leisure as being synonymous with a unique mix of strategies of activism assertion and resistance, mobilizing practices, black spatial imaginary, and struggle for equal access to publicly owned space and private land ownership, for pleasure and amusement, community life formation, sometimes accompanied by entrepreneurial ventures and commerce. Long overdue are the accounts of the lives of these African Americans, who claimed space in the California Dream and were able to defy the odds of racial discrimination to become successful citizens with the ability to enjoy leisure and invest in real estate for their personal or business use during the Jim Crow era in the West. In this work I join other scholars of New Western History and heritage conservation to give a voice to pioneering African Americans who deserve attention and commemoration, not to deemphasize the stories of those who achieved less and had distressingly narrower opportunities. Rather, my extraction and analysis of their stories elucidates the diversity of the experience of African Americans in their participation in the larger, complex world of the U.S. West, and the expansion of the nation's democratic tradition through their struggle and contestation for freedom, equality, and rights as citizens and consumers and as agents in the making of their own history, as well as western and national American history.[23]

1 Historical Context of Leisure, the California Dream, and the African American Experience during the Jim Crow Era

Beautiful Southern California . . .
—*Eagle*, December 5, 1908

The American West and California have been investigated and mythologized as places of opportunity, hope, and a leisure lifestyle by scholars and writers, as well as by civic and business boosters of all sorts.[1] From the late eighteenth century to the dawning of the twenty-first century, throughout its Native American, Spanish, Mexican, and U.S. history, diverse groups of people from around the world have embraced this imagery, particularly those attracted as tourists and new residents to Southern California. Over the last few centuries people moved to Southern California for the mild climate and the landscape, accompanying various industrial employment opportunities in cattle ranching, mining, agriculture, petroleum, tourism, movies, and technology. In the last few decades of the nineteenth century, transcontinental train travel allowed the American West to become the tourist destination of choice, as the railroads were marketed to affluent Euro-Americans with leisure time. Railroads transported these consumers to swanky beach and inland resorts in California, as well as to luxurious rustic resorts built in national parks and similar locations. More water sources were being engineered, agriculture flourished, Los Angeles developed a deep-water harbor in San Pedro, and the Panama Canal opened by 1915, transporting more people and goods to California. Since this period, the region has consistently promoted a romantic ideal of leisure as a lifestyle or "as a permanent way of life" in Southern California, as well as an attraction for tourists and migrants. Leisure became a distinctive defining feature of place and of American citizenship and culture, as an integral part of the modern life that was a measurement of fulfillment, self-determination, and uplift.[2]

The nineteenth century was a time of transition in the U.S. economy, from self-employment in small-scale, competitive capitalism to bureaucratic, corporate employment of middle-class men. Working-class and immigrant men, as well as middle-class women, challenged middle-class men over who should control public power and authority, and, in turn, the nation's destiny. Victorian ideals of self-restraint, self-control, and postponed gratification were changing and, as historians Cindy S. Aron, Gail Bederman, and Kay Davis note, American men and women used leisure in the performance of various sorts of religious, intellectual, and therapeutic social practices as leisure became a way of defining class identity. Middle-class men in particular used their leisure time to participate in strenuous, active, and competitive physical endeavors, and to display their economic success, reinforcing their newly evolved sense of manliness and patriarchal power. Similarly, middle-class women exercised new forms of personal autonomy in experiencing a wider range of amusements and pleasures, along with new forms of social intercourse than were normally unavailable to them at home.[3]

As historians James J. Rawls and Walton Bean have observed, the advertising campaigns of the railroads and the contributions of independent writers promoting "California's charms and embellished . . . romantic heritage" propelled Southern California as a major tourist attraction and contributed to several real estate booms. Influential in the development of the region was the idea that "California offered leisure as a way of life." Charles Lummis, a writer and Southern California booster, popularized this notion in books and articles in the magazines *Land of Sunshine* and *Out West*. Lummis envisioned and promoted leisure as a defining ideal, as central to social life as work, eating, and sleeping. He and other boosters, including the new Hollywood entertainment industry of the early twentieth century, showcased the regional landscape in weekly film and newsreels and extolled "Southern California as the playground of the world, a place where Americans would finally learn to embrace leisure." Through their work and social routines, residents could improve themselves and their community in the process. Others could gain the benefits of the region by visiting.[4]

But as Californians undertook leisure, many found it limited, and themselves excluded from "the way of life." Racial and ethnic group communities (African Americans, Chinese, Japanese, Mexicans, Native Americans, and Jews) encountered restrictions by the white majority population, which prevented them from fully taking advantage of the state's opportunities and amenities. From Lummis's time well into the twentieth century, race, power, privilege, and wealth often inflected leisure opportunities as well as determined who was able to take advantage of economic and social opportunities in Southern California. Leisure became a site to separate, segregate, control, and regulate people, places, and opportunities. White boosters broadcasted this rhetoric of leisure lifestyle pleasures through the mass media, speaking to white consumers to create a sense of place in the California social and physical landscape that excluded Jews and communities of color. In the white boosters' messages, communities of color were situated—if at all—as laborers, rather than as neighbors or social equals.[5]

The African American making of leisure in Southern California built upon a long history of human pursuit of recreational experiences, as well as upon the struggle for freedom and equality. Not until after the industrial revolution in the nineteenth century, however, did vacations become a pursuit that Americans beyond the wealthy or elite could imagine undertaking, as critical markers and entitlements of middle-class status. As soon as African Americans could afford extended leisure after their freedom from enslavement, they traveled to Euro-American resorts, first on the Eastern seaboard, and later in other places domestically and overseas.[6]

African Americans became part of the development of resort towns in the nineteenth- and early twentieth-century United States, as year-round residents, service workers, or entrepreneurs in such places as Newport, Rhode Island; Saratoga, New York; and Cape May, New Jersey. By the late nineteenth century a small but growing African American middle class could afford to travel for vacations, mirroring the resort-based leisure consumption of white middle- and upper-class Americans. Several vacation sites throughout the United States catered to an African American clientele during this period, with varying degrees of success and longevity. Hillside in the Pocono Mountains of Pennsylvania; Sag Harbor, New York; Highland Beach, Maryland; and Oak Bluffs on Martha's Vineyard in Massachusetts were open for business in the mid-Atlantic and northern coastal states. Idlewild, Michigan, was one of several retreats in the Midwest. The South featured more than one beach area that served African American vacationers, including American Beach at Amelia Island, Florida, and the Gulfside Resort outside Biloxi, Mississippi.[7]

Ideas, practices, and expectations of leisure in the United States informed and challenged the vision and practice that African Americans pursued in the Southern California region early in the twentieth century. As historians have analyzed and interpreted leisure as a cultural production of social practice and consumption, they have recognized the leisure of African Americans as a product of distinctive initiative and resourcefulness, cultural self-expression, self-determination, and political activism amid systematic exclusion and dispossession of public rights. African Americans made leisure integral to culture, community, and struggle in California during the twentieth century. This history is layered with stories about group and individual circumstances, and chronicles about migration patterns, socioeconomic status, cultural practices, educational and employment opportunities, and social power. These multifaceted stories took place in both private and public spaces, and the narratives of these experiences and histories intersect and overlap. They are inseparable from one another in their composition and reflection of the structural racial exclusion and class exploitation imposed on African Americans along with other peoples of color.

Historical remembrance and analysis of leisure generally has focused on sites owned and patronized by whites, while African American leisure spaces have been mostly unrecognized. African Americans, like other Americans who moved to California, embraced the booster dream of a leisure lifestyle and contested attempts of what the *California Eagle* newspaper identified as "confinement to . . . sordid forms of recreation and play" to assert self-determination in leisure. Astute African American entrepreneurs and civic builders recognized how this embrace of leisure combined with real estate and other business opportunities could create income and wealth. As was the case with leisure and residential resort spaces near Eastern, Midwestern, and Southern cities with relatively large African American populations that sprouted up in the early twentieth century, the race-specific leisure spaces of Southern California grew, because there were entrepreneurs and residents in particular areas offering services and accommodations to African American visitors. African American regional social networking and community building, as well as cultural traditions and economic development around leisure pursuits, occurred at these sites, marking a space of black identity on the regional landscape and social space. From this, as historian Andrew Kahrl asserts, "the development of attractive and accessible black beaches and leisure sites free from white harassment emerged as a major political issue in the long civil rights movement."[8]

Black Angelenos asserted self-determination to participate in popular leisure and cultural, social, and economic trends that were considered modern by the 1920s, including activities in exurban communities that they built so they could control the property for their enjoyment of these activities and contest white racism. Particularly, they were challenging the white racist labeling of African Americans as laborers and as inferior.

Scholars have argued that leisure and resorts, while produced by the social economy of industrial capitalism, created a novel cultural political form. Resorts and leisure spaces, as sites of transitory recreational consumption, depended on a market of visitors mostly from other communities. Entrepreneurs and civic leaders captured attractive public space and amenities in order to attract these visitors. Sources of resort life and their production have therefore typically been geographically diverse and fragmentary, reflecting distinctive aspects of the place of their making—conditions that may complicate many scholars' research in African American leisure making and the contention against it.[9]

In contrast to the city where black Angelenos lived, these California waterfront and pastoral places where they went to relax included Bruce's Beach in Manhattan Beach; Santa Monica's Bay Street beach near Pico Boulevard (a.k.a. the "Inkwell"); Lake Elsinore in Riverside County; the

Parkridge Country Club in Corona, Riverside County; Val Verde in Santa Clarita Valley, Los Angeles County; and a few others.

Established white racism in Los Angeles, when manifested in recreation space, was most consistently targeted at African Americans, though the racial and ethnic mix of the Southern California region included whites of various European ethnicities; Americans of Mexican, Latinx, Japanese, Chinese, Filipino, and other Asian descent; and California American Indians and Native Americans from other regions, as well as African Americans. While the structural discrimination of Los Angeles and the region was constant and tough, the color line was fuzzy due in part to the inconsistent definition and observance of California's 1893 statute and other subsequent legal reform by the 1920s that legally abolished most forms of racial discrimination. African Americans proved this discrimination more readily contestable than elsewhere in the country (such as the South, where there were actual discriminatory laws regularly and consistently enforced by public authorities) through everyday assertions of presence in the use of space and facilities, as well as other forms of challenge, such as civil disobedience and legal action. As the shape of race and racism shifts depending on historical time period, geography, and context, scholars are just beginning to investigate and comprehend the distinctive history of the varied ways that experiences of discrimination impacted different communities of color and marginalized groups, and that the narrative about the Los Angeles region—and the greater American West in general—during the Jim Crow era had important differences from those in states in the East.[10]

The modern era, of African American building of California, particularly for the more educated and resourceful class, began in the exodus from southern states in the 1890s, in what historian Douglas Flamming has identified as a "quiet, persistent procession" due to the racial inequality, political violence, disenfranchisement of black voters, lack of economic opportunities, and de jure Jim Crow segregation perpetrated and condoned by white southerners. California presented a complex web of laws and practices regulating housing, land ownership, labor, and marriage for communities of color, but when compared to the prospects in the Jim Crow South, these barriers did not dissuade African Americans from settling in California, or from launching leisure consumption businesses there. As historians Lawrence B. DeGraaf, Kevin Starr, and other scholars have observed, many of these black residents were drawn to California for the same dreams and reasons as whites: hope, opportunity, freedom, economics, better schools, better quality of life in a temperate climate, and a sublime landscape. Many in the African American population by the 1920s, as well as those who continued to migrate to the region until 1940, had the resources to enjoy life and leisure pursuits in Southern California.[11]

This Pacific Coast place presents a way to consider African Americans' dynamic reconstruction of social and political life in the rapidly changing twentieth-century U.S. milieu. As DeGraaf and Taylor assert, since Asian Americans and Mexican Americans had a much larger numerical presence in the Far West, this has led observers to largely ignore African Americans' presence until World War II—a pivotal period in their history in the state. This time of extraordinary growth of the black Angeleno population specifically suggests that the experience of African Americans offers an especially important window into the transformation of California in this era. From 1920 to 1940 the population of Los Angeles grew explosively from 576,700 to 1,504,277, while the African American community grew even more rapidly from 15,579 to 63,774. By 1950 as the population of Los Angeles reached 1,970,358 (a growth of 30 percent), African American numbers grew by almost eleven times to 171,209. This larger population of black Californians, led by civic luminaries who captured regional and nationwide recognition, built on the community's earlier contestation history to become a major visible subject of civic discourse and action.[12]

By the mid-1920s Los Angeles became the most important urban center for African American life, politics, and business in the West. Since 1900 Los Angeles had maintained the largest black population in California, of just under 2,200 (less than 1 percent of city's population), and it was one of the two substantial African American centers in the western United States. These initiatives contributed to defining and promoting the Southern California metropolis as a place of opportunity for African Americans in that era. This progress was symbolized by the 1918 election of Republican Frederick Madison Roberts (1879–1952) as the first African American assemblyman in California, representing the 62nd District in Los Angeles (1918–34). This California Assembly District, which included the Central Avenue district of Los Angeles, was where most African Americans in the region lived until the post–World War II years. While whites continued to make up the majority and ethnic Mexicans and Japanese were equal to African Americans in numbers, Flamming observes, "culturally and politically, black Angelenos [prominently] placed their stamp on the district" by the mid-1920s. The characteristics of the people and social dynamics within the black Angeleno community were different in many ways from eastern and northern cities to which African Americans migrated in the twentieth century's early decades.[13]

The Los Angeles region did not have an industrial base like the U.S. Northeast in the years leading up to the Great Depression and World War II. Flamming asserts that African Americans migrating to the Los Angeles region in the early decades of the twentieth century "were less interested in factory wages available in the North than in the general good conditions in Southern California." Most African Americans who migrated to California during this period were generally of the working classes that had been steadily employed before their arrival. As Flamming has argued, no matter what their educational or professional accomplishments before arriving in Los Angeles, most could only gain service jobs due to racial discrimination by whites, creating a constant tension with their values of respectability and ambition in their view of themselves as "the better class of Negroes."[14]

Some change in the economic status of the black working class in Los Angeles occurred in the 1920s and 1930s, as it slowly began to enter emerging industries. Angelenos contributed to a national trend in employing African Americans in government, providing for greater workplace freedom, inclusion, opportunity, and economic advancement. These black Angeleno migrants had been southern city dwellers who came with some savings to invest in real estate, and DeGraaf asserts they "were optimistic about their ability to make a better life for themselves in the West." These early twentieth-century African American émigrés paved the way for all their black compatriots who moved to the Southern California region during World War II and in its aftermath.[15]

In spite of their working-class wages, this was a "black bourgeoisie" with middle-class aspirations, an enterprising spirit, and a determination to succeed. Despite facing racial insults, assumptions about black inferiority, and barriers to equal opportunity, some African Americans had experiences that seemed to justify a faith in the promise of upward mobility and the California Dream. As Flamming notes, with investment in real estate some developed considerable wealth, even as racially restrictive covenants stung their sense of justice and impacted their wallets. In the early decades of the twentieth century a higher proportion of African Americans in Los Angeles owned their homes than in other urban centers with substantial black populations, like Detroit, Chicago, and New York City. This sepia-toned group of migrants placed a premium on self-discipline and education. Additionally, more of the children of black Angelenos than in other metropolitan cities were in school.[16]

With the geographic opening and mobility in the 1950s and 1960s came the fading memory of exclusion and struggle that had preceded it. That memory loss included the vitality of African American resort and leisure ventures that had countered racial discrimination and exclusion. Additionally, as scholar Priscilla A. Dowden-White observes, the marginalizing effects of racial segregation, the basic life challenges inherent in the Jim Crow era itself, white supremacy, and all manner of discrimination have served to obscure more than reveal African American local community, neighborhood, professional, and entrepreneurial organizing activities. The same can be said for the part played in the struggle by those African American impresarios of social and cultural expression and their clientele, and the memory of what they contributed to the long struggle, to the growth and character of their local communities, to California, and to the nation. The stories unearthed in this work are ones that have been obscured and what scholars Luther Adams and Davarian Baldwin identify as more diverse sites of cultural expression created through business, sports, music, and movies, where discourse and debate occurred that gave life meaning.[17]

Historically, free time has been one of the most treasured parts of life. This has been especially true for African Americans, who have been determined to overcome the legacy of enslavement and its aftermath in order to enjoy the consumption of leisure and other cultural experiences. The ability to choose how and where we spend our free time in many ways lies at the heart of what we understand "freedom" and "opportunity" to mean. Alongside the oppression and resistance that are central to understanding the African American experience, comprehending the multiple perspectives of black life in the twentieth century is just as important as in the life of other American groups. African American history is more than how black people got along with white people in the larger, white society. African Americans and their institutions exist beyond their connection to whites and their response to white oppression. African American people and their history are obscured if there is no understanding of their embrace of life in all its complexity, including how they enjoyed their free time at recreation and leisure destinations of their creation.[18]

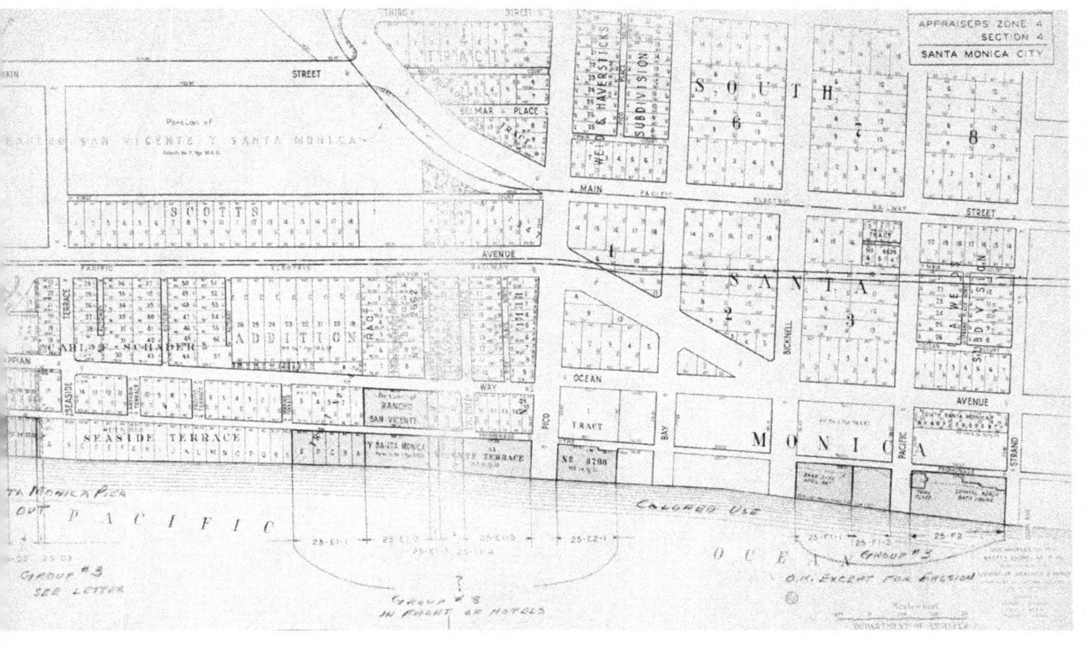

FIG. 2. City of Santa Monica, Los Angeles County Master Plan Map, 1947. State of California Department of Engineering, Department of Natural Resources Division of Beaches and Parks. Note the identification of the "Colored Use" beach section on the map regarding beach erosion. Courtesy University of Southern California Library Special Collections.

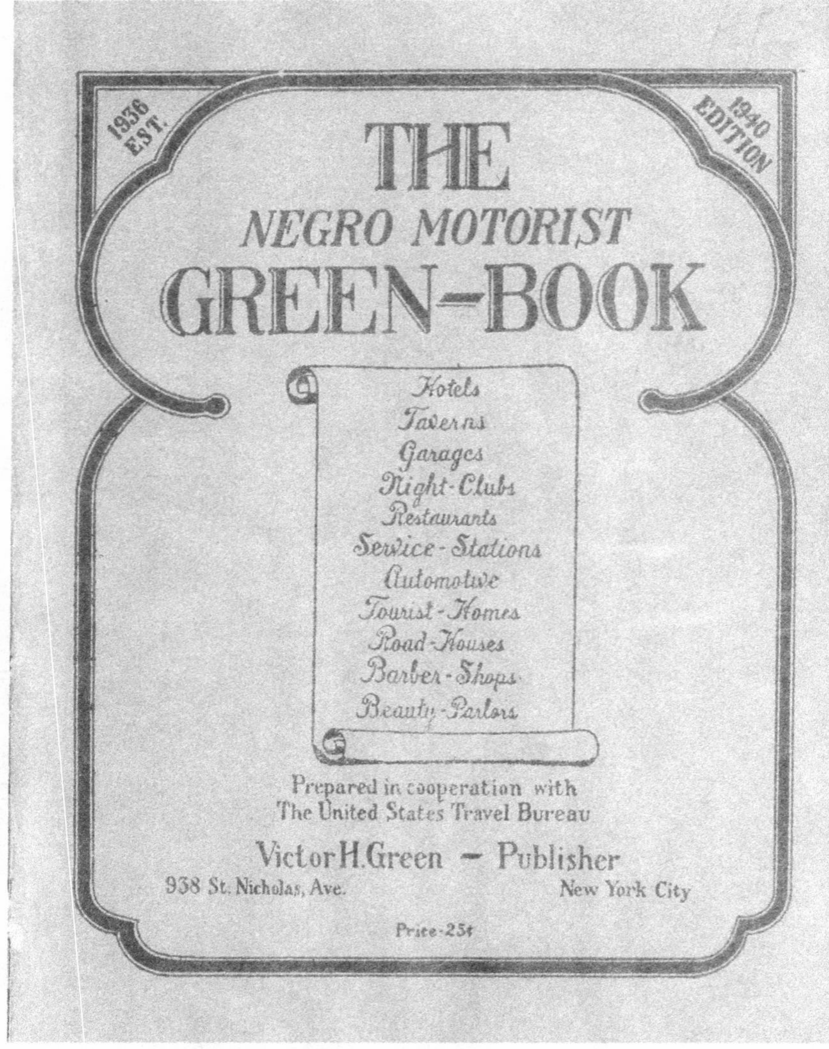

FIG. 3. *Negro Motorist Green-Book* cover, 1940 edition. Annually published by Victor Hugo Green from 1936 to 1963, this was the most well known of the guides listing accommodations that would serve African American travelers throughout the United States during the Jim Crow era and before civil rights laws were regularly enforced. Prepared in conjunction with the U.S. Travel Bureau, the 1940 edition cost 25 cents and listed "Hotels, Taverns, Garages, Night Clubs, Restaurants, Service-Stations, Automobiles, Tourist-Homes, Road-Houses, Barber-Shops, Beauty-Parlors." Over the years some accommodations at Southern California resorts were listed in the guide. Courtesy Schomburg Center for Research in Black Culture, Manuscripts, Archives, and Rare Books Division, New York Public Digital Library Collections.

FIG. 4. *Right to left*: Mrs. Willa Bruce; her son, Harvey Bruce; and Harvey's wife, Meda, under a pop-up wooden tent structure that served as the early place of business for what became Bruce's Lodge, later known as Bruce's Beach, in Manhattan Beach, California, ca. 1912–20. Courtesy California African American Museum.

FIG. 5. Visitors standing on the boardwalk north of Bruce's Lodge, ca. 1920. *Left to right*: Fannie Washington; Journee W. White and his wife, Mamie Cunningham White; and Elbridge Lee. The group are posing for a photograph during their outing at Manhattan Beach. Journee White was a leader in the investment group that bought the Parkridge Country Club. Photograph courtesy Miriam Matthews Collection, University of California, Los Angeles Library Special Collections.

MEET ME THERE!—WHERE?

Bruce's Beach

THURSDAY, JUNE 8, 1922

GRAND EXCURSION AND SUNDAY SCHOOL PICNIC

Given by the St. Paul Baptist Church

A grand outing and day of pleasure. Various contests are open and prizes worth your while will be awarded the winners at 3:00 P. M.

Note The Contests

Most Popular Miniser on Grounds; Most Popular Young Lady on the Grounds; Most Popular Married Lady on the Grounds; Most Popular Marriageable Young Man on the Grounds; Largest Family on the Grounds.

Fare

Adults—Round Trip, 75c; Children (6 to 12 years)—Round Trip, 40c.

Train: leave 4th and Hill Sts., at 9:50 a. m. and 1:00 p. m. —Return 5:30 p. m. and 6:00 p. m.

REV. R. N. HOLT, Pastor
Phone: South 4913.
C. L. COLES, Chairman General Committee
Phone: 271684.

Tickets on Sale at: California Eagle Office, 824 Central Ave.; Mattox & Sons Grocery, 5122 Long Beach Ave.; May's Sweet Shop, 20th at Hooper; Johnson's Pharmacy, Cor. Normandie and Jefferson.

FIG. 6. Advertisement for St. Paul's Baptist Church's excursion to Bruce's Beach in the *California Eagle*, May 27, 1922. The ad mentions nothing about Manhattan Beach. People in the know in the Afro-Angeleno community in this era were aware of the site's geographic location. Note that activities are mentioned for adults and families. One of the oldest African American newspapers in the West and based in Los Angeles, the *Eagle* covered news that its primarily African American readership wanted and needed to know until its final issue in 1964.

FIG. 7. Mrs. Willa Bruce (*left*) with her daughter-in-law, Meda (*center*), and her sister enjoying the sunshine at the seashore near Bruce's Lodge in Manhattan Beach, ca. 1920s. Courtesy California African American Museum.

THE TRUTH
about the
KU-KLUX-KLAN

ADDRESS BY
Dr. J. Rush Bronson
Nationally Famous Orator and Lecturer

Entrance to Pier
HERMOSA BEACH
Saturday Eve.
June 7—7:30 p. m.

Half Hour Band Concert
Public Meeting—All Welcome

FIG. 8. Klu Klux Klan meeting advertisement, *Manhattan Beach News*, June 6, 1924. An anonymous telephone intimidation campaign and other harassment was mostly organized by the Klu Klux Klan, or at least their sympathizers, to terrorize the Bruces and other African Americans who visited Manhattan Beach and the South Bay region of Los Angeles County. The newspaper ad states in the last text line "Public Meeting—All Welcome." In a public medium, this is an ironic tagline for use by a group with a well-known history of white supremacy and racial oppression, intimidation, and violence against black and other marginalized people in the United States and abroad. Kenneth T. Jackson indicates in his 1967 book *The Ku Klux Klan in the City, 1915–1930* that the group had suburban chapters in Redondo and Hermosa, cities near Manhattan Beach. Courtesy Manhattan Beach Historical Society Archives.

FIG. 9. A day at Bruce's Beach, Manhattan Beach, July 10, 1927. Sweethearts Margie Johnson and John Pettigrew pause in their enjoyment of the surf to strike a pose and create their photograph memory of this day at the crowded Pacific Ocean shoreline. This photograph and others taken of Bruce's Beach were featured under the title of this caption on a page in the scrapbook of LaVera White, who lived in Los Angeles for most of her life. Photograph courtesy LaVera White Collection of Arthur and Elizabeth Lewis.

FIG. 10. Anne Bradford Luke at almost three years old, with her father, Cornelius N. Bradford, having fun in Manhattan Beach near Bruce's Beach and their family property purchased in 1916, August 1939. Photograph courtesy Anne Bradford Luke Collection.

FIG. 11. Little Harold Peace Jr. sitting on a car hood, near the house of his grandparents, John and Bessie McCaskill, a few steps from Bruce's Beach in Manhattan Beach, ca. 1950. Photograph courtesy Harold Peace Jr. Collection.

FIG. 12. John and Bessie McCaskill entertaining family and friends in the backyard at their house, as they often did, in Manhattan Beach, near Bruce's Beach, no date. The McCaskills purchased their beach house in 1927 and sold it in 1976. Photograph courtesy Harold Peace Jr. Collection.

FIG. 13. Los Angeles area community member Eric Moore (*left*) and others standing in front of the new Bruce's Beach sign at the event held for the renaming of the park on March 31, 2017. The media and a few hundred California residents and visitors came to the site, overlooking the Pacific Ocean, to pay tribute to the African American pioneers who were dispossessed of their property and business ventures due to white supremacist actions in 1925. Photograph by and courtesy Karen Moore.

FIG. 14. Attendees of the Sunday School Convention of the Los Angeles District in front of Phillips Chapel Christian Methodist Church at Fourth and Bay Streets, Santa Monica, 1909. This was the first congregation building for the denomination on the West Coast, which before the 1950s was known as the Colored Methodist Church. The building was purchased from the Santa Monica School Board by Bishop Charles H. Phillips (*center, to the right of a woman wearing black*). Also pictured (*left foreground*) is Rev. James A. Stout, the Santa Monica church's first minister. Photograph courtesy Cristyne Lawson Collection.

FIG. 15. Santa Monica beach panorama, 1939. This aerial view shows beach and Crescent Bay Park areas just south of the three taller buildings at the Bay Street Beach, which in public memory is the location of the historical African American gathering place during the Jim Crow era. The built features, such as the colonnade and buildings, give physical definition to the site. Courtesy University of California, Los Angeles, Air Photo Archive.

Mrs. F. C. Warner, Mgr. Mrs. E. N. Warren, Prop.

LA BONITA

Single and Double Rooms; Two and Three Room Apartments
All completely Furnished

A Complete line of bathing suits and accessories. Hot and cold shower baths, and other accommodations.

RATES REASONABLE

Only two short blocks from ocean. Venice short line car, get off at Fremont, walk half block east, half block north.

Meals served—Good Home Cooking. Tennis Court for the guests or for all day club parties.

1811-1825 Belmar Place, Santa Monica Cal.

FIG. 16. La Bonita business advertisement in the *Los Angeles New Age* newspaper, August 28, 1914. This enterprise ad described the offerings of a black-owned bathhouse and lodge located at 1811–1825 Belmar Place in Santa Monica. Out-of-towners could rent a guest room, as well as a bathing suit, and buy a home-cooked meal. Segments of the business lasted into the 1950s under various management teams, and over the years the establishment was sometimes listed in the *Negro Motorist Green-Book*. Material courtesy University of California, Berkeley Library Special Collections.

Sun. Aug. 2 "24"

lub Casa Bel

me and Arthur

FIG. 17. *Opposite*: Newlyweds Verna Deckard and Arthur Lewis posing in front of the Club Casa del Mar sign during a day of enjoying themselves at Santa Monica beach, August 2, 1924. This photograph was taken on the Pacific Ocean shoreline area at Pico Boulevard (then Front Street), looking south. After the Casa Del Mar Club was built and opened in 1924, African American beach use shifted to the south side of the club. The shoreline between Bay and Bicknell Streets, identified in contemporary popular memory as the beach frequented by African Americans, was marked on the City of Santa Monica, Los Angeles County Master Plan map, 1947. Note in the background the Casa Del Mar Club's patrons and equipment on the right, and the shoreline, surf, and ocean horizon on the left. This photograph was among several made by Verna and her friends on many days at Santa Monica beach and featured in the pages of her scrapbook. At the time of the photograph Verna had recently moved to Los Angeles from East Texas. She married Arthur not too long after her move. He died of tuberculous before 1930. Photograph courtesy Verna Deckard L. Williams Collection of Arthur and Elizabeth Lewis.

FIG. 18. *Above*: The Cunningham family women appear here enjoying a relaxing day at the Bay Street Beach, no date. This is the Santa Monica beach area that became most associated with African American beach use after the Casa Del Mar Club was opened in 1924. Note the location's iconic colonnade in the background, which was still standing in 2019. Courtesy Mariam Matthews Collection, University of California Library Special Collections.

FIG. 19. *Picnic[k]ing at Santa Monica Beach*, Sunday, July 19, 1931. This photograph was one of a few made of friends enjoying the shoreline near Bay Street on a busy beach day and featured under the title of this caption on a page in the scrapbook of LaVera White. Nine of the ten friends in the photograph are identified as: (*top, from left):* Eona Moore, Eola Johnson, Margie Johnson, LaVera, and Dorothy; (*middle*): Margurite Robinson-Chapman, Velma White, Pearlita Johnson; and (*front*) Winona Wright. Note one of this beach location's defining features: the colonnade in the background on the left. Photograph courtesy LaVera White Collection of Arthur and Elizabeth Lewis.

2 The Politics of Remembering African American Leisure and Removal at Bruce's Beach

Bruce's Beach is in the limelight. On last Sunday a good day was reported and quite a few enjoyed a day at this pleasure place.
—*California Eagle*, July 18, 1914

In 2007 Bruce's Beach in the Southern California community of Manhattan Beach was formally commemorated with a park name and plaque. The site had not been known as "Bruce's Beach" since an African American resort business and surrounding settlement had been forced out more than eighty years before. With dispossession, the site's African American heritage disappeared from public discourse and retreated to private memory for decades. While officially recognized, the reemergence of Bruce's Beach heritage into public discourse continues to hold a contentious place in the social memory and collective consciousness of the Manhattan Beach community. This chapter examines the history and commemoration of the site and the social context that was the backdrop to the unfolding events impacting it.

African American entrepreneurs Willa and Charles Bruce established a successful resort service business, and by the 1920s a small community of black vacation homeowners had emerged in the vicinity. The small resort flourished despite white property owner resistance from its beginning in 1912. This resistance continued into the 1920s, when the protest of black actors forced city officials to discontinue discriminatory policies excluding African Americans from using the public shoreline at Manhattan Beach.

This peaceful but militant protest would be the first organized action of civil disobedience by the Los Angeles Branch of National Association of Colored People (NAACP).

The understanding of the significance of this place has evolved. From vibrancy in the 1910s and 1920s to silence by 1930, the memory of Bruce's Beach has remained muted for three quarters of a century. Then, in the subtext to a public discussion, private whispers of the demise of Bruce's Beach led to debate about the necessity to reclaim the history of the place and to its remembrance in the 1990s to 2000s. As new groups of citizens learned its history, discussion about memorializing Bruce's Beach grew louder, and commemoration ideas by citizens and elected officials surfaced. Memories of Bruce's Beach and the city's racist removal of the site came to contend with other messages leaders wanted inscribed on the site. The commemoration that resulted became a decorous sort of reclamation of history, designed to absolve contemporary white residents of the uncomfortable truths from the past that they found appalling and embarrassing. Their image of themselves was blemished and their respectability tarnished by the injustice of the African American community's dispossession. The commemorative plaque placed on the newly named park signage shows this absolution of contemporary white residents and a narrow portrayal of black actors' contributions to Manhattan Beach, demonstrating the complexity of the layers of the African American experience and history in Los Angeles, California, and the United States, and African Americans' struggle for public memory, generally.[1]

African Americans' claim to public space and practices of leisure met with opposition by white citizens who countered with forceful public assertions of property rights, deployment of local state power, and restrictions on public beach access to exclude African American beachfront resorts. Bruce's Beach became contested ground in the development of attractive beaches and resorts free from white harassment. In the Los Angeles metropolitan area, as in many other places around the nation, leisure presented a distinctive political concern and social meaning in the nation's long freedom rights struggle and civil rights movement.[2]

Scholarly recognition of memory as a site of political power alerts us that the memory of leisure in Southern California has also been the product of politics, requiring critical examination. Decisions about what is to be remembered and protected situate the narratives of cultural identity in the collective memory of and history about a place and remake the place in the process. This is evident in the case of Bruce's Beach and the century of its making, unmaking, erasure, and recovered memory in Manhattan Beach. Although recovery alone does not restore public presence and power in a place, participants in the memory and heritage conservation battle around Bruce's Beach have believed it has influence. In Manhattan Beach, the struggle to present the fuller story of Bruce's Beach for the public shows the difficult steps that must be taken to achieve a more complex and accurate public memory.[3]

Just as participants have had to reclaim their place in the making of the history of the American West, so has the social quest for leisure, which has become inextricably understood as a fundamental field of self-determination. As scholar Mark S. Fosters asserts, the lives of those African Americans, who were able to defy the odds of relentless oppression to become successful citizens with the ability to take vacations and possibly buy second homes during the Jim Crow era, deserve historical attention for their part in making leisure in order to reach a more complex understanding of the American experience.[4]

Manhattan Beach and Los Angeles

When Manhattan Beach was founded and the Bruces were purchasing their resort property, thousands of people, white and black and from varied backgrounds, migrated to "the mythical land" of promise. They came westward to California and the Los Angeles region in the early decades of the twentieth century for economic opportunities, health reasons, the climate, the beauty of the locale, and the freedom to create a better life for themselves. Over a generation, from 1900 to 1920, the population of the city of Los Angeles grew 82.2 percent from 102,479 to 576,673 people. Carey McWilliams has observed that the rapidly increasing population facilitated expansion of the construction industry and its payrolls. New industries emerged, more stores opened, and employment opportunities in the professions and service trades proliferated. While many came with money to invest in homes and maybe other real estate or small entrepreneurial business ventures, most came with only an optimistic determination to succeed. With employment earnings and savings, even Los Angeles migrants of modest means could purchase a house, and some became wealthy from real estate transactions.[5]

Of the towns in the southern section of the Santa Monica Bay coastline, Manhattan Beach, where coastal sand dunes melded into the inland hills, was one of the latest to begin development in 1902 and did not receive its name until the city was chartered in 1912. The first Santa Fe Railroad train ran into Redondo Beach in 1888, and in 1904 the Los Angeles Railway, later called the Pacific Electric Car, added the electric transit line from Marina del Rey to Redondo. Not until these two public transportation systems were constructed did development of Manhattan Beach begin.[6]

The city's south section was developed by Steward Merrill, the central section by Frank Daugherty with his associates in the Highland Land Company, and the northern track by wealthy Los Angeles area developer George H. Peck. The Bruce property was located in the Peck Tract, which ran along the coast inland to the crest of the dunes, where one had a "grand view." The original Manhattan Beach homes were wooden structures referred to as cottages, but many of them were little more than sheds. Water was available from two central wells and had to be delivered in buckets. Each of these developers offered promotions typical of the day to attract buyers to purchase lots in Manhattan Beach, including auto tours, as well as free train rides and lunches.[7]

In the early years of the city's development, people from Los Angeles and Pasadena could take the Pacific Electric car and arrive in little more than an hour at this summer retreat, where only twelve families lived year-round. The first pier with concrete pilings and decking was built in 1923, with a dance pavilion and bathhouse erected at its shore end. Sand was a symbol and a problem for early Manhattan Beach residents. As the wind would spread the sand in drifts, dunes shifted, boardwalks and streets were inundated, and homes were destabilized. The northern dunes in the Peck Tract, however, were more stable and even proved to be attractive for desert scenes filmed for Hollywood movies in the 1920s and 1930s.[8]

Manhattan Beach began as a residential community with little industry and commercial development. Even though it was subdivided early, it developed more slowly than other nearby areas, as the developers were not required to furnish all of the improvements, which became standard features of later subdivided tracts. Residents were required to pay for water, sewers, drainage, streets, curbs, and sidewalks, street lighting, and parks. A large percentage of the city's sanitary sewers were slow to be constructed, and more than 50 percent of the streets did not have gutters, curbs, or paving until the 1950s. The city's drainage system was not fully constructed, either, until after 1958.[9]

Until 1949 Manhattan Beach had a winter population of less than one-half of the summer population. In 1920 the population was 859. By 1931 it was 1,891, and by 1940 there were 6,398 people living there. Most of the city's growth occurred after World War II, with the aircraft industry springing up on Aviation Boulevard and population growth in the Los Angeles metropolitan area and freeway improvements making the district desirable and accessible for commuters. In 2017 the Manhattan Beach population was slightly under 36,000. Its barren sand dunes of yesteryear had evolved into "a prosperous, [overwhelmingly white] enclave of the South Bay with a prestigious address, a town that has become home to aging baby boomers building wood and mortar castles by the sand."[10]

African Americans visiting Manhattan Beach in the 1910s and 1920s either rode out from Los Angeles on the Pacific Electric Car or came by automobile or by minibus, and they congregated at the shoreline section that became known as Bruce's Beach. Patronizing the Bruce enterprise were mostly black Angeleno beachgoers of all professional and economic statuses employed in the public and private sectors. African American Angelenos were a varied group, as illustrated in a series of articles published in the *Los Angeles Times* on February 12, 1909, to commemorate the centennial anniversary of the birth of Abraham Lincoln, "The Great Emancipator."[11]

In one article about the educational progress of African Americans both in the nation and the Southern California region, Professor E. L. Chew reported that their education levels in the local region were varied, ranging from those who had finished what would be considered grammar school to others who finished high school to normal schools (approximately two years of college). Still others attended or finished at colleges or universities. None were illiterate, even if they had only manual labor training.[12]

Another article in this *Los Angeles Times* series, titled "Negroes Who Have Won Place or Fortune in Los Angeles and Pasadena," showcased the new migrants' individual employment, business development, and land acquisitions. African American–owned businesses described included real estate investment, storage and transportation, plumbing, cleaning and dyeing, rubbish collection, metal dealing, construction, and hotel keeping. Occupations described included positions with Los Angeles County as deputy county auditor, tax collector, and assessor, and in Los Angeles city as a police officer. Other jobs included head porters, expressmen, tailors, ironworkers, cooks and caterers, landscape gardeners, undertakers, store merchants, and ministers. The series spoke about the African Americans' social practices through their businesses and occupations, and the club and religious institutions they had established by the end of the twentieth century's first decade.[13]

African Americans' appreciation for books, music, and art were also mentioned. In addition, the series highlighted the accomplishments of a few African American professionals such as doctors, dentists, pharmacists, lawyers, newspaper entrepreneurs, a veterinarian, teachers, and musicians. As articulated in the articles, the small but growing African American community demonstrated faith in the promise of upward mobility. They saved their money to acquire real estate as soon as they could, as they simultaneously sought to enjoy various opportunities available to contemporary Southern California consumers. Those opportunities included material possessions and such experiences as riding out to enjoy the Pacific Ocean's shoreline offerings, including Bruce's Beach.[14]

Bruce's Beach, African American Leisure, and Los Angeles County Boosterism

In 1912 Mrs. Willa "Willie" A. Bruce purchased the first of two contiguous Manhattan Beach lots near the Pacific Ocean shoreline between Twenty-Sixth and Twenty-Seventh Streets (west of Highland Avenue) for $1,225 from Henry Willard, a white real estate broker from Los Angeles. In comparison to the cost of nearby lots, Mrs. Bruce paid a high price for her 32 x 100 ft. lot. The land she and, later, that other African American families purchased was undeveloped, as was the majority of the land in this section of Manhattan Beach. The deeds to the land purchased by Mrs. Bruce contained no racial restrictive covenants—a practice that did not occur in Manhattan Beach until later in the twentieth century, although other socially exclusionary practices, such as real estate agents refusing to sell land to African Americans, did occur. About six hundred people lived in the small, half-resort, half-residential, rural Manhattan Beach district that became a city a few months after the June 1912 Bruce enterprise opened.[15]

Mrs. Bruce (b. 1862); her husband, Charles (b. 1860); and their son, Harvey (b. 1889) moved to Los Angeles sometime between 1900 and 1910. Mrs. Bruce was born in Missouri, her husband in the District of Columbia, and their son in New Mexico. The family lived and owned their homes free and clear in Albuquerque, New Mexico, in 1900, and in Los Angeles at 1021 Santa Fe Avenue by 1910. At the time Mrs. Bruce purchased the Manhattan Beach property in 1912, her husband was a dining-car chef on the train running between Salt Lake City, Utah, and Los Angeles. Like many upwardly mobile and middle-class women of the era, Mrs. Bruce's housewifery skills such as cooking, ironing, and sewing, or managing the room rentals for a boarder or two at her home, could have provided her with personal income.[16]

Evidence does support that Mrs. Bruce's skills were the prominent ones engaging the black Angeleno beach pleasure-seekers at the new summer resort. The *Times* reported upon its opening that the Bruces' establishment featured "a small portable cottage with a stand in front where soda pop and lunches [were] sold, and two dressing tents with shower baths and a supply of fifty bathing suits." In 1913 the earliest building at the resort was constructed, first known as "Bruce's Lodge." By 1920 Mrs. Bruce had purchased the adjacent land parcel south of her original acquisition, from New York residents Charles and Anna Kraus and Jessie Carson Drake. Her husband was not recorded as an owner of either of the two properties, but his name does appear in select sources associated with the business. His name may not have been on the property deeds because Mrs. Bruce was the manager of the resort operation and, hence, the responsible party for this particular investment. By 1923 there were two structures on the original lot purchased in 1912, one of which was a two-story building with room upstairs for dancing and a café downstairs. On the second lot, purchased in 1920, another structure was built, which mostly included the Bruces' accommodations. The resort accommodated the needs of African American day-trippers and a few overnight guests who wanted to enjoy themselves at the seaside.[17]

The reaction of the white Manhattan Beach community to the African American presence was mixed. Within a week of the opening of the small resort enterprise in 1912, white landowners of adjacent land expressed agitation and took action with the invocation of public power to harass the Bruces' guests. A *Los Angeles Times* article of June 27, 1912, written on the Monday after a Sunday full of visitors at the Bruce resort, reported that landowner George H. Peck installed "no trespassing" signs on the strip of land in front of Mrs. Bruce's property. This meant the Bruces' customers could not reach the shoreline without walking a half-mile around Peck's supposed oceanfront land parcel. Simultaneously confronting Mrs. Bruce and her African American guests' beach usage were two deputy constables patrolling the "prohibited strip," warning them not to cross Peck's land in front of Mrs. Bruce's place to reach the ocean. Clearly intended to drive out African American users, the barricade and show of force had little effect on the beachgoers. The *Times* reported, "This small inconvenience . . . did not deter the bathers, . . . pleasure bent, from walking the half mile around Peck's land and spending the day swimming and jumping the breakers."[18]

Mrs. Bruce became the face of the new resort business and its spokesperson, as well as something of a cause célèbre and source of irritation to the local white supremacists. The same *Times* article reporting on white opposition to her venture described Mrs. Bruce as a "dusky proprietor" and "stout negress." A line drawing based on a photograph of "Mrs. W. A. Bruce" featured the caption: "Colored woman, who has created a storm at Manhattan Beach by establishing a seaside resort for the members of her race." Despite the Sunday harassment, when interviewed by the *Times* correspondent Mrs. Bruce emphatically asserted her property ownership and that her business catering to an African American clientele would continue. The correspondent mustered a little sympathy describing this situation, noting,

> [Mrs. Bruce] avers negroes cannot have bathing privileges at any of the bath-houses along the [Pacific] coast, and all they desire is a little resort of their own to which they might go and enjoy the ocean. [She asserted,] "Wherever we have tried to buy land for a beach resort we have been refused, but I own this land and I am going to keep it."[19]

Willa Bruce's business actions and response as reported in the *Times* in 1912 are evidence of her awareness of the challenges she would face in providing beachfront pleasures to her African American clientele. She was conscious of her pioneering status and was prepared, if need be, to fight to keep her property and business. Unidentified Manhattan Beach white landowners publicly stated to the *Times* correspondent that they "deplored the state of affairs" of the new resort and its clientele and vowed "to find a remedy, if the negroes try to stay." Though public action was dormant for a few years after this first exchange, the stage was set for several rounds of private and public contestation between the African American protagonists and white landowners.[20]

From its opening in 1912 to its forced closure in the mid-1920s, the Bruce resort became a popular seaside gathering place for weekend outings and summer vacations. Accounts indicate that Bruce's Beach was popular and, for its owner, a financially successful enterprise. Bruce's Beach was one of the only nearby places Los Angeles African American residents could enjoy the Pacific coastline offerings with minimal harassment.[21]

By 1926 six identifiable African American families, all residents of Los Angeles, had purchased property in the general vicinity of Bruce's Beach. With the exception of the Bruce enterprise and one other small lodging I will discuss later, these family-owned properties contained beach cottages used as vacation accommodations by their owners. Most likely these families had been introduced to the pleasures of Southern California seaside living due to previous visits to the Bruce resort. Otherwise, this was the most remote shoreline section in Manhattan Beach and almost uninhabited. North of Bruce's Beach and the small African American residential resort community, there was nothing but sand dunes for about four to five miles until just south of Mines Field (known today as Los Angeles International Airport).[22]

The Bruces' claim to the place through purchase, residency, and day-to-day commerce appears to have been the anchor of a growing community. Joining the Bruces in property ownership in the Peck Tract were several African American families: the Prioleaus with Elizabeth Patterson; Milton B. and Anna Johnson with their daughter Emma K. Barnett; and Mary R. Sanders (Washington). Retired Major George Prioleau (1856–1927) and his wife Ethel purchased a lot with their long-time friend Elizabeth Patterson, whom they knew from Kansas. By 1919, when they bought and developed their lot with a duplex, George Prioleau had already blazed many trails. He was a former enslaved person who after the Civil War graduated from Wilberforce University before he became one of five black U.S. Army Chaplains, serving from 1884 to 1901. As an African Methodist Episcopal (AME) chaplain, Prioleau was a major supporter of providing education, in addition to spiritual guidance, to the U.S. Army Ninth Cavalry unit, also known as the Buffalo Soldiers. The Prioleaus owned a home in Los Angeles at 1311 W. Thirty-Fifth Street.[23]

Down the block from the Prioleau-Patterson duplex, Mary R. Sanders (Washington) bought her beach cottage in 1923 from Frank Heron, one of the owners of the Hollywood Cemetery. A very successful caterer, Sanders and her family had moved to Los Angeles in the late 1800s from Windsor, Canada. In an interview, her grandson Eddie Atkinson recalled that Sanders married several times and was quite a good businesswoman. In addition to her catering business, during her lifetime she made multiple property purchases that were passed down to her descendants. Her home in Los Angeles was near Twelfth Street and Kingsley Avenue in the Temple Street area. She instilled in her children her entrepreneurial flair, and Sanders's descendants continue to live in Los Angeles.[24]

John and Bessie McCaskill, along with the Slaughter family, purchased property outside of the Peck Tract, but adjacent to the general location of the other African American families' and Bruce properties. McCaskill and his family lived on Forty-Eighth Street, near South Park in Los Angeles' Central Avenue district, where most African Americans in this era lived. He was a presser who moved to California from Pensacola, Florida, with his parents when he was a teenager. Mrs. McCaskill was a native of California who worked in catering. The McCaskills enjoyed entertaining, and Harold Peace, their grandson, remembers elaborate breakfasts at the beach house. The family owned their Manhattan Beach property from 1923 until 1973.[25]

In 1927 the Slaughters built a small apartment building on a lot next door to the McCaskills that for a time was known as the Slaughter Hotel. There were other black families who purchased property outside of the immediate section that became known as Bruce's Beach and the early African American settlement. The Leggett and Bradford families made property purchases nearby in the early decades of the twentieth century. In 2018 descendants of these families continued to own property in Manhattan Beach. Evidence supports that all the property purchased by the African Americans in Manhattan Beach in the 1900s and 1920s was located in various adjacent sections to Bruce's Beach in or outside of the Peck Tract. Not only were these African American families purchasing real estate in southwest Los Angeles County for their leisure enjoyment, but they were also betting on the path of growth in the urban expansion of the Los Angeles metropolis toward the South Bay and the Pacific Ocean shoreline: an investment for their future financial security.[26]

African American Property Owners and Manhattan Beach's Racism

By the early 1920s some "concerned" and increasingly vocal white citizens believed a "Negro invasion" was in progress at Manhattan Beach. At this time California had civil rights laws that made it illegal to discriminate against all citizens in public places, which would have included the oceanfront. Nevertheless, local legal sanctions and private actions were implemented to discourage African Americans from visiting and settling in Manhattan Beach.[27]

Even though illegal, white owners of the property adjacent to the Bruces, sometimes, roped off the beach so African American visitors would be confined to the shoreline directly in front of the Bruces' establishment. These visitors, especially if they ventured away from this beach space, were harassed and insulted, both on the streets as well as on other African American–owned properties nearby. Some returned to their automobiles to find their tires vandalized. "Mysterious" fires occurred at African American owned properties. These incidents included a fire purportedly set to a mattress under the Bruces' main building by a Ku Klux Klan (KKK) member. The local fire department extinguished the fire and prevented any physical damage to the Bruces' structure. Another African American family's home was destroyed by fire.[28]

Harassment also included schemes under the guise of the law. A white Manhattan Beach resident and board of trustees member interviewed by Robert Brigham in 1955 asserted that consideration was given to planting liquor at the Bruce resort. As Prohibition laws were in effect in the early 1920s, the idea was to report the violation, hence provoking an arrest of the people on the Bruce premises. This particular harassment scheme was never implemented, due to lack of support from the "concerned" white citizens.[29]

In another use of public power as a harassment tactic, local authorities placed a "10 Minutes Only" parking sign in front of the property of Mrs. Sanders to inconvenience her and her guests. On June 19, 1924, Manhattan Beach enacted new laws with fines or penalties for any violation of these ordinances, to prevent new or additional development of bathhouses and commercialized amusements near the Strand. Some observers saw these laws directly aimed at African Americans, to discourage their establishing themselves in the area. Ordinance 273 prohibited "public bath houses east of the Pacific Electric right of way," located west of the Strand. As an existing facility, Bruce's Lodge was situated east of right-of-way and was not immediately impacted by the new law, but it kept Mrs. Bruce from expanding her establishment. Another ordinance, 274, stated that managers wanting to operate any new bathhouses and other amusement places would have to make written application to the city's trustees. Additionally, the new law gave the trustees the power to regulate these businesses as they "deemed proper and necessary for the maintenance of public order, and the promotion of public morals."[30]

To discourage visitors to Manhattan Beach who might be "undesirable," or not have a host with property and a formal structure at the shoreline, Ordinance 275 was passed, prohibiting dressing or undressing in any automobile or other vehicle on any street or public place or in a tent or temporary structure on the beach. Additionally, various subterfuge measures revolving around city land leased to white citizens and posting of

"No Trespassing" signs were used to make "private" the beachfront near the location African Americans frequented. One observer even recalled a fence or a rope being installed to inhibit the African American beach-goers' usage of the shoreline in front of Bruce's Lodge. The private action of a cross burning—a symbolic use of terror and warning traditionally implemented by the KKK to claim place—also occurred near the property of one of the African American owners. Attempts to terrorize the Bruces in an anonymous telephone intimidation campaign also occurred.[31]

When the white supremacist harassment tactics failed to drive African Americans vacation property owners or visitors from Manhattan Beach, a proposal to condemn their North End neighborhood through eminent domain emerged. A campaign to create a public park was launched by private citizens and submitted to city officials. George Lindsey, a local resident and real estate agent, first approached the trustees in 1921, requesting action to discourage African Americans from establishing residency in Manhattan Beach. Although city officials were sympathetic to this line of thought, they were reluctant to act and privately stated that they did not want to be identified as bigots in the public record. After no action by city officials, Lindsey then circulated a petition requesting condemnation of the African American neighborhood for a public park and presented it to city officials on November 15, 1923. By the next Manhattan Beach trustees meeting, another petition was submitted by landowners of Block 5 and 12 of the Peck Tract, protesting the one filed by Lindsey. The signers of this petition against Lindsey's petition were not identified, but it can be assumed they included most or all of the African American property owners.[32]

During this same time the *Eagle* reported in a front-page article that the "Ku Klux Klan [was] operating unrestrictedly along the water front . . . of California." The correspondent issued a call of alarm that transplanted white supremacists from Texas were attempting to restrict "Colored Americans" from California's oceanfront, a location understood to be free for all. The article cited an incident occurring in May or June 1924 at a Redondo Beach pier where three African American men were fishing. They were approached by a white man who handed them a pamphlet titled "The Ideals of the Ku Klux Klan." Scrolled across the top of the pamphlet was

"Colored Folks beach three miles North." The African American men left, after no further harassment. Also citing the Bruce's Beach condemnation case, the *Eagle* called on its California "colored" readers to fight this sort of KKK propaganda and the legal actions to divest African Americans of their oceanfront property.[33]

The *Eagle*'s call to action appeared to have been grounded in the belief that the KKK was having undue influence on the Manhattan Beach trustees. As the Bruces had been some of the first settlers to this Manhattan Beach section, the *Eagle* admonished that their struggle was also "the fight of the [black] people[, and that] the NAACP and all organizations should look into this matter." The correspondent further chided readers that they must be vigilant in ensuring all African American property owners would be given a fair opportunity to continue ownership of their pleasure community sites. We can only speculate whether the KKK's activities may have influenced the Manhattan Beach trustees in the condemnation proceedings of the Bruce's Beach establishment and surrounding African American resort community. What is clearly supported by evidence, however, is that the rhetoric of southern exceptionalism did not match the situation unfolding at California's oceanfront and other places in the 1920s. White agitation at the opening of the Bruce resort in 1912 appeared not to have reemerged, at least not in the public discourse, until the 1920s eviction and condemnation actions.[34]

Eventually, on October 16, 1924, Manhattan Beach officials passed ordinances to condemn the property of the Bruces and other African Americans to create a public park under the Park and Playground Act of 1909. This action was sharply contested by some in the Manhattan Beach community. The African Americans and other community residents recognized the ploy to dispossess them. In court papers filed to fight condemnation of their property for a public park, black Angeleno landowners stated the situation was motivated by racial prejudice:

> The proceeding . . . is to divest . . . members of the Negro Race of their ownership of said land, and their residence in said City, and to banish them . . . from the portion of the said City which is nearly contiguous to the Pacific Ocean.

They also pointed out the illogical nature of creating a public park out of this section, as there was already a 144,000-square-foot land tract about a half-mile south, which had been given to the city for park usage. That park site was not only larger, but more centrally located to the city's population and required no condemnation. Further, the landowners pointed out, if there was need for a park in the city's North End, there was other property containing fewer buildings that could be condemned with less trouble and expense.[35]

Bruce's Beach and its visitors were not alone in facing extraordinary harassment and policy efforts to exclude African Americans from public beach usage. An effort to dispossess African Americans of their Santa Monica real estate was moving forward simultaneously. Just as in Manhattan Beach, Santa Monica used municipal action to stop African American real estate development ventures. In Santa Monica's Ocean Park neighborhood, African Americans were forced to give up a beachfront resort project in 1922 while retaining public beach usage on the oceanfront.

Legal sanctions and private harassment discouraged African Americans from visiting and settling in particular beach locales as the region's population increased during the 1920s. A second strategy for exclusion was also emerging from civic leaders, ironically involving claims of "opening" to exclude. Adversaries urged that the beaches should be preserved for the public, at least where African American land development projects were concerned. During the 1920s several "save the beaches" campaigns were implemented to keep African Americans from creating or maintaining beachfront resorts.

In 1925, a few miles north of Bruce's Beach, another African American beach resort plan received strong opposition. White citizens' groups blocked black businessman, attorney, and aspiring politician Titus Alexander from constructing a beachfront amusement park for the Los Angeles African American community at a proposed site in El Segundo (near Mines Field) on land owned by the city of Los Angeles. Local white businessmen obtained an injunction to prevent the city council from leasing a 200-foot beachfront section to Alexander, arguing it was an ill-advised handout to a private concern. They argued that Alexander's proposed facility not only opened the door to the full privatization of the county beaches, but also promoted segregation, because whites would not have access to a 200-feet section of the close to 400,000 feet (sixty-five miles) of Los Angeles County shoreline. As ingeniously as it was hidden in an ostensibly anti–special privilege and public openness argument, in fact it was race that motivated Alexander's opponents.[36]

In the 1920s Los Angeles's Department of Playground and Recreation estimated that on summer weekends and holidays a quarter or more of the total population of the county (500,000 plus) visited local beaches. Realizing beaches were a primary tourist destination, white city officials assiduously policed them and maintained their sanitation. In the 1920s the local public authorities began purchasing and managing oceanfront properties to assure public access and urged voters to support more coastal land acquisitions. African Americans were forced to pay taxes to buy up coastal land they might be discouraged or prohibited from using through explicit ordinance or by custom.[37]

Historian Lawrence Culver observed the fact that African American taxpayers "could stake a claim to the . . . recreational space that stood at the core of the [region's] civic life and identity made them seem more of a threat to white dominance than poorer migrants or immigrants." Ethnic exoticism at tourist attractions was encouraged by boosters. Tourist promoters used Chinese motifs, Spanish Revival architecture, and Mexican performers as theme elements at many area resorts. African Americans did not fit into this booster agenda, as they were a reminder of the national racial tensions of the 1920s. Systematized white racism in the Los Angeles region, when manifested in recreation space, was most consistently targeted at African Americans, although the racial and ethnic mix included whites of various European ethnicities, African Americans, Mexicans, Latinos, Japanese, Chinese, and Filipinos, along with California American Indians and Native Americans from other regions.[38]

Although whites were successful in taking land from African American owners in Manhattan Beach, this did not stop black Angelenos from using shoreline public space. After the Bruces' shoreline venture was taken by eminent domain for a park, city officials in 1927 leased city beach frontage and the pier to a crony, Oscar C. Bassonette, for a payment of one dollar for a period of twelve months. He placed a "No Trespassing" sign at the beach between Twenty-Fifth and Twenty-Seventh Streets as a way to deter people he later called "undesirables"—meaning African Americans—from using this beach section. He asked the local police to act as enforcers. These measures set in motion a series of harassment actions toward African Americans in Manhattan Beach that eventually bolstered some NAACP members' resolve to militantly press the issue of public beach access to African Americans.[39]

On Memorial Day the Manhattan Beach Police recorded the names and addresses of twenty-five swimmers in front of Bruce's Beach in a harassment action to dissuade them from swimming that day or in the future. Refusing to leave the water or the beach, the African American holiday crowd was told this police action had occurred because the swimmers were trespassing on privately leased beach frontage. An *Eagle* article with the headline "Attempt to Bulldoze Negro Bathers" articulated African American citizens' firm commitment to demand their civil rights "with both feet" in usage of this public beach.[40]

A California native and University of California, Los Angeles, African American student Elizabeth Catley, seemed to have internalized the *Eagle's* entitlement message. A member of a family that migrated from Texas, Mississippi, and Tennessee to Los Angeles in the early 1890s, on July 4, 1927, she was "hauled . . . jerked around . . . and pushed into an automobile" by Manhattan Beach Police, who arrested her for swimming at the same shoreline spot of the Memorial Day harassment. The *Eagle* report on the incident asserted Catley was swimming in the ocean alongside Japanese, Mexicans, and whites. She was held in her wet bathing suit at the police station until Mr. Slaughter, the father of some of the girls she was with on the beach, posted a ten-dollar bail. Her hostesses, sisters Willine and Estella Slaughter and other young women in their party, had not entered the ocean.[41]

At nineteen years old Catley was the oldest in her private beach party. Upon reflection about going into the ocean, she said to the *Eagle* correspondent, "I dared to do what I thought was my right [and] . . . was thrown in jail. . . . The real importance of the whole affair is just beginning to dawn upon me." As many other African Americans and young people of her age were beginning to do, Catley was demanding equal access to participate in all available urban public recreational spaces.[42]

On this same day, Roy Hilbert was also arrested for swimming in the contested area and released on a ten-dollar bail. Catley recounted to the *Eagle* correspondent that Mr. Hilbert was swimming in the ocean around Bruce's Beach as he did most every Sunday, and this was the first time he had been arrested. She also asserted that Police Chief Henry of Redondo (where Catley was most likely taken to jail) objected to the Manhattan Beach officers' incarcerating her. The Redondo police chief's purported reaction to the events gives some evidence that not all local citizens were of the same mind about using intimidation and harassment tactics toward African Americans to keep them off the South Bay shoreline. By allowing his jail to be used for the arrests of Catley and Hilbert, regardless of the chief's words on that day, his acquiescence supported Manhattan Beach Police use of aggressive intimidation to restrict African Americans public beach usage.[43]

On July 17, 1927, led by Los Angeles branch president, dentist, and attorney Dr. H. Claude Hudson (1887–1989), the NAACP entered the beach struggle with a dozen or so people willing to press the issue with a swim-in. Sixty-year-old Mrs. Sadie Chandler-Cole, an educated, cultured, militant, and stalwart member of the local NAACP, was one of the protesters, in what would be the branch's first organized action of civil disobedience. The daughter of a conductor of the Underground Railroad, a Fisk University graduate who became a social worker, music teacher, active clubwoman, and social activist, she would not tolerate racial restrictions. She moved to Los Angeles from Detroit, Michigan, in 1902 with her husband and their children to join her sister and other family members. Chandler-Cole's civic leadership accomplishments were numerous, including becoming the first woman to be elected vice president of the local NAACP branch in Los Angeles. The Chandler sisters and their extended relatives were pioneer African American families who made Angeleno history. Chandler-Cole once told writer Delilah Beasley she was determined to break up discrimination if she had to die in the process.[44]

Before the Los Angeles branch of the NAACP was formed in 1913, Chandler-Cole succeeded in having a sign with the words "Negro Trade

Not Wanted" removed from a Broadway soda shop. Her actions influenced Los Angeles Mayor Arthur C. Harper's order for all such signs in the city to be removed. Since Sadie Chandler-Cole was such a respected, determined, and committed activist in defense of racial justice, her participation in the beach protest was an important statement.[45]

Bissonette, the alleged white shoreline plot leaseholder with "belligerent" police officer enforcers, proceeded to have the African Americans ejected off the beach or arrested if they would not leave. NAACP members Hudson, John McCaskill (an African American Manhattan Beach property owner and taxpayer referenced earlier in this chapter), James Conley, and Romulus Johnson challenged the transparent expropriation of public land and were the only ones arrested for trespassing on what was alleged to be private beach property. They were officially charged with resisting a police officer and disturbing the peace. Others involved in the swim-in escaped arrest, including Sadie Chandler-Cole. Hudson and the three others incarcerated posted bond of ten dollars each and were told to appear in court on Tuesday, August 2, 1927. In the trial the four were represented by attorney Hugh MacBeth, who in his trial maneuvers called to the judge's attention the city's beach lease, Bissonette's failure to acknowledge the actual sum of money paid, and the fact that the only purported "undesirables" being arrested on the beach were African Americans. He further argued that the whole situation "reek[ed] with fraud, and deception, and [was] a blot on Americanism."[46]

Even given MacBeth's tactics, the four were still found guilty, with each sentenced to $100 fines or twenty days in jail. Upon appeal MacBeth got the judge to grant an arrest of judgment motion suspending the fines and releasing the men on a $500 bond. More important, the Manhattan Beach trustees revoked the private lease of the public beach and pier and secured a perpetual lease of its entire beach frontage, making it free for all the public's enjoyment. On August 16, 1927, the *Times* reported that Manhattan Beach trustees secured "two miles of foreshore, free from private exploitation or the erection of barriers, assure[s] residents and visitors an ocean playground in keeping with the spirit of democracy." Without direct reference to the recent beach scandal, the reporter argued that this action reflected the Manhattan Beach trustees' financial foresight and set an example for other Southern California beach cities. The victory by the NAACP's Los Angeles Branch energized the black Angeleno community. Also galvanized by the victory, the NAACP's national office proclaimed in a press release that this militant stand for civil rights in Southern California set a good example for the setting of the Nineteenth NAACP Convention, which would be held in Los Angeles in 1928.[47]

Around the United States, accessibility to beaches and resorts and demand for decent recreation space free from white harassment and intimidation became a political issue in African Americans' struggle against environmental racism and economic exploitation in the long freedom rights struggle and civil rights movement. Blacks continued to open businesses and other establishments for their social and physical welfare, as well as for amusement, entertainment, and lodging. As the twentieth century wore on, individual actors and local, state, and national groups, such as the NAACP, would increasingly utilize legal actions and public protests to dismantle legally sanctioned as well as informally enforced segregation and discrimination in public accommodations.[48]

Sustainability of the Bruce's Beach Resort Community

In this climate of mixed success and contestation for African American beach access, a lawsuit by the families challenging the condemnation of their properties in Manhattan Beach was unsuccessful. The landowners alleged the proceedings were arbitrary, oppressive, and inspired by racial prejudice. Their cottages and the Bruce resort were razed in 1927; the city moved quickly and preemptively before the legal challenge had been completed. Litigation lasted until 1929, and the African American landowners eventually settled for the most favorable sale prices they could obtain. Whether they were favorably, let alone adequately, compensated for their land has remained open to debate. These landowners were allowed to relocate to other places in Manhattan Beach, but not on the Strand (the beachfront). The Bruces chose not to relocate in Manhattan Beach, but did continue living in Los Angeles.[49]

In 1928 Mrs. Sanders purchased another vacation house at Twenty-Sixth Street and Highland Avenue, near her former property. She died in 1937 and left the property to her daughter, Ethel Atkinson. Mrs. Atkinson and her husband continued to use the property as her mother had, for both personal and rental use. She sold it in 1953, because her husband tired of driving to Manhattan Beach to care for it.[50]

Mrs. Barnett-Holt, the daughter of Milton B. and Anna Johnson, who were original African American landowners, purchased another home on Twenty-Third Street and Highland Avenue in 1927. She did not hold on to the property very long, because the neighbors were aggressively unpleasant and often grossly insolent. Mrs. Prioleau with Leslie King (who replaced Ms. Patterson as a partner in a duplex) moved the entire structure to the corner of Twenty-Fifth Street and Bayview Drive. Mrs. Prioleau enjoyed the new place for several years after her husband died in 1927. After she had been there a while, she learned that the new parcel had a restrictive covenant. Rather than risk the indignity of another eviction, she decided to trade the Manhattan Beach property for one in Los Angeles.[51]

The Slaughters who had erected a small apartment building, on land purchased next door to the McCaskills and across from the Bruce's Beach condemned property on Twenty-Sixth Street and Bayview Drive, were foreclosed on in 1930. They advertised it as a hotel after the eminent domain process began. Brigham speculated that the Slaughters possibly "hoped that their facilities would replace those the Bruces had been forced to abandon" and asserted they left the area due to animosity they received from their white neighbors. As "Negro" commercial establishment owners, they attracted larger numbers of blacks to the area who were non–property owners. Like the Bruces, the Slaughters may have been the recipients of more directed animosity from white citizens, because their establishment, although smaller and able to accommodate fewer visitors, was symbolic of the causes as well as an intentional promoter of the "Negro invasion."[52]

After the African American landowners who had their private property taken relocated to other parcels and Manhattan Beach authorities acquired the contested two blocks, they continued to be harassed in the same manner as before the eminent domain proceedings. The anti-Negro activity carried out included house burnings, intimidation, and the same quasi-legal maneuvers of posting "10 Minutes Only" parking signs. When a KKK burning cross appeared one night on the hill above Mrs. Sanders's house, the police did quickly respond to extinguish the fire.[53]

In an ironic twist, other African American landowners in Manhattan Beach during this time of their nearby neighbors' dispossession in the 1920s did not suffer the same fate and had no problems with the overtly hostile acts or vandalism. The homes or parcels they owned were outside of the two blocks where the affected families lived. The Leggett family purchased property for $1,600 in Manhattan Beach in 1916 and their descendants continue to own this property today. James and Anna Janet Leggett were both from Atlanta, Georgia, and met while at Howard University in Washington DC, while training to be pharmacists. From there they moved to Los Angeles in 1898. He and his partner owned Smith and Leggett's Drug Store in downtown Los Angeles at Fifth and Spring Streets, and the family lived on Ceres Street, where many African Americans lived in that era, in what today is the Flower District.[54]

Camelia Leggett Bradford, a teacher by profession, inherited the Manhattan Beach property from her mother, Anna Janet Leggett. (Camelia's husband, Cornelius "Neil" N. Bradford, a Los Angeles city police officer, also inherited Manhattan Beach property from his mother.) Mrs. Bradford was fully aware of what had taken place a few doors south of her family's vacation property. Her daughter, Ann Bradford Luke, remembers that there were regular inquiries as to whether her parents wanted to sell their Manhattan Beach land. More than a few times over the years while she was in grade school, Luke recalls men showing up unannounced at their home near Fiftieth Street and Western Avenue in Los Angeles to inquire about buying her mother's Manhattan Beach parcel. She remembers her mother was always a bit uncomfortable and agitated when this happened.[55]

Starting when she was a child, Luke's mother discussed with her the events of the Bruce's Beach community removal and considered the situation a social injustice. In an interview with the author, Luke indicated that her mother never had a good feeling about the Manhattan Beach community, because of both the seizure of the African Americans' properties and their general harassment by white Manhattan Beach citizens.[56]

When Luke inherited the family's property it was a vacant parcel. She developed it in 1974 into a four-unit apartment building. In 1995 she renovated and remodeled the structure to meet the desires of the contemporary renter interested in living in Manhattan Beach. Luke's mother always encouraged the investment in this property and other real estate around Los Angeles. The Manhattan Beach property is layered with pride and sadness: for the accomplishments of her family, and due to the unfortunate events of the 1920s. These sentiments have been carried forth into contemporary generations of the family living in the twenty-first century.[57]

Memory Erasure, Reclamation, and Park Creation

Thirty years of city inaction on the appropriated land glaringly proved that the only public purpose served by the actions of the 1920s was to forcibly evict and attempt to exclude African American entrepreneurs and makers of a leisure community. This idleness and vacancy worked as a history erasure of the vital place once called Bruce's Beach. A fear of history, of remembrance of past acts, prompted city officials to remake the unused space of the former African American community into a park around 1956.

In the 1950s the Manhattan Beach Recreation Commission had begun to worry that the descendants of the former Bruce's Beach property owners might sue to regain their land because it had not been developed for the purpose it was originally taken—to create a "public park." Periodically, in the intervening decades before the 1950s, city authorities received investor inquiries about purchasing this unimproved land for private development. City council correspondence and meeting minutes indicated these investors were informed the land was to be used as a public park and was not for sale.[58]

The heightened interest in developing a park may have been due to a Fresno State College graduate student, Robert Brigham, who was conducting interviews with local residents to write his 1956 master's thesis, "Landownership and Occupancy By Negroes In Manhattan Beach," and whose work may have triggered the city officials to independently act on the park project. City council meeting minutes for January 11, 1955, indicate that Brigham, in his role as a local city resident, was "the Secretary of the Recreation Commission." It is feasible that, while in the midst of his research and serving on the commission, Brigham's research implied or may have expressly pointed out to city officials that they needed to take action to fulfill their obligations to create a park from the expropriated private property at the Bruce's Beach resort settlement.[59]

A *South Bay Breeze* article of November 9, 1954, titled "Manhattan Beach Scans 27th St. Site for Fourth City Park" reported on a joint session between the city council and the Recreation Commission to discuss developing a preliminary park plan. The article indicated that the city officials had pointed out there were no available funds for this project, and another *Breeze* article later reported Recreation Commissioner John W. Campbell as saying the land was not appropriate for any use in developing a park or recreation space. Nonetheless, in 1956 the vacant sloping land of sandy terrain was graded and transformed into five terraces. Topsoil and fill dirt were brought in from nearby Pollywog Pond, and grass, shrubs and trees were planted. Bayview Drive was subsumed into a terrace level of the new park. Lacking an identity as much as a purpose, over the years the park has been renamed several times. A naming contest sponsored by the Kiwanis Club and supported by the Manhattan Beach City Council in 1962 established the site as Bayview Terrace Park. Prior to this the site was referred to as City Park and Beach Front Park.[60]

New interest emerged in this city park site, and in 1974 the city renamed the park after the city of Culiacan in Mexico to honor Manhattan Beach's first sister-cities relationship. "Parque Culiacan" became the latest name of the park developed from the African American dispossession. In a 1977 *Easy Reader* article titled "Parque Culiacan: a smoldering history," Robert Brigham recalled that city officials did not overtly refer to the park's history in their speeches at the rededication ceremony. Brigham recalled that Manhattan Beach City Council member Steve Blumberg "made some 'ambiguous remarks' about good human relations," and he "hoped the park's renaming would foster better understanding between people of diverse backgrounds and cultures." This was the extent of public comment reproduced in newspaper reports at the time, although one journalist's story on the rededication ceremony recalled the Bruces.[61]

Thirty years after the Parque Culiacan naming, a new chapter opened at the former African American resort community site. The Leadership Manhattan Beach Class of 2003 (LMBC 2003)—an educational forum to develop and unite existing and aspiring youth and adult community leaders to encourage more civic involvement—proposed a contest to rename Parque Culiacan. By 2003 Culiacan was no longer the sister city of Manhattan Beach (a new sister-city association was established with Santa Rosalia of Baja California, Mexico, in 1989), and the Leadership Class believed the name "Parque Culiacan" was therefore passé for the community. The group thought the park renaming project would be a fun way to involve residents in civic activities and support of community pride. The Manhattan Beach Parks and Recreation Commission, and the city council unanimously approved the contest idea in January and February 2003, respectively. The move to rename the site again opened the door to a longer view of memory and meaning.[62]

This new boosterism and local promotion could have set the stage to rebury the site's past and the city's public chicanery. In the "Renaming of Parque Culiacan Position Paper" written by the classmates of LMBC 2003, the introduction stated: "[The proposal] is not intended to change whatsoever the nature or ambience of this quiet park in any fashion." The *Background of Culiacan Park* section of this document stated that "the park began its life in the 1920s" due to "the City Council initiation of eminent domain proceedings to take the property located from The Strand to Highland Avenue, between 26th and 27th Streets." The document presented no other details about the 1920s property confiscation events. In his article of February 27, 2003, titled "Contest Set to Rename Parque Culiacan," *Easy Reader* reporter Jerry Roberts called this out, conveying that this opening text was an understatement about the actual events of the park's birth out of the ashes of misfortune.[63]

The theme of the park-renaming contest was: "To demonstrate the best of Manhattan Beach by celebrating the best of our past while encouraging the best for our future." Contest rules stated the park could not be named after an individual, and submissions had to be accompanied by a five-hundred-word-or-less explanation of how the name reflected the contest theme and would be appropriate for the park. A six-judge panel was selected from the Parks and Recreation Commission and local civic organizations to identify the top five names, and five alternate names to recommend to the city council for the final selection. The one-page "Rename Parque Culiacan Contest" form did not include a description of the park's "history." Only a few words were offered about the park's geographical features and landscape design in the form's narrative about the contest particulars. A $100 prize was offered to the person who submitted the winning name.[64]

The contest's promotion efforts included press releases sent to local media; advertisements on the city website, in local newspapers, and on the local cable television station; and circulation of the contest form throughout the community, including to schools. Downplayed but present in all the news coverage was the story of the 1920s African American resort community land dispossession via eminent domain proceedings undertaken by white Manhattan Beach city founders. The civil rights protests for shoreline usage, however, remained overlooked. The majority of the news and community outlets covering the contest offered the site history in their text as transmitted orally over fifty years from community members, and from interviews with Robert Brigham. Much of the news coverage mentioned Brigham's 1956 master's thesis covering the site's historical events, but it was not apparent in these stories whether the journalists had actually read the study. A few writers of these stories offered their own additions to the folklore of the Bruce's Beach site in the words chosen to frame or texture their social commentary around the facts of the site history, such as that African American landowners "ultimately settled for favorable sale prices." This framing was a distraction from the truth of the history of the Manhattan Beach founders' intentional use of state power in actions motivated by racism to evict their African American neighbors and was a self-serving attempt to absolve contemporary white citizens of their guilt about the shame of past moral tragedy. This reframing of public memory bid to tell the story of the community's past in a more positive light.[65]

In 2003 South Bay journalists did not solicit or conduct any new research to develop the retelling of the Bruce's Beach site historical narrative. The primary and secondary research sources are not robust and in some instances not easily accessible. The LMBC 2003 did undertake research in the city's archives and other local resources to learn about the "park" history after the 1920s eminent domain proceedings. If Brigham's master's thesis had been more thoroughly read (or read at all), there might have been more nuanced and detailed discussions of the actors and actions involved in the social injustice and justice events of the contestation between white bigots' maneuverings and African Americans' protests in Manhattan Beach. Furthermore, for the general public, the difficulty of research material access is a contributing factor as to why the Bruce's Beach story continues to be narrowly cast.

Over 120 entries were submitted from fifth graders to long-time residents, with most coming from students. In recommendations for new park names a restoration of Bruce's Beach was not considered, though oblique references to the 1920s eminent domain property evictions of the African American families did enter in the essays for Friendship Park, Ocean View Community Park, and Harmony Park. The others made reference primarily to the beauty of the ocean views and the experiences of spiritual rejuvenation and nature one could have while visiting the park, disregarding the historical origins of how the place became "public."[66]

Despite previous direction that the LMBC 2003 pursue the renaming project, after the elaborate contest proceedings on April 15, 2003, the city council voted to keep "Parque Culiacan" as the park name. Council members concluded they could not support the reasoning behind renaming the park, and that "while the intent was good none of the names proposed [were of] interest." During the public comment period before the council's vote, several residents, including long-time active members of the Sister City Committee, had voiced their displeasure about the renaming idea. Some of these citizens made their sentiments known in various newspaper interviews published around the time of this city council meeting.[67]

The city council accepted the LMBC 2003 gift of $3,600 raised for a new park plaque. They directed city staff to work with LMBC 2003 to develop text for a new plaque, while retaining the "Parque Culiacan" name and explaining the park site's history. Sandra Seville-Jones, LMBC 2003 co-project manager, suggested the plaque text writer should attempt to thematically combine the park's history with the sister-city ideals that enabled the Bruces to gain partial reentry to the public memory. Referred to as the "tragic" circumstances, the leading historical fact on the new park plaque identified Bruce's Beach as a resort that had been utilized by "African American Angelenos." Also noted was that "minority families" were "housed" in the two-block resort neighborhood and evicted by condemnation through eminent domain proceedings. The other tragic circumstance not illuminated in the 2003 plaque text was that there was no sense of the 1920s-era African American initiative or designation of responsibility for Manhattan Beach's public racism and injustice. No mention was made of the African American landowners' legal fight opposing the city's land grab, or of the black Angelenos' civil rights agency of the 1920s that forced city authorities to cease discriminatory land leasing policies illegally inhibiting African Americans from local public shoreline usage.[68]

The LMBC 2003 carried the city's public memory from no specific identification of their community's dispossessed African American pioneers in the "Renaming of Parque Culiacan Position Paper" to an affirmative step toward a more open and inclusive recognition of the site's history. Though still a partial story, for many of the Manhattan Beach polity the words on the new Parque Culiacan plaque discussing Bruce's Beach would be their first awareness of their town's African American resort pioneers. The new park signage and plaque were rededicated in July 2003.[69]

The 1920s-era public park campaign to halt the "Negro invasion" was successful. From 2003 to 2018 African Americans remained less than one percent of the city's population. In a nod toward diversity from a more inclusive local electorate, businessman and actor Mitch Ward was elected for his first term as a city council member in 2003, the first African American to serve in this capacity. He also identified himself publicly as a gay man who had been married to his partner for more than twenty years. Ward continued as an elected city official until 2011, and before finishing his service he would be Manhattan Beach's mayor twice. Ward's presence as a city elected official and his input would be pivotal in the next chapter of the park renaming and the public recollection of the once-popular African American beach resort site.[70]

Name and Public Memory Reconsidered, Again

The LMBC 2003's Rename Parque Culiacan contest resulted in new consciousness and a new park name plaque. It also opened another chapter in the park-naming saga and public remembrance of the site of Manhattan Beach's dispossessed African American resort community in December 2005. During a city council meeting a local resident and activist Patrick McBride requested consideration of "the renaming of Parque Culiacan in honor of civil rights leader Rosa Parks" who had died in October 2005 at the age of ninety-two. The city council directed the Parks and Recreation Commission to "discuss and consider" the request to rename Parque Culiacan because of Mrs. Parks's historical civil rights achievements. At the commission meeting on February 27, 2006, a lively public discussion among the members and the general public unfolded. The advocates for and opponents of a park name change presented their cases. Patrick McBride argued that, because of the removal of the African American resort settlement, the park had "a huge civil rights significance and deserve[d] the name of a great civil rights leader [like Rosa Parks]."[71]

Opposing this proposed name change, long-time Sister City Committee member and local resident Marge Crutchfield argued that the message of the Parque Culiacan plaque represented "understanding diversity, appreciating your fellow man no matter what his color is or where he comes from"—all things the Sister City program stands for. Bill Roos, a resident who lived near the park, suggested "the [city] should not get so political." Whether he recognized it or not, as a citizen offering his comments, Roos was participating in the "political" discourse of government in his community. His and the Sister City Committee's insistence to preserve the Parque Culiacan name, its symbolism, and its physical signage was a political act of power in selective remembrance and organized forgetting. Maintenance of this moniker strategically silenced the conflicting historical political facts and events of the park's site in the public sphere, and in the identity and self-definition of these town citizens. Roos further argued that the eight to ten thousand dollars the city would spend on new signage should be utilized for a new shower and drinking fountain at the park's shoreline edge, for which he had advocated the last three years.[72]

No evident suggestion appeared in the meeting minutes to contact a Los Angeles historian or other professional with expertise in these matters. A recurring theme in the commissioners' comments was a concern that if the park name was changed, the new moniker needed a local connection related to Manhattan Beach. Commissioner Kathleen M. Paralusz favored a name more inclusive in recognizing "our commitment to diversity." Commissioner Edward O. Lear's comments spoke for his colleague Paralusz's sentiments, "Culiacan might not be the best name, but the connection of Rosa Parks is not compelling enough to rename the park."[73]

During the February 2006 meeting, the city's Parks and Recreation director Richard Gill, an African American, suggested that Bruce's Beach would be a more appropriate name for the park, as he saw no direct connection between the city and Rosa Parks. Commissioners unanimously agreed that if a name change was to occur, they supported renaming the park Bruce's Beach, to reflect the local history. As Commissioner Lear noted:

> The Commission has an interest in sending the message that Manhattan Beach stands for, amongst other things, diversity and recognizes that the greatest blemish in our history is what happened in the 1920s at Bruce's Beach.[74]

McBride indicated that if the commissioners liked the name Bruce's Beach, he and others would respond favorably to this moniker. A motion was unanimously passed recommending to the Manhattan Beach City Council that the park's name *not* be changed to "Rosa Parks Park."[75]

At their meeting on March 21, 2006, the city council passed a similar motion. The next event of the park-renaming saga took place at the meeting on April 18, 2006, when Mayor Mitch Ward requested and the council directed staff to refer the renaming of Parque Culiacan back to the Parks and Recreation Commission for the exploration of a new name with historical significance to the city.[76]

In the midst of the city officials' discourse about renaming the park, a descendant of the Bruces spoke publicly about the possible park name. Bernard Bruce, a grandson of Willa and Charles Bruce, in conjunction with the Center for Law in the Public Interest (CLIPI/renamed the City Project in the fall of 2006) in a letter dated March 21, 2006, to Mayor Mitch Ward, urged the renaming of Parque Culiacan to Bruce's Beach to commemorate and honor the civil rights legacy of the Bruce family. CLIPI/The City Project also lobbied city officials to include the installation of interpretive panels and public art to accurately tell the story of the site once the park was renamed Bruce's Beach. CLIPI/The City Project, known for its work on equal access to public places—especially beaches and green spaces for underserved and underrepresented urban populations—recognized the power of history not only for reclaiming a place, but promoting the contemporary cause of equal access through celebrating the history of its assertion. These letters supporting the park renaming to Bruce's Beach most likely exerted some influence with Mayor Ward and the other city officials who may have reviewed them.[77]

The commission took up the matter of identifying a new name for Parque Culiacan again at their May 22, 2006, meeting. The very occasion alerted journalists, who, in their reporting for their readers, retold the story of Bruce's Beach and provided the contemporary community with an opportunity for renewed exploration of its history and interpretation. In his article covering the proceedings, reporter Deepa Bharath wrote that in the layered history of the serene and scenic park "lies a controversial past and an uneasiness and embarrassment that continues to this day," and that the matter of the park's renaming in 2003 and 2006 "caused a stir in the community." Bharath opined that the upcoming Parks and Recreation Commission consideration of whether to rename Parque Culiacan would ensure that its history, however unpleasant, would not be forgotten.[78]

The May 15 *Daily Breeze* article also featured comments from Mayor Ward. He expressed support for the park's name change to Bruce's Beach, a modification of his 2003 position to leave the park name unchanged. Ward noted, "It is pointless to change the name [of the park] to reflect a theme such as friendship or peace, however honorable they might seem. Rosa Parks, too, was a great leader. But there's little there in terms of relevance to local history." Other voices included Manhattan Beach Sister City Committee representative Marge Crutchfield, who continued to oppose another name change of the park site.[79]

At a commission meeting on May 22, 2006, those for and against a name change of the historic park site lined up to speak. As Deepa Bharath observed in his *Daily Breeze* article of May 24, 2006, the assembly was "an emotional meeting," permeated not just with words but imagery. He wrote, "Several residents . . . favoring the name change [to Bruce's Beach] wore t-shirts bearing the likeness of Rosa Parks with a pink paper heart with the letters 'BB' pinned on their shirts." The majority of the supporters for the name change advocated for the site to be renamed Bruce's Beach to honor the historic struggle that took place on the land. Resident Michele Murphy asserted that plaques could disappear overtime, but naming gave power to remembrance of the historic site.[80]

Naming a site offers shared civic commemorative recognition and acknowledgement of actors, actions, or other features, such as destroyed significant buildings. This identity and meaning allows a site to tell its stories and history to the public. As historian David Glassberg observes, "Places loom large not only in our personal recollections but also in the collective memory of our communities." In a few words, a name on a public site infuses history into the collective memory of the local and national culture. An oral heritage is transmitted with a name for people who never have the opportunity to visit a site and read a plaque text or other information about a location.[81]

New community opposition to the renaming of the park joined continuing opposition from those previously heard in 2003. The new voices argued that renaming the park Bruce's Beach would bring up bad feelings and tell a negative story. John Bushman, a life-long Angeleno and member of the city's Metlox, Police, and Fire Facility Committee argued that if the name were to change it should be something "non-descript" like Ocean View, Surf View, or Sunset View. The historically accurate Bruce's Beach as a name for the park was "too descriptive," as some citizens were increasingly recognizing the power of remembering this place. The marking of a place for history was too powerful for some, sustaining the shame of past wrong rather than repairing it by remembering.[82]

Historian Paul A. Shackel has observed that while many minority histories are about struggle, racism, and tragedy and many Americans see their commemoration as important, others continue to struggle with the inclusion of these stories in American heritage. Changing the park name to something "non-descript" or innocuous would be a symbolic act of deliberate re-erasure of the site's history and a continuation of the process of normalizing white hegemony in the community.[83]

Similar to his fellow citizen John Bushman, resident Jim Wagner had a problem with challenging the city's accepted history. Instead of diminishing the recognition of the site's history, Wagner was explicitly against remembering it at all. Wagner sarcastically suggested to the commission that the park should be named "Mea Culpa." As every city has its dark secrets, he did not understand why this beautiful park should make amends for an errant past. He commented that this was not Mississippi, and that he did not comprehend naming a park after something that has not contributed to the development of Manhattan Beach.[84]

Some would argue with Wagner that the making of a community devoid of African Americans and other people of color had indeed been a deliberate strategy for the growth of Manhattan Beach. As Brigham's 1956 thesis recounted, the unofficial, underlying reason for the 1920s Bruce's Beach resort community property dispossession was due to what some whites hyperbolically decried as a "Negro invasion." They had declared the African American presence as a threat to the city's property values and its ability to continue to attract Euro-Americans to the shoreline community. Of course, a mass influx of African American residents in the twentieth century was entirely unlikely due to varied socioeconomic and geographic conditions, but that did not stop the city from using its policy and powers to disrupt and dispossess the African American citizenry. Although Manhattan Beach was not Mississippi, it still had used some of the same white supremacy attitudes and exclusion policies that disenfranchised African Americans in Mississippi of their civil rights and their rights as consumer citizens. The park's renaming advocates recognized that Manhattan Beach's growth has exclusively been among an aspirational and higher-income white group, which was a product of harassment and removal of African Americans.[85]

A majority of the commissioners favored renaming the park Bruce's Beach and were unafraid of a more inclusive city history and commemoration of a moral tragedy. Others wanted to maintain the status quo. In a 4–2 vote, the Parks and Recreation commissioners recommended to the city council the renaming of Parque Culiacan to Bruce's Beach to reflect the historical events that took place at this site. A *Beach Reporter* article of May 25, 2006, titled "What's in the Name?" described the commission's action as a "controversial decision" that would go before the city council for "the final say about the park's name" at its meeting on July 5, 2006. At that time the council included some members of the 2003 council, who unanimously voted against renaming Parque Culiacan.[86]

The city-elected and staff officials and the public maneuvered through discourses of political avoidance, gamesmanship, and expediency in their deliberations about renaming the park. Mayor Ward urged his fellow council members to center the discussion on whether the park should be renamed Bruce's Beach. In his remarks before opening the meeting to the public comments, however, Mayor Ward shifted the focus of the discussion to the origin of the land itself in Manhattan Beach's history, and away from the Bruce family. To frame this point he cited a passage in the *Manhattan Beach Observer* newsletter of the all-volunteer Manhattan Beach Residents Association:

> When Manhattan Beach was incorporated in 1912 George Peck, bucking the then current practice of racial exclusion, opened up two blocks of land on the beach for African Americans to purchase. George Peck is remembered as a generous businessman who helped his black neighbors build a fishing pier (Peck's Pier) near the resort, which was the only pier open to African Americans in the area.[87]

Mayor Ward reiterated the evening's discussion should be "about the movement . . . the Bruce family generated as a result of the generosity of George Peck." Ward's words introduced a new dynamic to the site's interpretation narrative dialogue about renaming the park that until now had been about commemorating the city's African American resort community's dispossession and pioneering local entrepreneurs, not the white developer Peck who allegedly sold them the land.[88]

Twenty-three people eventually came to the microphone to offer their comments for and against the park name change. As they had at an early 2006 Parks and Recreation Commission meeting, many in the audience favoring the name change wore light pink and yellow hearts with the letters BB pinned on their clothing. The demographics of the public attending the meeting reflected the ethnic makeup of Manhattan Beach. Most everyone in the audience was a white person.[89]

The opposition voices from the Sister City program boosters were the most prevalent at the July 5 meeting. During the public comment period, speaking for many of her allies, Manhattan Beach Sister City Committee founding member and long-time local beauty shop owner Carmen

Daugherty expressed concern that the group's years of service would be forgotten if the park name were changed. Other program enthusiasts thought the name Parque Culiacan was a more recent and a more positive reference than Bruce's Beach.[90]

The Sister City program's claim for the park name raised issues of selection and compound meanings of place and memory. Historian David Glassberg reminds us that "the various senses of place in a community reflect not only it residents' emotional attachments to the local environment but also their position in a larger economic and political system." In Manhattan Beach, "marking" one's presence of the more contemporary white residents was pitted against the historic African American property ownership, dispossession, and civil rights actions as claims to preeminence and remembrance.

Resident Larry Grik offered another perspective to this chapter of the site's renaming. He and his neighbors who liked Bayview Terrace as a new name asserted that it reflected the park's location, topography, Bayview Drive (which once bisected the park), and the view of the Santa Monica Bay. Representative of a few others who spoke that night, Grik also argued there was no need to revisit a tragic historic event. These few people saw remembrance of the African American resort events as negative and a step backward. He indicated that, due to his lack of support for the park renaming to Bruce's Beach, some had characterized him as a racist. Mayor Ward offered reassurance that people were not saying he was a racist. Grik said he felt intimidated by citizens supporting the name change, because he did not endorse it. He claimed the situation was turning into a civil rights discussion.[91]

Whether or not Grik was a racist, his rhetoric presented a common conservative, neoracist argument of "white injury." His argued that, in recognizing the settlement history of dispossessed African Americans and their city forefathers' eminent-domain land dispossession, current citizens were "intimidated" and wrongly made to suffer. His resentment at joining this Manhattan Beach site to a civil rights narrative suggests he accorded power to place. Grik and his faction's "whiteness" status and privilege—dependent on what W. E. B. Du Bois called a "public and psychological wage" involving "public deference" and their preferential "personal treatment" by key social and political institutions—was being challenged. Others joined Grik in objecting to the name change of a public park to acknowledge the wrongs of former officials.[92]

The majority of the individuals who spoke up at the meeting favored the renaming. Some of their thoughts echoed those heard from the city council. Donna Warren, a native black Californian and Hawthorne resident, recalled that until she was twelve years old she could not go past Crenshaw Boulevard due to the existing racism and occasional racial harassment. A 2006 Green Party candidate for lieutenant governor of California, Warren insisted that our society has to accept the historic truth in order to move forward in friendship and as comrades. Local resident Bob Willett observed that property values were not at risk when the African American families lived in Manhattan Beach, and that it was a tragic and cruel mistake the families were pressured to leave. In my role at the time as a University of Southern California graduate student involved with scholarly research on the site who had been consulted by some citizens in favor of the renaming, I joined the debate, contending the renaming of the public park would tell an American pioneer story about successful African American entrepreneurs who serviced their community and recognize a more inclusive rich history that had been overlooked.[93]

Long-time city resident Gail Runk reminded those at the July 5 meeting that the past was not that far away, as there had been a cross burned on the lawn of African American residents in the 1970s. She noted that in the 1960s she was instrumental in the creation of the Manhattan Beach/Hermosa Fair Housing Council after discovering landlords would tell communities-of-color apartment seekers that none were available, but later lease to white renters. Runk asserted the renaming of the park was a positive action of acknowledgement.[94]

Thirty-year resident Grace Walters said it frightened her that the Bruce's Beach history was not widely acknowledged and kept undercover. Other comments added to the variety of interpretations regarding local knowledge of the site's historical truths and what residents thought might have relevance for commemoration. This community dialogue and process about the broader Manhattan Beach history and its significance was important in itself as a moment of public remembrance acknowledging the issues on record, formally and publicly.[95]

Many white and a few African American citizens are uncomfortable with discussion and recognition of racial discriminatory events. But, as scholar Robert Weyeneth has noted, these conversations are part of the education process to help societies think about the relevance of the past, particularly of events that remain controversial. These discursive acts acknowledge that history matters and its legacy continues to shape the present. Public hearings, apologies, memorials, plaques, site name changes, financial compensation, and days of contemplating the past are symbolic acts of recognition that offer moral reparations, provide a means for present generations to respond to the past and draw lessons for the future, and present a path toward healing and unity.[96]

Perhaps due to internal parochialism, the council at first indicated the majority were in favor of retaining the "Parque Culiacan," citing respect for the Sister City program, the recent plaque, the alternative of a formal apology, and compliance with the longstanding policy of not naming city parks or buildings after individuals. Ward used a bit of drama, theatrics, political gamesmanship, and his personal story to obtain his colleagues' vote.[97]

Among his remarks, Ward reminded all as the city's first African American elected official who was also a gay man that he was a minority on the council in more ways than one. Ward commented on how good the Bruces must have felt when they bought their land and built their resort. Once again, he invoked the legend of George H. Peck, noting that he wanted to honor the foresight of this visionary man, who had aided the Bruces' entrepreneurial endeavors. More political maneuvering and posturing ensued. Ward questioned council colleagues about why they valued the people from Mexico over the original American inhabitants of that property.[98]

After Ward turned the council's vote to 3–2 in favor of the name change, loud applause erupted from the audience. As Michelle Murphy noted in the *Manhattan Beach Observer*, many participants were convinced the park name change to Bruce's Beach might not have happened were it not for Ward. His words sufficiently soothed the anxieties of the polity, or at least of the council. As had the arguments of Warren, Runk, and Walters, Ward's presence as a contemporary African American Manhattan Beach pioneer reminded his constituents that the park renamed Bruce's Beach not only commemorates the past, but also the memory of the present and the future.[99]

One important change wrought by the public hearing was recognition of the Bruce's Beach resort settlers as Manhattan Beach pioneers themselves, who encouraged economic development through real estate transactions, property improvements, and leisure consumption. The previous discourse had depicted the African Americans solely as victims in relationship to the white city pioneers who evicted them, subject to the goodwill of the white people who helped them. In the newspaper discourse local polity members pointedly discussed the more challenging, less-spoken-about issues of the lost economic opportunities forfeited by the African American resort landowners due to their city fathers' 1920s land dispossession.[100]

Public Remembrance Narrative

Moving the new multifaceted discourse to the memorial plaque would not be automatic. The new language proposed for the 2006 plaque at the December 5 city council meeting included some new words, which changed the meaning conveyed by the original text. While some of the language of the 2003 plaque was semantically problematic, and the legacy of the nonviolent civil rights agency occurring at the site was not included, the overall text conveyed a public history memory of the site that offered primacy to the African American pioneers.[101]

Manhattan Beach polity members were still not satisfied with the newly edited language of the plaque text. While some saw it as not going far enough to tell the history and its meaning, others continued to contest any recognition of the historical wrong. In the public comment period local citizens Patrick McBride and Bev Morse suggested more effort should be put into deciding the suitable wording of the plaque, and the decision on the final language should be deferred. Sandra Seville-Jones, LMBC 2003 co-project manager, who was involved with the original text creation, indicated that the additional wording to the plaque raised questions. Shaped by the local elected political actors to suit their political and ideological agendas, whether intended or not, the new language of the Bruce's Beach plaque text changed the meaning of the site's public memory, as well as the commemoration of the black Manhattan Beach and Angeleno pioneers. The proposed language of 2006 changed the meaning of the site's public history remembrance.[102]

During the meeting of December 5, 2006, the city council unanimously voted to approve the new wording. With this approval, the opportunity to recognize additional significance of the Bruce's Beach site in the new plaque language was passed over for a narrative of political expediency that created new problems. The revised history text now glorified a white businessman, a city father who in fact had been disturbed by the Bruce resort opening in 1912. George H. Peck had tried to keep African Americans from using the beach with the installation of "no trespassing" signs and police deputies patrolling the area. Later, in 1924, his business associate and son-in-law Herb Culler roped off the shoreline at Twenty-Sixth and Twenty-Seventh Streets to discourage African Americans' usage in front of the Bruce resort. Peck's silence during the eminent domain eviction proceedings in the 1920s indicates support for the removal of African American resort community. Yet he was now being honored, as this new plaque language misrepresented historical events and their significance.[103]

The Next Chapter in Bruce's Beach Remembrance

For many Americans the stories of places like Bruce's Beach are what historian Edward T. Linenthal calls "indigestible" narratives: stories that "stick . . . like a fishbone in [a] city's throat." The terms used to characterize engagement with these sites and stories speak of processes of erasure: marginalizing, suppressing, concealing, masking. Linenthal asserts that "the enduring hunger for redemptive narratives smoothens any rough edges in these indigestible stories, insisting that other, more positive stories about [an uncomfortable historic event] . . . be told in the service of 'balance.'"[104]

In the controversy over the 2006–7 final Bruce's Beach signage, the historical understanding of the site evolved into a political contest to absolve contemporary white citizens' guilt about the 1920s land dispossession and racial discrimination. The new text featured the white city founder George

H. Peck in the first line as the hegemonic subject of the narrative. Peck was an important man in Manhattan Beach history. While he may not have placed racially restrictive covenants on two blocks of his new land subdivision, Peck was agitated by the African American presence in 1912 and was one of the white landowners who tried to aggressively discourage this presence. Contrary to what some local residents have passed down through oral history, evidence does not support that Peck directly sold or set aside any land to specifically be sold to the African American families at the Bruce's Beach resort area. Unfortunately, popular memory of historical events and actors in this situation has proven difficult to change, even with new scholarship, advocacy, and more enlightened historical and cultural civic leadership.

There is no record of Peck standing up to the bigotry of his fellow citizens in the 1920s. By his silence Peck at least condoned, if not supported their actions. Peck's prioritization in the new language diminished the symbolic life of the destroyed African American resort community and erased by omission their civil rights activism and agency.[105]

The plaque text made no mention of the nonviolent, but militant, NAACP civil rights agents of the 1920s who stood up in civil disobedience and whose actions aided in forcing the city government to discontinue discriminatory land leasing policies inhibiting African Americans from Manhattan Beach public shoreline usage. Stating that Bruce's Beach was "the only beach in Los Angeles County for all people" and identifying the other resort pioneers as "minority families" erases by substitution and misrepresents the African American history and public memory at the site. This site marks the place where an African American collective demanded justice and equality, setting the stage for the fading away of racial restriction attempts at public beaches, and for the opening of these spaces for all in the coming decades. The new plaque text reinscribed the historical meaning and commemoration of the past to subvert the apparent public intent of memorialization of the heritage of Bruce's Beach as a place where pioneering black Californians seized the initiative to participate in the fruits of the state's recreational and real estate offerings.

As many Americans continue to grapple with the commemoration of histories that include struggle, racism, and sometimes even tragedy, each marginalized group's commemoration is important, as it allows them to claim a part of the public memory and American identity. Linenthal asserts, "Conscientious remembrance is more than a necessary expansion of the nation's narrative. It is an act of moral engagement, a declaration that there are other American lives too long forgotten that count." Bruce's Beach was a site not only of African American presence, but struggle. Its remembrance forges production of a more inclusive and diverse American story in the local, regional, and national historical narratives of American history and cultural memory.[106]

On Saturday, March 31, 2007, a dedication ceremony was held to officially rename the park between Twenty-Sixth and Twenty-Seventh Streets, and Highland Avenue and the Strand, Bruce's Beach. Mayor Nick Tell and council member Mitch Ward officiated at the program. In spite of the inadequate language on the signage plaque, renaming the park Bruce's Beach spurred recognition of a more inclusive and diverse cultural heritage, and of some of the rich history that has been ignored. An American pioneer story about successful African American entrepreneurs has begun to be told, as well as that of the disenfranchisement of the small resort community. The public has received a small measure of education about California black pioneers through this site naming. The Bruce's Beach story has initiated the journey of becoming part of the local and national collective memory, even with the signage plaque text that dilutes, misrepresents, and partially omits the site's historical truths and understanding.

The next chapter unearths a different history and public memory of a beach destination in Santa Monica. North on the Pacific Slope a few miles from Manhattan Beach, the beach site became very popular with black Angelenos from the 1910s to 1960s due in part to a small yet significant and overlooked African American community that lived and owned property close by.

3 Race, Real Estate, and Remembrance in Santa Monica's Ocean Park Neighborhood

> The boulevards of [the] Los Angeles [environs] grip me with nameless ecstasy. . . . To sing with the sun of a golden morning and dip, soar and roll . . . out . . . to the sight of the sound of the sea—this is Glory and Triumph and Life.
>
> —W. E. B. Du Bois, *Crisis*, September 1928

"It was a summer weekend gathering place. You would see everybody . . . all your friends, there," Los Angeles native Ivan J. Houston (b. 1925) recalled of the beach in Santa Monica's Ocean Park district, where African Americans could enjoy sand, surf, and sociability during the de facto Jim Crow era of racism—an era that reigned into the early 1960s in Southern California. "It could be a very noteworthy, social event to go to the beach," especially as a young adult, Houston remembered. He liked to stay in the water a long time, swimming and bodysurfing on those hot summer day visits to the "Inkwell," the derogatory name whites gave to this beach a few blocks south of Pico, which was frequented by African Americans. This pleasure was not unbounded, however. Making the beach a site for African American leisure required assertion against racist opposition. Houston, a third-generation Californian and retired head of Golden State Mutual Life Insurance Company, vividly recalled a memory from his youth when the nearby Club Casa del Mar built a wooden and chain link fence out into the water (in the late 1930s to 1940s), allegedly to help stop beach erosion. Before its removal, Houston viewed that fence as a symbol of discrimination, which kept "people" from moving freely on the public beach in front of the exclusive clubhouse.[1]

As Houston's recollections suggest, the history of this beach frequented by African Americans in Santa Monica's Ocean Park neighborhood was one of continued assertion of authority to make the place for leisure. This popular beach area was established and defended and persisted as an African American place in the spatial imaginary in California's frontier of leisure, contrary to the experience of Bruce's Beach. Though public remembrance of African Americans' leisure activities at this site have dissipated since the end of the Jim Crow era, personal remembrances remain. Interviews with black Angelenos whose families have been in the region over most of the twentieth century reveal that this beach near the end of Pico had been a gathering place for African Americans more or less alongside whites since the 1900s. These residents indicate that this beach usage developed because there was a sepia "anchor" community living nearby in Santa Monica that drew African Americans from around the region to this beach. A number of African American families had settled in Santa Monica by the early years of the twentieth century. The continuous presence of Phillips Chapel, a church of the African American Christian Methodist Episcopal (CME) denomination in Ocean Park near the beach since 1908, indicates it was not merely a recreational outpost, but the site of community life. This local population's existence helped African Americans' beach usage to persist through all challenges.

Ocean Park's history shows that at a time when racially restrictive real estate covenants and laxly enforced civil rights laws prevented them from buying property in certain areas or using various public or private facilities, and when distinct social barriers and overt discrimination prevailed, African Americans nevertheless succeeded in claiming recreation and relaxation sites in Southern California. This Ocean Park beach remained an important recreational area for African Americans from the turn of the twentieth century through the racial conflicts of the 1920s, 1930s, and 1940s, into the postwar period when the sustained activism of the modern civil rights movement began to erode social and legal barriers.

Whites had begun complaining about beach usage by African Americans as soon as their gatherings became organized efforts to occupy public space, evidence suggests. Along many stretches of the California coastline, refusal to allow African Americans access to places of leisure constituted an "informal" policy that was sometimes forcefully asserted and physically enforced by white citizens and public authorities. As early as 1912 in Manhattan Beach and 1914 in Playa del Rey, complaints by whites about African American beach usage appeared in the local newspapers. These complaints did not result in distinctively newsworthy white antagonistic acts against African Americans. These news items even acknowledged that, under California laws, African Americans could not be prevented from using the public beach. In 1927, as discussed in chapter 2, African Americans did win clarification on their right to unrestricted public access to beach frontage in a Manhattan Beach court case that did not reverse the city's dispossession of the supporting leisure community there. Yet laws did not prevent systematic discrimination and exclusion at other recreation sites.[2]

When racial discrimination and restrictions reigned, African Americans made a place of sociability, special significance, warm memories, and some self-determination in the Ocean Park neighborhood of Santa Monica. Their formation and defense of leisure practices tells a fuller story that exposes their foundational and creative pioneering role in patterns of settlement and sense of community. This story grants further agency to African Americans, other marginalized groups, and their allies to pursue public initiatives to overcome continuing questions of who is authorized to claim and reclaim space. Against threats and exclusionary conditions, this place remained a site where African Americans composed a community of leisure.

African American families of all economic classes, professional and occupational levels, and social persuasions demanded and developed this Santa Monica beach as their leisure place by regularly visiting on day trips, and through guest room rentals for weekend outings and summer vacations. Some of the African Americans who came for recreation at this beach became permanent residents of the area. In Santa Monica little sign remains today of the Jim Crow–era leisure site. As is true of African American leisure sites across the region, documentation of these places has been neglected, and only one building in the Santa Monica beach area has been designated as a historic landmark associated with African Americans. Sites of African American leisure activities have faded from memory as white-determined leisure culture dominated the region's narrative and emerged as "original" to the place.[3]

Santa Monica and the Ocean Park Neighborhood

The Santa Monica Bay shoreline seems to have always been a popular location throughout California's history. The Tongva people (later renamed the Gabrielenos by the Spaniards) lived in villages scattered throughout the Santa Monica Bay area adjacent to the rivers and marshes, and near the Pacific Ocean. When the Portuguese explorer Juan Cabrillo first investigated the California coast for Spain in 1542, he claimed Santa Monica Bay for the king of Spain, but it was not until over two hundred years later, in 1769, that missionaries were sent to colonize California. Spanish settlement was limited in the Santa Monica area until 1821, when California became part of the Republic of Mexico.[4]

The area came under U.S. control in 1848, at the conclusion of the Mexican American War. North of Ocean Park, starting in the 1850s, the canyon and beaches of Rancho Boca de Santa Monica became popular with Angelenos and other Southern California residents for picnics, sunbathing, and camping. South of the canyon, Santa Monica's north side neighborhoods and Ocean Park developed somewhat independently of each other. Travel was difficult between the two communities, as they were separated by an arroyo or gully through which the Santa Monica Freeway now runs to join the Pacific Coast Highway, and a mile-wide unimproved tract that belonged to the Southern Pacific Railroad.[5]

In 1874 sheep rancher Colonel Robert S. Baker and Nevada senator and mining entrepreneur John Percival Jones began building a railroad and a port in northern Santa Monica, along with a town site by the ocean. Although their railroad was eventually sold to the Southern Pacific and the port idea never came to full fruition, in 1886 Santa Monica was officially incorporated and the city evolved into a resort community. Vacation leisure became a defining industry of the place, as numerous hotels and bathhouses were built on the north side for wealthy tourists and health-seekers. Pleasure piers were built, including today's municipal pier at

Colorado Avenue. Wealthy easterners and Santa Monica founders built homes in the architectural styles of Queen Anne, Eastlake, Shingle Style, and Colonial Revival that exemplified Victorian seaside living in California. Beginning in the 1880s through the early part of the twentieth century, north Santa Monica played host to many wealthy and influential business and civic leaders and, with the turn of the century, Los Angeles movie stars who sought recreation in the "freshness of the ocean air."[6]

The Ocean Park neighborhood, south of the arroyo, and northern Santa Monica were already known regionally and across the United States for their amusement facilities, entertainment, and beach resorts. The two sections of the municipalities developed to accommodate regional day-trip tourists along with both vacationers and year-round residents. The initial growth of the little city by the bay as the playground of the Los Angeles region was multiplied by its connection with the electric streetcar to Los Angeles, the railroad, and, later, the automobile. The electric trolley railway line from Los Angeles to Santa Monica and Ocean Park began service in 1896. The route followed what are known today as Sunset and Santa Monica Boulevards. By 1903 it extended through Santa Monica along Main Street and Neilson Way through Venice and Playa del Rey to Manhattan Beach and Redondo Beach. While these transportation conveniences were available, there were still dirt roads in Santa Monica into the twentieth century. The Ocean Park district of Santa Monica developed its own unique identity while evolving with permanent residents.[7]

Visionary and entrepreneur Abbot Kinney (1850–1920) and his partner Francis Ryan (d. 1898) bought large sections of waterfront property in 1892, which they subdivided for sale as modest residential parcels (twenty-five by one hundred feet). They developed a pleasure pier, racetrack, auditorium, and casino. By 1901 the small community, in unincorporated Los Angeles County, which was also called Ocean Park, had two hundred cottages, a post office, and a few stores. In 1904 Kinney split from his partners and began construction on Venice-of-America, a rival amusement park and residence community on the undeveloped land he obtained in the dissolution of the partnership, which opened in 1905. The entire coastline from the Ocean Park communities of Santa Monica and unincorporated

Los Angeles County (which would eventually be called Venice), became known as "the Coney Island of the West."[8]

The attractions situated in Ocean Park at the turn of the twentieth century made the area one of the most popular destinations in Southern California and provided work and tourist income to community members. As the area was oriented toward the beach, residential development was clustered on the streets closest to the ocean. Housing consisted of boarding houses, beach cottages, bungalow courts, and hotels built in a variety of styles, including Craftsman, Spanish Colonial Revival, and Mission Revival. Servicing permanent residents and visitors, Main and Pier became the commercial streets of the area. Banks, churches, libraries, schools, civic groups, and local businesses emerged.[9]

Pioneers in the Santa Monica Bay Cities

The first African Americans moved to Santa Monica in the late nineteenth century to join communities of Chinese, Japanese, old Californios, new Mexican immigrants, white Americans, and Jews, as well as immigrants of various other national backgrounds. Santa Monica became one of the few seaside cities in the region with a historical African American community, which continues today and still includes descendants of these early settlers. Drawn by opportunity as much as they were seduced by the lure of the resort town, the early black Santa Monica pioneers came from beyond California to seek their dreams of "El Dorado," just like the other migrants to the area. Trekking westward to widely advertised Southern California, African Americans moved west on the railroads and later in automobiles to the region and Santa Monica for employment opportunities, the climate, health, beauty, and a more liberated lifestyle. The majority of these black newcomers from the 1880s to post–World War II came to the Santa Monica environs from U.S. southern states. Like African Americans who moved to the northeastern part of the United States, those who moved to Santa Monica also acted to escape the worst of de facto and de jure Jim Crow–era racial restrictions.[10]

Many of the new African American émigrés who moved to Santa Monica in the first few decades of the twentieth century settled within walking distance of Phillips Chapel, the first African American institution established in the Ocean Park district. This local CME congregation was organized in 1905, the first spiritual outpost established by the denomination in California and on the Pacific Slope. The congregation bought its building in 1908.[11]

At this time, racial discrimination in the cities by the bay and in California generally was not as rigid as it would become by the 1920s and 1930s. Most African Americans lived in neighborhood clusters side by side with people from varied ethnic and racial groups within a few blocks of Phillips Chapel, as well as in the area that is now the Santa Monica Civic Center and part of the Santa Monica High School campus. Farther away, there were African American neighborhoods in northern Santa Monica, one a few miles inland and one south in Venice that also included families who participated in the Phillips Chapel congregation.[12]

As in other parts of the United States in the early twentieth century, most African Americans living in Santa Monica had limited occupational opportunities. Most were employed in service positions in domestic work, transportation, and the restaurant and hotel trades as maids, janitors, draymen, and, later, with the rise of the automobile, chauffeurs. Some were entrepreneurs running small enterprises such as boarding houses, barbershops, beauty salons, and other service-related businesses, such as hauling and trucking. A few established early businesses that serviced blacks as well as whites. Aside from a minister or two serving the African American congregations, professionals with formal education had few employment options; for the most part, teachers and medical professionals, for example, would not find employment in their trained professions in Santa Monica until the late 1940s to 1950s or later.[13]

Santa Monica's African American pioneers developed social life and churches, and a sense of place as members in good standing of the larger Santa Monica community. They developed a sense of community and were agents in communal leadership and resistance to racist challenges they faced. For example, when barber George W. Hunt died on August 18, 1916, a *Santa Monica Bay Outlook* newspaper article noted that he was "one of the oldest colored residents" and "a pioneer of the bay district [who had lived] in Santa Monica for a quarter of a century." The 1910 U.S. Census recorded that Hunt (age forty-nine) was born in Virginia and worked in his own shop. He was a homeowner living with his wife Clare (forty-eight, born in West Virginia) and their children (Camelia, twenty-nine; Tourseall, fifteen; and George Jr., fourteen) and a boarder named LaVerne Floyd (age seven), at 1548 Seventh Street in the north Santa Monica neighborhood between Colorado Avenue and Broadway. The timely mention of his death and funeral services in the local newspaper seems to acknowledge Hunt as a respected citizen among his white and black contemporaries of the Santa Monica community.[14]

Formerly of Woodville, Mississippi, Walter L. Gordon (1883–1949) established Gordon Day Work Company in Ocean Park in 1902, specializing in house and window cleaning and janitorial service. The resort town business lasted at least eight years and at one time had a multiethnic workforce of seventeen employees. Though successful in Santa Monica, Gordon moved to Los Angeles for more lucrative business opportunities. He worked for a time at the U.S. Post Office as a letter carrier and in other successful side business ventures. By 1923 he had left the post office to organize the Walter L. Gordon Company, a very successful real estate firm headquartered on Central Avenue in Los Angeles.[15]

As early Santa Monica residents, Charles E. A. Brunson (1881–1950) and his African American neighbors asserted full citizenship and contested derogatory treatment. Brunson arrived in Santa Monica in 1905 from Americus, Georgia, with little formal education. Yet as an entrepreneur he worked to achieve upward mobility for himself and his family and became an advocate for racial social justice. Historian Delilah Beasley has reported that Brunson took successful action to have an objectionable sign referencing African Americans removed from the Santa Monica Pier. Early on he earned a living with a horse and wagon, hauling construction material for builders, and by carrying tourists' luggage from Los Angeles train stations to the luxury hotels along the Santa Monica shoreline. Later in his life he would work in maintenance and janitorial services.[16]

Charles lived with his wife Selena McDonald Brunson (1881–1934) and their fifty chickens and two horses on Fifth Street, then a small dirt road five blocks from the beach. At the time, this was a neighborhood of shotgun houses and other small vertical wood board cottages. Some of these structures had been makeshift oceanfront vacation cottages with no plumbing or electricity that had been moved by horsepower to this area by residents. This is also where the Brunson's two sons, Donald (b. 1907) and Vernon (b. 1909), were born.[17]

The Brunsons divorced by the time Donald began school. The elder Brunson moved to Venice, and married Theresa Edwards Trimble (a widow), becoming a stepfather to her two daughters. Brunson's first wife, Selena, and their boys stayed on at the Fifth Street residence.[18]

Selena supplemented her child support payments with work as a piece ironer at Gallow's, a domestic hand laundry on Ocean Park Boulevard. Being a minister's daughter, she saw to it that her sons attended the only African American church in town, Phillips Chapel. The family later attended other churches in Santa Monica, including the Anglo Methodist Sunday School near Arizona Avenue and Lincoln Boulevard. In the 1920s, after the First African American Episcopal Church of Santa Monica was established inland at Michigan Avenue and Eighteenth Street, they remained active members there for the rest of their lives.[19]

Several other pioneering Santa Monica African American families resided in the neighborhood where the Brunsons lived, establishing a sense of community, which they would assert against racial and other challenges. By 1920 Santa Monica's total population had grown almost 50 percent since 1910 to 15,252 people, as had the African American community, growing from 191 to 282 members.[20]

Arthur L. Reese (1883–1963) and his family were early African American settlers in Venice. Originally from Louisiana, Reese came to Los Angeles as a Pullman porter in 1902. In 1904 he rode the streetcar out to Venice to see what kind of economic opportunities might be available for him through Abbot Kinney and the Venice-of-America operation. He started a shoeshine business, then a maintenance service that thrived. Reese then became the maintenance and later decorations supervisor for the Kinney properties and was involved with other business ventures in Venice. Eventually, he was supervising a workforce of a few dozen people, many of them family members he would have recruited to move to California. Members of the Reese, Tabor, and other families who worked for Arthur Reese's or Abbot Kinney's enterprises were the first African Americans to live in Venice.[21]

Reese had other notable achievements in his business and civic life. He was appointed to the election board and became a member of the Venice Chamber of Commerce in 1920. In this time period in the United States it was not a common occurrence for an African American businessman to be a member of a white organization of this type. Another of Reese's civic accomplishments was as a founding member of Santa Monica's Crescent Bay Lodge Number 19, an African American Masons Lodge formed in 1910. The lodge today continues to exist at its Eighteenth Street and Broadway site, which was purchased in the 1910s. Reese also served as president of the Santa Monica Branch of the NAACP in the 1910s.[22]

Reverend James A. Stout (1875–1932) began his tenure as the first minister of Phillips Chapel CME Church in 1909. He eventually became the presiding elder of the region and was involved with the formation of several CME churches in the West. Rev. Stout moved to Southern California from Texas accompanied by his wife, Mary (1872–1964); their daughter, Bernice (1908–2004); and his mother-in-law, Mrs. Ary McReynolds, in 1908. Rev. and Mrs. Stout were both graduates of African American colleges in Texas, where they both trained as teachers. During his lifetime it was said of Rev. Stout that "his . . . insight [is] keen, his spirit fearless, his heart generous and his personality [is] engaging." In addition to these admirable qualities, Rev. Stout was a handsome, physically imposing presence at over six feet tall who possessed a deep, musical bass voice.[23]

In its expansion the CME church denomination was endeavoring to keep up with African Americans' emigration from the South. The new church became an early anchor of the already established and emerging community of African Americans in Santa Monica. It created a formalized institutional space where African Americans could shape community to address their social, spiritual, political, cultural, and leisure needs. This institution, along with the clans of the Stouts, the Lawsons, the McCarrolls, the Brunsons, the Reeses, the Tabors, the Gordons, the Jacksons, the Spauldings, the Carters, the Maxwells, the Quinns, and others, played an important role in drawing African Americans from across the Southern California region and beyond for activities in Santa Monica.[24]

Paralleling other places around the United States, in Santa Monica African American social life was centered on family, the church, evolving social and civic organizations, civil rights groups, and the limited number of public places and private enterprises allowing them patronage. In these early decades, these new Santa Monica residents developed a beach culture in Ocean Park, while their attendance at other recreation centers, including municipal pools and theaters, was by local custom often times restricted.[25]

Following World War I, population growth in the region accelerated. In Los Angeles the population grew from 102,479 in 1900 to 576,673 in 1920, and in Santa Monica from 3,057 to 15,252 during the same period. In 1920, while the African American population in Santa Monica was only roughly 300, their population in Los Angeles was 15,579, up from 2,131 in 1900. Santa Monica's unique relationship as a playground for Angelenos brought many new tourists, day-trippers, and residents to Santa Monica.[26]

As Euro-Americans from southern states became more entrenched in California and the African American population increased in visibility in their pursuit of leisure activities, so too did institutionalized restrictions and racism. In the first few decades of the twentieth century racism in Los Angeles and Santa Monica was much subtler than in U.S. southern states. The state was more diverse than the black-white binary due to the presence of multiple racial and ethnic groups. It was unpredictable where African Americans would encounter discrimination. As in Los Angeles, in Santa Monica African Americans learned from experience that they were unwelcome at many hotels, restaurants, theaters, and other establishments, although it was not always stated explicitly. The racial restrictions experienced by multiple racial and ethnic groups in the West are a topic scholars did not begin exploring until the 1990s. Due to the recent nature of the scholarship, the Los Angeles regional experience of the Jim Crow era, and its similarities to and differences from what occurred in the rest of the nation, has often been overlooked.[27]

Beach Usage and Place-Making at Santa Monica Bay

In the first few decades of the twentieth century African Americans from Santa Monica and Los Angeles enjoyed congregating around the end of Pico, north of the Crystal Plunge site (a swimming pool), which was destroyed by a storm in 1905. They were relatively free to enjoy the shoreline, three quarters of a mile south to Ocean Park Boulevard. At this time most of the tourism activity was about a half-mile to the north and south of the Pico Boulevard area of central Santa Monica and Ocean Park. This area of Pico near the shore was not so densely packed, as it would become with the population growth, which brought new waves of tourists and residents to all of Los Angeles County, and specifically Santa Monica. By the mid-1920s, when the exclusive white beach clubs began to rise near the foot of Pico, the site remembered today as the principal gathering place for African American beachgoers during the Jim Crow era emerged around Bay and Bicknell Streets as its hub in the Ocean Park neighborhood, less than a quarter of a mile south of Pico.[28]

There is evidence of the African American community's enjoyment of other Santa Monica Bay beach locations in North Beach and Playa del Rey in addition to Ocean Park before the 1920s. Their usage of these sites appears to have stopped after a few years, at least for large social gatherings. A 1908 *Daily Outlook* front-page news headline read "Picnic of Colored People on July 27" to celebrate Emancipation at Santa Monica's North Beach (north of the Santa Monica Pier), the most popular "beach center for tourists, holiday crowds and 'hometown' parties." Promoted by William T. Simpson, an African American resident of Santa Monica, the event appears to have been scheduled on a Monday, when a smaller number of whites would likely have visited the beach. "Grand" entertainment for the night included "Leonard's military band of Los Angeles, a colored organization numbering about twenty pieces and singing by the Glenwood Quartet, a negro quartet of some note in this section." Advertised throughout the local Santa Monica community and in the bay cities' general newspaper, this promotion invited an audience that would not have been exclusively African American.[29]

Most of the *Daily Outlook*'s audience would have been white. As its July 10 announcement and an event-promotion article of July 25, 1908, headlined "Darkies Are to Have Big Time" suggests, the venture was intended to attract white as well as African American customers. The article's text noted that the North Beach Auditorium gallery would be reserved "for the white folk to witness the cake walk and dancing." The use of this demeaning and disrespectful term ("darkies") referencing African

Americans' skin color, as well as the mention that white folks were welcome in the auditorium gallery for the evening activities, is simultaneously curious, confusing, and exploitive. During this time period, "darkies" was acceptable among whites as a patronizing and racist term for African Americans. The evening activities of this Emancipation "celebration" appear to have been aimed at divergent promoter goals and audience expectations, which accepted African American presence and cultural initiative as they eroticized, demeaned, and depoliticized it.[30]

If pitched to whites as a consumable spectacle, Simpson's Santa Monica North Beach event promoted as an Emancipation celebration would also have been a stage for African Americans to exercise their agency in the creation of social practices, spatial imaginary, and new opportunities, including leisure. Black urban musical forms and dancing were featured in the evening for *all* North Beach Auditorium customers' enjoyment, even if the space was racialized. No sources are currently available showing that Simpson promoted the event in Los Angeles, which he would probably have needed to do to attract a large African American audience. The available sources provide evidence sufficient only to speculate about the rationale of African American promoter Simpson (maybe with partners not mentioned in the newspaper articles) for this type of event promotion. If Simpson was motivated by money, he was hedging his bets by diversifying the audience outreach to African Americans, whites, and anybody else that read the bay cities newspaper or heard by word of mouth about the event. He and any associates would have wanted to sell tickets to as many patrons as the venue could manage.[31]

On the southern side of Santa Monica Bay at the Playa del Rey oceanfront community, south of Venice and Bellona Creek, African Americans' leisure outings held in June 1914 were advertised in the *California Eagle*. "Railroad Day! Universal Conclave" was set for the area's New Germania Park on Thursday, June 4, 1914. Advertised on a page dedicated to news specifically for black railroad and affiliate workers (e.g., porters, waiters, chefs, maids, red caps, hotel men), the event was similar to those held for several years at the same location by Southern Pacific employees. The difference was that the African American workers who promoted their Railroad Day did not have a corporate sponsor covering the event costs, and it was advertised for African American industry workers and the general public to attend. The event offered ocean swimming and various games on the sand, barbecue, fish dinners, assorted refreshments, and dancing and entertainment in the Pavilion into the evening.[32]

The event was a success in every way, from the numbers drawn to the demonstration of orderly leisure it exemplified to the cooperation of public authorities in suppressing harassment. On June 13, 1914, J. Allen Reese reported in the *Eagle* that "Railroad Day was celebrated at the Beach by way of a picnic at Playa del Rey. Quite a crowd was in attendance, the majority from Los Angeles." In the same issue in the "Local Happenings" column, Matthew T. Laws, the president of the Pacific Amusement Club that promoted the event, declared it a success and publicly thanked Los Angeles Police Chief Charles E. Sebastian and officers along with the Pacific Electric Railway for their excellent service. Laws also added extra praise for Chief Sebastian's assistance in removing a few undesirables. He further noted the emerging battle against nationally surging typecasting of criminality to malign African Americans, suggesting that as they claimed beach space it was a deliberate demonstration of civic respectability and right to the place.[33]

While articles in the *Eagle* spoke of the successful Railroad Day Conclave, the *Daily Outlook*'s coverage of activities in Santa Monica bay cities was not laudatory. The June 24, 1914, front-page headline read: "Don't Want Picnics, Citizens Protest to Venice Trustees Against Negro Gatherings at Del Rey." This article from the "citizens" asserted that "a protest [would] be lodged with the Venice trustees against the negroes holding picnics at Playa Del Rey." The *Outlook* correspondent noted, "During the past year large numbers of colored folks picnicked at Playa del Rey and caused, according to the Venice police, a great deal of trouble." The article stated, in closing, "It is exceedingly doubtful under the state law if the negroes can be prevented from picnicking at the beach." This statement appears to be a begrudging recognition of African Americans' rightful presence on the beach, even as it implied that their presence attracted "trouble." The writer also suggests "trouble" came from the law enforcing their rightful presence.[34]

Development pressures (including some simultaneous residential building, road construction, oil drilling at the shoreline's edge, and the emerging aviation industry) as well as attempts at racial harassment and exclusion elsewhere were probably the major factors driving African American gatherings to Santa Monica's Ocean Park shoreline from other regional destinations in the 1910s to late 1920s. Additionally, disasters such as flooding and fire destroyed or damaged the Playa del Rey's tourist facilities in the 1910s and early 1920s. As the regional population increased, in Ocean Park racial exclusion and development pressure appear to have pushed the African American residential community further inland and their oceanfront gathering place south from its earliest incarnation centered at Pico Boulevard. But the African American community's leisure space at Ocean Park persisted. Black social networking, community building, cultural traditions, and economic development around leisure created this and other sites, marking a social space of black identity on the regional landscape.

Across the decades there were more confrontations and assaults, some of which turned violent, aimed to bar African Americans from public beaches. Activists mounted legal challenges to these discriminatory practices by whites. One such incident involved Arthur Valentine, a chauffeur from Los Angeles who was beaten and shot by three sheriff's deputies on Memorial Day, May 20, 1920. It was alleged that Valentine and his extended family trespassed on private ranch land adjacent to Topanga Canyon at the oceanfront. Other accounts suggest the African American group crossed into an area frequented by white beachgoers, several miles north of Santa Monica's city limits. A grand jury indicted the sheriff's deputies on assault with a deadly weapon and intent to do bodily harm. After several trial delays, in January 1923 the charges against all three deputies were dismissed due to insufficient evidence. This case suggests the inconsistency among authorities in enforcing the rights and privileges of all California's citizens of African American descent. Further, it indicates a complicated class- as well as race-based response toward African Americans' assertion of their rights and the disregard of white "rowdy" disorder and perpetration of violence toward African Americans.[35]

Even with such violent attempts by whites to evict African Americans from public beach space outside Santa Monica's city limits, African

American recreation and leisure occurred at these sites unabated. African Americans were discreet and mindful in their oceanfront visits, but undeterred by attempts to harass, molest, intimidate, or restrict them from Southern California public beaches.[36]

Another incident demonstrates both effective resistance to harassment and the deterrence that authority-claiming harassment could have. In 1937 an African American family was having a nighttime gathering near the beach at Pacific Palisades when a local white resident, R. A. Stephens, attempted to evict them from the area. Displaying a deputy sheriff's badge, Stephens approached the group, commanding, "Don't stop here, you'll have to move on." Shannon S. Wylie, a former Los Angeles Police detective who was among the group, informed Stephens that the law said his family and friends were within their rights to use the beach. Stephens threatened the group with violence, but, according to a *Pittsburgh Courier* newspaper article about the incident, "the colored citizens fearlessly answered, 'Use any means you see fit.'" Once Stephens realized the group would not leave, he was described as hurrying off to harass another Negro party some distance away. Harry Levette of the Associated Negro Press (APN) reported the other group left after their interaction with Stephens.[37]

As ineffective as Stephens's harassment proved to be when it met resistance, the second group's departure demonstrated the deterrent effect racist assertions of authority could have. The article described "Los Angeles Negro citizens" as calling on both city and county officials to investigate this attempt at establishing racial restrictions on a Los Angeles County public beach. They asked officials "to take definite steps in the matter and warn the guilty parties that they, as citizens, must not be molested." ANP articles were distributed to several African American newspapers around the United States, including those in Los Angeles, illustrating the desire of African American citizens to know about what was happening in the broader struggle for racial equality and access to public accommodations across the United States.[38]

These publicly reported vignettes of white intimidation and African American consumers' contestation of racial restrictions represent the possibilities and limits of action in the local struggle to dismantle racial discrimination. Citizen consumers fought against predominant racist practices for the right to use Southern California beaches throughout the early decades of the twentieth century. The level of demand for power over, and use of, recreation space varied according to the individuals involved, the particulars of the laws, and the dynamics of each leisure location and social situation. But, generally, the unpredictable nature of white reception to African Americans at beaches in Southern California's outlying exurban coastal areas influenced black Angelenos' greater use of Santa Monica's Ocean Park beachfront as a congregation place as the twentieth century edged forward.[39]

White reference to the Ocean Park beach as the Inkwell did not deter African American claim and development of the site. History suggests that white Americans probably first used the term to describe more than one U.S. leisure site associated with African Americans during the Jim Crow era. Some African Americans and, later, their allies took agency and repurposed the offensive term to describe these places they frequented and enjoyed, transforming the hateful moniker into a badge of pride or belonging. However, the name "Inkwell" has not been universally recognized by African Americans and their allies, with some refusing to use the name at all.[40]

The Santa Monica site likely began to be referred to by *some* whites and *some* African Americans as the Inkwell by the 1920s, given the rise in visibility of African Americans living in the region and visiting this beach. In interviews the author conducted with African Americans who enjoyed this Santa Monica leisure space during the Jim Crow era, the term "Inkwell" was not universally used to describe this Ocean Park beach. Many of these African Americans with lived experience at this site pre-1960 called it "the Bay Street Beach." Further, no articles in the local newspapers (African American or general population media) of the era reviewed by the author about the Santa Monica leisure site referred to this place as the Inkwell.[41]

The "Bay Street Beach" site continued to serve as a recreational outpost enjoyed by African Americans into the twentieth century's middle decades. Many a sepia-toned visitor from the Los Angeles environs may have stopped by Phillips Chapel for religious fellowship in the morning before heading for the sun, sand, and surf in the afternoon. Others may have headed to La Bonita, a black-owned bathhouse and lodge at 1811–1825 Belmar Place (a street that ran north and south, and does not exist today) between Pico and Main Street, where the Santa Monica Civic Auditorium is today, or at Thurman's Rest-A-While Apartments at Fifth Street and Broadway to the north, in the heart of Santa Monica. These establishments, where out-of-towners could rent a bathing suit as well as a guest room, and their amenities probably helped to further broaden the appeal of this beach for African American consumers.[42]

The La Bonita enterprise, which opened around 1914, appears to have been the venture of Frances and Moses Warner and their daughter, Helen Warren. Helen's husband, Ellis Warren, seems to have maintained the family residence in Los Angeles, while working as a foreman and a manager in a private company. The guesthouse was two blocks from the ocean and offered rooms, meals, bathing suit rentals, and other accommodation amenities for individuals and club parties. In the next decade an *Eagle* advertisement announced the opening of La Bonita Café in connection with La Bonita Apartments on Saturday, May 28, 1921, and also emphasized that the enterprise catered to "Auto Parties" and could arrange for "any SPECIAL occasion." This establishment was listed a few years in the *Negro Motorist Green Book*, the annual national guide published from 1936 to 1963. This guide and other handbooks for black travelers listed accommodations and safe places that would serve African Americans traveling through the Jim Crow–era United States.[43]

Thurman's was located in the early African American neighborhood in Santa Monica near the first location of Calvary Baptist at Sixth Street and Broadway. The Dewdrop Inn and Café, owned by the Paxton family, was nearby, at Second Street and Broadway.[44]

Visitors at one time could stop to pick up something to eat at the Arkansas Traveler Inn run by the Dumas and Griswold families at Belmar Place at Main Street. Their 1930 *Eagle* advertisements stated the eatery specialized in Southern-style barbecue with genuine barbecue sauce, and Southern-style fried chicken. The "New" La Bonita's paid advertisements in the *Eagle* in the same year noted the renovated amenities under the new management of Frank N. Miller, with supervision assistance from Mrs. M. L. Pitre and Mrs. C. Sims, and that all patrons at La Bonita facilities would be given the most courteous treatment and best attention. The advertisements went on to assure potential patrons that they could enjoy La Bonita's big picnic ground with a large pit for wiener bakes and private parties. The development of leisure at the Bay Street Beach supported the rise of African American ventures, a deepened community life, and more complex relations to the Ocean Park beach as an African American–made place.[45]

Racist Challenges in the 1920s

As the oceanfront around Pico drew increasing numbers of African Americans and businesses catering to them, the Santa Monica Bay Protective League, an Ocean Park neighborhood group of white homeowners, unsuccessfully "sought to purge" them from the beach in 1922 by prohibiting leisure business enterprises. Within walking distance of the black residential community and shoreline recreation space at Third Street and Pico—a few blocks east of La Bonita, on the southern edge of the today's Santa Monica Civic Center—George Caldwell's dance club hosted parties on Sunday nights, bringing large numbers of African Americans to the bay city. The evening socials got out of hand a few times, and complaints by neighbors and the Santa Monica Protective League influenced the municipal authorities to pass an ordinance prohibiting dancing on Sundays. Caldwell, who was an African American, responded by moving his dances to weeknights. The authorities then responded by "[adopting] a blanket ban on dance halls in residential districts" at the City Council meeting on July 26, 1922.[46]

In a *Los Angeles Times* article on July 27, 1922, titled "Fight Against Beach Dance Halls Success," a staff correspondent reported, "A delegation of negroes, headed by George W. Caldwell, voiced their protest to the passage of the ordinance, but it was adopted by a unanimous vote." Some seventy-five members of the Protective League, "which opposed the negroes encroaching upon the city," showed up to offer support for the passage of the ordinance. Many African Americans saw it as a case of Southern prejudice encroaching on life in California. Los Angeles attorney and civil rights activist Hugh MacBeth noted of the crowds at Caldwell's Dance Hall that the actions of a few individuals did not merit "wholesale discrimination and limitation" of all African Americans. He encouraged protest to prevent and eradicate this type of Southern-style discrimination.[47]

It is unlikely patrons at Caldwell's evening events were any more unruly than white patrons at similar establishments. Instead, such description was more likely an exaggeration to justify shutting down the dancehall. Similar situations elsewhere around the United States suggest the closing of this festive atmosphere was an overzealous way of policing and containing African Americans' leisure activities and freedom of expression because of broader white anxieties over this urban and upwardly mobile labor force and the ways its members chose to use their free time. This view helped to perpetuate white belief in a defined racial order predicated on distinct and immutable racial characteristics and an ideology of segregation. While the characterization of African American dance gatherings as disorderly enabled white use of local ordinances to harass and suppress leisure, historian Andrew Kahrl notes that "few images were more threatening to the emerging Jim Crow order than that of a black family relaxing on a beach, books in hand, in silence."[48]

At the same time Santa Monica Bay's Protective League was closing down Caldwell's Dance Hall in 1922, this same group also sought to block black entrepreneurs from carrying out plans to build a "first-class resort with beach access" near Pico Boulevard and the oceanfront. Charles S. Darden, Esq. (1879–1954) and Norman O. Houston (1893–1997), two civically active and enterprising black Angelenos, were president and secretary, respectively, of the Ocean Frontage Syndicate. The outfit had plans for their facilities to include a bathhouse, dance hall, and other attractions. To entice patrons, the business plan included advertising from Los Angeles to El Paso seeking to draw sixty thousand African Americans to the Santa Monica pleasure site.[49]

As in other parts of the United States, because they were barred in Southern California from employment with better wages and in higher-level managerial positions in corporate America, as Flamming and other scholars have noted, "ambitious African Americans gravitated toward entrepreneurial ventures, especially those that catered to the group population of [black] Angelenos." The "nationalist surge" of the early 1920s—when

Pan-Africanist Marcus Garvey and others spoke at organized meetings in Los Angeles and around the United States promoting black pride and political and economic self-reliance—strengthened this entrepreneurial trend. Carried forward from earlier decades, these same themes of self-development and self-determination had been promoted in one form by Booker T. Washington, as well as by other African American journalists, entrepreneurs, clubwomen, and ministers preaching race progress through enterprise.[50]

Most likely the Ocean Frontage investors were part of the African American population that had prospered after the end of slavery, despite obstacles and prejudice. During the Jim Crow era, successful blacks developed resorts and amusement facilities in other parts of the United States, similar to the one the group was attempting to build in Ocean Park, so they could relax and insulate themselves and their children from humiliating or unpleasant confrontations with whites. In providing this service to their community, African American entrepreneurs hoped to make a profit from their resort development endeavors.[51]

Attorney Charles S. Darden was a land use specialist from a prominent family in Wilson, North Carolina, where his father was the first African American undertaker. After graduating from Howard University Law School in 1904 and before settling in Los Angeles, Darden made a grand tour of the mainland United States, the Hawaiian Islands, and Asia. One of the earliest African American lawyers admitted to the California Bar, and the first of his race to take a case before California's Supreme Court, Darden was the first African American lawyer to successfully challenge the legality of racially restrictive real estate covenants that appeared on deeds of land sales. The 1915 court decision (*Benjamin Jones and Fannie Gautier v. Berlin Realty Company*) established a precedent, as it was the first decision obtained upon this question in a court of justice in the United States.[52]

Another important precedent-establishing decision Darden won in California was that a married woman could sell community property without the consent of her husband, especially when the title to the property was vested solely in her name (*M. Randall v. Jane Washington and Samuel Washington*). Practicing law in California for many years, Darden, like other black lawyers, worked on civil and criminal appeals before the California Superior and Supreme Courts. Darden was a reserved man, but socially popular. He was active with the Knights of Pythias, the Masons, and the Elks. In addition to leading the effort to develop amusement facilities and a resort in Santa Monica, Darden was also involved in a resort and expansion development plans for African Americans at Lake Elsinore in Riverside County (see chapter 4).[53]

The other syndicate leader, Norman O. Houston (1893–1981), was a second-generation Californian born in San Jose and raised in Oakland. He attended the University of California, Berkeley, and was commissioned as a lieutenant in the U.S. Army during World War I. In 1925 he cofounded the Golden State Mutual Life Insurance Company, which sold life and health insurance policies, and, later, mortgage loans for homes and businesses of varying sizes to African Americans throughout California. At its height the company became one of the largest African American-owned businesses in the United States. Although Houston's professional life has been most associated with Golden State Mutual and his numerous civic activities, he was involved in other successful business ventures. For instance, he was cofounder of the black-owned Liberty Building and Loan Association in 1924, and later in his career he was chairman of the Board of Directors of Broadway Federal Savings and Loan (a company that was founded in 1947 and still in business in 2019).[54]

Darden, Houston, and associates faced organized racist opposition to their project that moved beyond harassment and menace to determined public policy. An article about the formation of the Santa Monica Bay Protective League in the *Los Angeles Times* on June 9, 1922, reported the slogan of the organization as: "A membership of 1000 Caucasians." The article reported that the league was created to "eliminat[e] all objectionable features or anything that now is or will provide a menace to the bay district." The *Times* account also included a statement issued at the occasion of the group's election of officers:

> Inasmuch as a certain negro syndicate has announced through the Los Angeles press their intention of making this bay district their beach and bringing thousands of negroes to the beach cities, which we believe

> would be very detrimental to our property values and our bay district as a whole, this organization will immediately take up this problem which in its opinion is of vital interest to all citizens. We believe that they should procure a beach of their own at a point separate and apart from all white beaches—which would eliminate all possible friction for all time to come. We invite any and all citizens to notify the secretary of any menace, which needs the attention of this league.[55]

On May 1, 1922, the *Santa Monica Evening Outlook* reported the Santa Monica City Council refused to amend zoning ordinance 211, passed in February 1922, setting aside the ocean frontage for residence property, to permit the construction of the resort. On the morning of May 1, more than four hundred white citizens appeared at City Council chambers to protest the Ocean Frontage's group request for the change in the ordinance. In an earlier *Outlook* article on April 19, 1922, covering the Ocean Frontage group's petition for the ordinance amendment so they could move forward with their development, the petitioner included an appeal to the City Council's sense of fairness for all taxpaying citizens, even if they were black and used their own facilities separately from other U.S. citizens. The venture's investors claimed that African Americans' past usage and presence (of ten to fifteen years) at this beachfront site for their pleasure project was a political claim for policy continuity, against the opponents' contention that their project was a "disruptive" use of this location.[56]

An *Eagle* editorial described the text of a handbill sheet distributed in the bay city as unfairly playing to white racial prejudice toward blacks to stop the construction of the Ocean Frontage amusement venture. The editor expressed hope that Santa Monica's citizenry might be above this kind of negative race baiting:

> The [Santa Monica] officials . . . are high class gentlemen and would not for one minute stand for the whims of the cracker from Texas who, by the foulest methods possible seeks to stir up strife. The blatent [*sic*] misrepresentations in the vile sheet mentioned, comes not from any paper of standing but as forestated from a notoriety sensational hand bill guided evidently by a red neck from the South.[57]

A *Times* article dated July 30, 1922, with the headline "Settlement of Negroes is Opposed: Santa Monica and Ocean Park Blocks Plans for Colony of Colored Folk" reported that the Protective League influenced local authorities to pass the ordinance denying permission for the construction of the African American bathhouse and amusement center. The same article also reported the cancellation of the sale of the oceanfront property by the owners, Messrs. Harry H. Culver and Robinson.[58]

Thus a move was apparent in the white segment of the Ocean Park beach community by 1922 to bar African Americans from beach use, land development, and further home ownership. White owners of large land tracts in the district who had recently subdivided several lots of beach frontage "placed a Caucasian restriction on their properties, barring Negroes from ownership or occupation." Major Santa Monica and West Los Angeles real estate developers Robert C. Gillis and Charles "Roy" Leroy Bundy and their associates urged other property owners throughout the area to employ the "Caucasian clause" to prevent the leasing, occupancy or sale of any property to persons of non-Caucasian origin.[59]

California's civil rights laws affirmed it was illegal to discriminate against all citizens in public places, which included the oceanfront. Unenforced laws, legal sanctions, and private harassment actions dissuaded many African Americans from visiting or taking up residency at particular beach and other locales. Further, civic leaders began promoting the idea that beaches should be maintained for the public, as least when African American land development plans were involved. As described in chapter 2, the 1920s saw several "save the beaches for the public" campaigns emerge to keep African Americans from creating or maintaining beachfront resorts.[60]

Similar efforts to exclude African Americans occurred at other Southern California beach towns in the 1920s. In 1925, a few miles south of Santa Monica's Ocean Park and north of Bruce's Beach in the city of Manhattan Beach, African Americans were forced to give up on developing a beachfront resort at El Segundo. Numerous white-run civic and business groups, including some in Santa Monica Bay, supported the action against the proposed El Segundo beach resort plan. Other beach resorts suffered similar fates. The most violent intimidation campaign to evict African Americans from enjoying the beach was the destruction of the nearly completed Pacific Beach Club in Huntington Beach. In 1926 arsonists burned the beautiful new facility to the ground shortly before it was to open (chapter 6).[61]

The upwardly mobile African American population residing and migrating to the region in the 1920s through the 1940s had the resources for consumer pleasures and for enjoyment of the leisure offerings of Southern California. Even with economic racism, structural or institutional inequities, and a mishmash of laws that might restrict some of their freedoms, the conditions for the African American population were much better than in Southern and some Eastern cities. As discussed in chapter 2, white boosters and civic authorities viewed the beaches as the region's most important recreational and tourist asset. African Americans' private ownership of beachfront property and their claim on beach public space was viewed as a threat to attracting white Americans and to white dominance. Though the population of Los Angeles was a diverse, multicultural mix—of whites of various European ethnicities, and peoples of color—systematized white racism aimed at African Americans most consistently occurred at Los Angeles' recreation spaces.[62]

As the most popular summer weekend and holiday recreation spaces for residents, beaches became an important image for the promotion of tourism and the Southern California good life as early as the 1920s. As a primary tourist destination, beaches were patrolled and maintained by various municipalities in Southern California. To assure public access, local authorities began purchasing and managing oceanfront properties and strongly lobbying voters for support of more beachfront property acquisitions. This was at the same time as racial restrictions were imposed on African American taxpayers at the beach, forcing them to pay taxes to acquire coastal land they might be prohibited from using by law or custom.[63]

Ironically, amid the campaign to prevent construction of the Ocean Frontage Syndicate beach resort, it was white beach privatization that effectively bounded African American beach use to the Bay Street Beach area. In Ocean Park, racial exclusion and development pressure appears to have pushed the African American residential community further inland, and their oceanfront gathering place south from its earliest incarnation centered at Pico. A string of lavish, exclusive, and highly advertised beach clubs (and some private residences) were constructed beginning in 1922; by the 1930s they stretched north from Pico, about 2.5 miles, all the way to Santa Monica Canyon. The former Ocean Park Crystal Plunge site became the extravagant Club Casa del Mar (today the Hotel Casa del Mar). Opened in 1924, it was the first of three large private clubs, and the most successful opening in the vicinity from Pico north to the Santa Monica Pier. North of the Casa del Mar at the end of Pico, the Edgewater Club was built in 1925. A short distance north of the Edgewater, the Breakers Club opened in 1926.[64]

By means of public policy, the white racist "Protective League" had facilitated the denial of Darden, Houston, and associates their resort outpost. Racists recast mutual leisure into raced, segregated practice, which set the stage for inevitable conflict and enabled privatization of the public realm. Popular discourses of privacy, antigovernment association, and value of business-style management of all social ventures further supported privatization. Whereas at the public areas on the beach all classes more or less mingled together, at the beach clubs the members stayed within their own private fenced-in beach, reinforcing white notions of privilege and shifting the focus away from race as a primary motivation of exclusion. This did not, however, diminish the racist motivations. These private clubs imposed restrictions and open discrimination against African Americans, Mexicans, Asians, and Jews. The creation of private clubs at recreational spaces was a policy used to circumvent civil rights laws outside of the South, and throughout the urban North and West. In Santa Monica the African American beach site moved from the edge to the center of public activity. Down the hill from Phillips Chapel CME Church at Fourth and Bays Streets, near the pergola colonnade and park area known today as Crescent Bay Park, and just south of the Club Casa del Mar beach area, fanning out from Bay to Bicknell Streets, African Americans from the Santa Monica and Los Angeles environs continued to gather for parties and to socialize. Here they enjoyed the ocean breeze, swam, played games, and physically asserted their rightful presence with more success against racially motivated harassment than at other southland beaches.[65]

Remembrances of the Bay Street Beach, Sometimes Called the "Inkwell"

In spite of the unpleasant events in the 1920s the African American community's growth, persistence, and agency sustained their oceanfront usage in Santa Monica as it evolved over the twentieth century. While not necessarily welcoming African Americans with open arms, the lack of white violent resistance and resilient insistence by African Americans overcame the constrictive ordinances and harassment by white groups like the "Protective League" to maintain marginal racial coexistence in Santa Monica. African Americans maintained their right to occupy public space in their continued possession of this part of the beachfront alongside whites from varied economic classes. Simultaneously the unpredictability of racial discrimination by white groups at other beaches effectively limited where many African American groups seemed to feel they could safely use beach space beyond Santa Monica. Different stories of recollections—personal memory, public misrepresentations, and a recent resurgence of public remembrance—have emerged about this site due to the persistence of African American use over multiple decades through varied geographic, political, and social conditions.

The presence of the Casa del Mar facility, its history, and the perpetuation of its memory have erased the broader history and memory of the early African American beach site, while contemporary popular media and other accounts have preserved myths about explicit physical demarcation of the beach in Santa Monica for African American usage. Some of these accounts have arisen due to the limited sources available for review and incomplete understanding of the context and material facts of Santa Monica oceanfront cultural landscape and geography, pre- and post-beach clubs, as well as the region's history. Experiences and preferences of some black and white observers have also affected how the history of the site has been interpreted in commentary on the cultural landscape of the beach. Some interpreters have made remembered practices of beach space usage into mythical, explicit land demarcation at the Ocean Park beach landscape. They have "imposed" geographic limitation based on their fantasies rather than on what actually occurred in the physical landscape where African Americans were the most visibly distinguishable at this shoreline congregating place. Others have overlaid the history of the American South with its laws of systematic discrimination and segregation on California, mistaking the actual local history of discrimination. Popular memory of many historical events of the Jim Crow era, including the African American beach leisure in Santa Monica, has proven difficult to extricate or amend, even with new scholarship and public cultural administration.[66]

In the 1940s Los Angeles native Marilyn Williams Hudson (1927–2015) and her friends started a group they called "the Beach Club" at Bay Street. This group of established and financially secure black Angelenos continued the tradition of gathering there until around 1970. During this period Synanon, a substance-abuse rehabilitation center, occupied the nearby Casa del Mar. As a result, Hudson said, the atmosphere of the whole vicinity changed. Into the twenty-first century's early decades her "Beach Club" continued gathering for fun at the shoreline, though its members discontinued meeting at the Ocean Park location long ago. The buildings at Santa Monica beach around Bay Street began to look frayed, as did the population inhabiting these shoreline properties, Hudson recalled. These impacts, combined with the memory of the exclusivity of the defunct Casa del Mar and the development of beach leisure culture across Southern California as a white space, aided in erasure of the memory of the history of African American self-determination through leisure at this Pacific Ocean section of Santa Monica's shoreline.[67]

Hudson's Beach Club moved their activities south to Marina del Rey to take advantage of the new amenities and commercial accommodations, which were more upscale than what was available at the Bay Street environs. South of Santa Monica and Venice to the north of Playa del Rey atop a portion of the Bellona Wetlands, the newly developed area, Marina del Rey, opened in 1965. The public-private shoreline project included a pleasure craft harbor, public parks, fishing and beach areas, restaurants, shops and other businesses, hotels, and residential housing. African American groups from the region such as Hudson's Beach Club enjoyed new places to congregate and consume in Marina del Rey and elsewhere. Visibility, along with public memory of African American community life, declined as the social practices of African Americans faded from the beach at Bay Street. The memory of the area's pleasurable times and sense of place began to be mostly retained in the personal memories of groups like Hudson's Beach Club and other African Americans who experienced Santa Monica's Ocean Park beach during its heyday, while receding from the public memory.

In 2000, after Synanon closed and other organizations who occupied the building moved out, the Casa del Mar Club was restored as an elegant beachfront hotel. The club-turned-hotel site is now included in the National and California Registers of Historic Places. On the location where the African American entrepreneurs attempted to construct a "first class resort with beach access" in 1922 for black community patrons, a new, upscale Shutters Hotel on the Beach was constructed in 1993. The Crescent Bay Park and the pergola colonnade south of the hotels have not changed much. The Bay Street Beach area was partially taken up by a parking lot in the 1950s. Nonetheless, in general, the location continues to have its charming character and the defining vistas of the Santa Monica Pier, the Pacific coastline, the ocean, the Crescent Bay Park and pergola colonnade, the bluff, and the Casa del Mar, along with other buildings.

Until a recent commemorative plaque was put in place, few people visiting this stretch of Santa Monica's beach in contemporary times have had any idea that this section was once a place where African Americans had built a beach leisure culture and that it was sometimes referred to as the Inkwell. The shoreline has been transformed to protect for beach erosion, and the Casa del Mar fence dividing black and other non–club member beachgoers from affluent, white beach club members no longer exists. In the twenty-first century people from all walks of life can now enjoy "the best part of the beach."[68]

In Southern California and throughout the country, African American agency forced changes in discriminatory laws and social customs and enforcement of existing civil rights laws. This, combined with changes in leisure culture and new transportation infrastructure over the course of the twentieth century, created many more opportunities for all people, and especially African Americans, to enjoy a greater variety of recreational and leisure spaces at beaches. At the same time, in Southern California and across the United States, the painful reality of discriminatory practices (which sometimes included violence and intimidation), imposed and reinforced by both government institutions and white resistance limiting African American consumers access and economic development of the most coveted urban beach, recreation and other spaces, has been largely ignored or forgotten. The memory of African American presence and struggle was only resurrected by research, the revaluing of the personal remembrances of beachgoers, and the broader movement to reclaim African American history, generally, and of leisure, specifically, elsewhere around the southland.

Historians and the local community have collaborated to reclaim the Ocean Park beach site through memorializing African American beach culture at the Bay Street Beach. These historic African American beachgoers and Nicolas (Nick) Gabaldón (1927–1951), a Santa Monica resident who is one of the earliest documented California surfers of African American and Mexican American descent, were honored on February 7, 2008, with the installation of a commemorative monument at Bay Street and Oceanfront Walk. In 2004 and 2005 books with some mention of Santa Monica's African American experience began the contemporary scholarly reclamation of this history. My research extended their efforts in the community, with my public presentations on the Phillips Chapel CME Church and Southern California African American beach culture laying the foundation for the historic church to be landmarked in 2005. This work enhanced public officials' and local citizens' formal awareness of Santa Monica's diverse heritage, hence facilitating the commemoration of the Jim Crow era and the historical African American beach at the Bay Street in 2008.[69]

Folklore has it that Nick Gabaldón took his first swim in the Pacific Ocean at the Bay Street Beach. One of the few African American students matriculating at and graduating from Santa Monica High in 1945, he is said to have loved the beach and the waves. A handsome, athletic, and well-liked young man, Gabaldón and his friend Wayne King taught themselves to surf using the thirteen-foot rescue surfboard of a white lifeguard whom he befriended in the 1940s. A skilled recreational waterman rather than a professional competitive surfer, Gabaldón's legacy is an empowering story about overcoming bigotry, the pursuit of freedom, and the attainment of self-fulfillment. His story has inspired many, especially surfers of color, to consider him a role model. In 1951, at age twenty-four, Gabaldón died in a surfing accident at Malibu Pier. Though only traces of his life story are known, his passion, athleticism, discipline, love, and respect for the ocean live on as the consummate qualities of the California surfer.[70]

A local citizen supported by members of the Black Surfing Association suggested to the Santa Monica City Council that this beach site and Gabaldón be recognized in some way, and they approved. I had the honor of creating the text on the plaque monument and of serving as a speaker at the unveiling ceremony. As public memory work, this monument touches many people's lives and recasts for them the African American making of beach culture as they come to enjoy the oceanfront at this site. The plaque's text tells an American pioneer story about African Americans who, in spite of challenges, took agency to participate in the fruits of California. The American stories told about the Bay Street Beach and surfer Nick Gabaldón on this monument are being infused into the collective memory of local and national public culture.[71]

More interest developed in the reclamation and recognition of African Americans' participation in the California Dream and Santa Monica beach culture space. The "How We Roll: Cultural Influences in Skateboarding, Surfing and Rollerskating" exhibit appeared at the California African American Museum in Los Angeles' Exposition Park in 2010, featuring information on African American beach culture. Two documentary films, Ted Woods's *White Wash* (2011), and *12 Miles North: The Nick Gabaldón Story* (2012), by Richard Yelland and the Nike sporting goods company, were debuted. Both films examine black surfers, but through different lens and distinctive directions, and discuss the historical Bay Street Beach site.

When Rick Blocker first started surfing in the 1960s, he looked for African American role models who surfed, because he never saw any of his African American peers surfing. As the third generation of his family who grew up enjoying the Santa Monica's Bay Street Beach environs and other locations, he eventually learned about Nick Gabaldón. In 2013 Blocker commissioned a portrait painting of Gabaldón by Los Angeles–based artist Richard Wyatt. Best known for his contemporary murals and installations, many of Wyatt's usually large-scale works showcase scenes of people in the region's history in institutional spaces. Wyatt's interpretive vision of Gabaldón in street clothing places him in a classical center-of-canvas pose, looking directly at the viewer to illustrate his importance. A complex green-colored background behind the subject makes the viewer think of the Pacific Ocean. Blocker makes the portrait available for public viewing and media use in varied community programming efforts.[72]

Other contemporary efforts of some innovative educational programming are also connecting the public to these more inclusive and diverse heritage stories of Southern California. The Santa Monica Conservancy, Heal the Bay, the Black Surfers Collective, Surf Bus Foundation, the Black Surfing Association, the Malibu Surfing Association, and other groups, along with Los Angeles County public officials, have separately and jointly implemented public programs in community outreach efforts to inform and connect a broader citizenry to the African American heritage in the California Dream, ocean stewardship, and social justice concepts, intersecting with the joys of surfing and other beach recreation, and health and wellness. Santa Monica's Bay Street historical African American beach culture site, since 2012—has been a Coastal Cleanup Day location for this global program, and since 2013 Nick Gabaldón Day has been held to celebrate the African Americans who challenged racial hierarchies in the Jim Crow era in order to enjoy the beach.[73]

Inclusive of Nick Gabaldón and Coastal Cleanup Days, the Passport to Success LA: Life at the Beach Series field trip program emerged 2017 to bring South Los Angeles youngsters to visit the Santa Monica environs. Led by the Santa Monica Conservancy, with this author acting as the coordinator, these trips capitalized on the partnerships built in the other activities to expand the innovative programming. Field trips include visits to: the Santa Monica Conservancy's offices in a rehabilitated historic shotgun house; the nineteenth-century, Rancho-era Pascual Marquez family cemetery; the recently landmarked Malibu Historic District at Surfrider Beach; and the Santa Monica Pier Aquarium, along with the Bay Street Beach monument site. Additionally, a National Register of Historic Places listing nomination of the Bay Street Beach Historic District is in process for the site, led by Michael Blum of Sea of Clouds and this author. This National Register listing will aid in support of other programming developing to honor the legacy of African American beach culture that may be on the way to becoming regular events at the Bay Street historic site.[74]

The celebration of U.S., California, and Santa Monica heritage has yet to fully illuminate and embrace the complicated layers of national, regional, and local memory, at work in the history of African American leisure culture at the Ocean Park beach. As the case of this place illustrates, the lack of tangible material culture in the form of buildings to landmark in recognition of a group's legacy makes the recovery of a rich history that was made at a place more difficult, but not impossible. Through research, innovative ideas, and programs to memorialize marginalized groups, citizens and scholars in Santa Monica and beyond have begun to recover and recast a fuller history of African American invention, struggle, and persistence in the making of Southern California's beach leisure culture.

Moving from the beach, eastward to the Inland Empire, chapters 4 and 5 uncover the experiences of African Americans in their self-determination successes and challenges in maneuvering around Jim Crow–era practices at locations of two different forms of leisure making and land ownership and development scales in the Riverside County cities of Lake Elsinore and Corona.

FIG. 20. African Americans enjoying themselves at Lake Elsinore, ca. 1921. *From left to right*: Eddie DeQuir, Pearl Rozier DeQuir, Carolina Rozier Harrison, and Sarah Rozier Bryant. Note the concession sign, a landmark that also appears in many family group photographs at this Lake Elsinore shoreline location from this era. From Shades of LA Collection, Los Angeles Public Library.

FIG. 21. Boat races at Lake Elsinore, 1937. Spectators of many backgrounds parked their cars on Lake Shore Drive and on the beach to get a spot for viewing and enjoying the day's activities on the water and the shoreline. Courtesy Lake Elsinore Public Library Collection.

Persons with Tuberculosis or other Contagious Diseases not received

Rieves Inn

LAKE ELSINORE HOT SPRINGS

P. O. Box 96 Phone 532
Popular Prices Meals a la Carte

THE water of this famous Health Resort is unsurpassed for Nervous Disorders of all kinds, Rheumatism, Liver, Kidney and Stomach Troubles. Temperature of water 110°. Altitude 1350 feet.

Passengers from Los Angeles take Pickwick Auto stages at Union Stage Depot, Fifth and Los Angeles Streets, or the Santa Fe Railroad.

For further information write or phone

W. L. Burgess, Manager.

Elsinore, Riverside County, Cal.

May 20, 1924

Dear Mr. Ransom, —
Your letter received - Ever so glad to hear from you. Am glad to say that I am feeling much better.

FIG. 22. Rieves Inn stationery with a portion of a letter by A'Lelia Walker of the Madam C. J. Walker Company, to her corporate attorney, Freeman Briley Ransom, Esq., 1924. In addition to being used for correspondence, the stationery served as an advertisement for the offerings of Lake Elsinore hot springs and inn, and for travel arrangements from Los Angeles. The letterhead text reads: "Persons with Tuberculosis or other Contagious Diseases not received; The water of this famous Health Resort is unsurpassed for Nervous Disorders of all kinds, Rheumatism, Liver, Kidney and Stomach Troubles; Temperature of water 110 degrees; Altitude 1350 feet; Passengers from Los Angeles take Pickwick Auto stages at Union Stage Depot, Fifth and Los Angeles Streets, or the Santa Fe Railroad." Letter courtesy Walker Collection of A'Lelia Bundles.

FIG. 23. African American friends posing on a boat at Lake Elsinore, ca. 1946. On the left (*standing*) is Thomas R. Yarborough, Lake Elsinore real estate entrepreneur, civic activist, and city council member and mayor (1966–68) who was hosting his friends from Los Angeles. Seated (*third from left*) is Dr. Herbert Fairs and (*third from right*) Mrs. Towles. Her husband, Dr. H. H. Towles, is second from right. Dr. Towles loaned the use of an office in his building at 14th Street and Central Avenue to William Nickerson and associates in 1924 for the founding of the Golden State Mutual Life Insurance Company; he was an early member of the company's board of directors. Standing (*second from right*) is Floritta Ware. To her right is Leon Washington (*with hat*), the owner and publisher of the *Los Angeles Sentinel*, founded in 1933; he also owned property at Lake Elsinore. To his right is Kermit Brown, a retired Los Angeles Police Juvenile Division officer. Photograph courtesy Walter L. Gordon Jr. Collection of William Beverly Jr.

FIG. 24. Members of the Independent Church and entrepreneurs of Lake Elsinore, ca. late 1940s to 1952. Several of the people in this photograph were business proprietors who provided accommodations to African American vacationers when they visited Lake Elsinore. *From left to right*: Horace C. Hensley (Hensley Court on Riley and Sumner); Dan Wheeler; George Moore Sr. (George Moore's Chicken Inn on Pottery and Spring—the 1949 edition of the *Negro Traveler's Green-Book* suggested his place on Scrivener for accommodations); Pastor Arthur A. Webb; John Craig; William Hendrix (Hendrix Motel on Lowell); George Moore Jr.; Ms. Jennings; Gussie Hendrix, wife of William Hendrix; Viola Craig; Estella Hensley, wife of Horace C. Hensley; and Mildred Sterling (vacation guest cottage proprietress and owner of a bar in Los Angeles at 21st Street and Hooper Avenue). Photograph courtesy Independent Church of Lake Elsinore, collection of author.

FIG. 25. Youngsters Kerry Jackson, Kev Jackson, and Halvor Miller (*left to right*) playing in the "medicinal" mud, Lake Elsinore, 1948. Photograph courtesy Halvor Thomas Miller Jr. Collection.

FIG. 26. The Neal family reunion has taken place at Yarborough Park for many years, inspired by family members who were longtime resort visitors and by a few who became lake town residents. Lake Elsinore, August 13, 2005. Photograph by author.

Official Program . . . . Opening Celebration, May 30th 1928

PARKRIDGE

THE LARGEST COUNTRY CLUB IN THE WORLD OWNED AND CONTROLLED BY BLACK AMERICANS

HAVE YOU ever before had an opportunity like this? . . . an opportunity to belong to a country club ranking among the largest and most beautiful in the West . . . An opportunity to become a part of its fascinating life . . . to enjoy its round of social activities . . . to participate in its many sporting events?

To become a member of Parkridge is to take a step forward . . . a step that leads to the better things in life . . . wholesome fun and enjoyment . . . health . . . quickened interests . . . valuable friendships. Here, amid the atmosphere of refinement and surroundings of beauty the best in youth is developed. Sports to build up vitality and increase alertness . . . social contacts to develop personality and nourish seeds of ambition.

Here, in addition to playing on one of the finest golf courses in the South, you may enjoy the pleasures of shooting . . . riding . . . tennis . . . swimming in the hill-crest pool . . . dancing to joyful music . . . dining on the best in the land. Playgrounds are provided for the children and cozy bungalows offer accommodations for overnight guests.

Every inch of Parkridge's vast domain is dedicated to pleasure . . . for you!

To reach the club house drive out East Ninth Street, Los Angeles, to Fullerton, turn to your left through Corona, one mile to Parkridge.

THE ONLY MILLION-DOLLAR COUNTRY CLUB IN THE WORLD IN WHICH YOU CAN BUY A MEMBERSHIP FOR TWENTY-FIVE DOLLARS

APPLICATIONS TAKEN AT THE CLUB HOUSE TODAY

FIG. 27. *Opposite*: The Parkridge Country Club official opening day program bulletin cover, May 30, 1928. The African American owners of the club, the Nelson-White Holding Company, produced the four-page bulletin about the facilities and activities for the day. Note the picturesque photographs of and descriptive text about the facilities, as well as the hyperbolic sales pitch. The inside of the bulletin featured advertisements for Los Angeles businesses (mostly black-owned ones) supportive of the event and the order of the day's program activities. Names of the children, sports costumes, beauty parade contestants, and club management were listed. The California Eagle Publishing Company was mentioned as the designer and printer of the bulletin. Courtesy Anne Cunningham Smith Collection of the author.

FIG. 28. *Above*: Bathing beauty contest on opening day at Parkridge Country Club in Corona, May 30, 1928 (Decorations Day, later known as Memorial Day). A note attached to the back of the framed photograph's backing reads: "Many Central Avenue community residents joined L.A.'s first and only black country club. . . . Various factors, including harassment by local police, forced the club to close in its first year." The text goes on to say that "Verna [Deckard Lewis] Williams [*front row, center*] is shown wearing her bathing suit . . . purchased especially for the occasion." This text was added many years after the event, after Verna remarried and obtained the last name of Williams from her then-husband (Lewis V. Williams). Photograph by J. A. Ramsey, courtesy Verna D. L. Williams Collection of Arthur and Elizabeth Lewis.

FIG. 29. Friends, mostly from Los Angeles, pose in Pasadena, ca. 1920 (*front, left to right*): Cora Jordan, unidentified woman, Angelita Williams Nelson and her husband, Dr. Eugene C. Nelson; and (*back, left to right*) Dr. B. A. Jordan, Buell Thomas, and Ethel Miller Thomas. By the time Eugene C. Nelson, MD became a leader in the investment group that bought and opened under new management the Parkridge Country Club venture in 1928, he was divorced from Angelita. From Mariam Matthews Collection, University of California Library Special Collections.

FIG. 30. Eureka Villa Community brochure, ca. 1924–25. One side of this early two-sided, five-panel sales brochure with a cartoon map gave viewers an impression of the contrast between the city they lived in and the place they could go to relax, only a short distance from downtown Los Angeles. Featured is an artist's conception of the proposed clubhouse designed in Spanish Colony Revival–style with an insert box drawing that represented 1920s-era modern, elite tourist services. Note the names of the Eureka Villa advisory board, all prominent members of the Afro Angeleno community. The other side of the brochure features drawings of homes; farm and ranch products of chickens, eggs, grapes, corn, and other produce; a rolling and mountainous landscape with a road and vehicles; and small industrial buildings. This scene presents an integration of economic self-determination and healthy living through real estate investment in a bucolic environment that might in the future offer new economic development opportunities. Courtesy Aubrey Provost Collection.

FIG. 31. People relaxing at the Hi Hat Inn in the rustic yard nearby the establishment's cabins, Val Verde, California, January 1939. This was one business in the area where restaurant and overnight accommodations were available from the 1940s to 1960s. Courtesy Fay M. Jackson Memorial Collection of Dale Lya Pierson.

FIG. 32. At the Val Verde Park ceremonies and celebration, as boys from the Los Angeles Health Club look on, acclaimed actor Hattie McDaniel enthusiastically places a memento in the copper vault that was used to house all the mementoes placed in the cornerstone of the new swimming pool facilities, April 16, 1939. After it was built, the new Olympic-size swimming pool was the second largest in Los Angeles County. The development of Val Verde Park was a history-making event for black Angelenos and Los Angeles County officials, who marshaled local and federal government financing to construct the park improvements. Although most of the surrounding homes and ranches were owned by African Americans, the Los Angeles County park grounds and facilities were open to all citizens. Courtesy Fay M. Jackson Memorial Collection of Dale Lya Pierson.

FIG. 33. Cosmos Club members and their guests enjoying a meal, Val Verde, ca. 1948. *From left to right*: Felix Williams, Samantha Williams, Leroy Beavers Sr., Nathaniel Shaw, Norman B. Houston, Gloria Shaw, Sarah Grimes, Johnny Luke, Ivan J. Houston (holding his daughter, Pam), and a few others. In 1946, just after World War II ended, the club was founded by twenty male friends who had grown up together in Los Angeles. Still existing in 2018, younger members—some of them descendants of the original members—have been recruited to carry on this group's social traditions, which have a business networking and civic disposition. Photograph courtesy Cosmos Club Archive.

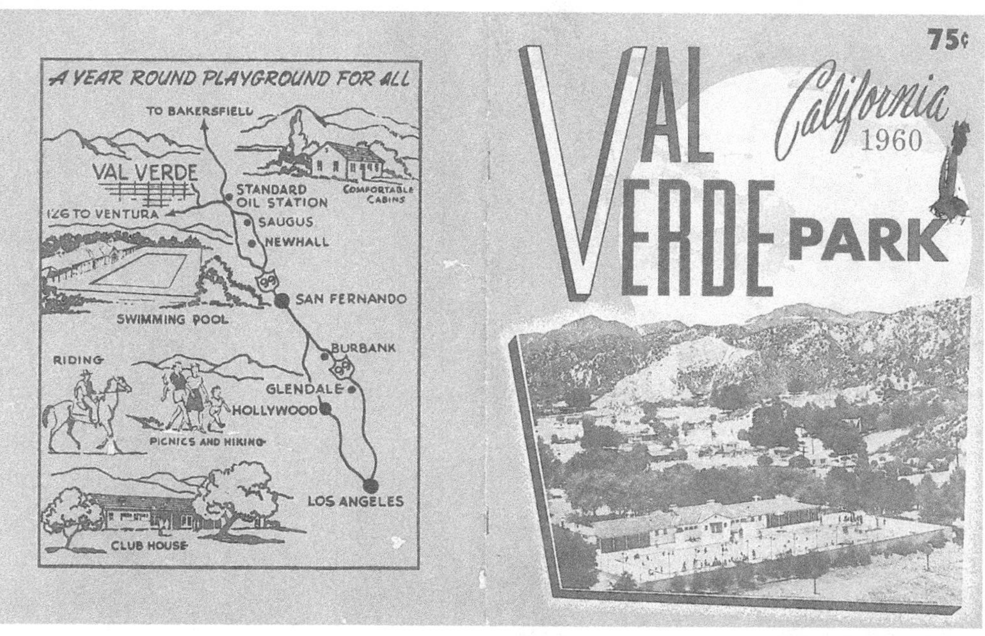

FIG. 34. Val Verde Park bulletin cover, 1960. Produced by the Val Verde Chamber of Commerce, this forty-page bulletin described the mission of the group as one "to improve business and build a better community" and listed the names of the leadership team members. The offerings and the history of the community and some of its civic builders were highlighted and described. Inside are pictures of important community events, such as the annual parade, holiday parties, fashion shows, sports competitions, social club activities, and a teenager record hop with renowned Los Angeles deejay Hunter Hancock. Several pages of advertisements of Val Verde and Los Angeles area businesses are included. Note the cover photograph image of the Olympic-size swimming pool with a view of Val Verde Park and environs. The bulletin's back cover highlights the offerings of the Val Verde rural retreat in close proximity to regional population centers of Los Angeles, Ventura, and Bakersfield. Material courtesy of the County of Los Angeles Department of Parks and Recreation Archive.

FIG. 35. Florence LaRue (*left*) won the contest for the title of Miss Val Verde in 1965 before she became a member of the popular Grammy-winning singing group the Fifth Dimension. Next to her is Bradley Polk, who won the contest for the title of Mr. Muscle Man that same year. These contests and the parade were popular annual Val Verde events for more than thirty years, ending in 1979. The LaRue family members were regular visitors, with Florence's parents owning a cottage in the leisure enclave. The *Los Angeles Sentinel* of May 23, 1965, was among the media outlets to publish this image. Photograph courtesy Frank D. Godden Collection of Salaam Mohammad.

4 A Resort Town Mecca for African American Pleasure Seekers at Lake Elsinore

> To the Colored citizen, Lake Elsinore, is comparable [as] . . . Palm Springs [is] to the wealthy white vacationist.
>
> —*California Eagle*, May 23, 1940

As African Americans were making leisure sites on the Pacific Slope at Bruce's Beach and the Bay Street Beach, they were also developing a vacation community of a different sort inland from the ocean. Remote from Los Angeles, in a scenic valley with a large freshwater lake and mineral hot springs, African Americans invested their labor, money, and recreation time in a health resort and garden agrarian community, Lake Elsinore. Well into the middle decades of the twentieth century, Lake Elsinore was a place of work, leisure, family, and communal life and memory centered on recreation and health for the African American community. Lake Elsinore's distance from Los Angeles made it more of a retreat or "escape" destination. The development efforts of its founders and first residents drew both black Angeleno good-life seekers as holiday visitors and vacation residents as well as established real estate investors and business owners providing services to African American consumers. Dr. Wilbur C. Gordon and Charles S. Darden, Esq., whose leisure and residential development visions at other locations around the southland had experienced the destructive use of state power to block their plans, proved undeterred in pioneering community-building efforts at Lake Elsinore. There, black social, communal, and business practices built a place of leisure and living relatively insulated from aggravated racial harassment and discrimination by whites.

African Americans joined a long line of travelers, settlers, homesteaders, and fortune and recreation seekers into the valley where the Elsinore Colony would be formed in the late 1880s. The longer history of the area shows the range of places imagined by those encountering it, and the attractions patterned on the successful promotion of other Southern California places at the end of the nineteenth century. Lake Elsinore was one of the many California and American West sites promoting health tourism and progressive agrarian smallholdings in the late 1800s to the early decades of the twentieth century that had varying life cycles of transformation, longevity, and decline. As aspiring settlers and developers purchased land for agriculture, leisure pursuits, and real estate speculation, cyclically inconsistent lake-water levels overlaid with real estate platting that supposed a more fixed water topography than ever existed in the valley ultimately shaped the community's history.

The Lake Elsinore Valley in California's Riverside County had long been known for its natural attractions. Many of those who have entered the valley have used it for social as well as subsistence endeavors. At different times Native peoples, Spaniards, Mexicans, and Anglos, along with African Americans and other groups, took in the valley's offerings to create a variety of transient, seasonal, and permanent communities. Situated in the Santa Ana Ortega Mountain range along the interior route between the cities of Riverside and San Diego, ninety miles from Los Angeles and inland from the Pacific Coastal towns of San Juan Capistrano and Laguna Beach, the valley has been appreciated for its beautiful vistas, climate, water, mineral deposits, adaptable soil, and natural hot springs. The Pai-an-che Indians, the earliest settlers, named the valley "Etengova Wumona," which means "Hot Springs by the Little Sea." The lake and the hot springs were very important to the spiritual traditions and subsistence of the tribe.[1]

In 1797 Franciscan Padre Juan Santiago was the first Spaniard to see Lake Elsinore. Assigned to Mission San Juan Capistrano, he entered the valley from the long-established trail used by Native Americans to traverse the Santa Ana Ortega Mountains from the Pacific Ocean side. In the early part of the nineteenth century few non–Pai-an-che used this trail, but as the century progressed the trail was more frequented by colonialists and other venturers. It became a favorite camping location for American trappers, due to the shade trees along the shores of the "Laguna Grande," as Lake Elsinore was known at that time. A Mexican land grant was issued to Julian Manriquez in 1844 for Rancho La Laguna, which included "Laguna Grande" and twenty thousand acres surrounding it.[2]

When California became part of the United States in the mid-nineteenth century, many a new group of couriers, adventurers, and other travelers rode through the Elsinore Valley along the old trail and stopped to refresh at the lake. Stagecoaches like the Butterfield stage mail and passenger line, used the valley passage as part of the overland trail connecting California to the rest of the United States. After a succession of ownership including Mexican Augustin Machado and American Abel Stearns (who both also owned rancho land in the Santa Monica Bay region of Los Angeles County), Rancho Laguna was purchased by Franklin Heald (b. 1864), William Collier, and Donald Graham sometime in 1882–1883. They established a town on the lake's north side, called Elsinore, and began to sell lots. By 1885 the town was on the Santa Fe transcontinental railroad line passing through San Diego.[3]

Heald recognized the potential of the hot springs, along with the Elsinore Valley's beauty, to attract "seekers of health, recreation and rest." By the 1900s various entrepreneurs had developed numerous hotels, apartments, and cottages, as well as several sanatoriums, to attract visitors from around the world to what became a popular vacation site for health and pleasure. The valley contained a number of different types of hot and cold mineral water wells said to cure various ills, such as rheumatism, gallstones, indigestion, kidney and liver trouble, skin rashes, and constipation. Varied social and recreation activities were promoted on land and in Lake Elsinore, including hunting, hiking, fishing, picnicking, swimming, boating, and dancing on summer nights.[4]

Real estate speculators like Heald were aware tourists were prospective residents and, when possible, capitalized on their enjoyment of the valley to sell them lots. Originally from Iowa, Heald was the developer of the Elsinore town site and region who had the most to do with its growth. He arrived in Pasadena in the 1870s with some familiarity with California and its development, as his uncle was a founder of Healdsburg in Sonoma County, near San Francisco. Franklin Heald was one of the region's late nineteenth-century pioneers who California historian Carey McWilliams views as coming to build a new land, who was a part of the progressive, enterprising, venturesome spirit that so impressed visitors to the region at that time.[5]

After buying out his partners in 1883–84, Heald kept approximately twelve thousand acres, for which he paid them $20,000 (approximately $1.67 per acre). Graham and Collier retained two thousand acres. The land was sold to the public in the range of $25 to $50 per acre in 1884. Heald's Quaker background was probably a strong influence on the way he and his partners chose to develop their "Elsinore Colony." From the start, this community was viewed as progressive. The founding pioneers were interested in "families of limited means" being able to afford a "place that promised to equal Pasadena and Riverside at about one-fifth of . . . [their] prices." Small lots were created for settlers in the town site, around the valuable hot springs, as the founders wanted to "form a dense community, where a mutual and neighborly interest [would] act as a stimulant and encouragement."[6]

The examples of Pasadena and Riverside, both rural settlements that had developed into resort towns by the turn of the century, were fresh in the developers' minds.[7] Lake Elsinore capitalized on the same bucolic, healthful, agrarian image that successfully launched Pasadena and Riverside. At Lake Elsinore,

> beyond the town site, citrus, walnut, apricot and olive groves alternated with groves of eucalyptus trees and open spaces where rabbits and coveys of quail made their homes . . . In the center of it all Lake Elsinore sparkled in the sun, or reflected the silver path of the moon, or flung its waters about in fury when strong winds blew from the ocean or desert.[8]

Featured in the book *Lake Elsinore Valley: Its Story, 1776–1977* by Tom Hudson, this description of the valley as it appeared in the early 1920s would predominate into the 1970s.[9]

Although by the early decades of the twentieth century Lake Elsinore Valley was popular for its beauty and health-giving attributes and for the adaptability of its soil for agricultural production, the lake was "once described as 'one of the most perverse, unruly and unpredictable bodies of water in California.'" Before manmade interventions, the lake was really a flood plain holding runoff from the surrounding hills and mountains, and an overflow site for the San Jacinto River. When full it was the largest freshwater lake in Southern California, at about seven miles long, two miles wide, and forty feet at its deepest point. When it was dry, it could be a dust bowl. The Colorado River aqueduct began delivering water to Southern California in 1941. But Lake Elsinore's water level would not be stabilized until 1964, with water flowing from the Colorado River and Lakeview aqueducts, the San Jacinto River through Canyon Lake, and local watershed runoff. Prior to this, the lake had regular cycles of wet and dry years coinciding with precipitation amounts. Later, manmade factors, such as various dams installed on the San Jacinto River and huge amounts of water pumped from underground to develop the region's farms and cities, further adversely affected the lake's water level.[10]

Even with the capriciousness of the water level, Lake Elsinore remained an attraction for visitors throughout the twentieth century, particularly to fashionable Angelenos, who first arrived by train and then by automobile. The community's economic development over the twentieth century waxed and waned with the lake level. In spite of this, the town survived and the residents stayed, sustained by faith in the future despite the realities of the vagaries of their natural environment.[11]

The 1920s were a prime era for real estate development in Lake Elsinore Valley. New buildings were constructed for local businesses, social organizations, country clubs, tourist lodging, and other facilities, including a golf course and campgrounds. Residential structures, including a few palatial homes, were built around the lake. Improved transportation lines were built, making it possible to drive on paved roads north to Corona, and south to San Diego. The many attractions of the valley and California were extensively promoted in a variety of publications. People came from all over to visit, buy property, and spend money. Like the town's founders, visions of economic opportunity lured an assortment of boosters and promoters, who continued their attempts to develop Lake Elsinore into a health and recreation center with the extra benefit of ideal home and business districts.[12]

Successful businessman Ernest Pickering, one of the developers of the Ocean Park section near the city of Santa Monica in unincorporated Los Angeles County, which eventually became Venice, bought the entire block of Lake Elsinore where the Lake View Inn and the Crescent Bath House stood around Spring and Limited Streets, along with a substantial parcel of lakefront land nearby. Clevelin Realty became Elsinore's biggest real estate promoter, selling lots on the lake's north and south shores, including at Country Club Heights (also known as Clevelin Heights) on the north shore. The company also constructed on the north shore what became known as the Aloha (Pleasure) Pier in 1926, and Clevelin Country Club, near the edge of town. Other real estate developments, which had varying degrees of success, were reported in the *Los Angeles Times* during the decade.[13]

African American Heritage in the Early Twentieth Century

By the 1920s establishments were open catering to African Americans seeking recreational and leisure opportunities in Lake Elsinore Valley. In 1887, when the town was first established, African Americans William Charles Burgess (1842–1913) and his wife, Hannah (1852–1947), came to the valley and began work as domestic service employees for the town founder Franklin Heald's household. From Missouri, the Burgesses bought property off Pottery and Spring Streets, a location then at the outskirts of the town center. They purchased additional property a little further out, including near Pottery and Kellogg Streets, where they grew oranges and olives. Eventually, Pottery Street became the main thoroughfare of the African American vacation and year-round community.[14]

The Burgesses and other early residents parlayed their labor in agriculture and service occupations into community stability, enterprise, and land purchases. By the 1910s and 1920s their efforts had established a resort destination that would attract leading African American professionals, successful entrepreneurs, and good-life seekers. William Charles Burgess was noted for his civic activities and employment history. Accounts described the senior Burgess as having worked as a cook for various individuals and on work details such as road-construction crews. Born in enslavement and a Union Army Civil War veteran, Burgess was at one time a color-bearer and treasurer of the Elsinore Grand Army of the Republic Post with other Civil War veterans. Other early African American families with permanent residences at this time in the Lake Elsinore environs made a living in the local economy in agriculture, construction, and other manual labor employment. A few worked in support jobs for the (Euro- and African American) resort infrastructure as masseurs, cooks, housekeepers, property caretakers, and small-lodging proprietors serving both Euro- and African Americans.[15]

From the 1910s to 1927 Mrs. Burgess and her son, William Lafayette Burgess (1875–1948), ran a small lodging known as Rieves Inn, built at the family farm near Pottery and Kellogg. Catering to African American leisure and health seekers, their lodging facilities began in a private residence and expanded to a larger hotel structure when they were sold to Mr. and Mrs. Kruse from San Diego. The Kruses had previously worked as managers of the café at the Douglas Hotel, a hugely successful African American establishment located in downtown San Diego and founded in 1924.[16]

A 1921 article in the *Eagle* speaks of the Rieves Inn as a "popular resort for health and recreation." The article describes a scene of a successful party with guests dressed in their finery. Mr. and Mrs. Maurice Hunter, from Oakland, California, are noted as being participants in the merriment that went on past midnight on a Wednesday evening. Robert C. Owens (1859–1932), the prosperous black Angeleno real estate entrepreneur and a descendant of Los Angeles pioneers Robert and Winnie Owens and Bridgette "Biddy" Mason, was reported as a party guest. The description of the soiree and socially prominent African American vacationers shows that Lake Elsinore not only attracted the well-to-do, but presented a public discourse of respectable social interaction like that appearing in city newspapers of the day. The *Los Angeles Times* often featured articles discussing similar incidents of socially prominent whites enjoying parties and vacations at popular resort hotels.[17]

A letter dated May 20, 1924, written on Rieves Inn stationery, from Ms. A'Lelia Walker (1885–1931) to a Mr. [Freeman Briley] Ransom [, Esq.], (1884–1947)—along with the *Eagle* article, noting visitors from Oakland—gives evidence that the Burgess's Lake Elsinore hotel was known to African Americans outside of Southern California. Ms. Walker's letter to Mr. Ransom, the attorney and general manager of the Madame C. J. Walker Manufacturing Company, informed him she was feeling much better and had been following the orders of her California physician, Dr. Wilbur C. Gordon, a respected black Angeleno medical professional, civic leader, businessman, and Lake Elsinore property owner. Walker was a prominent national figure, the only daughter and heir to the cosmetics empire and fortune created by her mother, Madame C. J. Walker (1867–1919), the first self-made African American woman millionaire. Before becoming New York residents, Walker and her mother had lived in St. Louis, Missouri, in the 1880s, and it is possible they may have been acquainted from that time with the Burgesses.[18]

By the mid-1920s several prominent black Angelenos purchased their own vacation homes at Lake Elsinore. A few ambitious entrepreneurs from the city also invested in resort and recreation spaces for their own and their African American compatriots' use. They were doing their part for race progress through enterprise at a time of Pan-African peoples' diasporic surge toward self-development, self-determination, and economic self-reliance (see table 1).[19]

The Rieves Inn served as a point of encounter and an inspiration to further enterprise and community building. The resort venture known as Lake Shore Beach, located on the north shore of Lake Elsinore, may have been launched after one of its founders was a guest at the Burgess establishment. In 1921 the Lake Shore Beach Company purchased a little less than fifty acres to build a resort at the northeastern corner of the lake, edging the town site just below Clevelin Heights. The investor group included several leading black Angelenos who wanted to ensure that African Americans had "a footing on the lake" so they would not be shut out by racial discrimination and white harassment.[20]

TABLE 1. Lake Elsinore African American resort community sites, 1920s to 1960s

PROPERTY	ADDRESS
1. Rieves Inn, 1920. By 1930 the Rieves Inn would be called L. C. Malanda's Burgess Hotel and Health Resort; from 1931 to the 1960s it was called the Elsinore Hotel or Inn	416 N. Kellogg at Pottery St.
2. Lake Shore Beach 1921–1940s	On Lakeshore Drive going toward the northeastern corner of the lake about 1.6 miles from Main St. in historic downtown Lake Elsinore near Manning St.
3. Mrs. Mildred Sterling cottage rentals business, 1920s–1970s	311 N. Kellogg
4. Love Nest Inn, a.k.a. Strider & Sons, 1925 (faded sign may still be there at private home)	N. Kellogg across from Lake Elsinore Hotel/Inn
5. George Moore Motel & Café (Chicken Inn) in Los Angeles; Moore also owned a service station and tire shop at 46th St. and Central Ave.	Pottery and Spring Sts.
6. Martinez Bathhouse	Riley and Sumner Sts., across from Hensley Court
7. Mundy's Court, 1940s	NE corner of Pottery and Langstaff Sts.
8. Hotel Coleman DeLuxe, 1926–1930s	Pottery and Lowell Sts.
9. LaBonita Motel, 1930. First owner: Jim and Inez Anderson. Later owner: Wyman and Rita Burney, who also had a lamp shop in the Hermitz Bldg. on Graham. Extant as apartments, but modified	Pottery and Riley Sts.
10. Brooks Health Baths and Spa and Café, 1930s, Al Brooks, proprietor	Pottery and Poe Sts.
11. Hensley Court, Horace C. Hensley, owner, 1940s. Tom Yarborough owned property before Hensley. Extant as apartments	Riley and Sumner Sts.

12. Nightingale Lunch Room & Deli, 1920s; Pottery Lunchett, 1930	415 Pottery and Poe Sts.
13. Smith's Grocery Store, 1930, A. Smith, proprietor	419 Langstaff St.
14. Leon Daniels's Court cottages	Riley St.
15. Hendrix's Court, 1930s, William and Gussie Hendrix, proprietors. Served family-style meals; Gussie was the mother of the Independence Church	309 Lowell St.
16. Clarence Muse, Muse-A-While Ranch	Hwy. 74 and Margarth St., Perris CA
17. Henry's, 1940s	Pottery, between Langstaff and Poe Sts.
18. Miller's Café, 1945–1980s, Andrew J. and Elizabeth Miller, proprietors. Rubin "Buddy" Brown's family lived next door on Pottery St.	SE corner of Pottery and Langstaff Sts.
19. Thomas and Kathryn Yarborough residence, 1920s–1960s	Pottery, near Silver St.
20. Judge David Williams residence	Silver, west of Sumner St.
21. Paul R. Williams residence	16908 Grand Ave. at Buena Vista St.; across the lake from the historic town center
22. Douglas and Mary Henderson residence. In Los Angeles, he was a pharmacist at Washington Blvd. and Central Ave. His wife, Mary Broyles Henderson, worked at the soda foundation in the Clark Hotel	Poe between Pottery and Sumner Sts.
23. The (Leon and Ruth) Washington family ranch; 30 acres, *LA Sentinel* newspaper owners	
24. Dr. N. Curtis King's ranch	Flint, off Chaney St.
25. H. Claude Hudson family residence. They also rented a house on Lowell before they built on Lewis; Barbara Anderson owns the house today	304 N. Lewis, Lewis and Sumner Sts.

26. Dr. Elvin and Olive Neal residence	Scrivener and Pottery Sts.
27. Thomas and Portia Griffith II residence	214 Lewis St.
28. Thomas and Judy Rutherford residence	On Lewis St.
29. Paul Payne family residence	On Lewis St.
30. The Oggs residence	Near M. Sterling on Kellogg St.
31. Rev. Hampton and Gertrude Hawes Sr. family residence, 1930s	Pottery and Scrivener Sts.
32. Second Baptist Church of Los Angeles Retreat	1548 Lakeshore at Lake Elsinore City limits between Townsend and Matich Sts.
33. Charlotta A. Bass residence, 1950s–1960s	709 West Heald, between Kellogg and Lowell Sts.
34. Hill Top Community Center, 1950s–1960s; later site of Yarborough Park	Off Pottery St. between Poe and Kellogg Sts.
35. Barbershop, 1940s. One owner: Sterling Jackson	Pottery St.
36. Beauty Salon, started in 1953; Miriam Hutchinson, owner. Arrived in Lake Elsinore in 1920s	Pottery and Lowell Sts.
37. Jones Fish & Tackle Repair Shop; Dollene Jones	Langstaff St.
38. Rev. and Mrs. Jones residence	Lewis, between Pottery and Sumner Sts.
39. Dr. Wilbur and Desdemona Gordon residence	Pottery, east of Main includes parcels across the 15 Freeway; off Adobe and Rupard Sts.
40. Burgess property	Pottery between Main and Spring Sts.
41. Independent Church (African American, 1920s–present)	Kellogg between Pottery and Sumner Sts.

Source: Created by author. Locations were identified from interviews, census records, African American newspaper advertisements, and travel and business directories.

The members of the Lake Shore Beach investment group were all civically active and highly regarded in the black Angeleno community, likely knowing one another through their business, social, and church affiliations. These associates were part of the black population who flourished after the end of enslavement, despite the obstructions and discrimination they confronted. As in the Eastern United States, successful, more affluent African Americans developed resorts like Lake Shore Beach to promote rightful leisure and health, insulated from racist confrontations such as enforced public proscriptions and violence of word or deed.[21]

As resort developers, these trailblazing California pioneers and entrepreneurs sought to use their money and civic connections to promote their vision of African American business ownership, wealth growth, and community life at a place where they and their paying guests could enjoy themselves without fear of insidious tormenting by whites. The head of the group, Dr. Wilbur Clarence Gordon (1880–1945), hailed from Ohio. He graduated from Howard University Medical School in 1904 and had a successful practice in Ohio until 1912, when he moved to California. From the beginning of his tenure in Southern California, Gordon was a leader on matters of racial social progress, medical and dental professional associations, and black business development. He was instrumental in organizing the Doctors, Dentists, and Pharmacists Association for Southern California, as well as the Ohio State Social Society. He was the chorister of Second Baptist Church, one of the oldest African American churches founded in 1885 in Los Angeles. He was already familiar with Lake Elsinore at the time the Lake Shore Beach Company was forming, as he and his wife, Desdemona, had purchased a 130-acre ranch there in the previous decade. His father and mother, Calvin and Arabelle Gordon, moved out from Ohio to California and operated the ranch for them (see table 1).[22]

Dr. Gordon was involved in numerous business and real estate development projects in addition to his medical practice and the Lake Shore Beach Company. Business ventures were one way Dr. Gordon used his personal agency to push for African American civil rights, as well as more black business-ownership and equal access for African Americans as consumers of California's offerings in this era. He persevered even while he and other black Angeleno entrepreneurs experienced state action and white bigotry that impeded some development projects. Another significant investor in this enterprise was attorney Charles S. Darden, a noted land litigation specialist. As mentioned earlier, Darden had also been one of the leaders in an African American resort development plan at Santa Monica beach. After graduating from Howard University and before settling in Los Angeles, North Carolina native Darden undertook purposeful leisure travel around the United States and the Pacific Rim. Another important investor in the venture, Arthur L. Reese, also mentioned earlier, was originally from Louisiana, and like many African American men of that era he came to Los Angeles as a Pullman porter in 1902. He eventually settled in Venice, California, where he developed several small business ventures, mostly in the Santa Monica Bay region, and worked with developer Abbot Kinney in several capacities. Reese brought his workforce of a few dozen people and civic connections, plus his professional network from his work with Abbot Kinney's resort enterprise in Venice to the Lake Shore Beach project (see chapter 3).[23]

Ernest Pickering, a successful white real estate developer who had worked with Abbot Kinney at the same time as Reese, also invested in Lake Elsinore property as Reese and his partners began developing Lake Shore Beach for African American patronage. While the venture could have been encouraged by the similar investment of Pickering, with whom Reese almost certainly had contact, it is unlikely Pickering's project had any direct influence on the Lake Shore Beach investment, as there was already an established tradition of African American property ownership and leisure use in the valley by the 1920s. This earlier African American land ownership is likely to have been more of an inspiration for the Lake Shore Beach owners land purchase at Lake Elsinore, with Pickering's interests noted as a good sign.[24]

One more Lake Shore Beach Company investor, Sallie Taylor Richardson (1878–1943), was a businesswoman active in the civic life of black Los Angeles. Born into an old Kentucky family of racial justice activists, she was the granddaughter of two conductors in the Underground Railroad who helped many African Americans escape enslavement. Raised and educated in Kentucky and Illinois, she moved to Los Angeles from Indianapolis, Indiana, with her husband, Alexander (d. 1922), a merchant who did some real estate investing with his wife. In Los Angeles, she studied to become a certified chiropodist and appears to have been successful with her practice and real estate investments.[25]

In addition to a wealth builder, Richardson was a clubwoman and an active worker for the Sojourner Truth Club in Los Angeles. The club was an early affiliate of the California Association of Colored Women's Clubs (CWC). A branch of the National Association of Colored Women (NACW), the CWC was the most important organization for African American women in the state. CWC clubs provided social services to their local communities and encouraged women to achieve economic independence. Completed in 1914, the Sojourner Truth Industrial Home (later called the Eastside Settlement House) was the first major "institutional" project undertaken by local African American clubwomen in Los Angeles. The site provided living quarters, job training, lectures, and other services to self-supporting women and girls. African American journalist and historian Delilah Beasley observed that the colored women's groups "wove together cultural conservatism and women's rights activism in ways that [were] . . . slightly disarming, but which made perfect sense given their precarious position in society." Now located in the West Adams District of Los Angeles, the Sojourner Truth Club continues to provide service to the community in the early decades of the twenty-first century.[26]

The CWC-NACW structure offered women a source of power and an arena for service unrivaled by mixed-gender organizations. The CWC and the NACW supported the NAACP, and some clubwomen became leaders in that body. A local NAACP stalwart, Richardson was a speaker at the 1928 convention hosted by the Los Angeles branch. Her session was on membership development and retention. By many accounts, including one from the national organization's cofounder W. E. B. Du Bois, the 1928 Los Angeles NAACP convention was one of the finest the organization had held up to that time.[27]

Although Lake Shore Beach was open for business in the 1920s, some resistance and hostility from Lake Elsinore's white community to the African American resort plans persisted. Some white citizens influenced the Southern Sierra Light and Power Company to refuse the furnishing of electricity to the site. The resort owners were planning a big Labor Day picnic when they received this unfortunate news. A few months before, the group had considered canceling the event, due to concerns about the greater community's lack of hospitality. However, the event was held, and, after successfully organizing this Labor Day affair, Lake Shore Beach eventually obtained their power and light connection in December 1922.[28]

The Lake Shore Beach owners during the 1920s had serious intentions to create a fine resort catering to the leisure needs of African Americans, particularly those from Los Angeles. Various board meeting minutes, beginning with an entry on January 20, 1922, and continuing into 1924, 1925, 1926, and 1928, reported that architect Paul R. Williams (1894–1980) was hired to design site plans that included landscaping, dining and dancing pavilions, a bath house, cottages, and a fifty-room hotel. This was early in Williams's career, before he became the most prominent African American architect in the United States by the late 1920s, a status he retained throughout his lifetime and in the years after his death. Williams became especially well known for the luxury houses he designed for several Hollywood film industry and wealthy patrons, as well as for his office building designs. Architectural historian David Gebhard asserts that Williams became "an eminent society architect in Southern California" due to his luxury house designs by the early 1930s.[29]

Williams most likely obtained the Lake Shore Beach commission because the African American resort owners personally knew him and his early success as an architect due to their mutual social, civic, and religious activities in Los Angeles. At the time of the writing of this book, Williams's drawings for this development have not been found. Although the design style of the Lake Shore Beach resort is not known, it can be inferred from the known buildings designed by Williams during the 1920s that the Lake Shore Beach resort would have been in one of the popular Spanish Colonial, Moorish, or English Tudor revival styles of the period.[30]

While the owners worked on raising the money to build the resort according to Williams's plan, a series of interim structures were constructed from materials salvaged from other structures and from Army surplus: small wood-framed tent cabins, a dining pavilion, a dance platform, and temporary toilets. Additional clapboard-sided and simple stucco-sided housing was also built during the 1920s. Through never fully built as the owners intended, Lake Shore Beach did create a memorable leisure community.

The late Milton Anderson, whose father, Charles C. Anderson, operated the concession for the resort during the summer season in 1925, fondly remembered the place. The whole Anderson family helped with the resort operations management. It cost ten cents per person each day to come through the gate to the beach. If you lodged or camped there, the price was of course higher. Sodas were sold from tin tubs filled with ice for ten cents each. The concession sold sandwiches, and guests could make reservations for dinner.[31]

"Everyone would hang out at the lake for picnics, swimming and some boating. It was like a paradise to go out to the lake," he reminisced about his visits during the middle decades of the twentieth century. As a child, Anderson learned to swim in Lake Elsinore, and he has nice memories of the evening bands and dancing. He remembered Arthur Reese out on his boat on the lake. He also recalled that, sometimes, the lake had three- to four-feet-high waves that could be a bit treacherous, whereby one needed to be careful if out in a rowboat.[32]

To encourage visitors who did not want to drive or did not have a car to make the journey, the various groups sponsoring affairs at Lake Shore Beach offered Hupmobile (a minivan of the 1920s) transportation to bring visitors from Los Angeles. The periods around the Independence Day and Labor Day holidays were especially busy for the town, as well as the Lake Shore Beach resort with overnight visitors and day-trippers. From the 1920s into the 1940s the Lake Shore Beach owners continued to renew and upgrade the site to accommodate the crowds and regularly repair floodwater damage to the property from lake-water rises. Due to the inability of the resort owners to raise sufficient funds for its execution, Williams's resort plan design was never fully implemented.[33]

Pleasure seekers from San Diego also regularly visited Lake Elsinore during the Jim Crow era. Barbara Anderson, a retired librarian of African American lineage, reminisced in a 2004 interview that as a girl growing up in San Diego she thought it quite an adventure to travel to Lake Elsinore with her family, because it was a four-hour drive through winding roads around the mountains. In the late 1930s to early 1940s her family camped in a tent and a camper at Lake Shore Beach, or at the free public beach, for several weeks each summer for many years. She and her two siblings, William and Jacqueline, helped their mother, Louise, pick and can apricots as one of their summer activities. Like many fathers of the era who could afford a vacation for their family, Anderson's father, Lorenzo, stayed home in San Diego to work during the week and joined the family on the weekends at their vacation location. Initially not welcome by whites in San Diego County's Chula Vista district, where they purchased a Victorian-style house and a small farm, the Andersons eventually became an integral part of the civic life of that community. The Andersons grew corn, beans, peanuts, peppers, lettuce, celery, cabbage, and other crops, which were often sold at local markets. Lorenzo Anderson also worked for local road crews and later entered the landscaping business, working with contractors on new housing subdivision developments in the greater San Diego-Escondido area. While at the lake, for their enjoyment and probably for a bit of useful extra income, Anderson's father and uncle would catch significant quantities of fish and take them back to San Diego to sell.[34]

"There was a group of people who came to the lake just after school let out for the summer," said Anderson. She remembers how friendly the (black) people were at Lake Shore Beach: "You would walk by people on the shore and they would say hello." Anderson now has a retirement home at Lake Elsinore, formally owned by civically prominent black Angeleno H. Claude Hudson (1887–1989). Originally from Louisiana, Hudson was a dentist, lawyer, civil rights activist, longtime president of the NAACP Los Angeles Branch, and a founder of Broadway Federal Savings and Loan (1947).[35]

At the same time that African Americans were enjoying their recreational and social activities at Lake Elsinore, white community celebrities and notables such as Carole Lombard, Clark Gable, Andy Devine, Bela Lugosi, Will Rodgers, Harold Lloyd, Sir Guy Standing, Eddie Foy, James Jeffries, and even former U.S. President Grover Cleveland also gathered there. The Catalina Island Wrigleys, along with their baseball teams, the Los Angeles Angels and Chicago Cubs, came for the winter to the valley. Aimee Semple McPherson, one of the most popular evangelists of the era, conducted services and built a palatial house she called "Aimee's Castle" in Clevelin Heights, which still stands today, overlooking the valley. At the same time, the lake became a destination for record-setting boat races and Olympic swim team training.[36]

Other leisure ventures illustrated what a thriving community Lake Elsinore was for African Americans for another few decades. Beyond Lake Shore Beach and the Rieves Inn, other black entrepreneurs offered visitor accommodations, and individual families bought vacation homes with some rooms to rent to paying guests. Opened in mid-1925, the Love Nest Inn, owned by Mrs. J. Strider and Sons, could accommodate fifty or more guests with rented rooms and meal service at all hours, and the management furnished entertainment on the weekends with space for dancing. Mrs. Mamie Young opened the Nightingale Lunch Room and Delicatessen, serving refreshments and meals at Pottery, near Poe. Also advertised was the new Hotel Coleman DeLuxe, established by the pioneering black Angeleno entrepreneur and social activist John Wesley Coleman (1865–1930) and his wife, Lydia (b. 1866). Billy Tucker provided accommodations for visitors, and the Taylors and R. C. Anderson at their Silvia Lax Springs offered treatments from the local springs. Others, like Mildred and Aaron Jackson "A. J." Sterling, who first visited Lake Elsinore in 1919, began their accommodations venture sometimes in the early 1920s (see table 1).[37]

The entrepreneurs of Lake Elsinore were capturing some of the economic growth of the period in their black radical vision to develop economic opportunities through providing comfortable and safe leisure accommodations to a growing African American population. These entrepreneurs were part of the important segment of ambitious, articulate professional- and business-class residents who joined the larger group of mostly unskilled Southern laborers migrating to Los Angeles between the 1890s and the 1920s. Some, like John Wesley Coleman, had become business, civic, and fraternal organization leaders, working for the betterment of Los Angeles's African American community. He and other valley proprietors leveraged those networks to build a clientele for their ventures: through their social relationships, individual and cooperative resort business write-ups and advertising in African American publications, and broad word-of-mouth from happy customers.[38]

The coterie of investors and kin made Lake Elsinore a leisure place for Los Angeles's leading African American public activists, professionals, and businesspeople. Along with relaxation, many social patterns (organized and informal) taking place in Los Angeles also occurred at the lake, including family parties, picnics, and barbecues, card games with the men or women's sewing circles, discussions about the issues of the day, musical performances, and religious services. More personal social interactions, like developing friendships, courting, celebrating marriage, and learning how to swim, hunt, or cook, also took place.

The late Jane Miller Cerina, Mrs. Sterling's niece, remembers from her childhood visits in the late 1930s and 1940s watching the goats grazing across the street from her aunt's property. According to Kerina, Mrs. Mildred Sterling took great pride in her vegetable and fruit garden, which included a grape arbor and watermelon patch. She and her brother, Halvor Miller, Esq., both remembered that there were always people from Los Angeles stopping by visiting the family during their summer stays at their aunt's place and also sharing, sometimes, in the bounty of her garden.[39]

Kerina recalled the Wednesday night pinochle games her uncles, Leon "Wash" Washington—who founded the *Los Angeles Sentinel* newspaper in 1933—and Loren Miller, activist, attorney, journalist, and later municipal judge, had every week, whether in Los Angeles or at Lake Elsinore. When he lived in Southern California, the poet Langston Hughes, a friend of Loren Miller's, regularly joined the pinochle group. In 1932 Miller and Hughes were part of the much-publicized and criticized group of young radicals of the New Negro Renaissance, who went to the Soviet Union to view life there firsthand. At the time both men were active in the Democratic Socialist movement in Los Angeles. Though Miller eventually evolved into a "mainstream liberal Democrat," his early radicalism probably prevented him from getting a federal judgeship.[40]

The 1930 U.S. Census count included fewer than 3,000 Lake Elsinore residents, and fewer than 60 full-time residents (or 2 percent) were African Americans. At the same time, the city of Los Angeles had a population of 1,238,048, and the black Angeleno population was 38,894, or around 3 percent. In Riverside County there were almost 81,000 people, of which 1,303 (less than 2 percent) were African Americans. The seasonal visitor count is not calculated in the U.S. Census, but it can be estimated from the literature that thousands of people—white, black, and from other communities of color—visited the valley, especially from the regional population centers. From the late nineteenth century to the early twentieth century, ads and stories about the beauty, resorts, and natural (exploitable) resources of Lake Elsinore were regularly featured in the *Los Angeles Times* and other newspapers, including black publications. The Lake Elsinore and Riverside County Chambers of Commerce, the Automobile Club, the Santa Fe railroad and resort businesses, and other regional entities with a stake in economic development distributed booster and travel materials all over the United States.[41]

Even during the Great Depression, holidaymakers continued visiting Lake Elsinore Valley in record numbers from the regional metropolitan areas. Throughout the 1930s the area received substantial rainfall, and mining and agriculture flourished. The lake was stocked with fish, speedboats set racing records that regularly garnered national attention, and the mineral baths remained popular. As it was hard won by the American industrial labor force, the cultural practice of vacationing increasingly became institutionalized by the World War II years, and in the following decades. In the 1920s, 1930s, and 1940s the African American community of year-round and vacation residents grew along Pottery Street, west of downtown near the Rieves Inn (which had a few name changes after the Burgess family sold their interests in the property). During this time, some small hotels and cottages sprang up that African Americans—mostly from Los Angeles and San Diego—rented for weekend trips and longer vacations. Lake Elsinore African American residents also continued renting space in their homes to visitors (see table 1).[42]

During this time the health resort's sulfur water also attracted a large, mostly working-class, Jewish, and other European immigrant population. The Jewish community created several synagogues and temples, along with the Jewish Culture Club of Lake Elsinore, for their religious and social needs. Jews also enjoyed other health resorts in Riverside County. Highland Springs in Beaumont was popular among the more affluent Jewish community. Gilman Hot Springs in San Jacinto, and a few places in Hemet and Murrieta, also accepted Jewish patrons.[43]

Prior to the building of the national freeway system, starting in the 1950s, motorists or those riding the bus looking for a resort within easy driving distance of Los Angeles or San Diego considered Lake Elsinore delightful, but a bit far away and somewhat off the beaten path, due to its location at the extreme western and southern part of Riverside County. It could take four to five hours to drive to the lake from various population centers around the southland. Most people who visited—whites, Jews, or African Americans—planned to stay overnight. The distance of Lake Elsinore and the overnight "vacation" leisure experience gave the place an air of exclusivity, especially among black Angelenos (see table 1).

Wallace Decuir has fond memories of Lake Elsinore in the 1930s, when black Angelenos' engagement with the era's popular leisure and health practices was flourishing. He recounted happy memories of excursions to Lake Elsinore in the Model T Ford of his friend Ballinger Kemp's grandmother, who had a vacation home there. He recalled that when he and Ballinger were playing by the lakeshore, sometimes they would collect mud at the request of older ladies sitting on the beach, to spread on their bodies for health treatments. "We didn't mind them interrupting our play because they would give up five to ten cents for the chore. We would have a little extra money to spend for cokes and candy," he laughingly shared.[44]

African American physicians, lawyers, government workers, ministers, teachers, newspaper editors, business owners, and others from Los Angeles who were prosperous enough regularly visited, and some bought vacation homes in the valley. Some of these people were leaders in their respective white- and blue-collar professions and in their community in Los Angeles. Many were middle-class in values, lifestyle, and aspirations more than in wealth. Although economic racism stymied their financial ambitions, black Angelenos held continued faith in the promise of upward mobility, and they embraced the Anglo booster rhetoric of American West freedom and egalitarianism and of the California Dream's leisure and health lifestyle. Taking a road trip or an extended vacation and buying property like a second home were certainly big components of American West idealism and the California Dream that middle-class black Angeleno boosters also promoted.[45]

The Post–World War II Flourish and Fade of Lake Elsinore

For many 1940s African American leisure seekers, Lake Elsinore continued to provide a sense of community, a retreat for accomplished professionals, and the persistence of family tradition, even as environmental changes and mismanagement, along with Sun Belt booms, set up the vacation area's decline and transformation. *Ebony* magazine's May 1948 issue touted Lake Elsinore as the "best Negro vacation spot in the state . . . and . . . the nation, according to many Californians." The Lake Elsinore Hotel, the biggest of the African American hotels at that time, exemplified the vibrant fulfillment of *Ebony's* "best" proclamation. Mrs. Mary E. Baker (ca. 1881–1962) and her daughter, Eula M. Reeves (ca. 1898–1971), operated this African American establishment on Kellogg near Pottery, which they acquired in 1931. In addition to its main building featuring fifteen rooms, there were four cottages and camping spaces available for rental, an area to play croquet, and a tennis court. *Ebony* cited the hostelry as "the oldest Negro venture in town, built fifty-six years ago by a couple who came to the valley for their health."[46]

The Lake Elsinore Hotel had a clientele of whites who patronized the dining room, along with African Americans who were overnight guests, other resort visitors, and Riverside County locals. One of the white patrons was the local sheriff, who regularly came by for lunch (which he paid for) and to visit with the owners and others he might know who were dining there at the time. Two full meals a day were served family style, and snacks were set out on a sideboard table all day. When required, Ms. Reeves's brother, Ted, would pick up holidaymakers needing a ride to the hotel from the nearby bus or train stations. In the winter months, Reeves closed the hotel and went to Palm Springs to work during the desert resort's high season.[47]

Betty Lucas-Howard remembers that on their trips from Los Angeles during the 1930s and 1940s her family would rent space behind the hotel for their trailer for the month of August. She relished the greater freedom and independence her parents allowed her at Lake Elsinore, over the limits they imposed in Los Angeles. Her father, Rupert, came on the weekends to join Betty and her mother, Beatrice. Lucas-Howard would sometimes go swimming, fishing, and hunting for doves and rabbits with her father. She recalled the Lake Elsinore Hotel as a big brick house, and both proprietresses as good cooks and hostesses. On Sundays the lady hotelkeepers would make homemade ice cream and peach cobbler for all. For the adults there was evening dancing in the parlor or on the outside dance platform, with music provided by a jukebox, especially on Sundays.[48]

Holidaymakers, local residents, and some news publications recall a few famous people in the African American community as visitors to the Lake Elsinore Valley. A 1949 *Ebony* article waxed about Dr. N. Curtis King's ranch, where he held frequent lavish parties in his barn attended by prominent guests such as actress Louise Beavers and Liberty Savings and Loan president Louis M. Blodgett. As a teenaged summer employee and holiday maker from Los Angeles, Edith Hawes-Howard remembers actress Hattie McDaniel (1895–1952), who won an Academy Award for her performance in the movie *Gone with the Wind* (1939), vacationed at the Lake Elsinore Hotel during at least one summer in the 1940s (see table 1).[49]

Longtime residents and visitors also remember musician, composer, and record company impresario Leon René (1902–82) and his relatives spending time at Lake Elsinore. The René clan moved from Covington, Louisiana, to Los Angeles in 1922. In the 1920s Leon led his jazz group, the Southern Syncopators Orchestra, as songwriter, pianist, and singer. His older brother Otis J. René Jr. (1898–1970) was a pharmacist at Thirteenth Street and Central Avenue, and also a member of the band. For several decades the two brothers wrote songs both individually and together and produced them for musical theater and Hollywood films, as well as for jazz, rhythm and blues and rock and roll artists. Some of the songs become very popular. Louis Armstrong made their "When It's Sleepy Time Down South" (also written with Clarence Muse) his anthem when he recorded it several times during his career. Leon René wrote "When the Swallows Come Back to Capistrano," which became a standard with recordings by the Ink Spots, the Glenn Miller Orchestra, Bing Crosby, Pat Boone, and other artists. The song's popularity catapulted the little Southern California town and its old Spanish mission to a much higher profile in popular culture and public memory.[50]

One of Leon René's best-known and bestselling songs was "Rockin' Robin," first recorded by Bobby Day in 1958, later by Michael Jackson of the Jackson 5 in 1972, and more than fifty other artists. On the West Coast, the René brothers were also pioneering record company owners, opening a few of the first independent record labels in the 1940s and 1950s. They recorded early rhythm and blues and rock and roll hits with innovators such as the Nat "King" Cole Trio, Ivie Anderson, Herb Jefferies, the Johnny Otis Orchestra, Charles Mingus, and numerous other artists.[51]

Evidence suggests that both Leon and his wife, Irma (1905–98), had deep affections for the lake community, as they, along with their two children (Rafael "Googie" L. René, 1927–2007) and Cecilia N. René Masserschmidt (1931–68), were interred at the Lake Elsinore Valley Cemetery. During their lifetime, word of mouth and media reports of the Leon René family's and other prominent individuals' stays at Lake Elsinore would have contributed to informal promotion of the location as an African American resort where one could potentially see and mingle with the Who's Who of black Los Angeles.[52]

For the African American year-round and vacation communities, a happening place to eat and hang out was Miller's Café and Pool Hall, which opened in 1945 at Langstaff and Pottery. Miller's had a big streetlight in front that helped to entice nighttime visitors for inside activities and street-front gossip gatherings. Other businesses catering to African Americans in the late 1940s fanning out from Pottery included a motel and steam bath owned by the Hensleys, LaBonita Motel, and Mr. Leon Daniels's court cottages and meal services. Mrs. T. J. Mundy had an auto court facility charging five dollars a day per person, with meals (see table 1).[53]

The 1949 and 1956 editions of the *Negro Travelers' Green Book* suggested George Moore's hotel on Scrivener for accommodations. Before running this establishment, Moore had a motel and café, George Moore's Chicken Inn, on Pottery and Spring, where the legendary entertainer Louis "Satchmo" Armstrong (1901–71) was a visitor. Prior to this, entertainment entrepreneur and *Eagle* movie columnist Earl Dancer, who was at one time married to Oscar-nominated blues singer and actress Ethel Waters (1896–1977), with his mother, Mrs. Eliza Mason, first leased the site from the Carrier and McLucas families to create the Chicken Inn that Moore eventually purchased. Quite the ambitious entrepreneur, Moore had a network of potential resort clientele who were his customers at his service station and tire shop in Los Angeles at Forty-Sixth Street and Central Avenue.[54]

As a little boy in 1928, long-time Lake Elsinore and Perris resident Rubin "Buddy" Brown remembers a time when boxer Archie Moore (1913–98) visited Lake Elsinore. According to Brown, Moore was acting as chauffeur of a Lincoln Zephyr for his passenger, an African American woman from San Diego. When he was not working, Moore sometimes played ball out in the streets with kids. Before he became well established as a professional boxer, Moore probably picked up employment where he could that did not interfere with his boxing training regimen and bouts in San Diego, which became his adopted home. Setting a record for knockouts during his long career, Moore was elected to the Boxing Hall of Fame in 1966. It is said by some that Moore's colorful personality and his advanced age as a career boxer were part of the inspiration for the 2006 movie *Rocky Balboa*.[55]

The thespian, songwriter, screenwriter, and activist Clarence Muse (1889–1979) owned a 160-acre ranch in the hills of Perris, which he called "Muse-A-While," a short distance away from Lake Elsinore. In 1948 *Ebony* reported that his ranch offered six cabins for rent, including meals at $6.50 a day per person. His overnight as well as day-trip guests enjoyed opportunities for relaxation and socializing, as well as horseback riding, hiking, and hunting (see table 1).[56]

Muse was the first African American to star in a Hollywood film. He appeared in more than two hundred films, including *Huckleberry Finn* (1931), *Porgy and Bess* (1959), *Buck and the Preacher* (1972), and *Car Wash* (1976). He was an advocate for better and more equitable treatment for African American performers and a steadfast supporter of the controversial television series *Amos N'Andy*, because he thought, even with the caricatured leading characters, the show permitted African American actors to play doctors, bankers, judges, professors, and other parts that they could not in general get to play.[57]

In the valley resort town, Thomas R. Yarborough (1895–1969) found business and civic engagement opportunities, as well as relief from his asthma. He and his wife, Kathryn, became year-round residents in 1929, after living in Los Angeles for ten years. Yarborough was born in Arkansas, but he grew up in Greenville, Mississippi. He went to Straight University (today called Dillard University), an African American institution in New Orleans, from 1911 to 1912, and his wife was a graduate of Oberlin College in Ohio. Yarborough became a successful real estate operator. Before creating his own property management enterprise in Riverside County, Yarborough worked as a chauffeur, with building contractors, and in furniture making. He was a caretaker for evangelist Aimee Semple's estate when he arrived to take up lake town residency. His successful real estate strategy included buying inexpensive land at tax sales in Riverside County to sell later at better prices, or to develop for year-round and vacation rentals (see table 1).[58]

As a civic leader Yarborough served as a member of the Elsinore Planning Commission, the board of directors of the Chamber of Commerce, and the executive board of the Property Owners Association. Yarborough's path in civic leadership had a few hiccups that he had to overcome in the late 1940s. When he was appointed to the Planning Commission by then–Elsinore Mayor James Tarpley, he "was promptly the target of a recall campaign by lily-white old-timers," but he retained his seat with a vote of 378 to 286, as reported in *Ebony* in 1948. He was also a founder of the Progressive League's Hill Top Community Center, which was a hub for social gatherings and charity work. As African Americans and Jews became more visible in Lake Elsinore in the 1940s, and more confident in standing up for their civil rights, there were a few discrimination situations against individuals of both groups where establishments along Main Street refused them service. Yarborough rallied Jewish leaders in a common cause to fight these Jim Crow tactics, so that anyone could patronize any establishment for a drink or a meal in the business district without fear of discrimination. As a pioneer in local town leadership, Yarborough also helped to form a businessmen's association that included all community groups in its membership. Traveling to Los Angeles for their meetings, he was an active supporter of the NAACP.[59]

When elected to the Lake Elsinore City Council in 1948, Yarborough was the first African American to be voted into that office in California. He served his first term until 1952, but was defeated when he ran again in 1956. Yarborough was then appointed to fill a vacancy on the council in 1959 and was reelected in 1960 and 1964. In both of the later contests he received the highest vote count of all the candidates. His fellow city council members selected him as mayor in 1966, making him one of the three African American mayors of California cities at the time. When he retired from public service in 1968, the local citizens named a city park in his honor, to recognize his contributions to their community. The Thomas R. Yarborough Park was constructed on the property where the Progressive League's Hilltop Community Center used to stand. The park is one of the only landmarks to the African American community's historical presence (see table 1).[60]

Despite the capriciousness of the lake level, the agency and hospitality of the various African American proprietors—entrepreneurs like the Burgesses, the Lake Shore Beach owners, the Colemans, the Sterlings, Ms. Reeves and Mrs. Baker, Yarborough, and others—were in all likelihood the biggest factors in the ongoing inspiration for black Angelenos, and others throughout the Southern California region and from outside the locale, to visit the valley, with some continuing to build homes and ranches.[61]

A 1948 *Ebony* feature article on tourism in California noted the fifty-year history of the "favorite U.S. playground, [where] some five million sun-hungry tourists trek to Southern California to enjoy its well-ballyhooed 300 days of Ol' Sol annually." The reporter estimated that 300,000 of those visitors were expected to be African Americans with pockets filled with the wages of the post–World War II employment boom to spend on "a host of new facilities and resorts—many opened to colored vacationists for the first time by wartime exigencies." Lake Elsinore was extolled as "the brightest spot on the California vacation map for Negro tourists." Speaking to a national audience, the *Ebony* writer, under an article subheading titled "Elsinore Offers," described the beauty of the environs and expressed the place was one California resort where a Negro could easily find accommodations and "relax in warm sunshine without worrying about discrimination."[62]

All this enthusiasm in the Pan-African American community about visiting a safe place where they would not face embarrassment or humiliation due to discrimination while relaxing was happening during a period of many changes for Lake Elsinore. Beginning in the mid-1930s, during the Great Depression, the discontinuation of railroad service, drought, an earthquake, a disastrous storm that caused significant property damage due to flooding from high lake water, foul odors from dying fish when the lake was low, and delinquent taxes on lots depleting local revenue, adversely affected visitation rates and local services. In addition, federal and local officials vacillated between making Lake Elsinore a county park or maintaining it for a role in national defense. Many people from Southern California metropolitan areas continued to visit in record numbers, but during the World War II years the crowds, particularly of whites, began a pattern of decline that would continue into future decades. The people that did visit the lake spent less money and were not interested in buying property. There were many vacant houses in the community, which became home to the families of the men serving at Camp Haan Army Base a few miles away in Perris, across the highway from March Army Air Field. During the war years the lake and the surrounding area were used for army maneuvers and new equipment tests before it was sent overseas to be used by U.S. soldiers. Douglas Aircraft opened a small machine shop that employed five hundred women and men working in crews rotating over three shifts, manufacturing the wings of B-17 bombers.[63]

Even with Lake Elsinore's changing fortunes pivotal life moments and social practices took place alongside relaxation for African Americans during this era. Ivan J. Houston, in addition to remembering the hot weather and joy of swimming in his formative years in the 1930s to 1940s, also recalled his parents telling him that they had spent their 1920s honeymoon at Lake Elsinore. Jan Miller Cerina recalled that, in the mid-1940s, when she was an early adolescent, African American soldiers came to the lake's north shore one summer day on a big transport truck to watch singer Lena Horne perform. Cerina remembered the soldiers and others who came to hear the free show sitting and standing around at the lakeshore while Ms. Horne entertained from a makeshift stage provided by a truck transport bed. "She [Horne] was a very pretty, unassuming woman who also brought her children for vacation with her at the lake," recalled Cerina.[64]

Los Angeles native Price M. Cobbs, MD, remembered when he was about ten years old, on one of his family's summer visits in the late 1930s, seeing Dexter Gordon (1923–90), who was about seventeen years old at the time, before he became a renowned jazz musician who played tenor saxophone, driving his 1935 Ford Convertible around the lake. "I remember thinking how cool Dexter must be," said Cobbs, as he thought about who he would be and how he would be viewed when he was an older teenager. Young Cobbs with his parents, Dr. Peter Price Cobbs, MD, Rosa Ellen Cobbs, and Price's siblings, Prince and Marcelyn, would go for summer stays at Lake Shore Beach and at Mrs. Sterling's place. Several people I interviewed fondly remembered Dr. Cobbs, the elder who had provided someone in their family with emergency care while at Lake Elsinore. The recollection of lively day-to-day social relations show that the Lake Elsinore's self-determined vacation leisure extended the bonds of community across lines of class and status.[65]

The 1940s began the slow death of the resort, due to the economy and the impact of nature and humans on its water source. As cycles of little rainfall for several years at a time diminished the lake's level, two dams were put into service upstream on the San Jacinto River, further depriving it of a steady water source. There was escalating drainage of the underground water supply for use in the communities of San Jacinto, Perris, and Lake Elsinore that fed into the river, which eventually supplied the lake. In 1948 the combination of low water and overpopulation of fish caused depleted oxygen in the lake. Large numbers of dead fish washed up on the north shore due to the winds and had to be hauled away. Despite these events, the town population continued to grow. In 1950 the population had grown to just over two thousand people, with probably as many people living outside the town limits. At this time, serious discussion began regarding creating a public entity that would have the power to deal with the lake's problems. It would not be until the early 1960s that the major management issues of Lake Elsinore would be resolved.[66]

The problems and concern for future town development in the 1940s continued into the 1950s. By 1955 the lakebed was dry and dust storms were a regular occurrence. Except for 1958, the lake stayed parched for the next ten years, until, in 1964, Colorado River water was pumped in to partially fill it. Although many people left or did not visit because of these conditions, some stayed, a few visitors still came, and some even continued to buy land and build houses in the valley.[67]

The historic Lake Elsinore African American resort community had much in common with other sites around Southern California and the rest of the nation where prosperous American Africans successfully built a place of leisure to insulate themselves and their children from rude treatment and repeated affronts to their dignity from whites. These particularly determined African Americans eagerly pursued the respectable culture of vacation leisure and real estate opportunities in a similar manner to their white counterparts. Vacationing together at selected resorts provided African American families the opportunity to reinforce their relationships, make new acquaintances, and renew old ones. They were pioneering African Americans, carving out spatial imaginary and public spaces in recreation, leadership and public policy, and identity.[68]

As was the case with black resorts that sprouted up near other U.S. cities with relatively large African American populations in the early twentieth century, the Lake Elsinore Valley race-specific leisure space grew because there were entrepreneurs and residents who offered services, accommodations, and leadership to visitors. Relatively remote from the larger Southern California metropolitan areas, the lake community included African Americans as part of the early American settlement in the late 1880s. Evidence suggests that the presence of this family was a decisive factor as to why an African American leisure community emerged in this area, as it was a factor in the development of many others around the United States. Though the area was popular, it was never as coveted by whites as other Southern California resort areas. The African American (and Jewish American) leisure retreats coexisted around the margins of the white resort community in the valley, with few documented unpleasant confrontations between the different communities. Other African American Southern California resorts projects were not so fortunate in their start-up and endurance, making the Lake Elsinore community's success all the more noteworthy.[69]

With the onset of the Great Depression, World War II, federal legislation that made discrimination and segregation illegal, and stronger legal protection of public places open more or less to all, many African American resorts and leisure spaces began to suffer waning attendance and economic hardship. The Lake Elsinore African American retreat was no different in this regard, and the situation was exacerbated by the unfavorable environmental factors. As Southern California African Americans were presented with a broader array of vacation and leisure options, they began to patronize newly accessible places and stopped going to Lake Elsinore.[70]

Changing historical, sociological, and cultural significance does not diminish the importance of Lake Elsinore and other African American vacation retreats. On the contrary, the societal changes only make these sites more intriguing, because of the brave pioneers who persevered in seeking the good-life experiences in public, despite recurrent rebuff, hostile environs, and even bodily hazard. African American leadership has been associated with martyrdom, toil, and sacrifice, and also with advancing obvious racial causes and civil rights more associated with political and economic opportunities. This recognition is appropriate. But determined African Americans demonstrated by their own example that part of the right to freedom and self-determination was the right not only to work, but to leisure, to enjoy the fruits of their labor when and where they choose. These citizens' determination also advanced the universal search for human dignity, civil rights, and consumer equal access for all in the United States.[71]

By the 1960s healing-water resorts became less popular, and at Lake Elsinore the sulfur water baths became a relatively minor part of the local economy. Such places had a certain lifespan, determined by public fancy and changing ideas of leisure as much as by weather and the availability of transportation. Further, the change in consumer leisure tastes has been very much a product of its promotion and deliberate commodification as novelty and fashion, as promoters have cultivated "new" over "old" leisure in the exploits of capitalism. For Lake Elsinore, changing environmental factors accelerated the change in promoted tastes and the decline in the area's leisure lifespan. If not for the multifaceted environmental issues and socioeconomic factors and the lake's unpredictability that enticed successive visionaries and boosters, Lake Elsinore would probably have grown into a sizable town surrounding the big lagoon. As it was, the valley lost some of its "retreat" attraction as it began to feel less rural due to new residential community developments bringing population centers nearer, and the expansion of the influence of three nearby metropolitan areas encouraged by the enlarged regional freeway system that came to envelop it.[72]

The Lake Elsinore community has experienced many transitions since the twentieth century's middle decades. Public acquisition of the lake-bed lands occurred in 1957. No longer the vacation site it once was, the area is now a small suburban style housing family community, a mix of the old town site, rural areas, and new master-planned communities of houses built on land parcels that were once part of the lake, used for farming or as open land. Residents are for the most part retired, or commute to work locations around the southland in Riverside, San Bernardino, Orange, San Diego, and Los Angeles Counties. Today, the Lake Elsinore city and Chamber of Commerce websites promote the area's natural scenic and recreational attributes, social practices, and the memory of extreme sports venues and world-famous thermal winds for aerial sports, as well as the small, historic downtown district for dining and boutique shopping. They advertise the city's over 1,100 acres of freeway frontage available for new commercial and industrial park development, its lower housing and land costs, its relatively close proximity to skilled labor and universities, and its strategic location within the Southern California market.

People can legally camp at designated lakeside locales, but not currently at Lake Shore Beach. Promoted as the "Action Sports Capital of the World" by the city of Lake Elsinore, some public parks along the shoreline and throughout the city are maintained. A private company is contracted to manage the lake area campgrounds, boat launch and marina, day use areas, concessions, and other services. The Lake Elsinore and San Jacinto Watersheds Authority manages lake-water quality, wildlife habitats, and improvements. The lake itself is maintained at 3,300 acres, or 2.5 miles long and 1.5 miles wide, with ten miles of shoreline, less than half its size in the years of abundant water flow early in the twentieth century.[73]

None of the hotels serving white or African American visitors during the first half of the twentieth century are open now, nor are they much a part of the local public memory. Many of the vacation cottages and small hotels built during this period have been torn down, or dramatically altered for year-round use by residents. Descendants of some of the African American families who came to live in Lake Elsinore in the early part of the twentieth century continue to live in the valley environs. A few black Angeleno descendants who vacationed at the lake when the place was popular as a healing-water resort have taken over the second homes their ancestors occupied for their year-round residences. While memory remains in the form of their presence and in the recollections of past participants, an active, collective public characterization of the place's history as a product of African American leisure development success is absent from the landscape.

Today, in the early twenty-first century, many recreational visitors to the valley come for skydiving, hang-gliding, and other aerial sports, as well as water sports of wakeboarding and windsurfing—not for the therapeutic waters. Pottery Street is no longer the hub for African American life at Lake Elsinore, nor is any other street. The city has grown in landmass, and from a majority white population of about 3,000 in 1930, to a more diverse population of around 60,200 in 2017. At 51.9 percent, the Latinx population makes up the largest percentage of the residents, while African Americans make up about 4.4 percent and Asian Americans make up 4.3 percent. Following many cultural and environmental changes, the Lake Elsinore Valley continues to be a charming and beautiful place to visit and live, but with very different cultural nuances.[74]

5 African Americans and Exurban Adventures in the Parkridge Country Club and Subdivision Development

> Folks: This is just another way of spelling Parkridge, and our strong bond of district restrictions compel us to create new fields, new districts, and build a community that we might expand for the sake of prosperity—therefore, Parkridge.
>
> —*California Eagle*, August 31, 1928

"Land, by group ownership, means wealth collectively, and power politically, and with these two requisites you will help materially in solving a most critical economic situation which is fast gaining a strangling hold on Black America," declared the advertisement in the *Eagle* in late summer 1928. "It is your most sacred duty, people," it proclaimed, "to acquire land, not only residential lots, but beach frontage and farm land as well." With this analysis and charge to its readers, the principals of a new recreational and real estate ownership venture, the Parkridge, planted its purposes firmly in the ground of black Angelenos' quest for equality through leisure and economic self-determination.[1]

With the Parkridge Country Club project, a 1920s-era Southern California leisure site and subdivision development, promoters invoked racial uplift rhetoric to engage African American consumers in large-scale, organized efforts for leisure pursuits, wealth development through land ownership, and social and economic self-sufficiency. This project was unique because its black principals reimagined the previously unsuccessful white-owned elite leisure landscape of the Parkridge project for a new group: African Americans, as well as whites that might like to participate. This material landscape presented participatory inclusion as an assertive rejection of regional Jim Crow practices, as it aimed to realize for African American Californians modern citizen consumerist values embodied in leisure, ownership, and mastery of time. It presented to its members and the world at large evidence of esteem attained by socioeconomic success. In participating in this project, African Americans were simultaneously contesting their exclusion; creating their own images of a cultural island of economic power, social status, dignity and self-affirmation; and, on some level, maintaining the status quo of their individual and group conditions in the American cultural hierarchies.[2]

In more recent generations the Parkridge has been remembered as a place of local civic pride, an attempted location for African American suburban expansion, or not at all. Located in the Inland Empire city of Corona, this site is recalled less for its being enjoyed by African America than for its association with white America. In 2006 historian Jose M. Alamillo created a broader picture of Corona's history, with the publication of his rich narrative about the labor and leisure of Mexican American workers in the city's lemon industry, the dynamics and impact of the discrimination they faced, and their civil rights struggles from 1880 to 1960. Yet when the Parkridge is recollected at all in Corona local history and booster narratives it is as an architectural attraction and a failed Euro-American country club. On the website of the Corona Historic Preservation Society, the Parkridge is remembered as one of "Corona's lost treasures," and for the 1960s Cresta Verde Golf Course facilities and subdivision development that stood on the site in 2016.[3]

The remembrance of the architectural grandeur of the Spanish Colonial Revival style of the Parkridge clubhouse has obscured a more interesting and important historical significance. For example, writer Diann Marsh's account in the book, *Corona, the Circle City* (1998) and the publications by the Corona Historic Preservation Society declare that the country club existed only from 1925 to 1928, after which it was a sanitarium for a short time. In Marsh's brief account she mentions that Dan Gilkey built the club and sold Golden Life Membership cards for $500. These Corona local history accounts do not mention the African American purchase and ownership of the Parkridge site after Gilkey failed. On the Corona Public Library's "Brief History of Corona" webpage, the Parkridge is not mentioned at all among the culturally significant markers of Corona's identity. This memory misses moments of visionary leadership, of enterprise and political struggle, and of a more complex and inclusive community definition in excluding the African American initiative at the Parkridge.[4]

These African American venture leaders envisioned infusing new life into a once-failed project to build an exurban community of refined leisure pursuits. In addition, they hoped the venture would grow in value, building wealth for the principals and their patrons, while asserting full, unexcludable African American "membership" in the emerging consumerist citizenship of the early twentieth century. We can understand the venture by examining its regional social context and its place in the milieu of relevant Southern California leisure spaces, subdivision developments, and social history as they relate to Los Angeles and ethnicity. Additionally, I probe the booster rhetoric, racialized issues and discourse, and racist practices (and resistance) in the history of the Parkridge.

Southern California and the Citrus Belt

California's largest city by the twentieth century's second decade was Los Angeles. The establishment of new communities throughout the region expanded Los Angeles County and the nearby counties of Orange, Riverside, San Bernardino, and Ventura as the twentieth century evolved. Subdivision opportunities arose on large land tracts as ranching operations closed, promoting early regional suburban growth as local boosters prompted people from around the world to look more closely at Southern California as a land of opportunity. From within the region, African American entrepreneurs envisioned opportunities for self-determination beyond the city and the ocean's beaches, imagining a modern, leisured, and civilized "country" on the perimeter.[5]

In the 1920s and 1930s the southland region saw financial success from the oil and movie industries, as well as from the automobile revolution and the aviation industry. The transcontinental train lines brought many new visitors and future residents lured by the weather, scenery, and the chance for a new life. According to historian Carey McWilliams, the largest internal migration to the Southern California region in American history occurred during this time, and the population began to spread to new areas. As the population of California increased from 3.4 million in 1920 to 5.7 million in 1930, with most of the growth occurring in the southland, new industries and residential districts began to take over orange groves and agricultural lands. New cities multiplied.[6]

Established in the 1880s, by the 1920s Corona was a young city seeking economic sustainability and expansion. The Parkridge Country Club project was a new land use pattern of business and leisure site for this small city and its promoters and investors. Both city officials and businessmen had big ambitions for this venture in leisure-based home building in the Inland Empire district.[7]

Opened in the fall of 1925, the Parkridge was a half-million dollar leisure development endorsed by the local Chamber of Commerce as a "great asset to [the] citrus belt," due to its distinction of having what the city boosters regarded as the finest championship golf course in California, and possibly the entire country. In the local newspaper, the *Corona Daily Independent*, city boosters boasted that great golf tournaments held at the Parkridge would accrue national and international recognition for their citrus belt community and generate publicity benefits that would attract tourists. Once in the district, the boosters ventured, these visitors would gain an awareness of the beauty of the region, the excellent opportunities its promoters believed it afforded, and some of these tourists would become new residents.

When most people think of Riverside County history today, they think of its agricultural and residential real estate development. But from the 1880s to the 1960s numerous resorts were spread out over the landscape, "offering rest, relaxation, activities, and even recuperation to thousands of people both local and far away." By the late 1920s Inland Empire booster and mayor Guy Bogart of Beaumont proclaimed Riverside County in the *Corona Daily Independent* as the "Empire of Recreation and of Health." The hot springs resorts are the ones most remembered today. Situated along the numerous geographic faults that crisscross the county, resorts such as Glen Ivy, Lake Elsinore, Murrieta, Eden Gilman, Soboba, and Desert Hot

Springs offered their guests healing hot and cold mineral waters to soak and drink while luxuriating in the Southern California sunshine. There were also medical resorts, or sanitariums, and various-sized hotels offered visitors relaxation and vacation in the congenial southland climate at the Mission Inn in Riverside, the Robertine in Perris, the San Gorgonio Inn in Banning, the Vosburg Hotel in San Jacinto and others.[8]

The Corona Valley was part of this resort culture. Located in the proximity of the Old Temescal Canyon Road (which today parallels the Temecula Valley-Interstate-15 Freeway route), near the Santa Ana Mountains pass (today the Riverside-91 Freeway route) in western Riverside County, about sixty miles southeast of downtown Los Angeles on the inland route to San Diego, Corona Valley's geological attractions distinguished the place for first settlements. Native American use of nearby hot springs in Temescal Canyon and Lake Elsinore set the stage for the area's Glen Ivy and Lake Elsinore resorts in the 1880s. These establishments were part of California's emerging health tourism industry, which became one of the defining service industries of the region. Native Americans and Spanish, Mexican, and early California American explorers and settlers had traveled through the Corona Valley on foot and horseback, in wagons and stagecoaches, anticipating the automobile traffic that would follow later in the early twentieth century.[9]

The Parkridge Country Club topped "scenic slopes" with "awe-inspiring" views of the Corona Valley just outside the city limits at the intersection of the main inland transportation arteries in the southern foothills of the Santa Ana Mountains and the Cleveland National Forest on a delta basin near the Temescal Wash and Santa Ana River. With the development of the citrus industry in western Riverside County, Corona had become known for the "quality and quantity of lemons" the district produced. According to a 1926 *Los Angeles Times* article, the city with a population of 6,000 shipped more lemons than any other in the United States. By the 1920s Corona passengers and freight were served by the Santa Fe, Southern Pacific, and Pacific Electric railways, as well as three buses with almost hourly service to any regional Pacific Coast location. In addition, from the district drivers could motor along thirty miles of paved highways to reach the closest beach.[10]

Several already successful Iowans had organized the city in 1886 during the period of increased migration to California in the 1880s after the Southern Pacific Railway had reached Los Angeles. Robert B. Taylor, Adolph Rimpau, George L. Joy, A. S. Garretson, and Samuel Merrill created a land development company known as South Riverside to build an agriculture colony from 15,000 acres of the Spanish Rancho La Sierra and Rancho El Temescal, purchased from various owners. "Colonies" were cooperative enterprises where wealthy (or sometimes not-so-wealthy) investors jointly purchased large land tracts. They would subdivide the land among themselves and build an agricultural economy to subsidize schools, churches, government buildings, a water supply, and other necessary amenities.[11]

During the booming 1880s many towns were founded in California; some survived and others did not. Corona flourished because there was an artesian basin and a climate favorable to growing citrus crops and producing other agricultural products. Clay mining and manufacture of sewage pipes, bricks, and other products, along with rock quarry operations, also provided some additional economic opportunities. In 1896 residents voted to become an incorporated city with the name "Corona," a Spanish word for crown or garland. Alamillo observes, "The Spanish name evoked not only the region's romanticized Spanish past but also the shape of a citrus fruit and the town's unique circular design."[12]

Proclaiming a "white" racial identity, early settlers sought to create a community reflecting their Protestant mores and temperance beliefs. Yet, as a single industry town, dependent on an agricultural labor force of different background and beliefs, Corona's citrus industry relied on mostly Mexican and Sicilian immigrant workers, who, until the 1940s, were integrated into a labor system stratified by class, division of labor, ethnicity, and race. Alamillo contends that

> although Italian immigrants encountered prejudice and discrimination, they were structurally positioned as "white" in the U.S. racialized social system. By the 1930s, Corona's Italian Americans had gained greater economic and residential mobility, whereas Mexican Americans still faced economic and political road-blocks and were relegated to the nonwhite racial status of "Mexican."[13]

A small but powerful group of Euro-American citrus growers exercised substantial influence on the lives, housing, health, recreation, and education of their workforce, on the politics of multiple levels of government, on civic affairs, and on the layout and use of public space. The growers worked to keep competition and unions out of Corona and labor wages low. Those Mexican American and immigrant workers who lived at the citrus ranches were subject to a system resembling industrial plantations or feudal relationships, where their work and leisure activities were controlled by their white American supervisor or employer. Those Mexican workers who chose to live in Corona were pushed into a residential barrio in the northern part of the city within the circular platted town bounded by Grand Boulevard near Sixth Street. Italians lived nearby in neighborhoods on the north side of town.[14]

In the twentieth century's early decades, racially restrictive real estate covenants were attached to property deeds on land south of Sixth Street. Home listings included explicit instructions of "Do Not Show to Mexicans" for fear of depreciating property values. Also, in the 1920s, Mexican children who lived at the citrus ranches and in Corona's northern section were all sent to the same elementary school. The Italian children, along with the children of the two African American families who lived on the north side, were also sent to this same school. When the municipal pool opened in 1925, Mexicans, Italians, and other "foreigners" could only swim on Mondays: the day before the "dirty" pool water was changed, on Tuesdays, so it would be "clean" for whites to swim.[15]

Cultural discrimination and segregation in Corona limited employment opportunities and constrained public space for community organizing and leisure. Mexicans and Italians, like descendants of African Americans, Chinese, Japanese, and other ethnoracial groups in other parts of Southern California, relied on family, kinship, and neighborhood ties to create a vibrant community life. Many of these marginalized groups turned segregation into forms of congregation and developed their own separate institutions, organizations, and leisure activities. The contributions of these groups to the development of Corona and other local communities and the nation are gradually becoming more fully documented and recognized, alongside the narratives of white American elites.[16]

Until the shift of large sections of agricultural land in the 1950s to residential real estate development, the production of lemons and the manufacturing of a variety of lemon by-products was the largest industrial employer in Corona. By the 1920s, with prosperity from agriculture, Corona citizens had established a civic and commercial center with a variety of buildings, businesses, and civic institutions. The town contained a city hall, schools, a library, hotels, a municipal swimming pool, churches, a few movie theaters, a hospital, two English-language newspapers, business blocks, houses, and civic, charitable, and fraternal organizations.[17]

Parkridge Country Club Makes Its Debut

During the 1920s the Corona growers were very active in founding and developing Euro-American fraternal organizations and country clubs. In 1925 the Parkridge Country Club opened to cater to an elite, exclusive Euro-American membership of males and their families. The recreational and resort facilities combined with the stately, Spanish-Colonial-Revival, Mediterranean-style clubhouse, accented by a colonnade in front framed with arched openings and a prominent tower, was from the start a popular gathering place for Corona growers and other native white southland elites. The Parkridge project, created by its promoter and owner, Dan Gilkey of Long Beach, California, was a private business endeavor set up to make a profit through the proposed sale of country club estate lots on the nearby hills and memberships for the sports and social center. The local boosters supported this country club model of recreation as both a community amenity and a mechanism for promoting residential development.[18]

The 1920s in the United States were "the golden age of country clubs," a social and architectural form that emerged in the 1880s. These private recreational and social centers paralleled the rise of suburbanization and mass transportation. They had historical roots in the exclusive city clubs, spas, summer resorts, and elite sports clubs of the wealthy in the nineteenth century. Those who patronized country clubs sought a place of permanent organized space to spend their leisure time. Venues of elite status with a sense of community identity and traditions, these spaces enabled a way for white families to separate their collective leisure life from everyday life in the city, combined with physical security and social superiority. In the 1920s country club memberships were restricted to white American elites by selective administration procedures and high initiation fees and dues. Admission was denied to Jews, African Americans, and members of other marginalized groups, regardless of wealth or background. African Americans were occasionally hired as service staff, as were people of Mexican and Asian descent. In some places real estate developers like Gilkey linked country clubs with real estate ventures such as planned subdivisions to attract upper- and upper-middle-class white homebuyers. These integrated planned developments of clubs and homes are now recognized as the prototypes to the gated communities of the later twentieth century.[19]

In the years following World War II, many whites moved to these new suburban housing development communities and eventually to gated communities, spreading out from urban cores all around the United States. Segregated along class lines and excluding African American and other communities of color until the civil rights laws of the 1940s to 1960s opened up housing and other markets, many of these new upper-class white suburban subdivisions organized private swim and other recreation clubs rather than fund public facilities. Residency requirements and membership fees imposed class and racial exclusion, hence limiting the membership's social makeup of the community in a similar manner to the more elite country club projects. In these new communities with privatized recreation facilities, class and racial separation and discrimination was constructed and supported by private behavior, market practices, and public policies. These exclusive and exclusionary communities reinforced notions of white privilege and white supremacy and solidified social differences along class lines against other less affluent whites as well as racial lines against African Americans. These exurban white communities treated African Americans moving in as a criminal transgression, and residential segregation was enacted as part of a white spatial imaginary. African American desires for adequate housing, leisure, community amenities, and upward mobility were not viewed as part of the California Dream or American Dream in these exurban communities of the 1920s.[20]

A *Los Angeles Times* article touted the transformation by an elaborate irrigation system of a "wasteland" of "uninviting hills . . . to lovely, rolling greens" and "beautiful scenic slopes." The same article reported the project costs as almost $400,000 at the date of publication. The few available 1920s-era photographs of the place highlight tastefully appointed architecture and décor and a variety of recreational amenities on its seven hundred acres. The clubhouse building, constructed in the 1920s California style–inspired Spanish Colonial Revival of Mediterranean architectural design, evoked the region's romanticized past. This leisure palace overlooked a "championship" golf course designed by J. Duncan Dunn, a large swimming pool, a rifle range "declared to be one of the most complete in the West," cricket grounds, tennis courts, and a landing field and a hanger for airplanes. Overnight guests could be accommodated in fifty bungalows. A *Times* article of August 18, 1927, noted the Parkridge dining experience as being "conducted with an elaborateness and finish hardly equaled in the West."[21]

On January 3, 1925, the *Times* reported the new affiliation of the Corona Club and the Parkridge Country Club. The article also noted that the Corona Club was not disenfranchising its organization by joining the Parkridge; rather, they were taking advantage of the "outstanding additional benefits," including a golf course and a beautifully decorated clubhouse offered by the new facilities.[22]

The Parkridge management marketing strategy appears to have targeted potential members throughout the Southern California region, not only in Riverside County. The Inland Empire venture received extensive coverage and rave reviews in the local and regional newspapers, including the *Times*, presenting a vision of Parkridge social life to readers.

Many of these articles highlighted the well-known golf course's architect and the Parkridge course's design. One *Times* article, on March 8, 1925, was titled "Parkridge Club Is Hailed As The Best." The *Corona Independent* on March 2, 1925, listed the names and titles of various regional civic and business elites who visited the site for a "Community Frolic." Men identified as hailing from Corona, Riverside, Fullerton (Orange County), Los Angeles, and Long Beach (Los Angeles County) offered praise. Their approval helped publicize the facility and bolster its credibility for a regional white elite constituency, from whom the Parkridge Club management sought membership purchases and patronage. Although not explicitly stated in these booster-style newspaper articles, the inference was that these influential southland men were "white Americans," and the sought-after audience for patronage was an affluent, "white" constituency.[23]

Although the newspaper portrayed the Parkridge as being well received in its efforts of catering to the recreational and leisure needs of the Southland's elite, after two years the resort's finances were in poor health. In 1927 Gilkey found himself in financial difficulties, with outstanding personal and corporate debts of around $250,000, including a $122,000 mortgage against the club. In a *Times* article of August 18, 1927, the clubhouse and improvements were reported to have an appraised value of $600,000. The promoter contemplated bankruptcy proceedings, and, on August 19, the *Corona Courier* described Gilkey's efforts to make a deal with the club creditors and members to relieve his financial obligations. Gilkey informed the club members that if they "would relieve him of his obligations and would make a mutually satisfactory deal with the creditors he would turn over all of his club holdings, receiving nothing for himself."[24]

Apparently, Gilkey could not come to a satisfactory agreement with his club creditors and members, so he pursued another course of action to relieve his debt obligations. In August 1927 he sold the fashionable club and valuable property to an African American syndicate, the Nelson-White Holding Company, based in Los Angeles. The sale meant the new owners would not only own the property, but also manage the club's services for its existing and future membership. Gilkey's attorney, Welburn Mayock, informed the *Corona Daily Independent* that the new property ownership by the colored financiers would not interfere with the privileges of the current membership holders.[25]

The white club members' bitter contestation of this transaction, which began within days of confirmation of the Parkridge sale to the African American businessmen, took numerous forms. They would engage in a campaign to devalue and demonize this venture's credibility and legitimacy in the maintenance of their ideas of white spatial imaginary. As the *Courier* stated, "It is understood every possible legal recourse will be used by the club members to prevent the sale from going through."[26]

The publishers of the general interest daily newspapers in Corona and other Southern California cities geared their coverage to an audience assumed to be native white Americans. The tone of the newspaper coverage and the actions taken by the Parkridge club members and Corona citizens to stop the "negro invasion" were inflammatory, alarmist, reactionary, and resentful. The rhetoric about the club events making its way to the local newspaper pages was relatively indirect in word choice, but not in meaning. The local white newspaper writers used the tactics of associating blackness with the fear or phobia of being overrun by "some monstrous collectivity," which George Lipsitz and other observers identify as a master sign of "a fearful relationship to the specter of Blackness" constructed in U.S. culture to aid in maintaining white privilege and spatial imaginary that unfortunately persists in the twenty-first century. The news reporting and editorial pieces used both veiled and obvious racist attacks against African American citizens, denoting white privilege and entitlement betrayal if the sale occurred. The Euro-American attacks were couched in community-protectionist notions and verbiage against the rights of the African American syndicate and population in general.[27]

An editorial in the *Independent* on August 22, 1927, titled "Keeping Our Record Clean," opined that local citizens did not object to African American families who might move to Corona for employment. Claiming to speak for the sentiments of the majority of local citizens, the writer argued that these "industrious, honest and law-abiding" African Americans would have a place when work called them to the city. The implication was that since there was no employment they could be hired for, there was no place there for African Americans. The writer contended that Corona, and every other southland city, would object to and fight against "the coming of arrogant and uppish Northern negroes, who would make a playground in our midst. . . . We want no Central Avenue in this city." The "Central Avenue" reference indicated the writer's fear about the possibility of a vibrant cultural and economic hub like the one in the African American community of Los Angeles from the 1920s to the middle years of the twentieth century.[28]

The writer of the August 22 editorial paradoxically warned white readers that African Americans were creating a settlement that would decrease property values, though these African Americans were wealthy enough to have summer and winter homes with club privileges in the

Corona community. Whites and blacks could not mix in the privileges of club membership, the editorial opined, especially in a facility owned and controlled by African Americans. The objection of whites to African Americans' ownership of the Parkridge was about whites' inability to control and define the social, residential, and economic mobility of African Americans, along with their recreation. Just as these native white elites and the newspaper discourse defined Mexicans as undeserving of upward mobility, they also included African Americans in this same category.[29]

Newspaper headlines appearing in the local papers included "Parkridge Members Planning Fight on Club Sale at Meeting Tonight, Interesting Disclosures Likely"; "Corona's Crisis"; "Negro Menace Is As Great As Ever"; "Fiery Cross Burns Near Parkridge"; and "'Mixed Club' Will Never Be Possible, Says Corona Citizen." On August 19, 1927, the *Courier* reported that "many citizens regard the sale of the Parkridge Country Club to the colored population as a decided blow to the future growth and prosperity of both Corona and Norco (a nearby city north of Corona). They regard it as the first inroad of a negro population in this community."[30]

The local newspapers printed announcements about public meetings to be held at the clubhouse, open to all interested citizens, whether they were Parkridge members or not. At these meetings, the committee representing the members that became known as the Parkridge Protective Association discussed the actions to be taken in "their attempt to keep the . . . club from falling into the hands of a colored syndicate." As an August 19, 1927, editorial in the *Independent* ventured:

> Ask any citizen of Elsinore what he thinks of the situation there and you have in the answer what Corona may be expecting in the future if these things shall come to pass.
>
> During the past two years Corona has enjoyed a splendid growth. New citizens . . . have sought a home in the Southland where they might enjoy life amid pleasant surroundings amidst their own people—a happy and contented community. . . .
>
> One dark spot on the horizon will keep these people away and Corona cannot keep apace with her prosperous and growing neighbors.[31]

This reference suggests white elites' awareness of African American leisure sites elsewhere in the region. The remark about Lake Elsinore refers to the African American use and enjoyment of a section of lakeshore property owned by a black syndicate in the nearby town. In an article highlighting the comments of a Parkridge committee member from one of the meetings, Vern Tyler (head of Riverside Petroleum Company) is noted as saying, "Eight thousand negroes took possession of Lake Elsinore on July 4." Tyler's inflammatory rant declared that a similar gathering could happen at the Parkridge if the African Americans obtained possession of the site—the implication being that their site usage would be an undesirable event.[32]

The white membership of the Parkridge Club—which remained open during the contestation of ownership—"Organized For Protection," as stated in a sub-headline of an article in the *Independent* on August 20, 1927. To protect their interests, the members' committee and the creditors filed for bankruptcy proceedings to throw the club into receivership for the amount owed to creditors. (The white life-membership holders viewed themselves as among the creditors.) Another legal action filed in the Riverside Superior Court by "Golden Life" members charged Gilkey and the club creditors with violating the state securities act in the selling of life memberships with the intention to defraud them. Attorneys volunteered their services, and money was raised from the community "to carry on the fight to a finish" to keep "the white spot white." The white protectionists charged theft and had Gilkey arrested.[33]

Even after instructions from Gilkey, the white club caretaker refused to turn over the keys to the new African American property owner representatives (Dr. Wilbur C. Gordon and Journee W. White) after the sale of the property. In an unlawful, obstructionist vigilante maneuver, Corona's white male citizens, carrying guns, were recruited to serve as guards around the clock to prohibit lawful entry to the new proprietors of the Parkridge Club property. Signs were placed on the private road leading from Corona to the club, on the property owned by the firm of Kuster and Waterbury, stating that its use was "limited to . . . members of the Caucasian race only and their servants. All others subject to trespass law."[34]

Gilkey took some actions of his own to protect his interests in the sale of the Parkridge to the African American syndicate by making a few bylaws changes and sending official notifications to the members. Dan Gilkey and his wife, Eva, owned almost all of the Parkridge capital stock. At the stockholders meeting in August 1927, shortly after the sale and before Gilkey was arrested, the bylaws were amended to define a Parkridge member as a person who held a membership. The official notification of the removed restriction clause stating only whites could obtain club membership was the overt act that the white Parkridge members needed to obtain the court-ordered appointment of a receiver. Clarification was also made in the bylaws stating that members had no voting rights and no interest in the property or assets of the Parkridge project. Those members in the arrears on their club dues were also notified that they were dropped from the membership rolls.[35]

In Gilkey's testimony at his trial for grand theft, he stated that he warned the African American investors "the Corona people would resent the purchase of the club. . . . [It] might be blown up and . . . there might be bloodshed." They replied that race prejudice was something they always had to contend with wherever they bought property. This investor group indicated they were not deterred by the prospects of the ugliness that might occur in their purchase of the Parkridge. Two white Los Angeles detectives were also reported to have been at the club mingling with patrons, watching out for the interests of Gilkey and the new owners before they were able to take possession of the property.[36]

A small article in the *Independent* on August 20, 1927, reported that at a members' committee meeting a Corona resident suggested a "Southern gentleman" should be placed at the head of the combined municipalities of Corona and Norco to get things under control in the area. One night a flaming cross appeared atop a hillside across from the Parkridge, visible to those leaving the club, motorists on the road through town, and Corona Valley residents. As reported in the *Independent* on August 22, 1927, a few days later, a purported representative of the local Ku Klux Klan delivered a statement denying responsibility. Whether they were members of the hate group or not, we can safely surmise the local white citizens who positioned the upright burning cross on the hillside were well aware that this was an intimidation symbol for the KKK organization in their nationwide revival of the 1920s. In Southern California, the KKK aimed its intimidation tactics at limiting the rights of people of color, religious minorities, immigrants from southern and eastern Europe, and other new residents from purchasing homes and participating in employment in certain areas. In some Southern California districts, the KKK aimed at restricting Mexican American citizens to manual labor employment and from participating in community politics.[37]

The newspaper reference to "gentlemen of the South" handling things, along with the flaming cross, were veiled threats directed toward the African American investors or anyone who might help them to gain possession and use of their new property. Local newspapers suggested it was time for consideration of Jim Crow measures to keep Corona an inviting southland city. It was reported that many around town thought it time for Corona citizens to ruminate on placing restrictions on where nonwhites could live and play, as some of their white neighbors in nearby towns had done. Corona's whites may have hoped for a twofold benefit with this cross burning to signal their hostility towards the African Americans who were attempting to become a part of the community and to intimidate Mexicans "to stay in their place."[38]

On November 9, 1927, Dan Gilkey was found not guilty of the charge of grand theft. Though Gilkey was acquitted, there continued to be a few other unresolved legal matters, such as the receivership proceedings. In an August 1927 article, the *Independent* reported on the superior court's approval of the receivership orders and its ruling that the receiver was to be placed in charge of the Parkridge operations. The article read, "The . . . order states that only members of the Caucasian race shall have access to the club during the time it is in the hands of the receiver."[39]

Once the judge lifted the receivership order in April 1928, the stage was set for the African American investors to resume their negotiations for the Parkridge Country Club property. A *Los Angeles Times* article on April 21, 1928, stated that the appointed receiver, attorney T. T. Portous, had resigned several weeks before, as he declared, "It was hopeless to attempt to make the club a going concern." The white members committee and creditors continued in collaborated efforts to keep the African Americans from gaining complete control of the club while they awaited the court's decision against Gilkey regarding the changing of the club bylaws and the debt collection. The time finally arrived for the African American syndicate to take their turn to make a success of the palatial Parkridge. Financial tangles during Gilkey's ownership and white Corona citizens' legal and extralegal contestation of the new club ownership and patrons would remain a shadow over the eventual African American ownership, possession, and management of the Corona leisure site, as well as its clientele's enjoyment.[40]

"The Largest Country Club Owned by Black Americans"

The Nelson-White Holding Company signed the deal to purchase the Parkridge on August 13, 1927, from owner Dan Gilkey, for $575,000.[41] Completion of the transaction and close of escrow on the sale occurred quietly on November 7, 1927. Until at least the receivership matter of the Parkridge Protective Association and creditors' legal maneuvers were worked out, the African American investors were hindered from taking actual possession of the property. On May 4, 1928, days after a Riverside court judge formally accepted the receiver's resignation, the Nelson-White Holding Company took physical possession of the Parkridge.[42]

At this point, the new owners—Dr. Eugene C. Nelson, Clarence R. Bailey, and Journee W. White, respected members of the Afro-Angeleno community—were ready to show off the property. Like Gilkey, the African American syndicate planned to sell not only Parkridge Country Club memberships but also estate sites. They ran simultaneous advertisements for both activities in Los Angeles African American–owned press, such as the *California Eagle*. The syndicate's first big promotional event, billed as a grand gala opening, was held on Decoration Day (or what we know today as Memorial Day), May 30. Who were these ambitious, African Americans investors in the 1920s buying a luxurious resort in Riverside County? Their individual and cooperative economic efforts were part of the new forms of black social existence and spatial imaginary challenging the boundaries of racial progress before the Great Depression. Their efforts would carry over into the New Deal era, World War II, Cold War nationalism, the classical civil rights era of the 1950s and 1960s, and into Black Power militancy.[43]

Born and reared in Charleston, South Carolina, Dr. Eugene Curry Nelson (1888–1962) graduated from Prairie View State Normal College (today Prairie View A&M University) near Houston, Texas, and received his medical training at Meharry Medical School in Nashville, Tennessee. Like many other African Americans in his generation pursuing higher education, he worked his way through medical school by waiting tables in the dining rooms of steamboats and railroad cars. After graduating from Meharry in 1911, Nelson worked assiduously to earn money to purchase the equipment needed for his chosen profession as a physician and surgeon. He began his career in Virginia, before moving to and settling in Los Angeles in 1914 to build up his large medical practice, which served African Americans, whites, and patients of other ethnicities. During this time, it was not unusual for African American physicians in Los Angeles to have a clientele made up of various ethnicities, even while they and other African Americans were discriminated against in other professional and social situations.[44]

Nelson had a light-colored complexion and hair texture more straight than tightly curled, though he made no effort to conceal his racial connections to African Americans. Several written accounts waxed that the handsome Nelson was always "carefully groomed" and "elegantly tailored." In a 2011 interview, 102-year-old Walter L. Gordon Jr., a retired Los Angeles attorney, recalled Nelson as a handsome man with a nicely trimmed mustache who dressed well. Gordon remembered Nelson drove a convertible Pierce-Arrow automobile, an expensive and stylish vehicle during that era.[45]

Nelson was identified as "one of California's wealthiest Negroes" in a 1924 article by Noah D. Thompson in the *Messenger*, a nationally circulated African American monthly published by Chandler Owen and A. Phillip Randolph in New York. Before the Parkridge venture, in addition to practicing medicine, Nelson invested in several businesses in finance, real estate, manufacturing, oil, and amusement. Around the time of the Thompson article, Nelson had recently founded the Commercial Council of Southern California, dedicated to fostering business enterprises and civic participation among African Americans for individual and group benefit. He was also a founding member of the board of directors of the African American-owned Liberty Building-Loan Association in 1924, a financial association that encouraged African Americans to become homeowners. That same year Nelson was the principal organizer and president of the Unity Finance Company, a banking outfit for the African American community. Nelson also grabbed the opportunity to invest in oil, the world's new black gold. Some of the investment capital for these business ventures may have come from Nelson's trade of his Pierce-Arrow automobile with an acquaintance when an opportunity arose to buy stock constituting 1 percent in a particular oil well. Sometime in the summer of 1923, oil started gushing out of the ground at this site at a rate of nine thousand barrels per day.[46]

Other African American publications identified Nelson as "one of Los Angeles's leading Negro citizens and the Merchant Prince" due to his success in business. Mingling his own interests in entertainment with a business endeavor, he opened—with the assistance of Mrs. Tessie Patterson as manager—a sumptuously decorated cabaret called the Hummingbird Café. His "elaborate temple of pleasure," as Chandler Owen called it in a *Messenger* article, featured live music and other entertainment for the amusement of local African Americans and tourists. The article also contained photographs of Nelson and his then-wife, Angelita, and their two smiling daughters, Wildred and Ramona.[47]

In the midst of the Parkridge purchase, Nelson married Helen Lee Worthing (1905–48), a white entertainer once called the "Golden Girl" of the American stage. A Ziegfeld Follies star in New York, she was once "the toast of Broadway." As one of the "three world—famous artists" of the follies, and "considered one of the five most beautiful women in the world," in the mid-1920s, Worthing made her way to Los Angeles and to the Hollywood scene. She appeared in several silent movies including *Janice Meredith* (with Marion Davies), *The Swan* (with Adolphe Menjou), and *Don Juan* (with John Barrymore). After Worthing married Nelson, her movie offers dropped off. Some have observed that the white star's career was over once her interracial relationship was out in the open, rather than a clandestine association. The Nelson-Worthing marriage ended in 1933. In this union, they both had to battle intolerance, bigotry, and race hatred. Nelson was accustomed to fighting this "dragon," as he called it, but Worthing never comfortably figured out how to fight it.[48]

Nelson's partner, Journee W. White, was the public spokesperson for the Parkridge management. Born in 1890 in Louisiana, White was a proud, commissioned officer and World War I hero. He left his real estate business in 1917 to serve in France with the 367th Infantry of the 92nd U.S. Army Division, also known as the Buffalo Soldiers. His bravery and heroism in a decisive battle at Metz earned Lieutenant White, along with the First Battalion of his regiment, the Croix de Guerre (a French military cross decoration created to recognize French and allied soldiers who were cited for their exceptional gallantry).[49]

White hoped that the world, and particularly the United States, where he was a citizen, would recognize the achievement of these African Americans, as well as their loyalty. Like leaders such as W. E. B. Du Bois, who called for the "Close Ranks" strategy in an editorial in the *Crisis*, the NAACP's official magazine, White argued that this demonstration of World War I patriotic service and sacrifice should translate to greater social and political gains for all African Americans. As in other parts of the United States, the World War I service of African Americans did not halt open discrimination and racism against black Angelenos; thus, the local as well as the national fight for social equality continued. Riots occurred in several U.S. cities to roll back African American citizenship and the economic gains of the World War I era. White and several other black Angelenos were intensely interested in development of locally controlled and carefully executed financial investments, which led the economic renaissance of black Los Angeles in the 1920s.[50]

Journee W. White used his U.S. Army title, "Lieutenant," along with his World War I hero and patriot status, to his advantage. In the 1920s he was active in Los Angeles's Benjamin J. Bowie Post (black chapter) of the American Legion. The group's Legion Club, with White sometimes acting as the management's representative, took over the space of Dr. Eugene C. Nelson's Hummingbird Café, near Twelfth and Central, after the local police commission finally revoked its dance license "because of [what they viewed as] 'damnable conditions in which members of the white and black races misconducted themselves.'" In his *Chicago Defender* column titled "Coast Dope," Ragtime Billy Tucker ventured that, upon investigation, white club owners noted that many of their former clientele were patronizing the Hummingbird Café. As a measure to get back this lost clientele, Tucker concluded, the white owners started filing complaints with the authorities to revoke the Hummingbird Café's dancing license so its business would evaporate. Tucker's speculation may be correct, as late 1920s-era Los Angeles exhibited substantial police corruption and brutality, especially as it related to African Americans. Further, with the lax enforcement of statewide antidiscrimination laws, there were increased incidents of both subtle as well as more overt racism toward the growing African American population. The masked racism allowed white supremacy to be executed without obviously contradicting the state's civil rights laws or replicating the South's explicit system of hate and the armature of Jim Crow laws that gave formal structure to racism.[51]

The Legion Club, operated by the Benjamin J. Bowie Post of the American Legion, was closed by the police commission a year later, in January 1927. The Bowie Post management operating the Legion Club was charged with "flagrant violations of the Wright Act [1921–22]," California's ratification of the Volstead Act (1919) passed by the U.S. Congress establishing prohibition and a national ban on alcoholic beverages.[52]

In defense of the Bowie Post management of the Legion Club, Journee W. White testified at a police commission hearing regarding the suspension of the club's permit in an effort to have it restored. He testified that a certain policeman "had threatened to put the café out of business so a new club could get the patronage." The Legion Club was probably doing a visibly good business, and the most likely cause of its closure was the police department's racketeering network's inability to line their pockets with enough protection money or bribes from the club's management. In this situation and others, due to their various business activities and apparent civic network, White and the other Parkridge proprietors showed a sense of self-direction, justice, and community.[53]

In addition to the Parkridge and other business endeavors, White was involved in a few high-profile African American real estate development ventures, which were written about and advertised in the press during the 1920s. These deals included Gordon Manor (Torrance) and Eureka Villa, also known later as Val Verde (Santa Clarita). White also succeeded in other business ventures, indicating that he was intelligent, personable, fearless, and obviously ambitious. He appears to have been respected and well connected in Los Angeles and other communities.[54]

White's first marriage was to the socially popular Mamie V. Cunningham White (1884–1941). Her father, David Cunningham, was the first African American bricklayer and later a building contractor who worked on noteworthy buildings in Los Angeles. Her mother, Minnie Cunningham-Slaten, was a distinguished clubwoman, active at the Sojourner Truth Club and other organizations for the betterment of African Americans. Mamie and her several siblings were educated in the public schools of California. Earlier in her work life, Mrs. White was a clerk at the main Los Angeles post office. Later, after her marriage, she owned a successful employment agency located near Twelfth Street and Central Avenue. For a time she also assisted in editing the African American-owned *New Age* newspaper, published by Frederick Madison Roberts. Mrs. White participated in the women's auxiliary of the Benjamin J. Bowie Post. In August 27, 1927, the *Chicago Defender*'s "California News" column, which featured happenings in Los Angeles, noted, "Mrs. Journee White was among the fourteen women elected to attend the American Legion convention in Paris, and the only Race [meaning black] woman to be elected."[55]

Later in his life, Journee W. White would be involved in a few civic leadership endeavors in a similar spirit to his efforts with Parkridge, advancing the cause of racial equality, employment, and wealth development opportunities. In 1940 "Lieutenant" White was the head of the Committee on Labor and Industry of the Eastside Chamber of Commerce in Los Angeles, which exposed the prejudice against and the exclusion of Americans of color and religious minorities (including African Americans, Mexicans, Jews, and Portuguese) in violation of the federal and state laws forbidding such discrimination in national defense programs. The committee headed by White contended this discrimination was unpatriotic and presented specific evidence the National Youth Administration, the California State Relief Authority, and various trade schools were systematically excluding Americans of color and religious minorities from aircraft mechanical training opportunities. White and his committee members were in sync with labor leader A. Phillip Randolph's and other locally and nationally organizations fighting for defense industry opportunities for all Americans.

The pressure of their collective efforts finally forced President Roosevelt to sign Executive Order 8802 on June 25, 1941, declaring discrimination based on race, creed, color, or national origin in defense industries to be illegal. The order also created the Fair Employment Practice Committee (FEPC) to oversee compliance through investigation and exposure of racial discrimination charges.[56]

Clarence R. Bailey (1889–1975) was the third identified principal in the Nelson-White Holding Company's Parkridge venture. Bailey moved to Los Angeles with his parents and siblings from Birmingham, Alabama, between 1900 and 1910. His father, Samuel G. Bailey, was a builder. Clarence R. Bailey was listed as a self-employed painter and building contractor from 1910 to 1940 in the U.S. Census, and he may have continuously engaged in other business activities unreported to the census taker. He was married to Pearl P. Bailey by 1920, and, by 1930, Clarence and Pearl had five children (one girl and four boys). In census records he is identified as being either black, Negro, or mulatto. His wife and children were identified as white in the 1930 Census.[57]

By 1927 Bailey was involved with real estate transactions in addition to his building trade activities. The *Eagle* reported on September 23, 1927, that oil was discovered near land Bailey owned, located in the rapidly developing oil field in eastern Long Beach around Signal Hill in southeastern Los Angeles County. Available sources do not indicate who became Bailey's investment partners in this oil well project, or how much oil his drilling efforts actually raised. It can only be speculated that Bailey may have had some success with this project, because of the parcel's location in "proven oil land," in an area that became one of the world's richest oil deposits. What is known is that, in January 1929, Clarence R. Bailey and Journee W. White were partners in a three oil well where drilling was taking place ten to twenty miles southeast of Bailey's oil land parcel in Los Angeles County's Long Beach vicinity.[58]

Bailey and White were accused in a court case of not paying their (likely white) oil rig workers for wages owed them. The two partners were exonerated of any wrongdoing when the judge ruled that "a large part of the indebtedness consisted of indebtedness incurred by a former employer." No available sources give a clear indication of the degree of success of Bailey's and White's oil well projects. In any case, both Bailey and White were pioneering African American entrepreneurs directing capital into a range of ventures, including oil extraction, not unlike other nonblacks in similar circumstance in their era.[59]

The Nelson-White Holding Company principals had been part of other large real estate projects and were associated with investors who most likely were in some way involved in the Parkridge project. The Parkridge acquisition financing included loans from Euro-American banking and corporate entities and a corporate bond offering. A Parkridge promotion text stated that this type of equity and debt financing "mark a new era in the progress of our local Black Americans, being the first successful attempt of a deal of [this] nature by members of our group."[60]

White had also been on the team with Dr. Wilbur C. Gordon to develop an African American residential subdivision called Gordon Manor on 213 acres in Torrance, part of the South Bay section of Los Angeles County. While that project was undermined by wealthy and connected whites mobilizing state power, Gordon had simultaneously been involved in the resort development plan for African Americans at Lake Elsinore in Riverside County discussed in chapter 4, not far from Corona.[61]

The *Eagle* announced that Norman O. Houston and L. P. Grant, through the Parkridge Country Club Corporation, would sell the four thousand lots of the Parkridge Estates subdivision. A second-generation Californian, Norman O. Houston had been one of the leaders of a failed venture to develop a resort and amusement facility for African Americans in Santa Monica in 1922, and he continued to participate in business projects for African Americans. Belonging today to the city of Los Angeles, the Norman O. Houston Park is named for him. As a colleague in other ventures, White may have been involved with the effort to build the Santa Monica leisure resort with Houston and the other Ocean Front Syndicate investors, though no evidence has been uncovered to identify the names of other investors in this project.[62]

The purchasers that White, Nelson, and Bailey expected to join the Parkridge reflected the African Americans who migrated to the Los Angeles region from the 1890s to 1930s, many of whom were families of city people who were more educated, ambitious, and affluent, with a middle-class outlook. They were more likely to be professional people, like teachers, ministers, doctors, dentists, newspaper editors, and businesspeople, whether or not they found employment in these professions in their new home. Some African Americans who worked in the usual urban service employment open to them during this time, such as porters, domestics, custodians, and labors, also had upward mobility aims, often saving their money to invest in real estate. Others who might be able to pay for the club offerings and estate sites were a few men and women engaged in the underground economy, whispered or known to be in the vice business. Their business interests were in the numbers game and other gambling activities, speakeasies, illegal drugs and alcoholic beverage trafficking, and prostitution, mixed with other business interests including barbershops, dining establishments, real estate, and auto service stations. In many circles, some of these businesspeople would have been considered respectable citizens of the 1920s era and the later black Angeleno community.[63]

Scholar, activist and NAACP *Crisis* magazine writer W. E. B. Du Bois, as well as other observers following his lead, broadly viewed this generation of more educated, ambitious, and affluent African Americans that migrated out of the South between 1890 and 1915 as the Talented Tenth of the African American population, and as race leaders. The number of African Americans who migrated to Los Angeles and the American West in this era in general were more modest than the numbers that went north, with the Los Angeles black population growth rate staying the same in the 1920s as it had been since the 1880s. In the migration of the late nineteenth and early twentieth centuries, the black Angeleno population was not unlike those in other cities around the United States in their response to the process and formation of institutions such as churches, clubs, mutual benefit societies, and fraternal and other organizations. Tied to the formation of a new black elite, these new institutions articulated the philosophy of race pride and racial unity. Their complex collection of responses included self-determination, economic self-help, and "uplift." Determined to achieve fuller participation in American society, the Nelson-White group investors and patrons were the embodiment of the ambitious New Negro class of the 1920s, who built on varied brands of social, political, and economic self-reliance nationalism with respect to their community, generally through enterprise.[64]

When the black Angeleno syndicate purchased the Parkridge, Los Angeles was the center of the African American population, politics, culture, and business in California, and the Far West (outside of Texas). This was symbolized by the 1918 election of Angeleno Frederick Madison Roberts as the first African American assemblyman in California, and the cultural and political imprint African Americans literally stamped on the Central Avenue district of Los Angeles. High-profile African American businesses joined Roberts to generate immense pride within the local black community and attracted comments and contacts from outsiders in the white as well as Pan-African American community nationwide.[65]

The ideas, vision, and circumstances of Parkridge proprietors and their expected investors for this leisure project emerged from and fed off the growth and dynamism of the burgeoning black Angeleno community's expansion during the early part of the twentieth century. The Central Avenue district featured African American-owned residences, churches, theaters, nightclubs, savings and loan associations, automobile dealerships, newspaper offices, and retail businesses. The only black hospital, the Dunbar Hospital, opened in 1922. The largest African American–owned business in the West until well into the middle decades of the twentieth century, founded in 1925, the Golden State Mutual Life Insurance Company, made its home in the district. The Liberty Building-Loan and Unity Finance companies were established in 1924. The Angelus Funeral Home was founded in the district in 1925, which exists today at another location, on Crenshaw Boulevard. The beautifully appointed Hotel Somerville (later known as the Dunbar Hotel) opened to host the 1928 NAACP National Convention in Los Angeles, within months of the Parkridge purchase by African American investors.[66]

The images of the political, business, social happenings, and cultural expression of the African American community in the Los Angeles region, as well as the lures of the West, were transmitted and promoted via the black press regionally and nationally in the *California Eagle*, the *Chicago Defender*, New York's Harlem-based monthly *the Messenger*, the NAACP's *The Crisis*, other periodicals, and by word of mouth. Descriptions of

Southern California's endless summer lifestyle and the picturesque landscape were also circulated. By the 1920s the West Coast's jazz culture was headquartered on Central Avenue and exported nationally and internationally through the black and other press, Hollywood movies, performance tours, and other media. But the black press also presented a frank portrayal of the challenges of the hypocrisy and frustrating restrictions imposed by the dominant white mainstream, which undermined African American advancement. Even with this caveat, talented and driven African Americans received the message that they could acquire their version of the good life in Los Angeles with fewer restraints than in other parts of the United States. The Parkridge was presented in national black media discourse as consistent with and emblematic of the attainment of the community and heralded for its assertive enterprise in the face of opposition, and for its vision of African American leisure and business ownership.[67]

With the leisure palace in their possession, Dr. Eugene C. Nelson, Clarence R. Bailey, and Journee W. White put the Parkridge project into heavy marketing mode to their potential patrons and investors with promotional events, newspaper advertisements, and story placements. The management hoped to attract an integrated club patronage that included black and white Americans—or, at least, the management was hopeful that this invitation to southland whites to continue patronizing the Parkridge would reduce harassment to black visitors by Corona locals. Or perhaps, based on the experience of the Hummingbird Café, the new management did have real faith they could develop a multiple ethnic clientele. Having a broader patronage base would certainly have been beneficial to the financial situation of the Parkridge project, and the local community generally.

From the postbellum period to the middle of the twentieth century, African American business opportunities were limited by what African American entrepreneurs and insurance company executive Merah Steven Stuart (1878–1946) in the 1940s first observed as the "economic detour." In the United States African Americans faced an environment where they were restricted from involvement in business and as economic agents in the open market by state policies, local custom, and sometime even acts of violence, as in the cases of the destruction of black business districts in Wilmington (1898) and Tulsa (1921). At the same time that whites and other ethnic groups could do business with whomever they pleased, black businesses were not allowed entry into any but all-black markets and were excluded access to greater and more lucrative markets, except in a few rare situations. These effects of the economic detour had a harmful impact on the capability of African Americans to build and sustain flourishing businesses. Even so, African Americans did create prosperous businesses under hostile conditions. Using their skills and ingenuity, the African American owners worked to develop their new Parkridge project into a thriving venture, despite the obstacles in their path.[68]

In April 1928 Journee W. White, as the secretary of the club, sent a letter to white members, confirming that the African American syndicate was taking possession of the Parkridge. In the letter, which was also published in the *Corona Courier* on April 20, 1928, White invited the Euro-American members to continue to patronize the club, by extending an invitation to "all persons, regardless of race, color, creed or denomination" to join. He informed previous life members they could cancel their memberships and get their money back if they did not want to continue to participate. His letter reminded the local white community that all visitors to the Parkridge had legal rights, including African Americans. He expressed that the club owners expected respect from the local community, no destruction of their or their guests' property, and no abuse of the club's visitors. As White was aware of the hostility the local community had expressed against the African American entrepreneurs, his letter notified the members and, by extension, the local white community that his team was not afraid of them. He articulated his faith in the syndicate's business acumen, (on some level) the legal system, and the prospect that interracial sport and recreation activities could easily take place at the Parkridge for those who wanted to participate. He and his team identified themselves and their potential patrons as American citizens entitled to exercise their rights to equality in leisure and consumption.[69]

The *Courier* reported that local white citizens were "greatly incensed" by White's letter. The newspaper reporter fulminated in response to White that the idea of "race mingling" was impossible and would be bitterly contested by the people of Corona. Some citizens continued to complain that the African American possession of the club "was but the beginning of encroachment of an undesirable class of colored people in the community." White challenged the people of Corona to be "good citizens."[70]

Judging from the newspaper account, white Coronans did not seem inclined toward that, or toward a more inclusive social environment and the social mobility of African Americans in their community. The *Independent* ran an article with a headline that could be viewed as a threat of destructive use of state power against the new Parkridge owners: "County Can Condemn the Parkridge Club for Public Park Purposes, Suggested." Corona's white citizens were aware of the successful use of state power against other high-profile African American land ownership and development projects in Los Angeles County. Riverside County officials could follow the same course of action regarding the Parkridge situation, the reporter suggested. But the black investors legally owned the site, at least for the foreseeable future. At this point the white locals could only protest and harass the African American businessmen, and possibly their future patrons.[71]

Beginning in May 1928, the Parkridge's new management advertised the events and offerings of the club extensively in the pages of the *Eagle*. In addition to the ads, some editorial features and paid promotional text about upcoming events and reviews of happenings also appeared. Similar promotions and coverage were featured in other local African American periodicals, such as the *New Age* and the *Pacific Defender*, and in the out-of-town black press, such as the *Chicago Defender*. The advertisements, paid promotional texts, and editorial offerings featured booster rhetoric not unlike what one might have seen in any number of publications of the day. The new club management geared their marketing toward the more affluent black reading constituency whom it expected would want the California leisure lifestyle, luxurious facility access, and social status and would find the means to pay for it. The grapevine and the transregional networks formed by African American professionals as well as anyone else reading the black press throughout the country no doubt communicated information about the lavish Parkridge, which also would have encouraged interest in the place.

An elaborate half-page ad in the *Eagle* on Friday, May 4, hailed the Parkridge as "The Million Dollar Playground," "California's Finest and Most

Distinctive Recreational Resort and Playground," and "the Biltmore for the Race." The ad announced the opening invitation for visitors beginning May 6, and the May 30 grand opening of the club under Nelson-White Company management. The sports facilities were explicitly and invitingly described, much as they had been under the efforts of prior owner Gilkey in pitching to an exclusively white audience, using words to illustrate their fine quality, such as "championship golf course," an "elaborate Gun Range," a "modern Flying Field" and "superb Tennis Courts." The opening sports events included a golf tournament, tennis matches, and swimming races, with prize money being offered to the winners of many events. When the matches were finished, the swimming pool would be available for recreational use. Visitors could rent one of the fifty available bungalows for $1.50 per weekend. Also available on site was a children's playground. Additionally, the *Independent* reported that the people of Corona and previous club members were welcome, and that numerous Riverside County and Corona officials had been personally invited to attend the festivities. Without saying it explicitly, the correspondent expressed the economic benefits that were accruing to Corona due to the upcoming event, noting that the Parkridge management had placed an order with a local bakery "for three hundred loaves of bread for sandwiches and a meat order of approximate size."[72]

A beauty contest to decide who would be "Miss Parkridge" featured the largest and most extravagant prizes of the opening event: $500 in cash and a massive silver cup as well as "a $1,500 Founders membership in the Parkridge Country Club which includes a beautiful lot and cabin on the magnificent . . . estate, a regal country home to spend the week-ends and a piece of valuable property."[73] It was advertised that the pageant would be filmed for a newsreel to be shown at movie theaters to promote interest in land and membership sales for the country club project. Miss Parkridge and her court were the honored guests at the invitation-only "Grand Ball and Entertainment" fete to celebrate the progress African Americans had made in Southern California with the acquisition and opening of the leisure palace under the new management.[74]

In addition to reviewing or accessing the sports and social spaces and making acquaintances with potential economic opportunities, there were many opportunities for potential matchmaking at the Corona leisure palace. This club and its events exemplified glamour as well as leisure, seeing, and being seen. The black syndicate surely hoped the excitement and success of the Parkridge opening event activities would continue, so they could draw people who would patronize their new club and purchase lots within the subdivision.

On the day of the big Memorial Day event, the Corona Police Department, in what has the appearance of being an effort to inconvenience and harass African Americans visiting the Parkridge, issued many traffic citations. In the days immediately following the event a dispatch was "alleged" to have been sent from Corona via an unidentified correspondent of the United Press news wire service, stating that "a near race riot developed in Corona on Memorial Day" when long lines of African American visitors to the area were held up due to the issuance of over two hundred traffic tickets. There were also reports of multiple arrests and heavy traffic going to and from the Parkridge. The Corona newspapers offered clarification of, and indignation at, this story, which they viewed as unjustly exaggerated, stating that Corona law enforcement issued only fifty or so traffic tickets, mostly to African Americans, for minor violations, and that there were no arrests. Journee W. White called the news dispatch deplorable and affirmed he would investigate who the United Press service obtained the information from.[75]

The *Independent* reported that the Parkridge management and attorneys were "alarmed . . . [when] several complaints reached them that negro drivers had been stopped by traffic men and 'ticketed' on minor violations. The district attorney's office in Riverside had been requested to make an investigation as to whether or not discrimination had been shown."[76] This wire service dispatch sent all over the nation resulted in newspaper articles in Los Angeles and other southland and eastern cities, including Boston. Details of even more egregious acts of harassment directed squarely at the African American management also emerged in the local press following the Parkridge opening fete.[77]

While representing Parkridge patrons and the club's management in the Corona Police court, Attorney Donohue of Los Angeles revealed that a nefarious plot had been uncovered. Someone was going "to plant liquor in the colored club." If state authorities had found liquor at the Parkridge, the establishment could have been closed, as this was the Prohibition era. As reported by the *Independent*, upon learning of the plot details on May 29, Los Angeles Sheriff's officers thwarted the would-be perpetrators. Attorney Donohue revealed the harassment plot and the Los Angeles Sheriff's swift action of deterrence when he addressed the court regarding the traffic violation citations and how they should be handled. The Corona newspapers reported that local officials registered "distinct surprise" upon hearing of this attempt to plant liquor at the site, as they had not received any information on the matter from Sheriff William Traeger's office in Los Angeles. The newspaper discussions evidenced Corona officials' surprise and some embarrassment at this event, and the other situation of the unfavorable national media coverage, which resulted around the harassment of the Parkridge patrons.[78]

In building his case for leniency regarding the traffic violation citations, Donohue noted the revenue the Parkridge was generating for Corona businesses. He stated to courtroom observers and Judge C.D. McNeil that "the books of the colored club showed the negroes to [have] spent more than $3,000 among Corona business houses since the [new management began operation]."[79] Additionally, Donohue said, on Saturday, June 2, "*We* [my emphasis] held a beautiful dress ball at the club . . . attended not only by the best colored people, but representatives of the governor of the state of California, as well as some of your best people from the district attorney's office and sheriff's office."[80] He presented the evidence of racial harassment, the possibility of white investors' involvement (or at least his own involvement) with the club project, the economic benefit to the Corona community, and the club's connections to upstanding citizens in varied (Euro- and African American) communities of interest and power in the state and Southern California region.

Donohue was also reported to have indicated that the African Americans only wanted to be left alone. These citizens and their proxy, the Parkridge management, along with their white associates, were all upstanding citizens who expected to be treated as such when they were visiting the club and Corona. Following his argument, Judge McNeil dismissed the majority of the traffic citations and reduced the fines on the others. Journee W.

White, representing the Parkridge management, paid the fines for all those that were not dismissed.[81]

Was the exaggerated news wire story released as part of a conspiracy to malign the African American venture and their patrons or the Corona police? Both Corona citizens and the Parkridge management were unhappy over the hyperbole in the dispatch—with the misrepresentation of a near-race riot in Corona. The local newspaper writers seemed to have at one point sympathetically observed that this was not only unjust to Corona residents and officials, but also to the African Americans attempting to make a go of the club. Alternatively, were Corona leaders really only indignant and embarrassed because they were not in control of the message presented about their community and the new African American business venture as they had been over the last year? Or were they trying to erase the public exposé of their local citizens as bigots in the regional and national press by calling the news stories unjust, even sensationalized?[82]

An investigation by Journee W. White and his associates determined the exaggerated story was transmitted to the United Press correspondent via some disgruntled African Americans who felt they had been maltreated because of the traffic citations. The Corona press noted that the United Press correspondent did not fact-check the events of May 30 with the Parkridge management or the Corona authorities. While the Southern California office manager of the United Press wire service, after learning more of the facts of the May 30 events, came to recognize the number of traffic citations and arrests was inflated and the racial tensions in Corona were over dramatized, he nonetheless stood by the story. Though there were problems with the correspondent's fact-checking, African Americans were indeed harassed with traffic citations by bigoted white Corona police. At the same time, the United Press appears to have been more concerned with profit than the reliability of its journalism and less concerned with the incalculable damage these types of embellished stories might have on social dynamics and the public trust.[83]

Regardless of the impressions the white press created about the events of May 30, for the remainder of 1928 the Parkridge continued holding promotional events, including sporting matches, musical performances, dances, and dining offerings. More elaborate versions of these activities were planned around major occasions and holidays. A full-page ad in the *Eagle* on June 29, 1928, invited "the NAACP delegates and friends to visit Black America's Million Dollar Playground" for Independence Day. The 1928 NAACP Convention in Los Angeles presented black Angelenos with an important platform to promote their accomplishments and the region's offerings to a national audience of delegates, along with the people around the nation and the world who were reading about this meeting. Labor Day, Halloween, Armistice Day (or Veterans Day as it is known today), and Thanksgiving were also holidays used to promote the Parkridge, in addition to the continual advertisements of subdivision lots for sale.[84]

Despite the gala promotions and presswork, by January 1929 the African American–owned Parkridge Country Club and subdivision had financial difficulties due to lack of patronage and lot sales. There was also an issue with the compensation owed the local white labor force working at the property. The African American syndicate was also unable to raise the capital they had anticipated through the debt (bonds and loan) and equity (stock) financing program they instituted. Compounding their troubles, the debt entanglements from Dan Gilkey's ownership era of the Parkridge property had not been resolved.[85]

Parkridge Country Club and Its Public Memory

The Parkridge Country Club project finally went into bankruptcy, with creditors taking charge of the property to protect their interests in early 1929. In a meeting at the Parkridge clubhouse in July 1929, the receiver presented a plan the bankruptcy court approved, whereby the facilities would "revert back to the original and new members of the club, should they wish to consider it." As an *Independent* article about the meeting made clear, the original and new members being offered this opportunity were "those of the 'caucasian race' [as] explicitly . . . set forth in the original bylaws of the club." Eventually the property was sold to satisfy the creditors' claims, after remaining in receivership into the 1930s. The boom of the 1920s was fading fast, and one of the most dramatic economic downturns in American history was beginning. Many country clubs around the nation were hit hard by the Great Depression, with this industry only beginning to recover in the post–World War II years.[86]

For the next thirty-five years, until it was demolished in 1964/65, the club property's ownership changed hands several times. Alongside twists and turns of the Parkridge's occupancy and use, contestation and financial difficulties continued into the 1930s and later. The building also faced periods of vacancy and neglect. Mostly trespassers inhabited the clubhouse, and a speakeasy took over the building, serving a white clientele until Prohibition's end in 1933. The site was considered for a California state prison for first-time offenders in the early 1930s, and in 1931 the property was acquired from receivership to transform the building and grounds into an elite military academy. The school was named Pershing Military Academy in honor of U.S. Army General John J. Pershing (1860–1948), but this venture was unsuccessful.[87]

After 1937 the clubhouse became a sanitarium on and off until it finally closed in 1961. The once-lavish leisure palace was empty and deteriorating when its new owner, the Parkridge Development Company, took it over in 1964. Renaming the area Cresta Verde, the new owners built 522 homes and a new 18-hole golf course on 252 acres of the site. As part of the new subdivision, a new clubhouse was built to replace the original structure. The new owners determined it more cost-effective to build a new structure, instead of repairing the older Parkridge Country Club building.[88]

As historian Lawrence B. DeGraaf notes in a 1970 article on black Angelenos, the Parkridge and other similar leisure destinations, mostly in beach areas, were places where African Americans attempted "to join the urbanization of outlying areas" for "new housing and long range opportunities for residential expansion and race enterprise." According to DeGraaf, the endeavors of African Americans to join the 1920s housing boom in suburban areas was thoroughly rebuffed. In that conclusion he includes the Parkridge, not by name, but as a white country club in Corona, between Riverside and Los Angeles, taken over by blacks in 1928 as an interracial recreation area that failed for lack of patronage. As I would agree, he argues that these recreation centers "generally had the dual aim of providing a 'more cultured and sophisticated recreation' and of being nuclei for black residential colonies." The Parkridge exemplified this, as well as demonstrated entrepreneurial skill. Even when they were unsuccessful, these ventures evidenced a resourceful turn to leisure as a site for asserting the full rights of African Americans as citizens and consumers.[89]

The African American leisure lifestyle and suburban developments in the outlying areas DeGraaf speaks about in his article were hindered or stopped by whites due to racism, articulated through practice and public policy such as racially restrictive real estate covenants, as well as their fears of a "negro invasion." This concept of "negro invasion" was actively communicated in the media of the 1920s. White hostility toward African American upward mobility, racial equality, and interracial association was an inhibiting factor and deterrent to the black population's ability to gain employment, develop investment opportunities, and acquire residential housing. As discussed in other chapters of this book, places where African American Angelenos from the 1910s to 1920s attempted to establish leisure and amusement centers and were rebuffed included Santa Monica, El Segundo, near the present-day Los Angeles International Airport; Manhattan Beach and other sites in the Torrance district of Los Angeles County; and Huntington Beach in Orange County. In the case of the Parkridge, the African American principals were able to go around this resistance, if not totally overcome it, to gain ownership of the project without any physical violence. And, when harassed upon their club's opening by local police, they resourcefully mobilized law and publicity beyond the local authorities to counter the oppressive tactics.

The African American leisure resorts that did enjoy popularity for a longer time at Lake Elsinore, Val Verde, and Murray's Dude Ranch were not as coveted by whites as other Southern California resort areas, particularly those imagined by whites as integral to a locale's identity as the Parkridge was in Corona. The importance of the leisure ventures—which flourished more briefly—and their actors is not diminished. Like the Parkridge, they should be defined by the radical vision and resourcefulness they presented and the struggle they surmounted in the face of virulent opposition by craftily employed public power. Ultimately, for the purposes of this study, these African American actors should be defined by the composition and meaning of the leisure they imagined in a fuller definition of personal and community freedom, equality, and cultural expression.

In the case of the White, Nelson, and Bailey proprietorship of the Parkridge, its erasure from Corona's past has produced a void in understanding the evolution of the regional cultural landscape and the African American experience in constructive and legitimate business development, the different agents who attempted and participated in varied entrepreneurial endeavors, and the complicated layers of social dynamics of race, space, power, and capitalism in California's frontier of leisure that this distinctive story illuminates. The exclusion of this history from public memory also erases the African American principals' accomplishment of overcoming the resistance of the Corona citizens on top of the difficulties the white business operators had with this kind of endeavor and would certainly have faced as White and company did in the first waves of the Great Depression. Expanding our knowledge of various places and the actors associated with them, while exploring historical experiences from the multiple vantage points associated with them, makes history more fascinating and tells a more accurate and inclusive story about America and its citizens. The reassertion of the memory of African Americans and other marginalized groups in contemporary Southern California history is especially important because it claims broader civic community identity and belonging.[90]

As African Americans and other communities of color battle to have their histories documented, recognized, and remembered, and to claim a part of the public memory, it is not surprising that this struggle continues. As Trouillot argues, over many years historical narrators have engaged in the banalization and silencing of the history of such groups as African Americans through erasure of a history that cannot fit into Western historiographical traditions heavily guided by nationalism dogma and the interest of national state actors. In the long term, counterinterpretations and discourses such as those presented in this book have some impact on the structural nature of the problem of the exclusion of more diverse voices in history accounts. The Parkridge project was a site of African American history possessing value for local, regional, and national collective memory.[91]

The vision of the White, Nelson, and Bailey partnership, in offering an elite leisure landscape to African Americans and anyone else who chose to participate in this endeavor, was groundbreaking in its implications for social history. These African American entrepreneurs imagined a business opportunity and pursued it, all while contesting white assertions of inherent African American racial inferiority and subordination and the danger of public interracial mixing. These men were of the New Negro class of their era, shaking up the older order of social heritage, changing its relationships, shifting its center of gravity, and breaking stereotypes of who African Americans were or could be in their American identity and accomplishments. As with the other sites discussed in this book, the Parkridge project was a symbol of African Americans' assertion of the civil and consumer rights they were as entitled to with respect to places of leisure, profit-making, aspiration, and hope, like any other U.S. citizen. It is important to remember these persistent African American pioneers who took their own destiny in their hands to make places for self-directed African American leisure, despite repeated rejection, hostile environments, physical danger, and sometimes business failure in the first half of the twentieth century.[92]

While endeavoring to provide African Americans with community, recreation, and investment opportunities in the Parkridge—White, Nelson, and Bailey acted upon a capitalist ethos of seeking profit and valuing commercial culture. Involved in California's great oil boom as well as real estate promotion in their leisure building, they were broadly based contributors to the development of Los Angeles and Southern California in the post–World War I decade. These men and their patrons were trailblazers in their resolve to achieve broader fulfillment and participation in American life, and for their courage and determination to fight discrimination and demand respect in their development of leisure and attempts at exurban residential development in Southern California. Like other leisure sites discussed in this book, not only does the Parkridge story speak to struggles around leisure in the African American experience, but in the collective story of the making of Corona and of the Los Angeles region and American West in responding to the political, economic and social conditions of the late 1920s.

The next chapter examines the evolution of Eureka Villa, later known as Val Verde, located in the foothill canyons of the Santa Clarita area in north Los Angeles County. This formally planned, rustic resort community was originated in the mid-1920s by African American and white boosters, landowners, and developers from Los Angeles, who marshaled private as well as public resources to promote the area's growth for use by African Americans in the Jim Crow era, and later for the broader public. Chapter 6 also briefly discusses other competing Southern California leisure land development projects with similar social and economic goals as the Eureka Villa project, which emerged and failed for various reasons before 1930.

6 Race, Leisure, Subdivisions, Promoters, and Gambling on the California Dream at Eureka Villa

Never Another Opportunity Like This!
—*California Eagle*, February 13, 1925

Here nestled among the beautiful mountains, we offer an opportunity to build up a beautiful community, which will not be only a credit to our group but will be a credit to the great State of California.
—*California Eagle*, July 3, 1925

In the 1920s African American Angelenos set out to create resort communities of various models and different forms of leisure than what they experienced in their city life. The intent was to develop locations where they could enjoy freedom from discrimination in the pursuit of healthy outdoor activities and social life, as well as business opportunities. In the case of some leisure destinations, promoters also dreamed of incorporating new and permanent residential communities. In so doing, they joined the struggle for leisure to that of open and better housing, and the quest for economic self-determination, while they reimagined leisure in the process. As in the case of the Parkridge, selling residency with leisure was crucial to the venture's success. Lot sales as much as membership were calculated to finance the facilities and amenities' construction costs. Between 1905 and the 1920s leisure land-development ventures, some with the words "country club" and "subdivision development" attached as a descriptor, invited African American leisure seekers outside of Los

Angeles's city limits to Eureka Villa as well as the Parkridge Country Club and the Pacific Beach Club. For various reasons such as legal and public obstruction, criminal destruction, and the economic crisis, as the decade turned most ceased to exist in the 1920s. Yet, others, including Eureka Villa, persisted in some form until the end of the Jim Crow era in the 1960s.[1]

At its inception in the 1920s, Eureka Villa (later known as Val Verde) commixed leisure as industry, and residential and vacation housing, with some parcels accommodating agriculture and livestock. Founders embodied in practice a progressively modern vision of leisure and land development at the core of the California Dream for their African American audience. This view of the community has lived on in the public memory over other now-defunct African American places of leisure in Southern California.

This chapter examines how Eureka Villa's history represented another aspect of the African American leisure lifestyle spaces associated with the California Dream, different from the oceanfront resorts, lakefront retreat, and country club with modern recreational amenities discussed in this book thus far. Envisioned for leisure and work in everyday living for some and vacation visits for others, this African American project of a rustic inland resort community was ambitious in its articulated vision of recreation, land development, and wealth generation potential. As did the other sites discussed in this book, the 1920s Eureka Villa project developed in an American society characterized by urbanization, prosperity, leisure, technological advances, consumerism, and major shifts toward modern values as well as a struggle against Jim Crow racial discrimination. The automobile, recently available to the masses, created entirely new forms of mobility and was fundamental to the vision, creation, growth, and sustainability of Eureka Villa, because there was no public transportation to access this place.

This modern leisure venture—of rustic, recreational amenities and housing land development—was similar to another type emerging during this era and marketed to whites, which later evolved to become suburban residential communities. Eureka Villa, though, was designed by its founders to be exclusively African American, and not as ostentatiously expensive as some of the combined, planned communities of clubs and homes beginning to be promoted to whites around the nation, such as the original Parkridge project. Although the potential African American clientele may not have been as wealthy, Eureka Villa was premised on the expectation that they shared values similar to their white counterparts in seeking a place to spend leisure time socializing and networking with family and friends, as well as in creating a sense of community identity and traditions. African Americans also sought a place of shelter and security from the racial hierarchy stresses of their everyday lives, an aim distinctively different from anything their white counterparts experienced in deciding upon living and leisure places.[2]

These African American leisure sites and exurban housing community developments like Eureka Villa started during the period when Pan-Africanist Marcus Garvey's ideals about black pride and political and economic self-reliance rose to prominence across the nation, even after his deportation to Jamaica, the land of his birth. Others such as Benjamin Singleton, Booker T. Washington, and, in California, Allen Allensworth and William Payne had encouraged all black towns and land development schemes for economic self-sufficiency across the decades since the end of the Civil War. The rise of Pan-African Americans and the global "New Negro" in the 1920s intensified the local expressions of race consciousness, community self-determination, racial uplift, and sometimes self-defense as part of a larger international context to break free from the local, national, and global order of white supremacy. Davarian L. Baldwin describes these "local expressions of race consciousness" as "the product of multidirectional conversations and collective action that crisscrossed the globe." This was also a time when the presidential administrations of Wilson, Harding, Coolidge, and Hoover (1921–32) continued to alienate African America from participating in U.S. politics and refused to endorse anything related to civil rights.[3]

In the tradition of African American colonies like Allensworth, founded in 1908 in California's central San Joaquin Valley, Eureka Villa promoted the possibility of becoming an independent, self-sufficient township centered on providing the social and economic infrastructure for African Americans' consumption of leisure activities and economic development in a bucolic California and American Western frontier-style setting. Not all Afro-Angelenos supported the separate-town dream as they saw their freedom as exercising equal rights within mainstream society. But under the right circumstances, they were willing to participate in "Negro projects." Even after Eureka Villa's initial use faded from view, its recurring remembrance has demonstrated it is a site of African American and U.S. history that possesses value for local, regional, and national collective memory and identity. The creation of this and other separate spaces was a resistance strategy, which refuted white suppositions that blacks were not worthy of commercial amusements and other forms of public accomodation.[4]

Eureka Villa also represented African Americans' anticipation of growth in Southern California and their claim to a role in determining it. Aspirational citizens of all colors invested in land in the direction they believed the city of Los Angeles would grow. Transportation connections, the promise of public services, and natural environment features could enhance the monetary value of land for real estate investment. The flamboyant real estate entrepreneur Sidney P. Dones marketed Eureka Villa in the isolated San Martinez Chiquito Canyon of the Santa Clarita Valley in northwest Los Angeles County as situated "among the most beautiful mountains to be found in this wonderful [California] state," and as the last "great opportunity" for African Americans to buy a large swath of land "to build up a beautiful community." The jury would be out for a long while before answering this question of whether purchasing land at Eureka Villa was a "great opportunity" for African Americans.[5]

Promotional ads and narratives in the *Eagle* and other newspapers in the 1920s reminded black readership that several years ago "acreage on the Beautiful Pacific" could have been bought at "a ridiculously low price, [to build] homes of our own. [But] today that opportunity is GONE FOREVER." For Dones and at least some of his associates, Eureka Villa was their health and leisure spot, with "land prices that [were] five years below the prices of other property that came near equaling Eureka Villa." Dones challenged African Americans to look beyond the "crabs," as he called the investment skeptics, and to not be satisfied with being discriminated against at every resort in the state. In his sales message he admonished African Americans to look further than Central Avenue for better jobs and better communities. From the beginning, at least, as evidenced by the rhetorical language promoters used in their black press advertising, Eureka Villa was a place of contestation and investment opportunity alongside a place to have fun. The Dones-led promotional theme of investment and development control offers part of the reason, along with an unbroken history of occupancy, that there has continued to be some public memory of this early African American community of Eureka Villa (as Val Verde) in the twenty-first century.[6]

"Santa Clarita, Valley of the Golden Dream"

The Santa Clarita Valley, from which the black enclave of Eureka Villa sprung, may have been fifty miles from downtown Los Angeles, but Angeleno leaders and boosters always saw the northwest county area as essential in connecting the city's transportation, goods, and people to other parts of the state.[7] By the time of Eureka Villa's founding, the area was envisioned as both an early satellite community and a place of leisure retreat from Los Angeles. From the days of California's indigenous inhabitants through the Spanish and Mexican periods and the white Americans who followed, groups settled the Santa Clarita Valley as an intersection for travel and commerce. Connecting Mexico, the Pacific coastline and Channel Islands, Northern California, and other areas of North America, Santa Clarita Valley routes began as footpaths and were later altered to accommodate horses, wagons, and stagecoaches. Some of the routes would become railroad lines, followed by roads accommodating motorized vehicles for the California Aqueduct and twentieth-century travelers. From the beginning of the American invasion in the 1840s to the early decades of the twentieth century, people endured bust and booms as well as droughts, earthquakes, fires, and other disasters in the Santa Clarita Valley region, where they went to make a living from agriculture, ranching, water, gold and other minerals, oil, real estate speculation, transportation infrastructure improvements, temporary worker and traveler accommodations services, and the movie industry.[8]

These ventures created employment, which increased opportunities for shops, stores, restaurants, accommodations, and service trade businesses to provide goods and services to permanent residents and temporarily housed workers, as well as travelers. Travel time to Los Angeles was greatly reduced as a result of the train and automobile, facilitating access to city markets, family, friends, and attractions. With these changes, the valley also developed as a leisure place, in response to Los Angeles's and the area's imaginaries of the real and mythical American West. Money generated by movie production, oil, and tourism launched a real estate boom in Southern California. Santa Clarita Valley took part in its investment speculation, and Eureka Villa was one of the many themed resort community promotions emerging in Southern California during the era. Boosters of all persuasions, including those of Eureka Villa, combined leisure with promotion. In 1925 Eureka Villa was a rustic resort, but some of its boosters thought the place might become a bedroom community to the city of Los Angeles.[9]

Eureka, They Founded It!

There are different versions as to how Sidney P. Dones came to found and promote Eureka Villa. At the time, the area was no more than a crossroads northwest of the intersection of the historic Ridge Route (now Interstate Highway 5) running between Los Angeles and Kern Counties, and north of the road (now Route 126) running from Santa Clarita Valley through Ventura County to the Pacific Ocean. The site had been known earlier as Val Verde (Green Valley), a short-lived boomtown that sprung up after gold was found in 1843 at Santa Feliciana Creek, the site of California's first gold rush.[10]

The most likely version of events posits Eureka Villa's founding as an African American leisure and recreation center begun in the 1910s by a wealthy white woman, Mrs. Laura C. Janes from Pasadena, whose family then owned a secluded ranch in San Martinez Chiquito Canyon. After World War I, Janes was purported to have opened her family's ranch to African Americans as a result of her dismay at the discrimination they confronted in Southern California, especially around use of many parks and recreation areas. Whether it was motivated by her dismay at the discrimination African Americans faced or more by her interest in financial gain, Janes's San Martinez Chiquito Canyon ranch soon became a "weekend picnic spot for black Angelenos" as an editorial in the *Eagle* attested on February 6, 1925. Through lot sales of this secluded ranch land to African Americans mediated by Dones, Janes and other white landowners—including Harry M. Waterman, who joined her in this process—gained financially.[11]

The February 6 editorial spoke glowingly of Mrs. Janes for offering the land for sale and the impact her actions had on encouraging other (I assume white) landowners to also sell lands to African Americans in the Chiquito Canyon area. The editorial lauded Sidney P. Dones for "his discovery of this owner and intercession with her for this great body of land for his people." It was not his ownership and resale of land that was touted, but Dones's timely and foresighted business deal with Janes. Dones's venture secured one place for black America at the time when several regional exurban efforts for pleasure use and investment were underway. Recognizing and incorporating the amenities of the popular country club into an idyllic place of leisure residency, Dones promoted at Eureka Villa what he would call a "country club subdivision."[12]

African American investment groups had attempted to build leisure and recreation facilities for black Angelenos for a few decades. These Los Angeles area entrepreneurs extended this self-determination to develop leisure and pleasure accommodations in exclusively African American communities, which contested confinement and exclusion. An *Eagle* editorial on April 24, 1924, titled "Club House Movement Endorsed," declared the project "[would] be a monument to Negro enterprise, an expression of race progress, and an uncommon tribute to all responsible for its success." Using racial uplift rhetoric, editor Joseph B. "Joe" Bass's boosterism in support of country clubs summed up the way black Angelenos of the era could potentially find playground opportunities without discrimination, contest white racism through property control and community determination, and prosper in the classic Los Angeles way through owning, buying, and selling real estate.[13]

As the editorial observed, in the 1920s black citizens of Southern California wanted participation in what the text portrayed as "the average every day man" recreation and luxury dream that country clubs could offer. In addition to dissatisfaction with available recreation venues, African Americans increasingly faced "the cruel hand of segregation and discrimination in a way, never felt before on the Pacific Coast" due to the poisonous, racist propaganda spread especially by new white migrants from U.S. Southern states who provoked a few violent altercations. In addition to the attack by off-duty white sheriffs on Arthur Valentine and his family on a public beach discussed earlier in this book, another widely publicized example of violence and intimidation toward black Angelenos was that of a white mob destroying the property of a black family who moved into a district of mostly lower-income whites. Further, a major issue of contention was the change in City Parks Commission policy limiting black Angelenos' swimming pools use. Black Angelenos responded to these challenges to their freedom to consume leisure in Southern California as white racial hostility rose and the African American population grew in the 1920s. Throughout the third decade of the twentieth century in Los Angeles, as in other parts of the United States, African Americans resisted and contested prejudice, segregation and exclusion through direct action at particular black- or white-claimed accommodations and spaces, the legal system, and in the creation of black-owned leisure spaces.[14]

Both black and white entrepreneurs attempted construction of recreational playgrounds and subdivisions outside Los Angeles's city limits in the 1920s, with varied levels of success and longevity. Norman O. Houston and Charles S. Darden, Esq., led the effort in 1922 to build a leisure clubhouse and other recreation facilities on the Pacific Slope in Santa Monica, which the city council thwarted through prohibitive ordinance. Frustration at their exclusion due to white discrimination was duly voiced in the *Eagle* and other black press outlets as an affront to all peoples' ability to enjoy the liberty and pursuit of happiness guaranteed to them under the U.S. Constitution.[15]

An April 18, 1924, article in the *Eagle* advised "the colored people of the State of California are not to be denied an opportunity to keep abreast of all modern movements" in their "social and economic life." As this newspaper quote demonstrates, black Angelenos' participation in the "new movement" was a demand for their rights to consume leisure and recreation, a foundational feature of the 1920s version of the California Dream, popular cultural trends of leisure lifestyle imagery, and real estate development business opportunities in the region.[16]

The Peaceful Valley Country Club formation was one of the leisure land development ventures announced in spring 1924. It was located within a two-hour automobile ride of downtown Los Angeles in the western part of Los Angeles County, six miles from the city limits, in the area known today as Calabasas. On Las Virgenes Road, off Ventura Boulevard on a 100-acre land tract "plans . . . formulated for the construction . . . of a most up-to-date Country Club containing all those modern [recreation and athletic facilities] features," with a large and elaborate clubhouse for use by members and guests for socializing year-round, shade trees, and mountain trails for hiking. A portion of lot sales proceeds were to be set aside for facilities and grounds improvements. A large section of the tract was reserved for cabins, and charter members each received clear title to an individual cabin site. In a May 9, 1924, *Eagle* advertisement the promoters asserted that "The Rush Is On" to become members of Peaceful Valley Country Club.[17]

In the Peaceful Valley Country Club ads, Sidney P. Dones topped the list of real estate agents to contact for information and purchasing memberships. There was also an advisory committee including *Eagle* editor Joe Bass, which characterized the development as a class project, lending additional validity to the venture by including "leading citizens" of the city and county of Los Angeles. A narrative news feature-advertisement in the *Eagle* on May 9, 1924, portrayed the advisory committee members as united "in praising this forward looking plan to provide the people with the facilities for pleasure and health that are naturally due to every resident in Southern California without discrimination." Dones and associates promised a playground for all people with profit possibilities.[18]

The Eastside Realty Company, run by brothers F. L. and O. L. Banks, also began promoting the 240-acre Castaic Country Club subdivision in Charley Canyon of the "Thousand Canyons District" as the "Playground of Angelenos" in the spring of 1924. The new development was located less than ten miles north of Eureka Villa in what is known today as the Castaic section of Santa Clarita Valley. The *Eagle* described the area in picturesque vocabulary as "nestled in the bosom of Charley Canyon, one of California's most beautiful spots with . . . wooded retreats, mesas, gurgling springs and babbling brooklets fanned by a constant breeze of pure mountain air."[19]

The Castaic developers enlisted black Angeleno and rising architectural star Paul R. Williams to design the clubhouse. For a newspaper ad, this in-demand architect rendered a "beautiful, spacious clubhouse of Spanish design" with hills, trees, and a lone golfer strategically positioned for lifestyle imagery and sales enticement.[20] A portion of the funds raised from lot sales was to be spent on building the clubhouse and other facilities, including modern sport recreation venues, as well as on grounds improvements, such as shaded paths leading to cabin sites. The purchase of any cabin sites with lovely view of the surroundings at a $150 opening price included a free lifetime club membership with full available privileges. Readers and potential buyers were advised that terms were "within reach of all." Castaic project promoters advertised the site's close proximity to the Forest Reserve (renamed the Angelus National Forest Reserve in 1925): "California's choicest hunting Reserve, where deer and game of all descriptions abound." Prospective buyers and club members were further enticed by the only forty-two-mile, one-and-a-half-hours' auto ride (probably more like a two-to-three-hour automobile ride, at best, during this time period) from downtown Los Angeles.[21]

Instead of an advisory committee endorsement, the Castaic promoters offered up the success of their business history as pioneer subdividers and lot sellers of the Central Avenue Gardens and Central Avenue subdivisions in Los Angeles. Written in capital letters, a series of ads emphasized that the Castaic project was "A RACE ENTERPRISE, FOSTERED AND OWNED BY RACE BUSINESS MEN—FOR RACE PEOPLE."[22] This fact of the subdivision being a black enterprise not only proclaimed the place as one of African American purpose and collective benefit, but could have allowed *Eagle* readers dreams of the continual possibilities California offered them when discrimination's constraints were surmounted, as they contemplated the possibilities of Castaic Country Club membership purchase and the subdivision promoters' legitimacy.[23]

In *Eagle* editorials and ad campaigns, both the Peaceful Valley Country Club and the Castaic Country Club promoters observed that there had been several attempts by different groups of African Americans in California to establish country clubs for their group that for various reasons were not realized. All the land development promoters promised a handsome return to buyers on their monetary as well as social capital investments in the projects as the regional population and land values increased.[24]

Peaceful Valley would be short-lived. In June 1924 an *Eagle* ad for the Castaic Country Club project informed readers that "all Purchaser[s] in Peaceful Valley Country Club" could receive transfer "credit for the amount paid to . . . the Club (not exceeding the down payment of $30) on the purchase price of a cabin site," for a Castaic Country Club site.[25] Before the end of 1924, Rialto Park and Lincoln Gardens, both in Los Angeles County and another resort near Redlands in San Bernardino County, in addition to Peaceful Valley and Castaic Country Club developments, had *sprung up overnight and died.* Available sources provide evidence sufficient only to speculate that these land development projects most likely failed due to a combination of inadequate capital financing and public response.[26]

Eureka Villa meanwhile, persisted. Its founding visionary and business leader, Sidney Preston Dones (ca. 1888–1947), was an entrepreneur whose primary occupation during his lifetime was buying and selling real estate as a broker and an agent. His business repertoire encompassed more, including loan financing (i.e., cash money lending), and life and fire insurance sales. In addition, he was a pioneering member of the Democratic Film Corporation, starring in films such as *Reformation* (1920), which he also directed, and *The Ten Thousand Dollar Trail* (1921), which he also wrote. He was also a music dealer. Born in Marshall, Texas, Dones grew up in a farming family and community in rural East Texas, where he obtained an education in local public schools. He went on to study English at nearby Wiley College, founded in 1873 during Reconstruction as effectively the first African American higher education institution west of the Mississippi River. While attending Wiley preparatory school before he could take college courses, Dones picked cotton or anything else on the local rural farms to pay for his educational expenses. Young Dones left his college studies after a few years, coinciding with his father's death, to help support his family.[27]

Seeking a better life for himself and his relatives, Dones first traveled to Los Angeles around 1905. After working for a year as a day laborer, he went to El Paso, Texas, to join the team promoting the New Day Colonization Company, a venture attempting to secure fifty thousand acres of land for colored people in Mexico from President Porfírio Diaz before the Mexican Revolution (1910–20) ended their plan. After spending several years in Mexico, Dones returned to Los Angeles around 1910–12 and opened his first real estate office. To pay his own office space rent and to help support himself and his extended family, Dones worked as a janitor for the building housing his new business and at Manual Arts High School, where he earned twenty-five cents per hour. He continued his education, studying law with the La Salle Extension School of Law at Chicago and at Southwestern University in Los Angeles.[28]

By 1915 Frederick M. Roberts's *New Age* dubbed Dones "Los Angeles' most popular young businessman." The newspaper waxed, "[He] is enjoying the greatest real estate and insurance business of any race man in the West." Dones married musician Bessie Williams in 1913, and in a few years they had a daughter, Sydnetta and a son, Preston. Dones divorced and remarried another musician, Louvenia Harper, by 1920. He would divorce, remarry, and divorce again before the end of the 1920s.[29]

By all accounts, Dones was charismatic, courteous, hardworking, always the showman, and an effective self-promoter. He identified with and used racial uplift rhetoric as a booster for African American–owned business development and community and, in turn, for support of his own enterprises. In the *California Eagle's 1930–1931 Los Angeles Negro Directory and Who's Who,* Dones was cited as "perhaps the best known broker among our group [meaning African Americans] in Los Angeles, . . . and is considered an expert in the law governing real estate and finance. [He] has built up one of the largest businesses of its kind east of Main Street." Always one who expressed belief in the credo "help others and you help yourself," it was said Dones was especially friendly to the African American working-class people who were a substantial part of his client base. An *Eagle* editorial opined that Dones's success was also in his "conduct[ing] business [in a manner] as to win the confidence and respect of the better class whites."[30] It seems those observing him had admiration for Dones as a person and for his skills in winning friends and influencing others to do business with him.[31]

Throughout his lifetime, Dones was active in civic and political affairs, and as a philanthropist who donated to many worthy causes. He ran unsuccessfully for city and state elective offices several times, beginning with a run for Los Angeles City Council in 1917, and for California State

Assembly seats in 1928 and in the 1930s. In the interwar years leading up to World War II, Dones became a special investigator for the U.S. government on confidential missions to Mexico and the Hawaiian Islands. His outstanding service and achievements on these missions earned him civilian honors for his work.[32]

In the marketing campaign for the initial 480-acre new leisure community at Eureka Villa, Dones enlisted journalistic expertise to garner attention. He enticed people to visit and enjoy the outdoor setting, buy lots, and build residential and business improvements through frequent and sometimes elaborate advertisements as well as narrative marketing features. These advertisements ran in the black press of Los Angeles and other cities in the early years of the project's sales push, including on several pages of the *Eagle* each week. Dones and other supporters of Eureka Villa, in a manner similar to some of the other leisure-development marketing efforts mentioned earlier in this chapter, described the place in its physical manifestation with such race rhetoric and California lifestyle imaginaries as

> situated in a beautiful valley continually fanned by the cool breezes from the canyons leading to the Ocean . . .
>
> One of the greatest and most high class projects ever put before our group. . . . A community center and club that the entire race will be proud of . . .
>
> California Colored People's Greatest Achievement. . . . The Most Beautiful Townsite and Community Center in the USA.[33]

As further enticement and as assurance to the black public of the resort enterprise's legitimacy, as was often the practice of the era, Dones presented the roster of his informal advisors and official board of advisors, who were described as "some of the most influential and respected citizens of Los Angeles." On December 26, 1924, a Eureka Villa Improvement Association ad in the *Eagle* included a photograph of each of the advisory committee members. Their names, professional and community standing, and association affiliations that were published with their photographs represented community affirmation, as well as business legitimation to buyers, stressing their prominence and respectability to the black public. This encouraged the social practices of such leisure activity as respectable, and financial investment for pleasure and business purposes at Eureka Villa as solidly supported, forward-looking, and serving African American community advancement.[34]

The collection of people, their institutional affiliations and responsibilities on the association advisory committee, and an elaborate sales brochure's pictures and text reinforced the themes of *health, wealth, and happiness* that were the branding message in Eureka Villa marketing. A full-page insert, which ran for a good part of 1925 in the *Eagle* and other black publications, included expansive narrative marketing articles, photographs, testimonials, little bits of gossip, lists of visitors and purchasers, and the promotions of lot sales and businesses. Advertised in the black press were a variety of lot-giveaway promotions as prizes in a beauty pageant, big community barbeques and picnics, and Sunday afternoon dances held at Eureka Villa to entice people to visit.[35]

As voiced through board member and chair of the publicity committee Joe Bass's editorial commentary in the *Eagle* after a big picnic on September 28, 1924, dedicating the clubhouse grounds and opening of ranch properties for inspection, the promoters viewed its rise as a pioneering effort for Black America with "great possibilities . . . and a rare opportunity . . . to test the capacity of our group to demonstrate their ability to do something for themselves along the line of real progress." The early newspaper sales pitches focused on this project as a black business venture for an African American patronage, the building of a clubhouse and recreational facilities, the possibilities of athletic and social activities, a town site, and an industrial and business center. Then and now, whether the location was indeed ideal for all of these features would be relative to one's tastes and vision, aspirations, and access to opportunities for leisure and investment.[36]

The Eureka Villa sales pitch in the black press featured the development of leisure improvements and economic infrastructure along with the beauty of this California countryside and its available water for health and daily use. The promoters touted a $100,000 fund, or 20 percent of the gross sales of all lots, to be set aside for recreational facility improvements, "to make it the most desirable playground in Southern California."[37] Forty acres were allocated for these improvements, including building a sizable Spanish-design clubhouse to cost $50,000, a large swimming pool with lockers and dressing rooms, pigeon-shooting traps for gun marksmanship activities, tennis courts, a baseball diamond, picnic areas, a playground for children, and other recreational features. Eureka Villa sites of 50 feet x 80 feet and larger were offered for $75 and up, with full deed and title to the land. Included with each purchased site came a fully paid lifetime membership in the community club, entitling the holder to all available privileges. Noted in more than one newspaper pitch was the covered open-air dance pavilion, constructed at the early stages of the marketing push, and opportunities for hunting quail, rabbit, and foxes, along with hiking trails to see some of the area's natural wonders in sites such as Job's Peak and Zephyr Cave. Transportation advertisements described the availability of bus service from Los Angeles to Eureka Villa and the accessibility and timetables of two Southern Pacific Railroad trains, which stopped a few miles from the retreat every day.[38]

A combination endorsement and narrative sales pitch by Bass in the *Eagle* on September 19, 1924, made explicit the participation as well as the enthusiasm of the publisher for the new community. The "Hon. J. B. Bass, a member of the Advisory Board of Eureka Villa, who has always been in the front ranks for things along progressive lines for members of the race," asserted an industrial expert, was making plans to construct a large laundry and a canning factory. These two industries alone, he noted, could employ more than seven hundred of "our people." The article with Bass's photograph at the top reported that carpenters were already at work at Eureka Villa, with "it [being] a known fact that nothing but Colored carpenters will be employed provided they can secure enough carpenters to work." Announced also was an additional 160 acres (later identified as the Val Verde Tract), adjacent to Eureka Villa Tract, subdivided into one-and-a-half-acre lots and made available for chicken ranches and truck farms.[39]

Dones and his associates envisioned integrating all the basic components of both a leisure resort and a residential town infrastructure in Eureka Villa. In the black press they frequently reported their accomplishments to this end to entice people to visit, enjoy themselves, buy lots, and build improvements. Practical concerns for a residential town site like a new schoolhouse and a place for church services were advertised, along with transportation and water infrastructure. A finance and building company was organized by Dones, which would build two-to-three-room houses at a starting price of $400. Businesses opened by those who bought lots within the first year of Eureka Villa's inauguration provided services and accommodations to visitors and potential lot buyers. Their parties were given extensive coverage in the *Eagle*'s regular feature "Eureka Villa News."[40]

Extensive marketing in the black press in California and select cities across the nation, brochures, information meetings in Los Angeles, and promotional social events at Eureka Villa and in Los Angeles were complemented by Dones's promotional tours to several U.S. cities. The *Eagle* reported that Dones spoke at the Negro Business League's national conference and chapter meetings with the "hopes to interest eastern capitalists and building manufacturers in industries of all kinds at Eureka [Villa]." On two different trips in 1925, Dones visited Tuskegee Institute (Alabama), Tulsa, Kansas City, Richmond (Virginia), New York, Atlantic City, Chicago, and Memphis, among other places. A December 19, 1924, *Eagle* article reported that Dones, before this national tour, commissioned professional photographs of "[Eureka Villa's] grounds . . . park . . . the many beautiful oaks and cabins" that were to be distributed in advertisements for various African American businesses throughout the United States. This article also added that Eureka Villa newsreels were to be made and distributed in the near future.[41]

Dones also stopped to visit the 10th U.S. Cavalry (Buffalo Soldiers) at Fort Huachuca, Arizona, where Mrs. Mary E. Carver (the wife of Chaplain Monroe S. Carver) was recruited as a representative to distribute information concerning Eureka Villa to black soldiers. Some noncommissioned officers and enlisted men bought lots early. Chaplain Carver and his wife purchased lots there and in Los Angeles for their retirement. Chaplain Carver seems to have been encouraging soldiers to secure land and homes for their own retirement in this California area. Two ambitious officers from Fort Huachuca purchased "a beautiful site" to build the "Buffalo Hotel." The *Eagle*'s "Eureka Villa News" section on September 28, 1925, reported that this structure would cost $75,000 and would "be one of the finest erected by any group in America." Other African Americans from across the United States were mentioned in the *Eagle* as visiting and sometimes purchasing lots. Dones and his associates were leaving no marketing avenue and potential lot purchasers unexplored within their resources to make the project a success.[42]

Pacific Beach Club and Eureka Villa Compete

In the dawning months of 1925, during the height of promotion, lot sales, and early improvements, the rustic leisure retreat contended for recruits with a new beach club project for black Angeleno consumers. Accessible by the Pacific Electric's Balboa Car, less than two hours by automobile and thirty-five miles south from Los Angeles, near Huntington Beach in Orange County, the Pacific Beach Club development and construction was announced in February 1925. Membership promotion began almost immediately, with a sales force, brochures, and announcements in the black press—both locally and nationwide—and a groundbreaking ceremony was held on Sunday, March 22, 1925. In an *Eagle* article on March 20, 1925, enticing people to attend the opening-day program, Mr. Peace, the Pacific Beach Club's sales manager, boasted that "the Colored people of Southern California will inaugurate one of the foremost progressive steps ever entered into by the race in any part of the country." The same article linked the development to the struggle for public space, declaring, "This opening will be a monument to many race leaders who have worked for many years to obtain for their people a piece of the Pacific with its surf and sands where they may go and enjoy a day on the beach." For African Americans as citizen consumers to finally obtain a place of their own at this premier "frontier of leisure" location, a California beach, was indeed a momentous occasion of group pride and social mobility. Even as it contended with Eureka Villa for attention and membership, the African American ownership and agency in developing the Pacific Beach Club project was another significant moment of contestation of the era's racial hierarchies and African Americans' exclusion from the consumption of leisure and other privileges.[43]

On April 3, 1925, an *Eagle* editorial gave enthusiastic support to both

Eureka Villa and the Pacific Beach Club. Titled "Fortunate Indeed," the editorial explained that, just like Euro-Americans, African Americans in Southern California and visitors from other parts of the nation could enjoy Eureka Villa and the Pacific Beach Club "for seasonal pleasure and amusement." Just as with the Eureka Villa promotion, Los Angeles's leading black newspapers' ownership and editorial departments at the *California Eagle*, *New Age*, and *Pacific Defender* had business, civic, and personal relationship stakes in the success of the Pacific Beach Club. These newspapers reported and promoted these leisure ventures not only for their own reasons, but as news that their primarily black readership would want to be informed of and pay for.[44]

Both sets of promoters were vying for black consumption of new safe places to spend their leisure time in different kinds of lifestyle locations. Both ventures sought black investment dollars in land and improvements that could potentially increase tremendously in value over the years if the Southern California population grew in the directions of these specific leisure projects. The Pacific Beach Club, however, was not envisioned as a residential community development, though residential housing might develop in the vicinity, as some staff would need places to live outside the club grounds. Southern California black leaders and the venture promoters of both projects asked African Americans to be bold and fearless, to have vision and invest in their own current and future pleasure and prosperity, as well as that of their community.

Editors Joseph B. Bass, Frederick M. Roberts, and Fred C. Williams supported the Pacific Beach Club project lead by E. Burton Ceruti, Esq. (1875–1927), president of its board of directors. Born in Nassau, the Bahamas of the West Indies, Ceruti's family moved to New York when he was four years old. A founder of the NAACP Los Angeles Branch and its legal advisor, Ceruti began practicing law in the state in 1912. Historian Delilah Beasley called Ceruti "the most competent attorney among the colored profession in California." He was very successful fighting criminal and discrimination cases about housing and refusals to serve African Americans in public accommodations like movie theaters and restaurants. As an advocate for the NAACP, he prominently assisted in suppression of D. W. Griffith's film *The Birth of a Nation* (1915) as well as Roy W. Neill's

Free and Equal (1918), and led the effort to end discrimination against African Americans by the Los Angeles County Hospital's Training School for Nurses (1917).[45]

Hal H. Clark, a white lawyer and businessman, worked with black Angeleno leaders and financiers to launch the Pacific Beach Club. In a syndication deal with the black investment group, Clark provided more than seven acres, one thousand feet along the ocean frontage between Huntington Beach and Newport Beach, for lease along with the majority of the initial financing to develop the Pacific Beach Club, a pleasure ground organized exclusively for African American membership and use. The syndicate would take full control of the beach property at the expiration of a ten-year period and the fulfillment of some financial terms. The Pacific Electric and Southern Pacific Rail lines, and the then-new Coast Boulevard, bordered the property. It is unclear whether Clark was recruited by, or sought out, the African American partners for the business venture. Further, it is unclear what Clark's previous business relationships may have been with Ceruti or other African American investors.[46]

Clark proceeded with the project over strongly registered objections raised by various organizations in Orange County such as the Huntington Beach and Newport Beach chambers of commerce, and the Huntington Beach City Trustees. Clark had to use an obscure statute "[to petition] the State Railroad Commission for an order authorizing the construction of a private right of way to the property . . . shut off by other lands" to obtain access rights across the tracks from the Pacific Electric Railway and Southern Pacific Railroad.[47] Clark's petition to the commission occurred after the two companies rescinded their original permission to construct a concrete underground crossing for easy and safe access to the grounds, due to opposition pressure from Orange County groups. Huntington Beach officials tried to keep electricity and water services from being extended to the club. Repeated efforts were proposed to and by Orange County supervisors to take the property through condemnation and eminent domain proceedings for public use as a (whites-only) park.[48]

The Pacific Beach Club's leadership included many of black Los Angeles's affluent and well-established medical, dental, and legal professionals and aspirational business owners. Other prominent black citizens, who were leading supporters and eventually became members of the club's board of directors, included several doctors who were also deeply engaged in other community-building and civic endeavors. One of them was Dr. Wilbur C. Gordon, who was involved in Lake Elsinore and the Parkridge Country Club and the developer of the Gordon Manor residential subdivision. Another was Dr. Albert Baumann, who owned several pharmacies and was civically active during the 1920s and 1930s as chairman of the board of management of the YMCA, president of the Urban League, and other civic groups. Baumann and Gordon were both founders and board members of the Liberty Building-Loan Association. Whether a marketing ploy or a self-reflecting expectation, an *Eagle* ad described the promoters as having lofty hopes that "the membership of the Club [would be] filled with doctors, musicians, artists and business men of the Country."[49]

In an *Eagle* ad soliciting membership sales for their exclusive African American club, the promoters effusively proclaimed that this project "initiates the beginning of the very foremost step of progress that the colored people have ever attempted." Like the Eureka Villa promoters, they viewed their venture as a monumental accomplishment for all black America. They pronounced the Pacific Beach Club "a permanent landmark to the ever forward and aggressive spirit of those tireless leaders of Southern California."[50]

In the 1920s there were only a few African Americans living in Orange County. Sometimes there were social mentions and news of their activities from Fullerton and Anaheim contributors to the *Eagle*. To stake out a claim on prime beachfront property, in an area experiencing growth due to the era's oil boom over objections by Orange County residents, on land that was many miles from Los Angeles' Central Avenue District, was an ambitious and bold move by these African American investors and their white ally. This project may have also provided stiff competition for the Eureka Villa promoters.[51]

The description of the club's buildings and their intended use indicates that the planners had a grand and luxurious vision for their beach leisure site. Billed in ads as the "Queen of the Pacific," the planned improvements were projected to cost $250,000 for several buildings elaborately decorated in Egyptian Revival–style architecture with an electrically lighted boardwalk. Once it was built, the clubhouse was described in a newspaper ad "[as a] gorgeously decorated palace" and called a "Mother of Pearl Fairyland." The building was touted as offering plenty of room to accommodate five thousand people for lectures, conventions, concerts and other theatrical performances, dances and balls, and banquets. There were also smaller lounges for more intimate group socializing, billiards, and smoking. Balconies for entertainers and people-watching, stage fountains, and rest rooms were also celebrated in an *Eagle* advertisement. The modern and sanitary bathhouse, featuring generous sunlight, was to accommodate one thousand men and six hundred women, with two thousand lockers, showers, and dressing rooms.[52]

Finished in beautiful mother-of-pearl-colored paint in the interior and creamy stucco on the exterior, the clubhouse pavilion was to be topped with a roof garden behind glass enclosures complemented by electrically lighted towers where patrons could look out at the Pacific Ocean and see Catalina Island on a clear day. The plans also included a 450-seat auditorium with a huge stage, concession area, restaurant, drug store, and small grocery store. Two hundred and fifty tent cottages were to be constructed for patrons to rent for a week or more for a nominal fee, as well as a children's playground. The club property was to be surrounded by a six-foot-high ornamental steel fence, with parking space provided inside the grounds, manned by proper attendants. This security was necessary to maintain the property benefits for members and their guests, and to keep out undesirables, such as whites who might try to harass and do harm to the grounds and its inhabitants. When possible, concessions were to be operated by club members and African Americans were to manage and perform all work upon the grounds.[53]

On Labor Day, Monday, September 7, 1925, several thousand people attended the first ever Bathing Girl and Children Contest and Beauty Parade given by African Americans on the Pacific Coast, waded in the surf, brought their lunch baskets and danced all day to a live band. The *Eagle* wrote that the event "was one wonderful gathering" and that "never before in the history of Western America have so many people of the Negro race gathered at one event." An Orange County newspaper, the

Santa Ana Register, reported the crowd was so large the local authorities requested assistance from the sheriff's office to manage the highway traffic. The black-owned newspaper, the *Eagle*, assured the programming ran with no confusion and the "conduct of the monster crowd was above reproach" and peaceful. The "exceptionally clear" moving pictures taken during the event of the beauties and crowd scenes was written about in the black press and displayed for a few weeks at the Rosebud Theatre in Los Angeles. A few photographs taken that day are the only known visual archive available of the event.[54]

The images of the New Negro, their style and beauty, race, class, identity, political assertion, and pride, as well as the Pacific Beach Club site, preserve these collective memories. In 1925 the moving picture and photographic documentation of the Pacific Beach Club event would have been a visual representation of African American contestation and resistance to being ascribed second-class citizenship. These images were and are empowering as a self-representation and rearticulation of aesthetic and ideological issues, in the same manner as the racial uplift rhetoric in the black press worked to promote the participation and desires of African Americans as fully equal citizen consumers.[55]

The Pacific Beach Club promoters aggressively marketed lifetime club membership sales and made steady progress toward a fully operational facility throughout 1925 into early 1926. Simultaneously, Eureka Villa promoters competed with the Pacific Beach Club project in their marketing and sales efforts to attract lot buyers. One promotion among many marked the first anniversary of Eureka Villa's founding on June 28, 1925, with a big parade down Central Avenue in Los Angeles and a special musical program at Eureka Villa by the very popular Sunnyland Band. Souvenirs and banners were furnished for all cars in the parade, and prizes were given to winners in various athletic contests. A ladies' sport suit contest offered a cash prize to the winner and the first payment on any residential lot in unit 3 at Eureka Villa. A free barbecue picnic held Labor Day (first Monday in September) at Eureka Villa, directly competed for much of the same audience's attention as the Pacific Beach Club's Bathing Girl and Children Contest and Beauty Parade and beach party promotion.[56]

The year 1926 was decisive for Eureka Villa and the Pacific Beach

Club. In the early morning of January 21, 1926, the Pacific Beach Club's clubhouse, bathhouse, and dance pavilion—built during the almost-completed first phase of construction—mysteriously burned nearly to the ground just weeks before formally opening on February 12, 1926, Abraham Lincoln's birthday. The fire was the culmination of a series of obstacles and attacks made by opponents to halt the project, including open threats by white Orange County citizens. Authorities investigated, but no arrests were ever made.[57]

After a lengthy consideration of all the options for the Pacific Beach Club grounds and a review of all the complications of the business transaction, a majority of the charter and other members voted not to rebuild. From Clark's insurance proceeds and his sale of the property to white investors, the black investors were fortunately refunded their money plus a 10-percent premium. All legitimate creditors also received the money they were owed, with 10-percent interest. The one bright spot in this whole affair was the contract drawn up with Clark by Attorney Ceruti and the syndicate's management had protected the interests of club members and creditors. This story of the Pacific Beach Club then went on to be mostly forgotten.[58]

Eureka Villa Emerges as Val Verde

Eureka Villa continued after the Pacific Beach Club's fire, despite financial troubles, legal entanglements, and new management. Sidney P. Dones, the early advisory committee he led, and the white landowner Laura C. Janes discontinued their management of Eureka Villa. The Eureka Villa Finance Corporation became the owners and underwriters of the area now consisting of 720 acres. Dones continued to sell lots in the original "Eureka Villa Tract," which he probably had personal interests in as an owner or a real estate broker. His name would become less associated with the place as the years went by.[59]

The pleasure site got a boost in 1927, when white businesspeople associated with the area gave fifty-three acres for a park to Los Angeles County. In future years, landowner and real estate developer Harry M. Waterman would become the white businessman most associated with the parkland donation and the area's continued development efforts. After money for improvements had vanished due to mismanagement by earlier developers, one thousand lot owners of Eureka Villa and white landholder Waterman petitioned Los Angeles County Supervisor Jack H. Bean (on the board from 1919 to 1928) for a $25,000 appropriation for needed improvements. The county of Los Angeles and Supervisor Bean's involvement provided a new foundation, as well as much-needed financial and other stimulus for the growth of the black resort and the north county area in general.[60]

With a new park and this Los Angeles County investment began another transition. "Eureka Villa" began to be known by the area's early name, "Val Verde." Immediately the county drew up plans to build, for the public, the amenities the early Eureka Villa promoters had intended exclusively for the pleasure of the lot holders and visitors. A beautiful clubhouse, landscaping, and an improved water system were planned. In an *Eagle* ad promoting a free barbecue on July 4, 1928, at the newly designated park "at Eureka Villa and Val Verde," these improvements were enthusiastically described as "making this one of the most beautiful recreation parks in Southern California." Like the Parkridge Country Club in Corona, Val Verde capitalized on the NAACP National Convention in 1928 by inviting delegates and the public to Val Verde to hear speakers and enjoy various forms of entertainment to celebrate America's Independence Day.[61]

The new Val Verde Park Community Clubhouse construction was completed in time to accommodate visitors for Easter services on March 31, 1929. This spring program became an annual event held at Val Verde for decades, and the clubhouse became a well-utilized facility for social events. In addition to Easter Sunrise Hill services, festivities planned for Decoration Day (Memorial Day), Independence Day, Labor Day, Thanksgiving, and Christmas would also bring larger crowds of families, social clubs, and other organizations, sometimes numbering in the thousands, to Val Verde's hills and canyons.[62]

From the visitors' names listed in the "Val Verde News" and those noted as signing the guest register at the clubhouse, black Angelenos and visitors from other places were most often of the socially active, more affluent professional, business, and entertainment classes. Other African Americans of the blue-collar class also visited, although they were less likely to be written about in the black press. The *Eagle*'s "Val Verde News" section cited people's varied accommodations for overnight stays and day trips. Visitors continued to slowly buy lots and build cottages or cabins. Some stayed with friends who owned places already, some camped in tents, and others rented accommodations. Still others made day trips for the festivities. They socialized, took hikes, barbecued, picnicked, played games, participated in athletic competitions, hunted game, rode horses and burros, and held various cultural events. Entertainers such as Ella Fitzgerald and Lena Horne sometimes performed at the nightlife establishments. A few opened businesses servicing visitors and some even had small livestock ranches. Some visitors even established permanent residences.

By the 1940s some dubbed the retreat the "black Palm Springs." Its persistence represented meaningful progress for African Americans' community pride and spatial imaginary in Southern California's public space after the struggle to build and sustain leisure projects in the 1920s and 1930s. Through organizers' initiative, eventual public support and funding, and interest in subdivision development aided by sympathetic white businesspersons, black Angelenos were able to construct a pleasure retreat practically of their own. For the most part black Angelenos did not embrace the black town concept and rejected characterization of Val Verde Park as a segregated facility. Yet they adeptly won government funding for a county park as a group excluded by the prevailing "Negro-only situation." The funding helped the rustic resort slowly blossom during the 1930s and renewed community interest in Val Verde. This resort launched by African Americans in Los Angeles as a response to the exclusion and humiliation they experienced from white Americans accepted this type of racial separatism.[63]

As scholar George Lipsitz argues, whites in Southern California and across the United States created segregated neighborhoods and schools, all-white workplaces, exclusive country club and subdivisions, and prosperous, properly gendered white suburban homes, taking advantage of massively subsidized services, amenities, tax breaks, and transportation opportunities unavailable to African American residents. Winning the government funding of park improvements in the same manner as whites had so many times before and after this period, African Americans in conjunction with white allies were able to take advantage of the taxes they paid as citizens "for resources, rights, and recognition." Black Angelenos put the government funding to advantageous use in developing the Val Verde retreat to create not only a place for leisure but new life opportunities and chances for the accumulation of assets.[64]

Having claimed and won a share of local funding, in 1936 Val Verde property owners and promoters pressed further through Los Angeles County Supervisor Gordon L. McDonough (on the board from 1933 to 1944) to obtain federal government New Deal Work Progress Administration (WPA) funding to build a bathhouse and a fully equipped, Olympic-sized swimming pool. The new pool opened in July 1940 with state and WPA funding allocations adding up to more than a half-million dollars for the bathhouse, swimming pool, and other park improvements. On February 1, 1940, the *Los Angeles Sentinel* highlighted that, while most of the surrounding home and ranch sites are owned by "Negroes," the area is not restricted to "the race." The article also went on to remind its readers that the public park grounds and facilities were always open to all citizens. The Great Depression may have been in full tilt, but it did not slow black Angelenos' social mobilization and resourceful politics in adaptively developing public and private spaces in Val Verde.[65]

More than 3,500 people attended the cornerstone-laying and dedication ceremony for the bathhouse and the swimming pool on April 16, 1939, including County of Los Angeles Supervisors Gordon L. McDonough and John Anson Ford, the Jefferson High School band, and film and television actors Hattie McDaniel, Louise Beavers, Clint Rosemond, and Ernest Whitman. Local and national black press reported that African American business and civic leaders in attendance included Norman O. Houston and George A. Beavers (leaders of Golden State Mutual Life Insurance); Dr. H. Claude Hudson and Rebecca "Betty" Hill (of the NAACP, Los Angeles Branch); Charlotta Spears Bass (*Eagle* publisher and civic activist); Frederick M. Roberts (*New Age* publisher, businessman, and former California Assemblyman); Louis George "L. G." Robinson (head of the maintenance staff for Los Angeles County, civic activist, and an Angelus Funeral Home co-owner); and Dr. Vadia Sommerville (dentist, businesswoman, and civic activist).[66]

The Val Verde Park project was a history-making event for black

Angelenos and the County of Los Angeles, Supervisor McDonough enthused in the letter he submitted for inclusion in the bathhouse building cornerstone time capsule. He wrote, "When the pool is completed this improvement will establish Val Verde Park as one of the major regional recreational areas of Los Angeles County." Although New Deal programs sanctioned discrimination against African Americans, there was a change in the status and perception of African Americans' rights as a substantive political issue for government and society in the 1930s. The park's development was one of the tangible benefits African Americans exacted from the federal government in the 1930s, part of the limited but greater public returns won over what occurred in previous decades. This project and others like it around the United States showed African Americans and their white allies potential for and hope in federal action against the public exacerbation of inequality, and the influence of their agency and activism.[67]

As Fay M. Jackson optimistically reported for the *Eagle* in an article on the new swimming pool facilities, it appeared that "this colony will become one of the most exclusive Negro gathering places in the country." Waterman had slowed his push to sell Val Verde lots in the lead up to the Park's latest improvements until they were just about completed. In a February 1, 1940, *LA Sentinel* article, he stated that he wanted potential buyers to view the area as attractive, as "an ideal country home and ranch site for small wage earners and retired workers." By the time the swimming pool opened, Waterman had built display homes lot purchasers could choose to have built. Accounts tell of Waterman going up and down Central Avenue in Los Angeles's main African American business district, recruiting people to visit Val Verde Park for the aquatic facilities cornerstone dedication ceremonies and to stop by his real estate office to put a five-dollar deposit on a "ranch site." He also hired buses to bring people from Los Angeles on the weekends to experience the San Martinez Chiquito Canyon retreat and to sell them lots and cottages. To use words from Dr. Emily B. Childress Portwig's speech at the dedication ceremony, all associated with Val Verde had faith in the community's potential and were "enthusiastic optimists" about its future development.[68]

When the swimming opened to the public in July 1940, the Great

Depression was giving way to national economic and military demand fueled by World War II. European immigration continued to be shut off, the nation's military increased, and defense and other manufacturers needed workers, which eventually would include previously excluded women, African Americans, and other groups. Even before the attack on Pearl Harbor in 1941, organized African American pressure had forced President Roosevelt to issue Executive Order 8802, forbidding racial discrimination in hiring by defense manufacturers and establishing the Fair Employment Practices Committee (FEPC) to investigate charges of racial discrimination. Black migration to defense industrial manufacturing centers rose dramatically and would have significant implications for the next thirty years of the long civil rights movement. Los Angeles and the San Francisco Bay area in California saw their cities transformed by a massive wartime migration. For black Los Angeles, this was its "first" Great Migration, rather than its "second" Great Migration, as was the case in Eastern cities like New York, Chicago, and other U.S. northern industrial centers. They had already experienced large influxes of black newcomers in the years pre- and post-World War I. This internal mass migration of blacks and whites mostly leaving the South would continue until the 1970s, with a larger percentage of African Americans making the move. In seeking better livelihoods for themselves and their children, African Americans had renewed aspirations for racial equality, and a shared loathing of the persistence of Southern racism.[69]

The 1940s was a watershed in the growth and development of Los Angeles's African American community and its influence on the city. By 1940 the black Angeleno population had grown to 63,774 from a population of 2,131 in 1900 and then nearly tripled in the next decade. By 1950 African Americans would grow to 171,209, or 8.7 percent of the total population of Los Angeles. They became much more visible in public spaces and civic consciousness and had more frequent contact with whites than in previous decades, while continuing to experience racial discrimination and white hostility, which limited their options in housing, education, employment, and other areas. At the same time, these latest migrants added new energy to the older and smaller African American community's contestation efforts, as historian Josh Sides asserts, in "challenging discriminatory employers, racist police, insensitive city councils and mayors, and obstinate white co-workers and neighbors through pickets, boycotts, protests, and organized electoral political activity." As in other large U.S. cities, African Americans were increasingly important agents of history in shaping Los Angeles in the mid-twentieth century and beyond.[70]

Expanded employment, rising income, and new discretionary income for many African Americans in Los Angeles infused new energy into Val Verde's recreational and residential development from the 1940s to the 1960s. After the swimming pool opened, Waterman made a more visible effort at selling lots directly through his company, rather than through brokers like Sidney P. Dones. For a period of time Waterman employed the well-connected African American journalist, publicist, and civic activist Fay M. Jackson to aid publicity for his operation, now called Val Verde Properties, Inc.[71]

No doubt both Waterman and Jackson wanted to capitalize on the goodwill Val Verde had generated and their individual respect in Los Angeles County's African American community and beyond to generate new lots sales and other business opportunities. An *Eagle* ad in May 1940 titled "Go West The Val Verde Way!" promoted Val Verde as "quaint and picturesque . . . where [owners of] charming rancheros get the most out of living the outdoor Western way!" This ad encouraged people to buy their choice of lots "on the hillside, along the main drag for business, or . . . hidden in secluded section of the canyon" at that moment in 1940 "before it develops into the city which is planned."[72]

Placed in the black press, Waterman's 1940s ads did not include the African American race-pride and uplift rhetoric used in the 1920s by Sidney P. Dones and his cohort. Rather, without explicitly naming African Americans as its target audience, these black press ads from Val Verde Properties extolled the economic, recreational, and social opportunities afforded by buying into this community-building project. Waterman's ads recycled the California Dream and Western ideal rhetoric of growth and prosperity in a peaceful and healthy environment for the era's more urban population wanting a country home getaway without the inconveniences. His May 1940 ad promoted healthy and scenic county outdoor living with "city-like modernity" and the conveniences of electricity, a system piping water to each lot, county-maintained graded streets, and telephone service.[73]

The then-new *Ebony* magazine recognized Val Verde as it promoted travel to California and other resorts around the United States and encouraged a black spatial imaginary to their mostly African American, national readership. Founded in November 1945, the monthly coffee-table magazine modeled after *Look* and *Life* focused on presenting positive images of African Americans in a world of negative images and in particular showcased their achievements. A July 1947 *Ebony* article titled "Where To Go Vacationing" placed California's Lake Elsinore, Victorville (Murray's Dude Ranch), and Val Verde on the list as "Favorite Resorts for Negro America." With employment and income at new heights due to the wartime financial boost, the *Ebony* writer observed that experts agreed all Americans were on the move to a record year for vacation travel. The article went on to say, "Never before have there been as many summer playgrounds open to colored guests and vacation-hungry visitors are expected to top all attendance records at these resorts." In a sign of the changing racial and social climate, *Ebony* informed its readers that many of these summer playgrounds were opened in the last few year to all races, and "whites [were] not barred" at Negro-owned and—patronized places.[74]

From its opening in 1940, Val Verde Park swimming pool became the retreat's main attraction during the summer months into the early 1960s. Some local residents who were not African American also enjoyed the facilities' use. The park, the local residents, and its new visitors opened up a wider public space and spatial imaginary, as well as social practices and employment and business opportunities for African Americans in recreation and accommodations in the region. From 1942 until his retirement twenty-two years later, Leon Perdue served as Val Verde Park's director. He was the first African American in California to gain a permanent appointment of this type in the County of Los Angeles Department of Parks and Recreation. He supervised the park's annual recreational and educational programming—and more—for local residents and visitors. In addition, he managed the County Department's cosponsorship of the signature events held in the park with the Val Verde Improvement Association, such as the Bathing Beauty Pageant and Muscle Man Show, the

Fourth of July Dance for young people, the Christmas program for children, and the Art Exhibit and Hobby Show.[75]

In the 1940s through the 1960s, businesses such as the Cartwright Cabins, Brown's Cabins, Carr's Rooming House, Casa de Baldwin, and Taylor's Ranch were available for overnight accommodations. Restaurants such as Scott's Tavern ("with its prized collection of cactus, fountain and fish pond"), Hi-Hat Inn, Maybel Henderson's Ranch, Lucille's Tumble Inn, the Val Verde Park Clubhouse Cafe, a small grocery store, and a few nightclubs such as Dudley's Inn (which also sold cold drinks and barbecue during the day) comprised the resort community commercial district serving residents and visitors. McCoy's and Goldsby's Ranch House rented visitors saddles and horses for all-day excursions, and Chet Hawkins supplied a merry-go-round for the "kiddies'" enjoyment. At one time there were three active churches holding services, First African American Episcopal Church, Salem Baptist Church, and the oldest Macedonia Church of God in Christ, pastored by Rev. Samuel Dixon. In 1980 the first of the Samuel Dixon Family Health Center locations was dedicated in a building behind the church in honor of the pastor's energetic service to the area. For a time, there was even a Val Verde U.S. Post Office.[76]

There were many people in the post-1940s era who contributed to the wider spatial imaginary for African Americans in Val Verde and Los Angeles. They made and shaped the Val Verde version of the leisure vision through their infrastructure development efforts, promotions of annual events, lot sales support, and persistent civil engagement and community-building leadership. Their persistence carried forward the leisure enterprise and social and cultural life of the area.

Alice Taylor Gafford (1886–1981), a resident of Los Angeles and Val Verde, was one of these people. She founded and organized for seventeen years what became the Annual Art Exhibit and Hobby Show at Val Verde Park. Staged for over thirty years and drawing people from all over Southern California as exhibitors and visitors, the event would eventually be called the Annual Alice Taylor Gafford Art Exhibit and Hobby Show, honoring her distinguished career and life as an artist, educator, civic activist, and a Val Verde Improvement Association member. The show was one of the first in the region to present fine art by African

American artists, as well as crafts and collectibles of various types. At Val Verde and through organizing across the community, Gafford nurtured individual black artists and cultivated the broader appreciation of consciously black art.[77]

Through her cultural expression and promotion of art, Gafford, like other African American artists, constructed what George Lipsitz identifies as "discursive spaces" that were "sites of agency, affiliation and imagination." As an artist and civic booster Gafford's efforts "[spoke] to the spatial aspects of racial identity," as Lipsitz discerns. Her efforts created "repositories of collective memory, sources of moral instruction, and mechanisms for transforming places and calling communities into being through display, dialogue, and decoration" in Val Verde and greater Los Angeles. As an artist and activist, Gafford opened new cultural and economic spatial imaginary development for Los Angeles County's African American community in her work at Val Verde, as she forged the broader inclusion of black culture in regional civic cultural life for artists and promoted art appreciation, then and into the future.[78]

One of Val Verde's most visible shapers and community builders in the post–World War II years was Frank DeWitt Godden (1911–2012). Arriving in Los Angeles in 1939 from Alabama's Tuskegee Institute with a bachelor's degree in commercial industries, Godden "wanted to get as far away from the South as possible," as he told the *Los Angeles Times* in a 1994 article about Val Verde. Once in Los Angeles, *Eagle* publisher and editor Charlotta Spears Bass hired Godden to photograph the 1939 Val Verde Labor Day celebration, "beginning . . . his life long love affair" with the place.[79]

While working with Waterman's Val Verde enterprises, Godden became a leader in the Val Verde Improvement Association, spearheading efforts to create a water district and a lighting district and to obtain additional street paving. His leadership was also important in the establishment and management of the Val Verde U.S. Post Office, which opened in 1956, and in the reestablishment of the association's newsletter and other community projects. He and others active in the association instituted the election of honorary mayors, the Hattie S. Baldwin Award for community service, and the maintenance of regular Val Verde town meetings. In the early

1960s, when he was president of the association, Godden was known as "Mr. Val Verde Park."[80]

Godden appreciated the Val Verde canyons' rustic charm and peaceful recreation and spent a good part of his lifetime trying to build it into an exemplary resort community. Though not precisely the kind of self-contained, economically self-determined community initially envisioned by its founders, the vision of Val Verde as a place of African American leisure freedom and community infused Godden's work. "I was trying to get something there that could be a point of pride," Godden told the *Times* in 1994. "I wanted to build a first-rate community where black people could come up and just enjoy—and they did for a long time." With the large influx of people to California from all over the United States from the 1940s to the 1960s, and Los Angeles's booming economy in the late 1950s, Val Verde's national reputation would help it to remain in existence for a while longer as a recreation area primarily patronized by African Americans. Many black newcomers joined older settlers in continuing to seek out the rustic canyon for communal bonding, networking, and the hassle-free leisure environment, where they would not be confronted with overt racism while they tried to relax and rejuvenate themselves.[81]

Personal Remembrance, Public Memory, and Contemporary Reality

Personal remembrances of Val Verde span the spectrum of appreciation for the natural features of the landscape and the views, the enjoyment of the social traditions created by family and friends, the relaxation offered by the peaceful environment, and the pride of individual and community accomplishments. There are also the memories of the leisure traditions that were created and led by community members—formalized, planned, community-building activities of physical group experiences at this place. The persistence of physical practices of leisure and community building activities in public and private over almost a century has made the public memory of Val Verde stronger than most of the other Jim Crow–era, Southern California African American leisure places that did not endure as long. Having not been intentionally erased, nor struggled over in reclamation, public memory has played a more consensual and subtly affirmative role in Val Verde community identity since the 1970s.

Personal remembrance suggests that the meaning of leisure community which residents derived from Val Verde informed their social engagement and lives beyond the place and moment. For California native and retired schoolteacher Alma Phillips Hill (1927–2015), that meant economic opportunity and participatory community building as well as leisure. Hill's family bought a vacation home in the canyon in the early 1940s. Some of her parents' friends also bought property, with some of those friends becoming permanent residents.[82]

"There was always something to do and there were lots of young people around," she recalled fondly. In addition to swimming for the teens there were games of baseball, tennis, cards, and billiards, hayrides, picnics, dances, and fishing nearby at Lake Piru. During the summer Hill loved to horseback ride early in the morning before it got too hot. "I remember one beautiful morning going horseback riding with about a dozen friends, boys and girls, and my mother cooking breakfast for us all," she said.[83]

Hill and her mother, Malvina Phillips, would leave their Los Angeles residence and spend most of the summer at their rustic retreat. Her father, Samuel Thomas Phillips, employed as a railroad waiter, would visit when he was not working. Her father also served as an honorary mayor of Val Verde for a time.[84]

Not surprisingly, social conviviality and the commonality of leisure was as much a valued feature as individual "escape" and vigorous recreation in the constructs of personal memories of Val Verde. When she was a young teen, Los Angeles native Marilyn Williams Hudson (1927–2015) recalled happy memories of summer stays at the "Not A Care" cabin, owned by early Val Verde property owner and booster Dr. Emily B. Childress Portwig. A Young Women's Christian Association (YWCA) counselor, Dr. Portwig invited the girls like Hudson who were YWCA members to stay at her rustic retreat.[85]

The Miss Val Verde Bathing Beauty and Mr. Muscle Man competitions, with a parade featuring simple floats, were the summer's biggest events from the 1940s to 1979. Florence LaRue won the crown in 1965, before she became a member of the popular Grammy-winning singing group the Fifth Dimension. The LaRue family were regular visitors, with Florence's parents owning a cottage. Actor James Earl Jones, who raised thoroughbred horses at his eight-acre Val Verde ranch on Rainbow Drive, awarded the last beauty contest prize in 1979.[86]

Grade-school teacher and sportswoman Marie Rogers (b. 1957) has a visceral sense-of-place remembrance of the retreat from her childhood in the 1960s. "I would know we arrived at Val Verde in the family car from Los Angeles, as I smelled in the air barbecue being prepared," said Rogers in an interview at her Los Angeles–area home. Rogers recalls visiting her family's modest cottage—situated on the hillside of the canyon adjacent to the park—as an elementary-school-age girl, and the smells of the cottonwood trees and other native plant life while playing outside with her brother, James Frederick Wilson III. She also remembers the smell of the chlorine from her regular frolicking at the Val Verde Park swimming pool, where her father, James Fredrick Wilson, Jr. (b. 1906), was employed as a seasonal lifeguard from the 1940s to the early 1960s.[87]

During their leisure time at Val Verde, family members passed a lasting appreciation of nature and outdoors activities down to their daughter and granddaughter. Rogers enjoys in her adult life riding horses, running marathons, hiking, and sailing. In addition, she has a menagerie of rescued animals as pets, including dogs, horses, chickens from different countries, and llamas, that she and her husband, Bill, board at their rustic home overlooking the Pacific Ocean in Rolling Hills, California, on the Palos Verdes peninsula. The black spatial imaginary that Rogers's elders surrounded her with during her formative years at Val Verde enriched and informed her, providing a place for young Marie to develop the self-confidence to engage as an adult with a variety of sportswomen, as well as intellectual and community pursuits.[88]

The good times, fond memories, and African American community-building efforts and pride of ownership existed alongside perpetual challenges and complications for Val Verde's expansion and sustained existence as an African American resort, or any kind of community.[89]

As the era of flagrant overt white racism and racial segregation eased in the 1960s, coupled with regional land development policies and new projects along with water supply issues, Val Verde began to fade as a popular African American resort and recreation site. African Americans started to spend their time and money elsewhere as more places of leisure and recreation opened up to them. The north Los Angeles County rustic-vacation community evolved into mostly a retirement community of African Americans who had moved there years before, and of former Los Angeles city dwellers whose vacation homes became their new permanent residences. Vacation home use by African American owners still existed, but this practice was declining rapidly. By the latter half of the 1970s many vacation-home owners had become absentee landlords, renting their small houses to Latinx farmworkers and their families, who shared cramped facilities. At the same time a few white families that were more affluent than the incoming Latinx families also began purchasing lots, building permanent residential dwellings and renovating others.[90]

Even with the challenges, some African American property owners did profit through renting and selling properties as Val Verde's historical African American vacation community transitioned from the late 1960s into the twenty-first century into a multiethnic community of permanent residents. These new residents live in a community with a mix of new and old houses on assorted large rural and city-sized housing lots that originated with the 1920s community. On the larger ranchette lots, some people continue to keep horses, a few chickens, livestock, and small vegetable gardens.[91]

As the population in Santa Clarita Valley expanded and urbanized, more people discovered Val Verde. In the late 1970s to the early 1980s, mostly white independent developers began purchasing vacant lots and building new, simple homes. In 1988 these new homes cost around $115,000, while houses just three miles away over the hills cost $350,000 and up. The buyers of these new Val Verde homes were mostly young, working-class white couples looking for affordable housing and a peaceful place to raise their families. By the twenty-first century the newer residents started including more of the young upwardly mobile class ("yippies") who built larger, custom-designed homes at a more affordable cost than elsewhere in northwest Los Angeles County. Many of these people worked in the Santa Clarita, San Fernando, and Simi Valleys. The district's diverse demographics did not appear to be an issue with new wealthier yuppies, who came from Los Angeles and other places outside of Santa Clarita

Valley. On the contrary, at least on a superficial level, along with the lower costs of housing, the multiethnic demographic appears to have been an attraction to the Val Verde community.[92]

The Val Verde Civic Association became reenergized with new community shapers and builders, as the construction of new homes and repair of dilapidated ones brought new people into the small, unincorporated area. From the 1980s into the dawning decades of the twenty-first century the ongoing mission of the association and its supporters has been to maintain the rustic ambiance and limit growth in Val Verde, despite the fact that most of the lots were subdivided into city-size lots at the community's founding in the late 1920s. Civic leaders also began advocating for quality, custom-designed homes and opposing cheaply designed "box-like" houses, modular homes, trailers, and multifamily housing.[93]

In the mid-1990s the association took an aggressive stance to fight the expansion of trash dumping at the small Chiquita Canyon Landfill, constructed in 1971 to serve the trash deposal needs of the Santa Clarita Valley. The association was concerned that turning this small landfill into a mega-pit, drawing in waste from Ventura to West Covina, would create airborne environmental contaminates, which could circulate around the area due to the prevailing ocean breezes. The issue of environmental racism proved an important concern, as all discussion of new landfills in the region met extraordinary "not in my backyard" (NIMBY) politics. On multiple fronts this concern requires complicated analysis.[94]

Fast forwarding to the twenty-first century, the once totally African American community made up of the spectrum of middle-class property owners has continued the trend of being racially integrated, as Latinx and white citizens with incomes from the lower to middle classes move in. A few of the younger descendants of older African American landowners have bought into the new rural lifestyle as residents. Many younger descendants who inherited the vacation property rent out the small houses built in the community's pre-1960s era or have sold their property. Some are unable to build on their land for economic reasons, property tax encumbrance, and hillside development rules.

"The change [in the population make up] has been gradual and not hostile," observed Elijah Canty (1911–2011) in 2004. "People still move to Val Verde for the sense of community and because they love the rural outdoors." Miriam Canty (1916–2001) noted in a 1990 *Daily News of Los Angeles* article that people then taking up residence appreciated the beautiful canyon just as the original community settlers did in the early years. The Cantys' views remained valid, if more tenuously so in 2019. Residents of the early twenty-first century seem to have been drawn to Val Verde's quiet, rural landscape with its access to nearby conveniences of commerce, local services, and an urban center. African American race pride, uplift rhetoric and economic self-determination no longer empower the community's self-representation and rearticulation of aesthetic and ideological issues in their participation and desires as residents, citizen consumers, and civic activists. More contemporary history now informs local public memory, revolving around their association's fight to keep the nearby dump from expanding and the mitigation money they won for their small rural enclave.[95]

Val Verde's African American population in 2004 was about 4 percent. It did not materially change in the decade to follow. In 2010 the total population reached 2,468, an increase of 67 percent since 2000. In 2010 the population was 61 percent Latinx, and 30 percent white. Some of the pioneering African American families are still represented as residents and nonresident property owners and landlords in this community. During the summer some African American families and groups from the Los Angeles environs continue to make an annual day pilgrimage for picnics to Val Verde Park.[96]

No extensive published narrative, exhibits, or historic preservation landmark designations have been developed concerning the history and heritage of the black Val Verde leisure community site. A few newspaper articles have been written, short television program segments occasionally appear on local public television, and some photographs of historical African American leisure escape seekers can be found in local institution collections and private scrapbooks. The memory of Val Verde's heyday for African Americans, and the importance the historic district had for those who experienced its pleasures and its sense of place, are mostly retained in the personal memories of those who visited the resort haven during the Jim Crow era.[97]

Generally, in the second decade of the twenty-first century, when the historical origins of the community are discussed, the description focuses on it being a contemporary "forgotten rural hamlet" with beginnings as a resort haven founded by black Angelenos seeking escape from the nation's Jim Crow–era discrimination. Sometimes the Val Verde Park and swimming pool complex as building projects of the 1930s New Deal Work Progress Administration are included.

Generally, the public memory does not incorporate the important element of the everyday leisure and economic independence integration that the founders imagined. It does not include the names of community shapers and builders, or details of the resourceful agency of these African American men and women, who developed a district where they could visualize themselves as full, equal citizen consumers. Suppressed in this public memory is the empowering self-consciousness and self-determination of this leisure practice and the radical visions of economic development opportunities the venture provided to generations of twentieth-century African Americans and their California Dream.[98]

Conclusion

> The challenge of history is to recover the past and introduce it to the present. It is the same challenge that confronts memory.
> —David Thelen, *Memory and American History*

> In the course of their struggle toward a position of equality among the nation's people, [African Americans] . . . have helped to make the West a part of America.
> —W. Sherman Savage, *Blacks in the West*

Through the research that led to writing this book, I learned a great deal about extraordinary community builders and the socioeconomic development experiences of black middle-class people of Los Angeles and California—doctors, teachers, lawyers, entrepreneurs, and strivers from other occupational backgrounds—living their lives during the period of my study about whom I and many others were not aware. Like other African Americans, this underrecognized segment of the population grappled with the issues of their time in a period of profound social, political, and cultural transformation in the United States in the twentieth century. Members of this group seized their sense of cultural entitlement to articulate their California Dream in creation of African American spaces of leisure and other activities, despite the unrelenting, caustic barrage of oppression. As a third-generation Afro Angeleno and a member of this segment of the population, I have been a beneficiary of their efforts in my lifetime.

My maternal grandparents, Dr. Peter P. Cobbs (1892–1960), and Rosa Mashaw Cobbs (1899–1989), and their children, who were born in Los Angeles—Prince (1925–2019), Marcelyn (1927–95), and Price (1928–2018)—bore witness to this time, due to a decision to migrate to Los Angeles, California, from Montgomery, Alabama, in 1925, to begin new lives and start their own family. Upon their arrival, my grandfather was one of the few black physicians in the city, and my grandmother had a teaching degree. Growing up, I heard stories from my mother, Marcelyn Cobbs Jefferson, about her life and those of her family members, as pioneering African Americans in the area. In the early stages of my research, I had the great fortune to have an uncle, Dr. Price M. Cobbs, who had written a memoir, which included some stories of his personal experiences growing up along with his view of his family's life and community in Los Angeles. Over the years anecdotal stories about visits to Lake Elsinore emerged many times in stories told by my elder family members and their friends and associates.[1]

When I was a small child, three generations of my family went on what I recall as one grand outing to Lake Elsinore, just after the lake's water refurbishment in 1964. Hearing my elders' remembrances over the years, combined with my own memory of this single day trip to Lake Elsinore, planted the seeds of curiosity to learn more about their and other African Americans' summer experiences at this place and other Southern California leisure destinations that were popular before I was born. This experience also initiated my journey of this later formal systematic research and learning, to share with the public the, in many cases, almost lost knowledge about the African American experience in Los Angeles, California, and the West. This book about the history and memory of the African American experience at Southern California leisure destinations is one of the professional results and personal rewards of this knowledge reclamation journey.

Today few traces of the African American resort communities discussed in this book survive to link us to the experiences, sentiments, tradition, and memory of these Californians' Jim Crow–era cultural production. Most of the buildings have been demolished, many of the people who enjoyed them in their heyday are dead, and those who are still alive reside apart from one another in many locales near to and far from these places. While a few photographs, pieces of ephemera, oral histories, some television footage, architectural ruins, and stories and advertisements from mostly African American newspapers remain, the small quantity of material and visible markers on the landscape pose difficult challenges to historians, community members, and the heritage conservation movement who seek to commemorate these spaces. Yet the stories of these leisure struggles speak not only to the African American experience, but also to the historical and ongoing formation of the region and the United States. The quest to reclaim this history for public memory has opened and informed contemporary life, drawing upon past struggles of people of these Southern California towns to build shared understanding in contemporary communities.

This book aims to expand our historical knowledge of the African American experience, the American West, and the United States in general through local studies of struggles for leisure in Southern California. The project adds to the illumination and reclamation of African American spaces and places of social and cultural history around leisure in the Jim Crow era and the long civil rights struggle, reconsidering the narrative of the Southern California experience as it restores erased participants and events to the cultural landscape. The history reconstructed in this research challenges the invisibility of African American presence after a century of removal, by restoring and reclaiming public history, and renewing the claim to place in leisure locations across Southern California. It reconnects the material and nonmaterial memory heritage of places, people, ideals, and events that resonate historically, intellectually, emotionally, and unconsciously, to deepen the landscape of national consciousness. These local historical narratives are the foundation for a richer, more accurate American public memory, or what Pierre Nora calls *lieux de mémoire*—sites of memory. Only through concerted action documenting the history of the African American experience around leisure practices in these Southern California communities has there been success, however limited, against the erasure and toward the recalling, reclaiming, reframing, and incorporating this history into contemporary place memory.[2]

To imagine and write the historical narratives of each site examined in this book required considerable historical reconstruction. All of the sites examined in this book have varied presences and absences embodied in sources that have influenced the degree to which and how the African American experiences have fared in its past incorporation into local cities and Southern California historical narratives and memories. There is a structured institutional nature to the paucity and exclusion of sources and the dominant narrative that absents them. The availability of rare and scattered material culture sources in archives or personal collections such as photographs, ephemera, other documents, and in situ buildings has been a significant factor influencing the extent to which these experiences have been incorporated. The scarcity and scant institutional initiative to collect oral history and other accounts recalling the details of leisure practices or direct testimony of events at these places by African Americans who enjoyed them have in many instances cast a veil of silence about the specific practices at these sites. Further, this missing history has increased through multiple generations due to the modesty of individuals of this community, who are accustomed to considering their lives historically inconsequential. In these Southern California towns, contemporary insertions aside, most local community histories have almost entirely omitted African American involvement, or have privileged some events over others that would not be emphasized by the African American actors of that era or in the present. These types of silences in sources, archives, the making of narratives, and the making of public history of the African American experience in the various Southern California communities show the "inequalities experienced by the actors [that lead] to uneven historical power in the inscription of traces" in the process of historical production. The expanded historical narratives about the sites in this book contribute to shaping—or, in some instances recasting—the history and memory of African Americans whose voices have been silenced, marginalized, or ignored in these communities and Southern California due to their relative lack of civic, political, and socioeconomic power.[3]

The stories in these chapters offer more complex views of sometimes surprising interactions of local citizens' relationships in Southern California. They illustrate and open to analysis the broader pattern of struggle over leisure consumerism as it became an important element of American life. Local history narratives have excluded and silenced regional African American pioneers' zealous participation in the civic life and socioconsumer life of these communities and the nation and erased the active thwarting of their efforts by others. African American entrepreneurs were in the mainstream of the American economic experience when they purchased goods, services, and land from nonblack businesses to support and shape their enterprises to meet the leisure needs of their clientele. Too typically, the histories of the communities examined in this book have privileged nostalgic views to celebrate a partial past, featuring white city founders to make safe history for current privilege. That history is set neatly apart from the history of African American community building, and from the present. These local histories miss these towns' original formation in, and persistence as, entities of economic and spatial discrimination and exclusion that is racial in origin, and in doing so perpetuate misunderstanding in the present. These narratives do not reveal the past African Americans' struggle against racial discrimination, harassment, and violence for equal access to occupy public space, as well as for housing and employment that in some of these communities has impacted their limited residential presence today. In the locations where these African American leisure sites existed and their history was marginalized or excluded, the more contemporary discourse has shown how history can have bearing on community understanding. These expanded discourses offer new understanding, showing how consciousness-raising and history have spurred communities in the direction of slowly building a different and more complete identity.

To counteract the structural nature of the problem of the lack of inclusion of multiple voices in local history accounts by historical narrators and obstinate elites, who have participated in the trivialization and silencing of the history of such groups as African Americans, continuous multifront efforts will be required to recover and represent the history and reclaim its place. Professional scholars, museum curators, members of the heritage conservation movement, and policy makers, along with journalists and other observers, will have to more frequently research and present these broader narratives to the general public. In a region of constant migration and continued assertion of leisure as a central part of the region's identity, it matters that we know the actual story of assertion, context, and creativity in the composition of Southern California leisure, for current and future practice. Illumination of these local stories can open up a spatial imaginary for more diverse participants to define, innovate, and participate in government planning and vision for leisure's future in these places. As minority groups become the majority in the United States, it is in the national interest that all citizens gain a more sophisticated, culturally diverse consciousness and understanding of the history and contemporary experience of communities of color and other economically, politically, or socially marginalized Americans. Research studies have shown especially positive impacts of multicultural education for white students who learn about communities of color and the issues of race already familiar to marginalized group students. For the practice of democracy, where everyone is included, it is essential that all citizens be incorporated in the American historical narrative and identity, especially those who have previously been kept on the periphery.[4]

An important avenue for addressing how to increase historical narrative diversity is education policy and practices of implementation of multicultural grade school and higher education curricula to counter Euro-American–centric perspectives and dismantle institutional racism and hegemonic structures that impede this knowledge. Multicultural education and the ethnic studies movements, which emerged during the modern civil rights movement of the 1960s and 1970s, have historical roots in the African American and ethnic studies movements pioneered by scholars Carter G. Woodson, W. E. B. Du Bois, José Martí, and others that emerged in the late nineteenth and early twentieth centuries. Even with this long history of labor by scholars and educators in the advancement of teaching multivoiced narratives, in the nation's K–12 system of education it continues to be virtually absent and, in some states, resisted by conservative legislators. Higher education has a better track record, as some form of multicultural or ethnic American studies are taught at most of the nation's universities and required at many, whether the majority of students take these courses or not. Consideration of leisure as a social location of power, contest, and memory has made no entry into curricula.[5]

The California State Legislature, the Ethnic Studies Now Coalition, National Education Association, and other groups have made new strides in addressing educating the citizenry with an understanding of the diversity of human experience in California and the nation. The community stories in this book could be especially powerful and effective education tools for transforming California of the twenty-first century, as they are about local African American agents in the history of the making of community and place, uses of space, the power and reclamation of memory, along with the inclusive composition of the constantly shifting identity of people. These stories are also about social and state power to silence and dispossess. The legislative and civic coalition projects are concentrated around expansion of the K–12 education curricula and textbooks currently dominated by Euro-American perspectives, to include the knowledge and perspectives of marginalized scholarship by and about African Americans, Latinx Americans, Native Americans, and Asian Americans that reflect narratives and points of view rooted in these group's lived experiences and scholarship. Students of color continue to demand the inclusion of the knowledge and perspectives of their ethnic and racial groups, and there are now more sympathetic allies in powerful policy-making positions who are actuating their demands through public policy for the construction of a more inclusive public culture and national identity.[6]

In the last decade the California Legislature has been engaged in revising legislation (the FAIR Act) in favor of a multicultural voice and inquiry-based instructional model for California K–12 history curricula. The FAIR Act expands the categories of history encompassed in social science education and makes stronger antidiscrimination policies in instructional materials and textbooks selected in the state of California. The revised bill as enacted states:

> Instruction [and instructional materials] in social sciences shall include the early history of California and a study of the role and contributions of both men and women, Native Americans, African Americans, Mexican Americans, Asian Americans, Pacific Islanders, European Americans, lesbian, gay, bisexual, and transgender Americans, persons with disabilities, and members of other ethnic and cultural groups, to

the economic, political, and social development of California and the United States of America.[7]

The American Historical Association (AHA) is an advocate of the California FAIR Act. On November 18, 2014, AHA submitted a letter supporting the revision of the California K–12 History–Social Sciences Framework. The organization urged those engaged in revising the curriculum to adhere to the parameters of the FAIR Act, in attempts to provide elementary school students access to a broad range of viewpoints in primary sources, thereby encouraging them to develop their own evidence-based arguments. The organization of history professionals concluded that this model education legislation "is a step in the right direction for history education"—a sentiment that all who support more inclusive history instructional programming would agree with. This type of educational curricula will aid structurally in improving California students' and eventually the general public's knowledge of the diverse experiences of the American people.[8]

Some of California's largest public school districts—Los Angeles and San Francisco, for example, and a smaller one in Pico Rivera—have already made taking an ethnic studies class a high school graduation requirement for all students. In addition to teaching about diverse cultures, research studies have shown these types of courses specially help students of color academically, in increasing student achievement and engagement, as well as socially, giving them a sense of empowerment and self-worth when they learn about histories of people who speak and look like them. These research studies also have found that ethnic studies courses help bridge differences across existing experiences and build discovery of human commonalities. Conceived in this way, as the basis of public, historical collective understanding, ethnic studies, including the stories of African American leisure places and community builders, are intended not just as the stories and experience of specific groups of Americans but that of all American people. The courses' intentions are to play a role in developing empathy and antiracism, toward building a more fully realized multicultural democracy and public culture in America's future. As California is one of the most diverse states in the nation, some observers consider the state's ethnic studies for high schools legislation "as a powerful model for the rest of the country."[9]

Many in the general public learn about regional and national experiences of America's people while visiting historic sites. At this time the National Register, along with state and local historic registries, are not reflective of the nation's history, let alone its changing demographics. The number of national, state, and local landmark designations reflecting the history of communities of color and women continues to be very small, and they do not reflect all the narratives in the American story. Less than 3 percent of the National Register's sites and approximately 1 percent of California's historical resources inventory are associated with ethnic and cultural significance. Less still consider the historical formation of leisure as an important determinant of contemporary society and culture. Cultural landmark designations and the public programming around them can infuse a cultural and natural resource site with complexities of human history and experience that strengthens both the heritage and nature conservation movements by giving these places a critical dimension beyond beauty, rarity, and environmental protection. From an environmental justice viewpoint, the inclusion of this history is symbolic of limited social change and pushes forth a sense of collective cultural belonging and common membership in American society that helps in forming a basis for social progress, learning, and action in the future.[10]

In the more recent decades, the heritage conservation movement has reconsidered the definition of what is worth protecting. For some in the movement, there is now an understanding of a need for a definition that goes beyond architectural significance in the traditional sense. The movement has slowly acknowledged that there are layers of history at sites that deserve recognition, even when those layers reconsider the original character of the building or when there is no building extant upon which to situate the history. Sense-of-place stories, intangible cultural heritage or social value, such as oral traditions, performing arts and crafts traditions, social practices, rituals, and festive events are the "heritage" that makes many historic sites important to communities of color. These types of social value sites remain a tough sell in many circles of heritage conservation, as well as in nature conservation movements. In order for the heritage conservation movement to be relevant in diverse communities, it is very slowly finding its way toward more recognition and affirmation of such sites and landmarks. The recovery and incorporation of the landscape of leisure in Southern California invites this sort of creative marking and mediation.[11]

There are still large influential segments of white America, even in California, that continue to have a problem accepting an identity as a more diverse nation, and the loss of "whiteness" as a defining feature of the American identity of the dominant group. Further, this group continues to lag in embracing painful aspects of the past and the breadth of human experience in the nation's history as a more complex multiracial and ethnic landscape in order to see a common destiny. Popular memory of many historical events and sites has proven difficult to extricate from white-centered narratives, or to enrich with new information, even with the advent of new scholarship and more enlightened historical and cultural-site administrators who began work in the 1990s.

The development of a more inclusive American national consciousness and identity is a slow process that is ongoing. Like some of the research in this book, other scholarship produced in the last forty years can be utilized by public and private policy making administrators and educators of Western states and municipalities, as well as the nation, to create more inclusive narratives about African Americans and other peoples of color in the curriculum of the education system that provides the young with knowledge and training. This scholarship should also be used in developing additional landmark designations of historical sites associated with these groups at the local, state, and national levels. Other types of public programming, which could include museum exhibits, information websites, and public lectures, also should be developed to engage the American citizenry in understanding the full experience of the nation's people. These acts would go a long way toward better instilling the history of overlooked, neglected, and marginalized groups of America's Western region into national consciousness or historical public memory, as well as into the American identity.

NOTES

LIST OF ABBREVIATIONS

BR	*Beach Reporter* (Los Angeles County)
CE	*California Eagle* (Los Angeles)
CMB	City of Manhattan Beach
CC	*Corona Courier*
CD	*Chicago Defender*
CDI	*Corona Daily Independent*
DB	*Daily Breeze* (Los Angeles County)
DNLA	*Daily News of Los Angeles*
DO	*Daily Outlook* (Santa Monica)
ERN	*Easy Reader News* (Los Angeles County)
EV	Eureka Villa
LSBC	Lake Shore Beach Company
LMBC	Leadership Manhattan Beach Class of 2003
LAS	*Los Angeles Sentinel*
LAT	*Los Angeles Times*
MBO	*Manhattan Beach Observer* newsletter
SDHS	San Diego Historical Society
SSJPF	Sandra Seville-Jones Personal Files
SBDB	*South Bay Daily Breeze* (Los Angeles County)
TPD	*the Pacific Defender*
VV	Val Verde
VVPFLA	Val Verde Park File, Department of Parks and Recreation, County of Los Angeles

INTRODUCTION

1. Noah D. Thompson, "These 'Colored' United States, No. 15–California: Horn of Plenty," *Messenger* 6 (July 24, 1924): 215, 220.

2. Thompson, "These 'Colored' United States, No. 15–California," 221; "Negro Cities—Los Angeles," *CE*, December 26, 1924, 1.
3. "Negro Cities—Los Angeles," *CE*, December 26, 1924, 1; Thompson, "These 'Colored' United States, No. 15–California," 215.
4. Culver, *The Frontier of Leisure*. The title of the book and phase "frontier of leisure," to be elaborated on in chapter 1, speaks to the consumption of leisure opportunity as a particular lifestyle and as new marker to delineate socioeconomic class that spread from California to the rest of the United States during the twentieth century.
5. I use the term "freedom rights struggle" to mean the broader "assortment of civil and human rights that emancipated African Americans identified as freedom" that "acknowledges the centrality of slavery and emancipation to conceptualization of freedom," as Hasan Kwame Jeffries articulates it in *Bloody Lowndes*, 4. I also use the term "heritage conservation" rather than historic preservation as it is a more inclusive term of the activities to preserve American "heritage" beyond the sole consideration of saving a historic building for its cultural significance. The group name used to describe African Americans has evolved over the years. In this book I sometimes use the words "Negro" and "Colored" to identify people of African descent in the United States during the Jim Crow era, as these are the names they and others would have used. I also use "black" and "African American" throughout the book. These are group identifiers for people of African descent in the United States and serve as universal group identifiers, which cross historical time periods. Wolcott, *Race, Riots, and Roller Coasters*, 3, 6; Hall, "The Long Civil Rights Movement and the Political Uses of the Past," 1–28.
6. Hayden, *The Power of Place*, 9, 43, 78; Couvares, Saxon, Grob, and Billias, *Interpretations of American History*, vol. 2, 17–18; Novick, *That Noble Dream*, 415–19, 595–97, 603–4.
7. DeGraaf, "The City of Black Angels," 348–49; Sugrue, *Sweet Land of Liberty*, 3–58.
8. Shackel, *Memory in Black and White*, 198–99, 209.
9. Like the layers of social and historical experiences, as Delores Hayden notes, the marking and remembrance of a place in a public past for any city or town is a political as well as historical and cultural process, regardless of citizens' intentions. Hayden, *The Power of Place*, 7–9, 12–13; Glassberg, *Sense of History*, 3–22; Trouillot, *Silencing the Past*, 1–30; John Hope Franklin in "The National Park Service and Civic Engagement," National Park Service, 2001, 5.
10. In a "multiracial" society, white privilege and white supremacy are part of a system of social practices and policies that maintain and strengthen white social dominance, order membership in a civil community, and create social differences along race, color, and class lines as a qualification for full citizenship rights. For more on white privilege, see Pulido, "Rethinking Environmental Racism," 12–40; and Harris, "Whiteness as Property"; and, on white supremacy, see Fredrickson, *White Supremacy*.

11. For early important works on the American West that exclude or minimize the African American presence, see Turner, "The Significance of the Frontier in American History" (1893); and Walter Prescott Webb, "The American West: Perpetual Mirage," *Harper's* (May 1957). See DeGraaf, "Recognition, Racism, and Reflections" for a historiography of works on African Americans in the West before 1975.
12. DeGraaf, "The City of Black Angels," 323; DeGraaf, "Recognition, Racism, and Reflections," 42, 47, 50–51; Taylor, *In Search of the Racial Frontier*; White, *It's Your Misfortune and None of My Own*; Limerick, *The Legacy of Conquest.*
13. Broussard, "African Americans in the West," 5; Flamming, *African Americans in the West*, 305–9; Lapp, *Blacks in Gold Rush California*; Tolbert, *The UNIA and Black Los Angeles*; Broussard, *Black San Francisco*; Daniels, *Pioneer Urbanites*; Taylor, *Forging of a Black Community*; McBroome, *Parallel Communities*; Lemke-Santangelo, *Abiding Courage*; Horne, *Fire This Time*; Moore, *To Place Our Deeds*; DeGraaf, Mulroy, and Taylor, *Seeking El Dorado*; Self, *American Babylon.*
14. Taylor, *In Search of the Racial Frontier*, 18–19, 21, (quotation) 23, 292. Taylor's U.S. West are the nineteen states west of the ninety-eight meridian included in this survey: North and South Dakota, Nebraska, Kansas, Oklahoma, Texas, New Mexico, Colorado, Wyoming, Montana, Idaho, Utah, Arizona, Nevada, California, Oregon, Washington, Alaska, and Hawaii. Taylor's reinterpretation of the African American experience in the West goes much beyond Savage's *Blacks in the West*, which is considered to be the first survey of the African American experience in the West.
15. Taylor, *In Search of the Racial Frontier*, 309–10, 313–15; Flamming, *African Americans in the West*, 10–11; Broussard, "African Americans in the West," 5.
16. Kevin Mulroy, "Preface," in *Seeking El Dorado*, ix, xi; Bunch in *Seeking El Dorado*, 130; Broussard, "African Americans in the West," 5.
17. Bunch in *Seeking El Dorado*, 130–31, 143–44; Flamming, *Bound for Freedom*, 128.
18. My study draws more from Bond, "The Negro in Los Angeles," than Marne L. Campbell's work, as his analysis focused more on the twentieth-century black Angelenos who were some of the leisure makers in the exurban communities discussed in this book; Campbell's *Making Black Los Angeles* offers new attention to gender, class, and race and argues that women were significant leaders in the formation of this community in the nineteenth century; Sides, *L.A. City Limits.* Although extensively researched, journalist Beasley's *The Negro Trail Blazers of California* has no footnotes, but is a sweeping compilation highlighting the accomplishments and contributions of African Americans throughout California up to the time of its publication, with particular attention to Los Angeles. My study also builds on and leads to the growing body of Western and urban history scholarship that discusses other communities of color in addition to African Americans. See Wild, *Street Meetings*; Kurashige, *The Shifting Grounds of Race*;

Brilliant, *The Color of America Has Changed*; Almaguer, *Racial Fault Lines*; Sanchez, *Becoming Mexican American*; Deverell, *White Washed Adobe*; Alvarez, *The Power of the Zoot*; Estrada, *The Los Angeles Plaza*; Cheng, *The Changs Next Door to the Diazes*; Laslett, *Sunshine Was Never Enough*; Avila, *Popular Culture in the Age of White Flight*; Lipsitz, *Midnight at the Barrelhouse;* Johnson, *Spaces of Conflict*; Hassan, *Loren Miller*; Cobbs, *My American Life*; and Daniels, *Lester Leaps In*.

19. DjeDje and Meadows, *California Soul*; Bryant, Collette, Green, Isoardi, and Young, *Central Avenue Sounds*; Smith, *The Great Black Way*; Bogle, *Bright Boulevards*; Widener, *Black Arts West*; Jones, *South of Pico*; Allmendinger, *Imagining the African American West*; Stevenson, *The Contested Murder of Latasha Harlins*; Hernández, *City of Inmates*; Hunt and Ramon, *Black Los Angeles*; Ruffin and Mack, *Freedom's Racial Frontier*; Glasrud and Wintz, *The Harlem Renaissance in the American West*.
20. Pierre Nora, "From *Lieux de memoire* to Realms of Memory," http://faculty.smu.edu/bwheeler/Joan_of_Arc/OLR/03_PierreNora_LieuxdeMemoire.pdf (accessed February 16, 2015), xv, xvi, xvii.
21. Thelen, *Memory and American History*, (Thelen quotation) ix, (Frisch quotation) xix; Shackel, *Memory in Black and White*, 198–99, 209; Kaufman, *Place, Race, and Story*, 11–12.
22. Stephens, *Idlewild*, 3–4, 26, 29–36; "The New Negro Movement—NAACP: A Century in the Fight for Freedom, 1909–2009" Exhibition, http://www.loc.gov/exhibits/naacp/the-new-negro-movement.html#skip_menu (accessed February 14, 2015); Locke, *The New Negro*; Culver, *The Frontier of Leisure*, 2, 6.
23. Foster, "In the Face of 'Jim Crow,'" 130; Chan, Daniels, Garcia, and Wilson, *People of Color in the American West*, v; Lipsitz, *How Racism Takes Place*, 51–70.

1. LEISURE AND THE CALIFORNIA DREAM

1. Prescript, the "Beautiful Southern California" title was featured with cover artwork showcasing a woman who probably represents Queen Califia, the mythical warrior queen for whom the state of California is named, and the scenic and agricultural landscape of the region. Facing readers, the woman stands to the right of the page. Queen Califia is a character in the novel *The Adventures of Esplandián* (1500) by Garci Rodríguez de Montalvo. The *Eagle* (later known as the *California Eagle*), December 5, 1908, 1, Mayme A. Clayton Library and Museum Collection.
2. Culver, *The Frontier of Leisure*, 2, (quotation) 3, 4, 6–7; Rawls and Bean, *California*, xiii, 15, 206–7; Starr, *California*, ix–xiv; McWilliams, *Southern California*, 143–50; Bowman, *Los Angeles*, 216–18, 224, 227, 247–50.
3. Bederman, *Manliness and Civilization*, 12–15, 83–85; Aron, *Working at Play*, 3–4, 8–9, 46–47, 70, 72–73, 79; Davis, *Class and Leisure at America's First Resort*.

4. Rawls and Bean, *California*, 206; McWilliams, *Southern California*, 143–50; Culver, *The Frontier of Leisure*, 6, 16, 17, 35–36, 50–51, (Lummis quotation) 83.
5. Culver, *The Frontier of Leisure*, 8, 26–27, 41–42, 52–53, 66–68, 83.
6. Feifer, *Tourism in History*, 167; Aron, *Working at Play*, 5; Culver, *The Frontier of Leisure*, 7; Rosenzweig, *Eight Hours for What We Will*, 68–69, offers an in-depth discussion of the changes occurring in popular leisure in society and industrial communities of the United States from the nineteenth to twentieth centuries.
7. Armstead, "*Lord, Please Don't Take Me in August*," 18–22; Salvini, *The Summer City by the Sea*; Gatewood, *Aristocrats of Color*, 7, 200–201, 248; Aron, *Working at Play*, 10, 184, 207, 238, 248; Lofguen, *On Holiday*, 109–10.
8. "Club House Movement Endorsed/Editorials," *CE*, April 24, 1924, (quotation) 22; Kahrl, "On the Beach," ix; LeFebvre, *The Production of Space*, 30–53. I gained good insights into development of my research methodology from reading several resort community and residential recreational leisure histories, including Corbett's *The Making of American Resorts*; Culver, *The Frontier of Leisure*; Kanfer, *A Summer World*; Kahrl, *The Land Was Ours*; Phelts, *An American Beach for African Americans*; Walker and Wilson, *Black Eden*; Railton, *African Americans on Martha's Vineyard*; Stephens, *Idlewild*; Sorin and Rehl, *Honorable Work*; Bush, *White Sand Black Beach*; and Vickers and Wilson-Graham, *Remembering Paradise Park*.
9. Corbett, *The Making of American Resorts*, 3.
10. Such exclusionary customs and laws of maintaining racial restrictions were weakened by U.S. Supreme and California Court decisions between 1948 and 1968. It would not be until the U.S. Supreme Court decisions *Shelley v. Kraemer (1948)* and *Barrows v. Jackson (1953)* that the judicial enforcement of racially restrictive real estate covenants would be overturned and effectively abolished. These were the first of several legal victories toward the total abolition of all legal and vigilante racial restrictions and discrimination in housing, education, employment, and even recreation facilities. By the 1960s, at least on paper, the combined effect of *Kraemer* and *Barrows*, along with additional federal enforcement efforts—the U.S. Supreme Court decision *Brown v. Board of Education of Topeka* of 1954, the Civil Rights Act of 1964, the Voting Rights Act of 1965, and Title VIII of the Civil Rights Act of 1968—prohibited most forms of discrimination based on race, color, religion, or national origin. DeGraaf and Taylor, "Introduction," in *Seeking El Dorado*, 20; Bunch, "The Greatest State for the Negro," in *Seeking El Dorado*, 138; DeGraaf, "African American Suburbanization in California, 1960 through 1990," in *Seeking El Dorado*, 336–37, 415; Sides, *L.A. City Limits*, 100; Flamming, *Bound for Freedom*, 351, 367, 369, 373; Culver, *The Frontier of Leisure*, 66–74; Eleanor M. Ramsey & Janice S. Lewis, "Black Americans in California," *Five Views: An Ethnic Historic Site Survey of California*, California Department of Park & Recreation, Office of Historic Preservation, December 1988, http://www

.nps.gov/parkhistory/online_books/5views/5views2.htm (accessed September 25, 2015).

11. In Los Angeles, from the beginnings of the modern African American community in the 1890s, racial discrimination was present in housing, employment, and society. But the situation was complicated in that African American individuals and families did not share the same experiences in their obstacles to racial equality, because in their interactions with whites, some did not support racial discrimination, while others did. Additionally, racial discrimination by whites toward individuals and families in other communities of color groups had a similarly complicated situation with varying nuisances depending on the group; see Flamming, *Bound for Freedom*, chapter 2, for more on the improvement and decline of racial conditions and the blurriness of the color line in the sprawling, multiracial city of Los Angeles up to the 1940s and 1950s. Flamming, *African Americans in the West*, 12; Vivian, *The Story of the Negro in Los Angeles County 1936*, 32–33; Flamming, *Bound for Freedom*, 36; DeGraaf, "The City of Black Angels," 343; Broussard, "African Americans in the West," 5; Gregory, *The Southern Diaspora*; Starr, *Material Dreams*, 148–50.

12. From 1920 to 1940 California citizens grew from 3,833,661 to 12,206,849, and African American residents grew from 38,763 to 124,306. By 1950 the state's population grew by 30%, to reach 44,183,643, with African American citizenship increasing to 462,172. DeGraaf and Taylor, "Introduction," in *Seeking El Dorado*, 22, 27, 33; U.S. Census; DeGraaf, "The City of Black Angels," 232–324.

13. Even before 1915 the black Angeleno community was dispersed in several sections of the city of Los Angeles, where they were able to purchase land in less desirable areas. They resided in the northwest section of the city along West Temple Street, the northeast section in Boyle Heights, and the Furlong Tract in the southeast corner of the city. They also took up residence in an area west of the University of Southern California along Jefferson Boulevard between Normandie and Western Avenues, as well as on quite a few streets in the area south of First Street and Central Avenue. The early commercial districts servicing African Americans were in the area of First and Second Streets, near Los Angeles and San Pedro Streets in the central core of the city. A few miles south of the city's southern border there was also a black community in the incorporated city of Watts (which would be annexed to the city of Los Angeles in 1926). Bond's sociology dissertation (1936) is the earliest scholarly work on the beginnings of the modern African American community in Los Angeles: Bond, "The Negro in Los Angeles," 48, 67–69. DeGraaf, "The City of Black Angels," 323–24, 326n13, 328, 330–33; Taylor, *In Search of the Racial Frontier*, 19, 22; DeGraaf and Taylor, "Introduction," in *Seeking El Dorado*, 21–22; Flamming, *Bound for Freedom*, 66–67, 92–93, 308.

14. Flamming, *Bound for Freedom*, 8, 45–47, (quotation) 49, 367; Gregory, *The Southern Diaspora*, 1–79, 237–82; Wilkerson, *The Warmth of Other Suns*, 233.

15. Flamming, *Bound for Freedom*, 8, 45–47, 49, 367; Wilkerson, *The Warmth of Other Suns*, 233; DeGraaf, "The City of Black Angels," 330, (quotation) 331, 332; Sugrue, *Sweet Land of Liberty*, 3–58. For more on black Angeleno employment in the early decades of the twentieth century, see Johnson, "Industrial Survey of the Negro population of Los Angeles, California"; Charles Johnson, "Negro Workers in Los Angeles Industries," *Opportunity*, August 1928, 234–40; Vivian, *The Story of the Negro in Los Angeles County*. Washington DC: Federal Writers' Project of the Works Progress Administration, 1936, 33, 35.
16. Robert and Winnie Owens and Bridget "Biddy" Mason's families and their descendants are early, exceptional examples of African Americans who acquired substantial real estate holdings and became key leaders of the African American community of greater Los Angeles in the late nineteenth and early decades of the twentieth centuries. Flamming, *Bound for Freedom*, 8, 81; Sides, *L.A. City Limits*, 34; DeGraaf, "The City of Black Angels," 332–33, 341.
17. Flamming, *Bound for Freedom*, 35, 44; Kevin Mulroy, "Preface," in *Seeking El Dorado*, xi; Gregory, *Black Corona*, 5–6, 9–10; Foster, "In the Face of 'Jim Crow,'" 130; Dowden-White, *Groping toward Democracy*, 4, 19; Baldwin, *Chicago's New Negroes*, 5, 13, 19; Adams, "My Old Kentucky Home," 389, 402.
18. Aron, *Working at Play*, 131, 135; Slaton, Randl, and Van Demme, *Preserve and Play*, xiii.

2. REMEMBERING BRUCE'S BEACH

1. My discussion of contemporary white identity, absolution from complicity in and benefit from past societal racism, and the inability to recognize that "moral" white people can be racist is informed by scholarship from DiAngelo, "White Fragility," 54–74; Rymer, *American Beach*, 70–72.
2. Kahrl, "On the Beach," ix.
3. My discussion of collective memory in this paragraph is informed by scholars Paul Connerton and Martita Sturken—from Connerton, his ideas about the importance of the practice of historical reconstruction as a guide and shaper of the memory of social groups, about communal memory production being formed through more or less informally told narrative histories, and individual interconnecting sets of narratives as the story of groups from which individuals derive their identity (*How Societies Remember*, 14, 17, 21), and, from Sturken, her ideas about memory as a provider of individual and cultural identity that gives a sense of importance to the past and to understanding of a culture because it indicates collective desires, needs, and self-definitions (*Tangled Memories*, 1–2). See also Hayden, *The Power of Place*, 7–9, 12–13, 52, 61; DeGraaf and Taylor, "Introduction," in *Seeking El Dorado*, 27.
4. Aron, *Working at Play*, 131, 135; Slaton et al., *Preserve and Play*, xiii; Foster, "In the Face of 'Jim Crow,'" 130.

5. 1900 and 1920 U.S. Census; Jules Tygiel, "Introduction," in *Metropolis in the Making*, 7; DeGraaf, "The City of Black Angels," 333; McWilliams, *Southern California*, xii, 134; Bond, "The Negro in Los Angeles," 129.
6. Grenier, *Manhattan Beach*, 1–3.
7. Grenier, *Manhattan Beach*, 2.
8. Grenier, *Manhattan Beach*, 5, 8; "The History of Manhattan Beach: Earliest History," Manhattan Beach Public Library, Historical Document Files, 8; Cecilia Rasmussen, "City Smart," *LAT*, November 29, 1996, 2.
9. "The Growth and Progress of the City of Manhattan Beach," Manhattan Beach Public Library, n.d.
10. "The Growth and Progress of the City of Manhattan Beach," Manhattan Beach Public Library, n.d.; "The History of Manhattan Beach: Earliest History," 9; Rasmussen, "City Smart," 2; Manhattan Beach QuickFacts from the U.S. Census, 2018, https://www.census.gov/quickfacts/fact/table/manhattanbeachcitycalifornia/PST045217 (accessed July 5, 2018). The family of Judge Joyce Karlin and William Fahey (also a lawyer and later a jurist) reside in Manhattan Beach. Karlin was the California Superior Court judge in the controversial 1991 voluntary manslaughter case involving the murder of an African American, fifteen-year old Latasha Harlins, in which she gave a light sentencing to the shooter, Korean shop owner Soon Ja Du. This case and the aftermath of the Rodney King beating case decision were underpinnings of the spring 1992 Los Angeles uprising and the traumas of inequity in the modern United States. Karlin served as a Superior Court judge for five years. Using the surname of her husband, William Fahey, she was later elected to the Manhattan Beach City Council, where she served a rotation as mayor for two terms, per the system used by this city (1999–2007). Described later in this chapter, Joyce (Karlin) Fahey was a City Council member when the efforts to commemorate Manhattan Beach's African American pioneers occurred. For information on Joyce (Karlin) Fahey, the decedent, the defendant, the account of the 1991 case, and its aftermath, see Stevenson, *The Contested Murder of Latasha Harlins*.
11. John S. M'Goarty, "The Emancipated," *LAT*, February 12, 1909, section 3, 1; DeGraaf, "The City of Angels," 341–42; Flamming, *Bound for Freedom*, 8, 70–78; Sides, *L.A. City Limits*, 23–26.
12. E. L. Chew, "Educational Progress of Negro in College and School of Land is Remarkable," *LAT*, February 12, 1909, III-5.
13. "Negroes Who Have Won Place or Fortune in Los Angeles and Pasadena," February 12, 1909, *LAT*, III-6; M'Goarty, *LAT*, February 12, 1909, III-1.
14. In 1909 in Los Angeles the average home building would have been valued at less than $2,000. Chew, *LAT*, February 12, 1909, III-5.
15. In 1916, depending on the proximity to the oceanfront, lots were ranging for sale between $200 (farthest from the ocean) to $450 (nearest the ocean); *Manhattan*

Beach: 80-Year Anniversary, 1993, 9. We owe a debt to Robert L. Brigham, who might be called a "memory activist," for his 1956 master's thesis. Telephone interview with the author, November 7, 2004, Los Angeles; Brigham, "Landownership and Occupancy by Negroes In Manhattan Beach," 15, 17, 21, 24; "Colored People's Resort Meets with Opposition," *LAT*, June 27, 1912, section 1, 15; "Manhattan Beach Dons New Municipal Togs," *LAT*, November 27, 1912, II10.

16. The Bruce family's 1910 residence was near the Los Angeles River, north of what is the 10 Freeway today. 1900, 1910, 1920, and 1930 U.S. Census; "Colored People's Resort Meets With Opposition," *LAT*, June 27, 1912, I15.
17. Brigham, "Landownership and Occupancy by Negroes in Manhattan Beach," 17–18.
18. "Colored People's Resort Meets with Opposition," *LAT*, June 27, 1912, I15.
19. "Colored People's Resort Meets with Opposition," *LAT*, June 27, 1912, I15.
20. "Colored People's Resort Meets with Opposition," *LAT*, June 27, 1912, I15.
21. Dennis, *A Walk Beside the Sea*, 105, 108; Brigham, "Landownership and Occupancy by Negroes in Manhattan Beach," 17, 18; Ivan J. Houston, Los Angeles resident and retired head of Golden State Mutual Life Insurance Co., telephone interview with the author, October 27, 2004, Los Angeles.
22. Brigham, "Landownership and Occupancy by Negroes in Manhattan Beach," 21, 25, 35.
23. Brigham, "Landownership and Occupancy by Negroes in Manhattan Beach," 24–26, 63; Glasrud and Searles, *Buffalo Soldiers in the West*, 74–78, 81. In Los Angeles, the residence of Major Prioleau and his wife was in a neighborhood where African Americans were able to purchase property early in the twentieth century, a mile or so west of the University of Southern California. "Chaplain Prioleau Crosses Great Divide," *CE*, July 22, 1927, 1; "Major Prioleau, Aged Army Chaplain, Buried With Honor," *PD*, July 21, 1927, 1.
24. Brigham, "Landownership and Occupancy by Negroes in Manhattan Beach," 25; Edward C. Atkinson II, grandson of Mary Sanders, interview with the author, November 21, 2009, Los Angeles, California.
25. Harold Peace, grandson of John McCaskill, interview with the author, November 21, 2009, Los Angeles, California.
26. Brigham, "Landownership and Occupancy by Negroes in Manhattan Beach," 78; Anne Bradford Luke, Manhattan Beach and Los Angeles property owner, interview with the author, October 30, 2009, Los Angeles, California.
27. Brigham, "Landownership and Occupancy by Negroes in Manhattan Beach," 43–44; Dennis, *A Walk Beside the Sea*, 108; From 1893 to 1923 California statutes and legislation were instituted extending to "all citizens within the jurisdiction of this State . . . the full and equal accommodations, advantages, facilities, and privileges of inns, restaurants, hotels, eating-houses, barber-shops, bath-houses, theaters, skating-rinks, and all other places of public accommodation or amusement,

subject only to the conditions and limitations established by law and applicable alike to all citizens." Gleaves, "Civil Rights," 563–64; Klein, "The California Equal Rights Statutes in Practice," 253–73.

28. Brigham, "Landownership and Occupancy by Negroes in Manhattan Beach," 40–41; Dennis, *A Walk Beside the Sea*, 108; "Colored Family's Home Twice Visited by Fire," unidentified newspaper, December 3, 1926, Manhattan Beach Historical Society Collection.
29. Brigham, "Landownership and Occupancy by Negroes in Manhattan Beach," 41–42.
30. Brigham, "Landownership and Occupancy by Negroes in Manhattan Beach," 36, 38–39, 82; Minutes of Meeting, Trustees, City of Manhattan Beach (CMB), June 19, 1924; "Important Ordinances at Trustees Meeting," *Manhattan Beach News*, June 6, 1924, Manhattan Beach Historical Society.
31. *Manhattan Beach News*, June 6, 1924; Minutes of Meeting, Trustees, June 19, 1924; Brigham, "Landownership and Occupancy by Negroes in Manhattan Beach," 39, 39n10, 41, 82, 85; "Oustings in Terrorizing Plot Loom," *LAT*, February 16, 1928, A-14; Jackson, *The Ku Klux Klan*, 189.
32. Brigham, "Landownership and Occupancy by Negroes in Manhattan Beach," 44–50, 58–59.
33. Cady, "Southern California," 194–99, 226–28; "Klans Operations," *CE*, July 4, 1924, 1.
34. "Klans Operations," *CE*, July 4, 1924, 1.
35. Brigham, "Landownership and Occupancy by Negroes in Manhattan Beach," 44–50, 58–59; Answer of Milton B. Johnson and Anna E. Johnson, *City of Manhattan Beach v. B. H. Dyer, B. L. Rice et al.*, 1924, Los Angeles County Archives.
36. See endnote 27 of this chapter for information on California statutes and legislation regarding civil rights and public space in the 1920s; Cady, "Southern California," 194–99; Brigham, "Landownership and Occupancy by Negroes in Manhattan Beach," 31–34, 44–47, 86; Dennis, *A Walk Beside the Sea*, 108; "Beach Suit Depending on Voters: Continuance Granted Until After Election, as Changes May Settle Issue," *LAT*, January 30, 1925; Culver, *The Frontier of Leisure*, 70.
37. Brigham, "Landownership and Occupancy by Negroes in Manhattan Beach," 33; Culver, *The Frontier of Leisure*, 70.
38. Culver, *The Frontier of Leisure*, 66–68.
39. "Negro Bathers Outraged at Manhattan Beach," *CE*, August 5, 1927; "Dr. Hudson, Three Companions Receive Fines in Trail at Manhattan Beach," *PD*, August 4, 1927, 1, in NAACP Branch Files, Los Angeles, California, 1913–39, University of California, Los Angeles, Library Special Collections; Brigham, 85.
40. "Attempt to Bulldose Negro Bathers," *CE*, June 10, 1927; "Negro Bathers," *CE*, August 5, 1927.
41. Brigham, "Landownership and Occupancy by Negroes In Manhattan Beach," 84; "Negro Bathers," *CE*, August 5, 1927.

42. Brigham, "Landownership and Occupancy by Negroes in Manhattan Beach," 84; "Negro Bathers," *CE*, August 5, 1927; 1920 and 1940 U.S. Census; Wolcott, *Race, Riots, and Roller Coasters*, 3–5.
43. "Negro Bathers," *CE*, August 5, 1927.
44. "Negro Bathers," *CE*, August 5, 1927; H. Claude Hudson Oral History, interview with Lawrence B. DeGraaf, January 10 and April 18, 1967, Center for Oral and Public History, California State University, Fullerton Collection; Brigham, "Landownership and Occupancy by Negroes in Manhattan Beach," 84–99; Flamming, *Bound for Freedom*, 271–72; Beasley, *The Negro Trail Blazers of California*, 212, 241–42; Sadie Chandler-Cole in *L.A. Negro Directory and Who's Who, 1930–1931*; 1910 U.S. Census; 1915 Los Angeles City Directory.
45. "Negro Bathers," *CE*, August 5, 1927; Brigham, "Landownership and Occupancy by Negroes in Manhattan Beach," 84–99; Beasley, *The Negro Trail Blazers of California*, 212, 241–42; Flamming, *Bound for Freedom*, 275.
46. "Negro Bathers," *CE*, August 5, 1927, 1, 6; "Dr. Hudson, Three Companions Receive Fines in Trail at Manhattan Beach," *PD*, August 4, 1927, 1; "Manhattan Beach Throws Open Beach Frontage to the Public," *PD*, August 18, 1927, 1; Hudson to Pickens letter, August 4, 1927, NAACP Branch Files, Los Angeles, California, 1913–39; "NAACP Wins Beach Victory," *CE*, August 19, 1927, 1; Flamming, *Bound for Freedom*, 274; Brigham, "Landownership and Occupancy by Negroes in Manhattan Beach," 84–99.
47. "Negro Bathers," *CE*, August 5, 1927, 1; "Dr. Hudson, Three Companions Receive Fines in Trail at Manhattan Beach," *PD*, August 4, 1927, 1; "Manhattan Beach Throws Open Beach Frontage to the Public," *PD*, August 18, 1927, 1; "Los Angeles NAACP Wins Against Bathing Beach Segregation," NAACP press release, August 20, 1927, NAACP Branch Files, Los Angeles, California, 1913–39; "Manhattan's Fine Example," *LAT*, August 16, 1927, A4; "NAACP Wins Beach Victory," *CE*, August 19, 1927, 1; Brigham, "Landownership and Occupancy by Negroes in Manhattan Beach," 84–99; Flamming, *Bound for Freedom*, 274–75.
48. Kahrl, "On the Beach," ix–x; Wolcott, *Race, Riots, and Roller Coasters*, 4–8; "Civil Rights in America Theme Study: Racial Desegregation of Public Accommodations," National Parks Service, U.S. Department of the Interior, https://www.nps.gov/nhl/learn/themes/civilrights_desegpublicaccom.pdf (accessed July 5, 2018).
49. Brigham, "Landownership and Occupancy by Negroes in Manhattan Beach," 58–59; Dennis, *A Walk Beside the Sea*, 109; Paul Silva, "The Secret of Parque Culiacan: History of North End Park Reveals Troubled Race Relations," *BR*, April 16, 1987.
50. Brigham, "Landownership and Occupancy by Negroes in Manhattan Beach," 77; Atkinson interview, November 21, 2009.
51. Brigham, "Landownership and Occupancy by Negroes in Manhattan Beach," 77–78; As it relates to the restrictive covenant on the new lot, it is not clear from

currently available research sources why Mrs. Prioleau and Leslie King were not aware of the racial sales restrictions when they purchased the lot to house their moved duplex, or how they learned of it.

52. Brigham, "Landownership and Occupancy by Negroes in Manhattan Beach," 60, 78; "Ousting in Terrorizing Plot Loom, Keyes May Act against Beach City Officials in Attacks on Negroes," *LAT*, February 16, 1928, A14.
53. Brigham, "Landownership and Occupancy by Negroes in Manhattan Beach," 82; "Ousting In Terrorizing Plot Loom," *LAT*, February 16, 1928, A14.
54. Luke interview, October 30, 2009.
55. Luke interview, October 30, 2009.
56. Luke interview, October 30, 2009.
57. Luke interview, October 30, 2009.
58. Correspondence between Frank L. Perry and the CMB, May 10, 1937, and August 18, 1937, Sandra Seville-Jones Personal Files (SSJPF); Council Meeting Minutes, CMB, March 4, 1948, SSJPF; correspondence between Richard G. Thompson, Hermosa Realty Company and City Clerk, CMB, March 5, 1948.
59. Minutes of the City Council, CMB, January 18, 1955, SSJPF.
60. "Park Development of Manhattan's 27th St. Property 'Too Expensive,'" *SBDB*, January 12, 1955; "Manhattan Park to Blossom on Weedy Land Near Ocean," *SBDB*, December 14, 1956; City Council Resolution Number 2353, CMB, 1962.
61. Minutes of the City Council, CMB, February 19, 1974; Mary Lynn Swenson, "Parque Culiacan: A Smoldering History," *ERN*, February 17, 1977.
62. Final Report of the Leadership Manhattan Beach Class of 2003, on the Rename Parque Culiacan Contest, SSJPF, the Leadership Manhattan Beach Class of 2003 Project (LMBC 2003), November 2009; Presentation of the Leadership Manhattan Beach Class of 2003, Staff Report, CMB, April 15, 2003; Leadership Manhattan Beach, www.leadershipmb.org (accessed November 2009); Cindy Yoshiyama, "City to Find Out What's in a Name," *BEACH REPORTER*, April 3, 2003; City of Manhattan Beach, Sister City Program, http://www.mbsistercity.org/ (accessed April 29, 2015).
63. "Renaming of Parque Culiacan Position Paper," SSJPF, LMBC 2003 Project, November 2009; Jerry Roberts, "Contest Set to Rename Parque Culiacan," *ERN*, February 27, 2003.
64. Final Report of the LMBC 2003, SSJPF; Staff Report, CMB, April 15, 2003; Yoshiyama, *BR*, April 3, 2003.
65. Roberts, "Contest Set to Rename Parque Culiacan"; Jerry Roberts, "Culiacan: Same Is the Name of the Game," *ERN*, April 24, 2003; Yoshiyama, *BR*, April 3, 2003.
66. A full list of the proposed new names for the park site are included in the Final Report of the LMBC 2003, SSJPF.
67. Minutes of the City Council, CMB, April 15, 2003; Manhattan Beach City Council Members in 2003 included Jim Aldinger, Joyce (Karlin) Fahey, Mayor Steven

Napolitano, Mitch Ward, and Linda Wilson; Roberts, *ERN*, February 27, 2003; Dennis Johnson, "Context May Plant New Name on Park," *DB*, March 18, 2003; Yoshiyama, *BR*, April 3, 2003.

68. Minutes of the City Council, April 15, 2003; Minutes of the Parks and Recreation Commission, CMB, February 27, 2006.
69. Minutes of the Parks and Recreation Commission, February 27, 2006.
70. Manhattan Beach QuickFacts from the U.S. Census, 2018, https://www.census.gov/quickfacts/fact/table/manhattanbeachcitycalifornia/PST045217 (accessed July 5, 2018). The Manhattan Beach City Council is comprised of five members, each serving a nine-month mayoral position during their four-year term; http://www.citymb.info/city-officials/city-council (accessed March 23, 2015). In 2010 Ward was also a candidate in an election to represent the California State 53rd Assembly District; "Mitch Ward, A Mayor for the Assembly," http://digital.library.ucla.edu/websites/2010_997_217/about.html (accessed March 23, 2015); Nick Green, "Candidate Profile: MB Mayor Mitch Ward Stresses Local Interests in 53rd Assembly Bid," *DB*, May 22, 2010.
71. Minutes of the Parks and Recreation Commission, CMB, February 27, 2006; Rosa Louise Parks [1913–2010] was nationally recognized as the mother of the modern day civil rights movement in the United States. Her refusal to surrender her seat to a white male passenger on a bus in Montgomery, Alabama, on December 1, 1955, triggered a wave of protest on December 5, 1955, that reverberated throughout the United States. Her courageous act broadcasted all over television and other media changed the country and its view of black people and redirected the course of history. "Rosa Parks," http://www.rosaparks.org/biography/ (accessed March 25, 2015).
72. My discussion here of collective memory, representation, selective remembrance, forgetting, and silences is informed by examination of these themes by Marita Sturken in *Tangled Memories* (1997); and Michel-Rolph Trouillot in *Silencing the Past* (1995). Cynthia Dizikes, "Culiacan Keeps Name, MB's Past Racism Revised," *ERN*, March 2, 2006; Minutes of the Parks and Recreation Commission, CMB, February 27, 2006.
73. Minutes of the Parks and Recreation Commission, February 27, 2006.
74. Minutes of Parks and Recreation Commission, February 27, 2006.
75. Minutes of the Parks and Recreation Commission, February 27, 2006.
76. Minutes of the City Council, CMB, March 21, 2006, and April 18, 2006.
77. Robert Garcia, Esq., director, the City Project (formerly the Center for Law in the Public Interest), interview with the author, March 22, 2014, Los Angeles, California; correspondence of Robert Garcia (Center for Law in the Public Interest/renamed to the City Project in the fall of 2006) and Mitch Ward (mayor, City of Manhattan Beach), March 21, 2006; letter from Robert Garcia, executive director, and Andrea Luquetta, law fellow, Center for Law in the Public Interest

(CLIPI) to the Honorable Mitch Ward, Manhattan Beach City Council Member, dated September 5, 2006. Los Angeles–based CLIPI (the City Project) engages in advocacy and litigation on a broad range of issues including parks and recreation access for underrepresented communities. Center for Law in the Public Interest, www.clipi.org (accessed May 10, 2010). Bruce's Beach, the City Project, http://www.cityprojectca.org/ourwork/brucesbeach.html (accessed March 25, 2015).

78. Deepa Bharath, "Name Change to Fit Park's Past Weighed," *DB*, May 15, 2006.
79. Bharath, "Name Change to Fit Park's Past Weighed"; Minutes of the Parks and Recreation Commission Meeting, February 27, 2006.
80. The park names for consideration are represented as listed in the Minutes of Parks and Recreation Commission Meeting, CMB, May 22, 2006. Deepa Bharath, "Parque Culiacan Renaming Endorsed," *DB*, May 24, 2006; Minutes of the City Council Meeting, CMB, May 16, 2006.
81. Glassberg, *Sense of History*, 19.
82. Dizikes, "Commission Recommends Changing Parque Culiacan to Bruce's Beach," *ERN*, May 25, 2006; Parks and Recreation Commission Meeting, May 22, 2006; Bharath, "Parque Culiacan Renaming Endorsed."
83. Shackel, *Memory in Black and White*, 198.
84. *Mea culpa* is a Latin phase for acknowledgement of a personal error or fault. Minutes of Parks and Recreation Commission Meeting, May 22, 2006; Bharath, "Parque Culiacan Renaming Endorsed"; Dizikes, "Commission Recommends Changing Parque Culiacan to Bruce's Beach."
85. Brigham, "Landownership and Occupancy by Negroes in Manhattan Beach," 44, 73, 96–98; Culver, *The Frontier of Leisure*, 67–68, 70.
86. Parks and Recreation Commission Meeting, May 22, 2006; Deepa Bharath, "Parque Culiacan Renaming Endorsed"; Dizikes, "Commission Recommends Changing Parque Culiacan to Bruce's Beach"; "What's in the Name?," *TBR*, May 25, 2006. 2003 City Council Members: Linda Wilson, Joyce (Karlin) Fahey, Mitch Ward, Jim Aldinger, and Mayor Steven Napolitano, Minutes of the City Council Meeting, CMB, April 15, 2003. 2006 City Council Members: Joyce (Karlin) Fahey, Nick Tell, Mayor Mitch Ward, Jim Aldinger, and Richard Montgomery, Minutes of the City Council Meeting, CMB, July 5, 2006. The author spoke in favor of the park name change to Bruce's Beach at the Manhattan Beach City Council meeting on July 5, 2006. At the time of the 2006 Manhattan Beach park renaming action, the author was a graduate student working toward earning a master's degree in historic conservation at the University of Southern California.
87. Recreation Services manager Idris Al-Oboudi evaded answering a question about whether additional research was done to learn more about the Bruce family by indicating staff reviewed the documents obtained from various sources. Video of the City Council Meeting, CMB, July 5, 2006, http://www.ci.manhattan-beach.ca

.us/Index.aspx?page=1804 (accessed May 1, 2010; Minutes of the City Council Meeting, CMB, July 5, 2006; Michelle Murphy, "Park and Recreation Commission Recommends Changing Park Name," *MBO*, June 2006, 6.

88. Video of the City Council Meeting, CMB, July 5 2006.
89. Video of the City Council Meeting, CMB, July 5, 2006; Kristin S. Agostoni, "Council Votes to Change Manhattan Beach Park Name to Reflect Community's History," *DB*, July 7, 2006; Minutes of the City Council Meeting, July 5, 2006.
90. Video of the City Council Meeting, July 5, 2006; Agostoni, "Council Votes to Change Manhattan Beach Park Name to Reflect Community's History"; Michelle Murphy, "City Council Renames Park Bruce's Beach," *MBO*, July 2006, 8; Dawnya Pring, "Parque Culiacan to be Renamed Bruce's Beach," *TBR*, July 7, 2006; Lisa McDivitt, "A Park by Any Other Name, Manhattan Beach Contemplates a New Name for Culiacan Park, Triggering a Debate on How Best to Recognize the City's Black History," *ERD*, July 13, 2006.
91. Video of the City Council Meeting, July 5, 2006; Pring, "Parque Culiacan to be Renamed Bruce's Beach"; Murphy, "City Council Renames Park Bruce's Beach"; McDivitt, "A Park by Any Other Name"; Agostoni, "Council Votes to Change Manhattan Beach Park Name to Reflect Community's History," *DB*, July 7, 2006.
92. Agostoni, "Council Votes to Change Manhattan Beach Park Name to Reflect Community's History"; Jacobson, *Whiteness of a Different Color*, 18; Video of the City Council Meeting, July 5, 2006; McDivitt, "A Park by Any Other Name."
93. Video of the City Council Meeting, July 5, 2006; Pring, "Parque Culiacan to be Renamed Bruce's Beach."
94. Video of the City Council Meeting, July 5, 2006; McDivitt, "A Park by Any Other Name." The hate of the past is still not far away in the twenty-first century. In 2015 a Manhattan Beach African American family's home was set on fire in the middle of the night when someone place an ignited gasoline-soaked rubber tire at their front door. At the time the family had lived in this community for eleven years. This event was the culminating act of several previous incidents, which made the family think the firebomb was a hate crime. Although the police were hesitant to label what happened to this family in this way, others in the community who were people of color also viewed this arson attack as a hate crime, due to their own unpleasant experiences in Manhattan Beach. The African American family chose to remain in Manhattan Beach after the incident and, at the writing of this book, the police have not solved the case. Joseph Serna, "Manhattan Beach Family Believes Suspicious Fire Was a Hate Crime," *LAT*, February 6, 2015; Malissa Clinton, "Why I Stayed After My House Was Firebombed," TEDx Talk, Manhattan Beach, December 9, 2016, https://www.youtube.com/watch?v=b5FawlfSdGU (accessed July 5, 2018); Ryan McDonald, "Staying Power: Manhattan Beach's Malissa Clinton Finds Strength in Spirit of Community," *ERN*, February 9, 2017.

95. McDivitt, "A Park by Any Other Name," *ERD*, July 13, 2006; As a resident of Manhattan Beach since 1965, Myron Puller offered that he knew nothing about the history being discussed until recently. Video of the City Council Meeting, July 5, 2006; Murphy, "City Council Renames Park Bruce's Beach"; Weyeneth, "History, Memory, and Apology," 32.
96. Weyeneth, "History, Memory, and Apology," 14–15, 24, 31, 35–36.
97. Murphy, "City Council Renames Park Bruce's Beach"; Video of the City Council Meeting, July 5, 2006; McDivitt, "A Park by Any Other Name."
98. Video of the City Council Meeting, July 5, 2006; Pring, "Parque Culiacan to be Renamed Bruce's Beach"; Murphy, "City Council Renames Park Bruce's Beach," 15; McDivitt, "A Park by Any Other Name."
99. Murphy, "City Council Renames Park Bruce's Beach," 15; Video of the City Council Meeting, July 5, 2006; Minutes of the City Council Meeting, July 5, 2006.
100. "Letters," *ER*, Thursday, July 20, 2006.
101. Minutes of the City Council Meeting, November 8, 2006; Minutes of the City Council Meeting, December 5, 2006.
102. Video of the City Council Meeting, CMB, December 5, 2006, http://www.ci.manhattan-beach.ca.us/Index.aspx?page=1804 (accessed May 9, 2010); Minutes of the City Council Meeting, December 5, 2006.
103. Minutes of the City Council Meeting, December 5, 2006; Video of the City Council Meeting, December 5, 2006.
104. Linenthal, "Epilogue," in *Slavery and Public History: The Tough Stuff of American Memory*, 213–15.
105. The author reviewed records in the County of Los Angeles Assessor's Map Books and Registrar-Recorder and U.S. Census to determine the ownership and ethnicity of the property owners who sold the parcels to Willa Bruce.
106. Shackel, *Memory in Black and White*, 198–99, 209; Linenthal, "Epilogue," 224.

3. SANTA MONICA'S OCEAN PARK

1. Ivan J. Houston is one of the sons of Norman O. Houston, a founder of the Golden State Mutual Life Insurance Company, who will be discussed later in this chapter. Ivan J. Houston also remembered, from childhood, his mother fondly speaking about Bruce's Beach. Ivan J. Houston, Los Angeles resident and former head of Golden State Mutual Life Insurance, telephone interview with the author, November 2004, Los Angeles, California.
2. "Colored People's Resort Meets With Opposition," *LAT*, June 27, 1912, I-15; "Don't Want Picnics," *DO*, June 24, 1914, 1; Flamming, *Bound for Freedom*, 274; Cady, "Southern California," 198–99; "Swimming Pool Suit Dismissed, Negroes Advised to Seek Injunction Against Rule for Colored Bathers," *LAT*, October 17, 1922, A5; Culver, *The Frontier of Leisure*, 66–74; For more on exclusionary customs

of maintaining racial restrictions and California civil rights laws, see chapter 1, note 10, and chapter 2, note 27.

3. Cathy Naro, "A Page from History, How Green Was My Valley: Southland African Americans Remember Hayrides and Golf Games in Val Verde," *Westways*, February 1995, 71.
4. Historic District Application for Third Street Neighborhood in Ocean Park, Santa Monica, California, prepared by the Third Street Neighbors, 1990, vol. 2, 11; Ingersoll, *Ingersoll's Century History*, 8–93.
5. Wolf and Mader, *Santa Monica*, 14; Scott, *Santa Monica*, 24–27, 32–34; Historic District Application for Third Street Neighborhood, vol. 2, 22; Ingersoll, *Ingersoll's Century History*, 252.
6. City of Santa Monica, "Historic Preservation Element, Final Draft," prepared by PCR Services and Historic Resources Group, December 2001, 11–12; Wolf and Mader, *Santa Monica*, 42–43; Scott, *Santa Monica*, 35–46; Ingersoll, *Ingersoll's Century History*, 128–30, 142–45, 157–59; Basten, *Paradise by the Sea*, 24.
7. Nina Fresco, "Ocean Park in Santa Monica . . . and that other Ocean Park (Venice, California)," March 10, 2018, unpublished paper; Historic District Application for Third Street Neighborhood, vol. 2, 21–22; Wolf and Mader, *Santa Monica*, 33; Ingersoll, *Ingersoll's Century History*, 185–209, 211–43, 244–63, 317–25.
8. Patterned after the Venetian canals and buildings of its Italian namesake, the Venice community was originally an unincorporated area of Los Angeles County, which was referred to first as Ocean Park. This area almost became part of Santa Monica's Ocean Park district. After the population grew and surrounding housing tracts to the Venice-of-America were annexed, the community changed its name to Venice in 1911 and then became part of the city of Los Angeles in 1925. In many earlier published reports, there has been some confusion about the origins of Santa Monica's Ocean Park and Los Angeles's Venice communities, which Santa Monica's former Landmarks Commissioner Nina Fresco has helped to clear up with her research paper. The public can request a copy of the document for review from the city's Planning and Community Department. Fresco, "Ocean Park in Santa Monica," unpublished paper; Historic District Application for Third Street Neighborhood, vol. 2, 27–30; Ingersoll, *Ingersoll's Century History*, 211–43, 245–63; Basten, *Paradise by the Sea*, 52, 59; Scott, *Santa Monica*, 64–65.
9. Historic District Application for Third Street Neighborhood, vol. 1, 3; Scott, *Santa Monica*, 50–53.
10. Scott, *Santa Monica*, 7, 47, 50–51; Nugent, *Into the West*, 212; Rawls and Bean, *California*, xiii. The Jim Crow laws and customs relegating African Americans to the status of second class citizens operated primarily, but not exclusively, in Southern and border states, between 1877 and the mid-1960s. Where segregation of the races was mandated, treatment and accommodations were usually

inferior for black Americans to those provided to white Americans, which led to the institutionalizing of many economic, educational, and social disadvantages.

11. Scott, *Santa Monica*, 7, 47, 50–51; Lakey, *The History of the C.M.E. Church*, 349; Historic District Application for Third Street Neighborhood, vol. 1, 3; City of Santa Monica, Historic Resources Inventory Sheet for Phillips Chapel, prepared by Leslie Heumann, 1992; Lungsford, *Looking at Santa Monica*, 39; 1890, 1900, 1910, 1920, and 1930 U.S. Census. As a result of this author's research, which made city officials aware of the site, Phillips Chapel CME Church was designated a City of Santa Monica landmark on October 10, 2005, by the Landmarks Commission and the City Council. A small plaque noting this fact was placed near the main entry to the church. The criterion for designation was based on the cultural significance of the site, rather than the building's architectural aesthetic. Phillips Chapel was remodeled in 1910 and the 1940s and continues to serves its congregation in contemporary times.
12. Farther north in Santa Monica, around Second to Sixth Streets, near Broadway, there was another neighborhood that included African Americans. This is where Calvary Baptist Church bought its first public meeting space from the white Seventh-day Adventists in the 1920s. As early as the 1920s African American families began to settle in the neighborhood between about Fourteenth and Twenty-fourth Streets, between Front Street (later Pico) and Santa Monica Boulevard. The First African Methodist Episcopal Church (of Santa Monica) also established its first meeting place in this neighborhood in 1921. Today the Calvary Baptist Church is located at Twentieth Street and Broadway in a building constructed in 1950, when Reverend Wilford P. Carter served as the congregation's spiritual leader. To the south of Ocean Park, the community of Venice also had a cluster neighborhood of African American families formed in the 1900s to 1910s. 1910, 1920, and 1930 U.S. Census; Robert L. Leake, "The History of Calvary Baptist Church," prepared for Calvary Baptist Church Men and Women's Day Program, October 28, 2001, Santa Monica, California.
13. Nancy Smith, "SM Blacks Develop Own Culture," *EO*, May 17, 1975, 8B, 10B; Russell Snyder, "Centenarian Generous Slice of Americana Revisited," *DB*, November 6, 1983, B1, B3; Scott, 55.
14. "Pioneer Barber Passed Away," *SMBO*, August 19, 1916, 1; The three younger members of the Hunt household were identified as being born in California in the U.S. Census. 1910 U.S. Census; *Santa Monica City Directory 1912*, 101.
15. Gordon's son, Walter L. Gordon Jr. (1899–2012), would grow up to be a professional pioneer and very successful attorney with his office on Central Avenue, for a time in the same building that housed the *California Eagle*, the oldest African American newspaper in Los Angeles. Walter L. Gordon, Esq., Collection, William Beverly Collection, University of California, Los Angeles Special Collections; *L.A. Negro Directory and Who's Who 1930–1931*, 79.

16. Santa Monica Historical Society, Oral History Program: interview with Donald Augusta Brunson, interviewed by Barbara Wurf, February 23, 1991, 1–5; Beasley, *The Negro Trail Blazers of California*, 303; 1920 U.S. Census; California Death Index.
17. Brunson interview by Wurf, 1–5; Marquez, *Santa Monica Beach*, 104, 108. Located in this area of the Brunson's homesite today are Santa Monica High School and the Civic Center complex.
18. Brunson interview by Wurf, 1–5; 1910 and 1920 U.S. Census. Theresa Edwards Trimble was a member of a family who had lived in Los Angeles for many years. Her first husband, the Rev. J. A. Trimble, was from Georgia. He had lived in Los Angeles for a time and then in Venice with his wife and children. A well-liked man and an appreciated speaker from the Baptist pulpit, he died quickly following a sudden illness at age forty in 1915. The Trimbles were some of the earliest African American property owners in Venice to erect one of the first homes and small buildings on Broadway Avenue where he and his wife accommodated beach visitors. No Title, columns 1 and 2, *CE*, February 13, 1915, 1; "Episodes: Notes From the Beaches," *CE*, March 28, 1914, 7.
19. Brunson interview by Wurf, 1–5.
20. Smith, *SMEO*, May 17, 1975, 8B; Snyder, *DB*, November 6, 1983, B1–3; U.S. Census.
21. Alexander, *Abbot Kinney's Venice-of-America*, vol. 1, 1–5, 215; John Tabor, Las Vegas resident and retired Venice, California, businessman, telephone interview with the author, April 2005, Los Angeles, California.
22. Alexander, *Abbot Kinney's Venice-of-America*, vol. 1, 1–5, 215; Following Charles A. E. Brunson's successful effort noted in this chapter to have an objectionable sign referencing African Americans removed from the Santa Monica Pier, Arthur L. Reese, as president of the NAACP, sent on August 12, 1918, a typed letter to the City of Santa Monica commissioners Berkeley, Carter, and Townsend, demanding that another discriminatory sign be removed from the merry-go-round on the Looff Pier, which operated under a city license. This sign read: "Colored people welcome on Monday evening after 9 o'clock." The letter noted "[not] only have the Negro citizens of Santa Monica . . . been insulted and humiliated [by] this objectionable sign, but [we] have information that Colored women and children have been refused the privilege of riding on this device." He goes on to state to the commissioners: "We know it is within the province of those refused to institute civil procedure, but we think the needs of justice would be served to a greater advantage if you gentlemen, our commissioners, would see to it that management in question realize that these signs are an outrage upon a class of Americans." He continued: "These signs were first displayed under the regime [1906–15] of Mayor [Thomas H.] Dudley. The latter, perceived this gross injustice to our people," and successfully ordered them removed. In the left margin of Reese's letter a handwritten message dated August 13, 1918, reads: "Sign to be Removed."

The Brunson and Reese efforts for social justice and civil rights in public accommodates indicates the persistence and vigilance that African Americans in this era had to sustain to have their citizenship rights recognized in Santa Monica, California, and the nation; Arthur L. Reese to the Commissioners of the City of Santa Monica, August 12, 1918. Santa Monica Museum Collection.

23. Phillips Chapel CME Church File Papers, 2005. Rev. James A. Stout was educated at what was known then as Prairie View Agricultural and Mechanical State Normal School for the Training of Colored Teachers (known today as Prairie View A&M University), near Houston, Texas. There, Stout earned a state teaching certificate in 1894. He taught school in Texas, before going on to Tillotson College (known today as Huston-Tillotson University) in Austin, Texas, where he continued to teach to pay his school expenses, and where he graduated with honors in 1899. To educate formerly black enslaved people, both Prairie View and Tillotson were founded in the mid-1870s by the state of Texas and the Methodist Church, respectively. He entered the ministry of the CME Church after teaching for ten years. Likewise, Mary McReynolds attended Prairie View before she married James A. Stout in 1907. She also was a schoolteacher in Texas before becoming a partner in her husband's work. James A. Stout, *Pills and Pearls: A Collection of Sermons, Lectures and Addresses*, 1919, "The Author" section, Cristyne Lawson Collection; Cristyne Lawson, resident of Santa Monica, California, interviews with the author, February 17, 2006, June 2009, and November 6, 2010.

24. Lakey, *The History of the C.M.E. Church*, 349.

25. Lonnie Bunch, "The Great State for the Negro," in *Seeking El Dorado*, 142–43; Flamming, *Bound for Freedom*, 4; Smith, *SMEO*, May 17, 1975, 8B.

26. U.S. Census; Basten, *Paradise by the Sea*, 99.

27. Bunch, "The Great State for the Negro," 138; Scott, *Santa Monica*, 55–56; For an examination of the various ethnic and racial groups and classes and their historical relationships over time in different locations of the North American West, see White, *It's Your Misfortune and None of My Own*; and Almaguer, *Racial Fault Lines*.

28. Basten, *Paradise by the Sea*, 99; Marquez, *Santa Monica Beach*, 169, 172, 174–80; Scott, *Santa Monica*, 62; Flamming, *Bound for Freedom*, 271–72; "Negroes Ask Zone Change to Build S.M. Bath House, Syndicate Asks Council to Amend Ordinance to Permit Amusement Resort on Beach," *SMEO*, April 19, 1922; U.S. Census. There were few other recreational water sites around the nation that were called the Inkwell. More explanation of these locations will be discussed later in this chapter.

29. "Picnic of Colored People on July 27," *DO*, July 10, 1908, 1; "Darkies Are to Have Big Time," *DO*, July 25, 1908, 1; Basten, *Paradise by the Sea*, 26; Marquez, *Santa Monica Beach*, 25.

30. Scholar Paul Von Blum asserts that these types of derogatory names and imagery appealed to whites, who thought of them as "humorous depictions of obvious racial truths" and who "rarely encountered contrary images of African American dignity." The auditorium gallery seats reserved for white people would have allowed them separation from the music, dancing, and socializing on the floor below to watch ordinary African Americans enjoying themselves as an entertainment spectacle, like a minstrel show in a theatre. "Picnic of Colored People on July 27," 1; "Colored Picnic Will Be A Big One," *DO*, July 24, 1908, 1; "Darkies Are to Have Big Time," 1; Von Blum, "African American Visual Representation," 41–42, 45.
31. "Picnic of Colored People on July 27," 1; "Colored Picnic Will Be a Big One," 1; "Darkies Are to Have Big Time," 1.
32. For several years early in the twentieth century, in addition to being appreciated for oceanfront access, Playa del Rey was known for its wooden track auto racing at the Motordrome, which burned down on August 11, 1913, and was not rebuilt. Additionally, some of the first airplane flight exhibits were held nearby due to the location of the emerging airplane industry, including Hughes Aircraft and Mines Field (a.k.a. Los Angeles International Airport). The Railroad Day event promoters Bernard F. Spivey (porter-Red Cap), Nicolas W. Gordon (clerk), and Matthew T. Laws (porter) all worked at railroad or affiliated companies. "Famous Race Course Burns," *LAT*, August 12, 1913, II4: "From Motordrome to Sugar," *California Outlook*, August 29, 1914, 16; *Los Angeles City Directory 1914*; 1920 U.S. Census; "Local Happenings" column/Pacific Coast Amusement Club ad and Pacific Coast Amusement Club leaders' invitation to fraternal groups to Railroad Day, *CE*, May 23, 1914; "Railroad Men's Picnic: Southern Pacific Employees Will Frolic at Playa del Rey and Context for Hundred Prizes," *LAT*, June 12, 1907, II7; "Pier Repairs Finished, All Damage Wrought by Recent High Tides at Play del Rey Has Been Overcome," *LAT*, June 27, 1908, II8.
33. "Railroad Day! Universal Conclave" Pacific Coast Amusement Club ad, *CE*, May 23, 1914; J. Allen Reese, "Venice-Ocean Park-Santa Monica News" and "Local Happenings" columns discuss successful Railroad Day event, *CE*, June 13, 2014.
34. After reading both media outlets' narratives about African American usage of Playa del Rey, the *Daily Outlook's* acknowledgement of the state of California laws about beach access for all citizens and patterns of history associated with the Jim Crow era, I have found that the available sources do not provide conclusive evidence that the "rowdy" people were racist whites using harassment and subterfuge to inhibit African American usage of the public recreation spaces in the Playa del Rey community, hence causing the problems the police assisted in stopping. "Don't Want Picnics," *DO*, June 24, 1914, 1.
35. Flamming, *Bound for Freedom*, 183–84, 202–4, 272, 275; "The Valentine Case on Trail," *CE*, March 11,1922; "Law Delays the Valentine Case," *CE*, April 22, 1922; "The Valentine Case," *CE*, Editorial Section, May 13, 1922; "Special Policemen and

Colored Deputy Sheriff Lock Horns Up in Topanga Canyon Over Bagatelle," *SMEO*, June 1, 1920; "Suspension of Deputy Sheriff Cooper Comes as Aftermath of Recent Fight in Topanga Canyon," *SMEO*, June 11, 1920. For more on law enforcement corruption and brutality toward African Americans in the 1920s, see Hernández, *City of Inmates*. Arthur Valentine's son, Arthur Jr., would grow up to marry a Tabor family descendent. The Tabors were one of the first African American families who settled in the Venice community in the early twentieth century. As of 2018 their daughter, Jataun Valentine (b. 1937), lives in the family home and nearby some of the Tabor relatives, who continue to reside and own real estate there. This newly unearthed information is good to know, even if it does not upend our understanding of the 1920s Valentine case. Austin Ringelstein, "The African Heritage of the Santa Monica Mountains," prepared for the Santa Monica Mountains National Recreation Area, National Park Service, September 16, 2018, unpublished paper.

36. Social Intelligence: Heard or Seen in Passing column, *CE*, June 27, 1924, 6; "Lunch on Beach," Social Intelligence: Heard or Seen in Passing Column, *CE*, September 11, 1925, 5; "At Huntington Beach," Social Intelligence, Heard or Seen In Passing Column, *CE*, July 10, 1925, 5; "Pacific Palisades Sight For 6th Annual Camp Of Urban League," *CE*, August 12, 1927, 1. Even with such white violence and attempts to evict African Americans from public beach recreation space outside the Santa Monica city limits, social mentions in the *California Eagle* featured descriptions of the beach excursions some African Americans continued to enjoy in these places. A June 1924 party at Venice Beach celebrating the fifth birthday of little Hugh Macbeth Jr. and twenty of his small friends was discussed. "Lunch on the Beach" was the 1925 heading topping a social mention of a "delightful lunch on the sands of Palisades Beach." Dr. G. K. Offut and a party of seven women and girls entertained themselves "with an auto drive over the Mulholland Drive and through Topanga Canyon" before reaching the beach for their lunch. From the description it appears that the Offut's party enjoyed themselves without any problems at the area nearby the location where Arthur Valentine and his family endured white violence and intimidation in an attempt to evict them from the beach near Topanga Canyon.
37. Harry Levette, "Attempt to Bluff Race Bathers From California Beach," *Pittsburgh Courier*, August 7, 1937, 2. The story "Jim Crow Reported on Los Angeles Beach" was also carried on the front page of Los Angeles's *New Age Dispatch*, July 23, 1927. Most African American Los Angeles Police Department officers worked out of Newton Station during this era.
38. Levette, "Attempt to Bluff Race Bathers from California Beach," 2; Wolcott, *Race, Riots, and Roller Coasters*, 3.
39. My analysis is informed by Victoria Wolcott's assessment of African Americans' demand for the right to use recreation and public space was about power and possession. Wolcott, *Race, Riots, and Roller Coasters*, 3–4.

40. Nelson, *Finding Martha's Vineyard*, 131. There is another beach area historically used by African Americans on the U.S. East Coast island of Martha's Vineyard in Massachusetts called "the Inkwell." There were also a few other recreational water sites around the nation that were lesser known nationally which were called the Inkwell for the same reasons as the two locations that are more well known. These same locations were also called other derogatory terms referring to the "blackness" of the skin color of its visitors.
41. Nat Trives and a few other local African American citizens shared with me that the Bay Street beach was called "Spook Beach" by some in the post–World War II years. Nat Trives interview with Alison Rose Jefferson, City of Santa Monica Beach Stories Initiative, July 10, 2009.
42. La Bonita served African Americans visiting the beachfront from around 1914 through the early 1950s. Flamming, *Bound for Freedom*, 272; Lloyd Allen, retired Santa Monica businessman and civic activist, telephone interview with the author, April 2005, Los Angeles, California; Smith, *SMEO*, May 17, 1975, 8B; "La Bonita" ad, *New Age*, August 28, 1914.
43. "Venice-Ocean Park-Santa Monica News," *CE*, August 1, 1914; "La Bonita" accommodations ad, *New Age*, August 28, 1914, 2; 1910 and 1920 U.S. Census; 1914, 1915, 1917, and 1918 *Santa Monica City Directories*; La Bonita" ad, *CE*, May 28, 1921; *The Negro Motorist Green Book*, 1936–63, Schomburg Center for Research in Black Culture, Manuscripts, Archives, and Rare Books Division, New York Public Library, New York Public Library Digital Collections, https://digitalcollections.nypl.org/items/9dc3ff40-8df4-0132-fd57-58d385a7b928 (accessed November 12, 2018).
44. Smith, *SMEO*, May 17, 1975, 8B.
45. "La Bonita" ad, *CE*, June 27, 1930, 2.
46. Flamming, *Bound for Freedom*, 272; "Caucasians Organize Protective League," *LAT*, June 9, 1922, 14; "Fight Against Beach Dance Halls Success," *LAT*, July 27, 1922, II-11.
47. "Fight Against Beach Dance a Success," II-11; Flamming, *Bound for Freedom*, 272; Hugh McBeth, "An Open Letter to the Los Angeles Forum," *CE*, August 5, 1922, 8.
48. Kahrl, "The Slightest Semblance of Unruliness," 26.
49. The Ocean Frontage Syndicate is also referred to as the Ocean Front Investment Group in some sources. "Settlement of Negroes Is Opposed: Santa Monica and Ocean Park Block Plans for Colony of Colored Folks," *LAT*, July 30, 1922, V7; "The Color Line at Santa Monica: Blacks Again Feel Iron Fist of Race Prejudice," *CE*, April 1, 1922; "Amusement Center for Negro Visitors," *LAT*, April 20, 1922, II6; "Reopen Hearing: Project of Negro Amusement Center Urged at Santa Monica," *LAT*, May 5, 1922, II6; "Negroes Ask Zone Change to Build S.M. Bath House," 1.
50. See, generally, Gaines, *Uplifting the Race*; Flamming, *Bound for Freedom*, 227, 231–32; Delores Nason McBroome, "Harvest of Gold: African America Boosterism,

Agriculture, and Investment In Allensworth and Little Liberia," in *Seeking El Dorado*, 149–80

51. Foster, "In the Face of 'Jim Crow,'" 131, 135.
52. Beasley, *The Negro Trail Blazers of California*, 197–200; DeGraaf, "The City of Black Angels," 337–38.
53. Beasley, *The Negro Trail Blazers of California*, 197–200; Smith, *Emancipation*, 485–86.
54. Flamming, *Bound for Freedom*, 255–58; *California Negro Directory, 1942–1943*, 215; *L.A. Negro Directory and Who's Who, 1930–1931*, 93; *The Negro Who's Who in California* (1949), 54, 59.
55. "Caucasians Organize Protective League, Segregation of Races at Beaches Object of Santa Monica Body," *LAT*, June 9, 1922.
56. "Negroes Ask Zone Change to Build S.M. Bath House," 1; "Council Denies Petition for Negro Bath House," *SMEO*, May 1, 1922, 1.
57. "Southern Red Neck Is Pumping Hot Air at Santa Monica: Endeavors to Stir Up Strife," *CE*, May 6, 1922.
58. "Settlement of Negroes Is Opposed," V7; "The Color Line at Santa Monica"; "Negroes Ask Zone Change to Build S.M. Bath House"; assessor's parcel map, County of Los Angeles; Sanborn Maps.
59. Flamming, *Bound for Freedom*, 272–73; "Settlement of Negroes Is Opposed," V7.
60. Cady, "Southern California," 194–99; Culver, *The Frontier of Leisure*, 66–74.
61. Cady, "Southern California," 196–98; Brigham, "Landownership and Occupancy by Negroes in Manhattan Beach," 21, 25, 31–35, 44–46, 82–84; "Beach Suit Depending on Voters: Continuance Granted Until After Election, as Changes May Settle Issue," *LAT*, January 30, 1925.
62. Culver, *The Frontier of Leisure*, 66–74; Flamming, *Bound for Freedom*, 8–9, 12, 37, 41.
63. As the twentieth century progressed, Southern California beach culture and sports emerged as a mass culture lifestyle with an even bigger global reach, influencing advertising, fashion, music, television shows, and movies. Books, music, movies, and shows such as the *Gidget* multimedia franchise (1950s to 1960s), the Beach Boys band songs (1960s–), *Beach Blanket Bingo* (1965), *Baywatch* (1990s), *Malibu CA* (1998–2000) and *The O.C.[Orange County]* (2003–7) are a sampling of some of the more well-known beach culture imagery promoting a vision of a romantic Southern California lifestyle that has influenced cultural development, regionally, nationally, and internationally. *Malibu CA*, http://www.tv.com/malibu-ca/show/1661/summary.html (accessed July 4, 2014); *The O.C.*, http://www.tv.com/o-c/show/16960/summary.html (accessed July 4, 2014); Brigham, "Landownership and Occupancy by Negroes in Manhattan Beach," 33; Culver, *The Frontier of Leisure*, 70–71.
64. Later, in the 1930s, the Edgewater was known as the Waverly Beach Club and the Ambassador Club in the 1940s. "Pier Repairs Finished, All Damage Wrought

by Recent High Tides at Play del Rey Has Been Overcome," *LAT*, June 27, 1908, II8; Marquez, 57–58; Basten, *Paradise by the Sea*, 99.

65. Marquez, *Santa Monica Beach*, 57; Wolcott, *Race, Riots, and Roller Coasters*, 19.

66. Here are a few examples of contemporary interpreters giving audiences a false sense of the history and geography of this African American historical site in Santa Monica's Ocean Park beach area. In a 2005 *LAT* article, Cecilia Rasmussen writes that there were ropes demarcating the African American beach site in Santa Monica's Ocean Park neighborhood in the 1920s. She does not appear to have a full understanding of the context of Santa Monica's beach culture and beach clubs during the era. The newly built beach clubs had at one time their own private, fenced-in beach areas for their members. These fenced-in beaches were to "exclude" anyone who was not a member and to note the "exclusivity" of their establishments. In this context, a roped-off beach area would have identified an exclusive site for African Americans at a popular center of public activity. She also wrote that the area "was marked 'for Negroes only,'" which again would be setting up a situation of exclusivity for African Americans rather than exclusion at the beach in this context and era. Rasmussen, "L.A. THEN AND NOW: In 'White Only' Era, an Oasis for L.A.'s Blacks, Inkwell in Santa Monica," *LAT*, July 3. 2005. Another example, a donated 1925 photograph in the Los Angeles Public Library's Shades of L.A. Collection, features several African Americans sitting on what appears to be breakwater rocks under a portion of a sign bearing the word "Prohibited." The photograph's donor said that the image was at the "boundary between the black and white sections of Santa Monica and Venice beaches." Since only a portion of the sign text is visible, it is impossible to know exactly what was "Prohibited." Most likely the sign indicated that "Walking," "Swimming," or "Fishing" was "Prohibited." Several contemporary interpreters have used this image in public projects to validate their narrative about the Santa Monica de jure Jim Crow era beach site to say that there were signs up marking this as a black recreation space. See image 00001726 at http://photos.lapl.org/carlweb/jsp/FullRecord?databaseID=968&record=1&controlNumber=5001106 (accessed August 4, 2014).

67. Marilyn Hudson is the daughter of architect Paul R. Williams and the daughter-in-law of dentist and civic activist H. Claude Hudson. Marilyn Hudson, Los Angeles resident, telephone interview with the author, November 2004, Los Angeles, California.

68. In 1947 the words "Colored Use" were used to identify this section of the beachfront on a map of a beach erosion and shoreline plan. Beach nourishment projects begun in the late 1940s have dramatically widened the shoreline frontage at this and other Santa Monica and Pacific Ocean beaches; City of Santa Monica, Los Angeles County Master Shoreline Plan map, Divisions of Beaches and Parks, Department of Natural Resources, Department of Engineering, State of

California, 1947, University of Southern California Special Collections; quote from Wallace Decuir, beachgoer and Los Angeles resident, retired fireman, and businessman, telephone interview with the author, November 1, 2004, Los Angeles, California.

69. See Scott, *Santa Monica*; Flamming, *Bound for Freedom*; Alison Rose Jefferson, "Nick Gabaldón (1927–1951): A Southern California Surfing Pioneer," The Ultimate History Project, http://www.ultimatehistoryproject.com/nick-gabaldoacuten-southern-california-surfing-pioneer.html 9 (accessed May 21, 2015); Designation of Phillips Chapel CME, LC-05-LM-005, City of Santa Monica Landmark Commission, http://www.smgov.net/departments/pcd/agendas/Landmarks-Commission/2005/20051114/Det_2001%204th%20Street.htm (accessed August 25, 2015).

70. Jefferson, "Nick Gabaldón (1927–1951)."

71. At the City of Santa Monica Council Meeting on February 14, 2006, "Ms. Rhonda Harper [with] inquiries and support from several members of the Black Surfing Association" are identified as making the request to recognize in some way the historical African American beach area at Bay Street and Nick Gabaldón. Members of the Black Surfing Association who led the recognition effort included Donald Stein III, Mary Mills, William Lamar, Rick Blocker, Andrea Kabwasa, Suyen Mosley, Max McMullin, Rosemarie "Rose" Garza Corley, and Tony Corley. Santa Monica Council directed staff to research options for creating a plaque for the site. Suggested language for the plaque was submitted by interested parties, and several drafts were circulated for review by citizens and history field professionals. This author wrote the final plaque text. At that time, in 2007, the author was employed as a historian at the Historic Resources Group in Los Angeles, California, and a graduate student at University of Southern California. In 2005 the author's research was used as the basis for the City of Santa Monica Landmarks Commission and Council to designate the Santa Monica's historic African American Phillips Chapel Church a city landmark. This research on Phillips Chapel included information on the Bay Street Beach-Inkwell site. Barbara Stinchfield, Director of Community and Cultural Services, "Information Item" to mayor and City Council, City of Santa Monica, City of Santa Monica Archives, September 7, 2007; Gary Walker, "Santa Monica: Plaque Is Dedicated at Historic Inkwell Beach, Once the Only Local Beach for African Americans," *Argonaut*, February 14, 2008, 3; Tony Corley, founder of the Black Surfing Association, telephone interview with the author, May 2015, Los Angeles, California.

72. The Nick Gabaldón portrait by Richard Wyatt is of acrylic paint on canvas, 30 inches wide by 24 inches high; Jefferson, "Nick Gabaldón (1927–1951)"; Mike Sonksen, "Richard Wyatt: Artist for Los Angeles," KCET, LA Letters, Departure Columns, February 7, 2014, http://www.kcet.org/socal/departures/columns/la-letters/richard-wyatt-artist-for-los-angeles.html (accessed May 21, 2015); Richard

Wyatt, Los Angeles artist, telephone interview with the author, May 2015, Los Angeles, California; Richard Wyatt Jr. Studio, http://www.richardwyattjr.com (accessed May 21, 2015); Rick Blocker, founder of BlackSurfing.com (www.legacy.blacksurfing.com), an information portal on African American surfers, telephone interview with the author, May 2013, Los Angeles, California.

73. At the Bay Street beach site, Nick Gabaldón Day has been held in early June. This celebration was begun by the Black Surfers Collective and since 2013 produced with partnership support from Heal the Bay, Surf Bus Foundation, the Santa Monica Conservancy, and other organizations. The first, Nick Gabaldón Charitable Paddlethon, was held in 2015, sponsored by the Black Surfing Association and the Malibu Surfing Association, with support from Heal the Bay and other groups. The Black Surfing Association was founded in 1976, and the Black Surfers Collective was founded in 2010. Both groups are based in California. In 2017 the population of Santa Monica was just over 92,300, with African Americans making of about 4 percent (3,692) of the population; Latinx 16.1 percent (14,861); and Asian/Pacific Islanders 10.1 percent (9,323). Santa Monica QuickFacts from the U.S. Census, 2018, https://www.census.gov/quickfacts/fact/table/santamonicacitycalifornia/PST045217 (accessed July 6, 2018).

74. Readers can learn more about the status of the approval of the National Register of Historic Places listing nomination of the Bay Street Historic District from the Sea of Clouds organization, www.seaofclouds.org, and at www.alisonrose-jefferson.com.

4. PLEASURE SEEKERS AT LAKE ELSINORE

1. In 1972 the town of Elsinore was officially named Lake Elsinore. Hudson, *Lake Elsinore Valley*, 3–5, 142; Zimmerman, *The History of the Elsinore Region*, 1–2; "Elsinore: A New Colony in Southern California" (Los Angeles: Times-Mirror Book & Job Printing Office, 1884), from the Riverside File, Seaver Center for Western History Research, Natural History Museum of Los Angeles County, Los Angeles, California, 12–13.
2. "Elsinore: A New Colony," 6–7.
3. "Elsinore: A New Colony," 7–9, 23.
4. As summed up a century later, "The hot springs and mineral waters brought visitors from all over, the Southern California land boom lured eager buyers to Elsinore and the arrival of the railroad added to the prosperity. "See "Lakes of California: Lake Elsinore," *PG&E Progress*, February 1972, Elsinore File, San Diego Historical Society (SDHS).
5. "Lakes of California: Lake Elsinore," SDHS; Zimmerman, *The History of the Elsinore Region*, 59; McWilliams, *Southern California*, 156; Culver, *The Frontier of Leisure*, 127.

6. "Elsinore: A New Colony," 3–4, 22; *An Illustrated History of Southern California* (Chicago: Lewis Publishing Co., 1890), 61, 132–33.
7. Starr, *Inventing the Dream*, 99, 102.
8. Hudson, *Lake Elsinore Valley*, 59.
9. Hudson, *Lake Elsinore Valley*, 59–60.
10. "Lakes of California: Lake Elsinore," SDHS; Zimmerman, *The History of the Elsinore Region*, 62–63; "Celebrating 50 Years of Water History," prepared by Mary Brown for the Elsinore Valley Municipal Water District, 2000; Rawls and Bean, *California*, 319; Hudson, *Lake Elsinore Valley*, 24, 55, 154–58.
11. Hudson, *Lake Elsinore Valley*, 78, 116–17; "Lakes of California: Lake Elsinore," SDHS.
12. Hudson, *Lake Elsinore Valley*, 61, 65, 68, 71, 73; "Lake Elsinore Healthy Place," *LAT*, June 27, 1928, A12.
13. Hotels and Apartments, Elsinore, *Southwest Builders and Contractor*, November 5, 1920, 19; "Lake Elsinore Healthy Place"; Hudson, *Lake Elsinore Valley*, 55–56, 61–62, 68, 71–72, 76; "Subdivisions and Subdividers," *LAT*, March 9, 1924, D1.
14. Sandy Stokes, "Elsinore Lacked the Look of Hatred: Black Family Going North Paused, Then Settled Down," *Press Enterprise*, February 13, 1996, B-2; Lake Elsinore Cemetery Records.
15. Stokes, "Elsinore Lacked the Look of Hatred"; history of Lake Elsinore compiled from newspaper stories by Altha Merrifield Cauch, 1956, Lake Elsinore Historical Society Collection, 307.
16. History of Lake Elsinore compiled from newspaper stories by Altha Merrifield Cauch, 1956, Lake Elsinore Historical Society Collection, 309–10; Richard L. Carrico and Stacey Jordan, PhD, Centre City Development Corporation Downtown San Diego African-American Heritage Study, Prepared by Mooney & Associates, San Diego, California, June 2004, vol. 40-V/46.
17. "Elsinore Notes," *CE*, September 21, 1921. After obtaining their freedom from enslavement, Robert C. Owens's grandparents settled in Los Angeles in the 1850s and prospered.
18. Bundles, *On Her Own Ground*, 16, 106–7, 165; A'Lelia Bundles, biographer and descendent of A'Lelia Walker, email interview with the author, Los Angeles, California, August 20, 2014.
19. See, generally, Gaines, *Black Leadership*; Flamming, *Bound for Freedom*, 227, 231–32; and McBroome, "Harvest of Gold."
20. Lake Shore Beach Company (LSBC), Board of Directors meeting notes, Arthur L. Reese Family Archives, Los Angeles, California, September 30, November 1, and December 13, 1921; July 2 and October 16, 1922; Milton Anderson, Los Angeles and Lake Elsinore resident, telephone interview with the author, Los Angeles, California, November 15, 2004; "Where Will You Spend Your Vacation," *CE*, June

27, 1924, 11; Robinson, *Problems in Training Adult Negroes in Los Angeles*, 71–72; 1920 U.S. Census.

21. It is noteworthy that several of these resort developers were viewed as distinguished citizens of their day, evidenced by their inclusion in Delilah Beasley's groundbreaking 1918 book, *The Negro Trail Blazers of California*. Foster, "In the Face of 'Jim Crow,'" 131, 135.
22. Beasley, *The Negro Trail Blazers of California*, 246–47; files on Wilbur C. Gordon, MD, California State Archives; 1920 U.S. Census.
23. Dr. Wilbur C. Gordon was a founder of the black-owned Liberty Savings and Loan Association, and its first president in 1924. This was the first black-owned financial institution of this kind founded in Los Angeles. In 1925 Gordon was among the initial investors in the Golden State Mutual Life Insurance Company, which went on to be one of the largest African American-owned businesses in the United States at its pinnacle. In 1925, with backing from Liberty S&L and the white-owned Commercial National Bank, Gordon and his personal realtor Journee W. White, along with several other African American real estate agents, worked to create a high-class residential subdivision for African Americans called Gordon Manor, near the city of Torrance, three miles east of Manhattan Beach in the southwestern section of Los Angeles County. As racists had done to the Bruces in Manhattan Beach, a group of wealthy white Angelenos who owned mansions and sizeable ranchette estates in the Palos Verdes hillsides several miles south of Gordon Manor convinced the Los Angeles County Board of Supervisors in 1926 to condemn the subdivison's land in order to build a park. African American architect James H. Garrett was a part of the Gordon Manor project team. For more on Gordon Manor, see Alison Rose Jefferson, "Leisure's Race, Power and Place: The Recreation and Remembrance of African Americans in the California Dream (PhD diss., University of California, Santa Barbara, 2015), 276–85. It is possible Darden and Gordon became acquainted with one another while matriculating in their respective professional education departments at Howard University as they were on campus during the same time period; *Negroes Who's Who in California* (1948), 59; *L.A. Negro Directory and Who's Who, 1930–1931*, 90–91; Tolbert, *The UNIA and Black Los Angeles*, 72; Flamming, *Bound for Freedom*, 74, 240, 238–42, 253–58; Beasley, *The Negro Trail Blazers of California*, 197–200; Charles Sylvester Darden, U.S. World War I Draft Registration Card, 1917–18; Charles Sylvester Darden, California Death Index, 1940–1997; "Gordon Manor" ad, *CE*, December 11 and 18, 1925, 2 and May 7, 1926, 2; "Eastside Realty Co. Opens New Sub-Division," *CE*, December 11, 1925, 1; George P. Johnson, Collector of Negro Film History, transcript of oral history, University of California, Los Angeles Library Special Collections, 1970, 87–89; Alexander, *Abbot Kinney's Venice-of-America*, vol. 1, 215; Lupoma,

Arthur L. Reese, 1–10; Sonya Reese Greenland, Arthur L. Reese Family Archives, interview with the author, August 2006, Los Angeles, California.

24. Hudson, *Lake Elsinore Valley*, 55–56; "Luncheon Honor as a Farewell," *LAT*, June 10, 1914, II8.
25. Beasley, *The Negro Trail Blazers of California*, 243; Sallie T. Richardson [a.k.a. Sally Richardson], California Death Index, 1940–1997.
26. Beasley, *The Negro Trail Blazers of California*, 243; Flamming, *Bound for Freedom*, 135, 138–39, 141.
27. Flamming, *Bound for Freedom*, 141, 281, 288–89.
28. LSBC, Board of Directors meeting minutes, January–December 1922.
29. LSBC, Board of Directors meeting minutes, September 30, 1921–1930s; Bardolph, *The Negro Vanguard*, 191; Hudson, *Paul R. Williams*, 22–23.
30. Hudson, *Paul R. Williams*, 21, 31–51, 104–5.
31. LSBC, Board of Directors meeting minutes, April 28, 1925; Milton Anderson, Los Angeles and Lake Elsinore resident, telephone interview with the author, November 15, 2004, Los Angeles, California.
32. Milton Anderson, telephone interview with the author, November 15, 2004, Los Angeles, California.
33. LSBC and various club event advertisements, *CE*, May–June 1922–25.
34. Barbara Anderson, Lake Elsinore resident and retired librarian, telephone interview with the author, October 30, 2004, Los Angeles, California. The Anderson family home in San Diego County's City of Chula Vista was designated as a local historic landmark in 2005. The Lorenzo Anderson House information sheet, Barbara Anderson Collection; Historic Sites List, Chula Vista Historic Homes (Lorenzo Anderson House, no. 68–3487), http://www.historichomesofchulavista.com/historic-sites.html (accessed October 20, 2014).
35. Barbara Anderson interview, October 30, 2004; *L.A. Negro Directory and Who's Who, 1930–1931*, 91; See chapter 2 for illumination of some of H. Claude Hudson's civil rights activities in the 1920s; Flamming, *Bound for Freedom*, 213–14, 273–75, 277–84, 281, 303, 373; "H. Claude Hudson, A Los Angeles Icon!," The African American Registry, http://www.aaregistry.com/african_american_history/2622/H_Claude_Hudson_A_Los_Angeles_Icon (accessed May 24, 2015); "Historical Notes on the Los Angeles NAACP," http://www.naacp-losangeles.org/history.htm (accessed May 24, 2015); "The History of Broadway Federal Bank," http://www.broadwayfederalbank.com/history.htm (accessed May 24, 2015); LSBC, Board of Directors meeting minutes, 1920s to 1940s.
36. Hudson, *Lake Elsinore Valley*, 73–74; Jeanie Corral, "Old Elsinore Boasted the Gracious Days of Hostelry and Cultured Elite," *Lake Elsinore News*, June 10, 1992, 4.

37. "Love Nest Inn, Elsinore Mecca for Pleasure Seekers and Tourists," *CE*, September 10, 1926, 4; Lake Elsinore advertisement, *CE*, July–August 1925; Coleman De Luxe Hotel advertisement, *CE*, March 12, 1926, 8; "Hotel Coleman De Lux, Elsinore," *CE*, May 7, 1926, 6; "Elsinore Alive with Visitors" and "Silvia Lax Springs, Elsinore, California," *CE*, September 10, 1926, 4; Exhaust Section, *CE*, September 10, 1926, 8; Coleman De Luxe Hotel ad, *PD*, March 8, 1928, 2; 1900 U.S. Census; California Death Index, 1905–39; Halvor Miller, Esq., Los Angeles resident, interview with the author, March 12, 2007, Los Angeles, California.
38. Fisher, "A History of the Political and Social Development of the Black Community in California," 163; DeGraaf, "The City of Black Angels," 327. Of the original African American community sites in Los Angeles, Boyle Heights was the most isolated that sprang up. In the late 1880s John Wesley Coleman (1865–1930) and his extended family were among the district's earliest African American pioneers, who acquired several land parcels and would probably have been the most active in selling area property to other African Americans during this period. Coleman's main business became a successful employment agency. His mother, Mrs. Harriett Owens-Bynum (b. 1850), was considered by some observers to be one of the most dynamic and business-savvy African American women of her era. For more on John Wesley Coleman and his family members, see Jefferson, "Leisure's Race, Power and Place," 298–305; Bond, "The Negro in Los Angeles," 1–39, 67–68.
39. Jane Miller Kerina, resident of Orlando, Florida, telephone interview with the author, August 21, 2006, Los Angeles, California.
40. Flamming, *Bound for Freedom*, 302–3, 369; Jane Kerina interview, August 21, 2006. For more information on Loren Miller, see Hassan, *Loren Miller*.
41. 1930 U.S. Census.
42. Hudson, *Lake Elsinore Valley*, 78, 85, 91, 96; "Lakes of California: Lake Elsinore," SDHS; George Brown, Lake Elsinore Valley and Alberhill resident and retired City of Riverside employee, interview with the author, October 30, 2004, Alberhill, California; Judge William Beverly, telephone interview with the author, October 2004, Los Angeles, California; Milton Anderson interview, November 15, 2004; Thomas Rutherford, Marina del Rey resident and retired electrical engineer, telephone interview with the author, August 18, 2006, Los Angeles, California; Aron, *Working at Play*, 238. There were a few larger-scale agricultural businesses owned by African Americans in the Lake Elsinore environs. In the 1940s the Wilson brothers from Los Angeles purchased from retiring rancher Jay D. Jenkins an industrial chicken ranch in Corona and his poultry market on East Vernon Avenue (at Ascot Street) in Los Angeles. At the present time the author has not found evidence of how long Jenkins ran his chicken ranch before he sold it to the Wilson brothers in the 1940s. "Chicken Farm: A GI Dream Come True,

Three Coast Brothers and Friend Parlay $5,000 into $250,000 Poultry Business," *Ebony*, February 1949, 62–65.

43. Stokes, "Elsinore Lacked the Look of Hatred"; Lech, *Resorts of Riverside County*, 52–57, 74–83; August Muymudes, Los Angeles resident and retired pharmacist, interview with the author, July 26, 2006, Los Angeles, California; Jewish Cultural Club File, Southern California Library for Social Studies and Research, Los Angeles, California.
44. Wallace Decuir, Los Angeles resident, retired fireman and businessman, telephone interview with the author, November 1, 2004, Los Angeles, California.
45. Flamming, *Bound for Freedom*, 5, 8, 58.
46. In some sources the Lake Elsinore Hotel is referred to as the Lake Elsinore Inn. Evidence suggests the Lake Elsinore Hotel was located on the earlier discussed Rieves Inn site that had been owned by the Burgesses. *The Green Book, 1959*, 8; Edith Hawes-Howard, resident of Talare, California, and retired chief, telephone interview with the author, March 2 and 5, 2007, Los Angeles, California; George Brown, Lake Elsinore Valley and Alberhill resident and retired City of Riverside employee, interview with the author, October 30, 2004, Alberhill, California; 1920, 1930, and 1940 U.S. Census; California Death Index, 1940–97; U.S. Social Security Death Index, 1935–2014; "California Vacation, Golden State Offers New Resorts to Record 1948 Army of Negro Tourists," *Ebony*, May 1948, 20–21.
47. Edith Hawes-Howard, interview with the author, March 2 and 5, 2007; George Brown interview, October 30, 2004; 1920, 1930, and 1940 U.S. Census.
48. Betty Lucas-Howard interview, 2006.
49. Dr. N. Curtis King founded Rose Netta Hospital in Los Angeles at Vernon and Hooper Avenues, where, in 1942, it was the first hospital where the Red Cross set up an interracial blood bank. *Negroes Who's Who in California* (1948), 32; *Los Angeles Classified Buyers' Guide, 1942–1943*, 11; "Ranches, Many Celebrities Flock to King Ranch, Best of Dozen Run by Negroes," *Ebony*, September 1949, 67–70. Louie Robinson, "Richest Negro Family: Blodgetts of L.A. Have Savings-Loan Fortune," *Ebony*, December 1962, 151–62. Edith Hawes-Howard (no relation to Betty Lucas-Howard) worked for the Lake Elsinore Hotel during her high school vacations and for several summers, which she spent at her family's cottage nearby on Pottery and Scrivener. Her father was Rev. Hampton Hawes Sr., the first minister installed at Westminster Presbyterian Church in Los Angeles, founded in 1904. Then located near Jefferson Boulevard and Vermont Avenue, this was the first African American church of the Presbyterian denomination in Los Angeles. Hawes Howard's younger brother was jazz pianist Hampton Hawes (1928–77), who was an important artist in the emerging "West Coast" school of jazz and recorded with Charlie Parker, Billie Holiday, Dexter Gordon, Art Pepper, Charlie Mingus, and others. Edith Hawes-Howard, telephone interview with the author, March 2 and 5, 2007, Los Angeles, California.

50. "Highlights of Black History of Lake Elsinore, 1982," prepared by Hilltop Community Center Program Bulletin, Lake Elsinore Historical Society Collection, 11; "Composer, Arranger Leon Rene Succumbs," *LAS*, June 10, 1982, A1; Leslie Berkman, "Song Ensures Home for Birds, Composer," *LAT*, June 7, 1982, B22; Cleo Joffrion, "Sleepytime Down South"; Author Leon Rene Revisits SU Campus," Afro-Louisiana Historical and Genealogical Society, http://www.alhgs.com/pub-sleepytimedownsouth.html (accessed November 15, 2014); "Leon Rene" in Nick Talesky, *Rock Obituaries—Knocking on Heaven's Door*, 544–45; Cox, *Central Avenue*, 67.
51. Berkman, *LAT*, June 7, 1982, B22; Bryant and Collette, *Central Avenue Sounds*, 335; Lipsitz, *Midnight at the Barrelhouse*, 26–27; Reed, *The Black Music History of Los Angeles*, 52, 73.
52. Talesky, *Rock Obituaries*, 544–45; " Composer, Arranger Leon Rene Succumbs," *LAS*, June 10, 1982, A1; Leon G. Rene, Find A Grave Memorial, http://www.findagrave.com/cgi-bin/fg.cgi?page=gr&GRid=16594921 (accessed November 16, 2014).
53. George Brown, interview with the author, October 30, 2004; Rubin "Buddy" Brown, Lake Elsinore Valley and Perris resident, interview with the author, March 3, 2006, Perris, California; Hilltop Community Center Program Bulletin, Lake Elsinore Historical Society Collection, 9; 1930 U.S. Census; "California Vacation, Golden State Offers New Resorts to Record 1948 Army of Negro Tourists," *Ebony*, May 1948, 21.
54. Louis "Satchmo" Armstrong was the orchestra leader at Frank Sebastian's Cotton Club on Washington Boulevard in Culver City from June 1930 to March 1931. Visiting Los Angeles often in his long career, from 1932 through 1945 he worked in sixteen Hollywood films as an actor or a musician. As black mobility and demand for leisure travel increased in spite of the racist restrictions and possible inconveniences, special travel guides were created by entrepreneurs and even the U.S. government to inform African Americans about services and facilities available to them as travelers on the road. As mentioned in chapter 3, the most well-known of these guides was *The Negro Motorist Green Book* (also called in some years *The Negro Travelers' Green Book*), published from 1936 to 1963. During this era the U.S. Department of the Interior published *A Directory of Negro Hotels and Guest Houses*; *1940 Negro Motorist Green Book*, 1. Prepared in conjunction with the U.S. Travel Bureau, the 1940 edition cost twenty-five cents, from "America on the Move," National Museum of American History exhibit, Smithsonian Institution, http://amhistory.si.edu/onthemove/exhibition/exhibition_11_3.html (accessed January 23, 2015); *1949 Negro Travelers' Green Book*, 12; *1956 Negro Travelers' Green Book*, 12; Wintz and Glasrud, *The Harlem Renaissance in the American West*, 9–10; Flamming, "The New Negro Renaissance in Los Angeles, 1920–1940,"

in Wintz and Glasrud, *The Harlem Renaissance in the American West*, 73; George Brown, interview with the author, October 30, 2004; Bogle, *Bright Boulevards, Bold Dreams*, 175–76; Rubin "Buddy" Brown interview, March 3, 2006; Hilltop Community Center Program Bulletin, Lake Elsinore Historical Society Collection, 9, 11.

55. Rubin "Buddy" Brown interview, March 3, 2006; "Archie Moore Dies at 84," *LAT*, December 10, 1998, 1; Archie Moore biography, http://www.encyclopedia.com/topic/Archie_Moore.aspx (accessed November 6, 2014); "Archie Moore's 1998 Death," http://www.infoplease.com/ipa/A0771452.html (accessed November 6, 2014); "Archie Moore Was a Colorful Boxer," The African American Registry, http://www.aaregistry.org/historic_events/view/archie-moore-was-colorful-boxing-great (accessed November 14, 2014); Archie Moore, http://boxrec.com/media/index.php/Archie_Moore (accessed November 14, 2014); "Archie Moore 1913–1998," Cyber Boxing Zone Newswire, http://www.cyberboxingzone.com/boxing/archie1209.htm (accessed November 6, 2014).

56. "California Vacation," *Ebony*, May 1948, 21; Halvor Miller, Esq., interview, March 12, 2007; *1956 Negro Travelers' Green Book*, 12; *1959 Negro Travelers' Green Book*, 8.

57. "Biography for Clarence Muse, Versatile Performer, Producer and Songwriter, Dies at 90," *LAT*, October 16, 1979, C3; "Clarence Muse, A Pioneer Film Actor," African American Registry, http://www.aaregistry.org/historic_events/view/clarence-muse-pioneer-film-actor (accessed November 8, 2014); "Clarence Muse," biography, IMDB http://www.imdb.com/name/nm0615617/bio (accessed November 8, 2014); "Clarence Muse," filmography, IMDB, http://www.imdb.com/name/nm0615617/ (accessed November 8, 2014).

58. *Negroes Who's Who in California* (1948), 66; Ken Overaker, "Elsinore Negro Mayor Retiring: Hopes to Work on Racial Peace," *LAT*, March 31, 1968, G1; Elbert Hudson, Los Angeles resident, telephone interview with the author, July 26, 2006, Los Angeles, California.

59. Thomas R. Yarborough was most likely a founder of the Elsinore Chamber of Commerce; *Negroes Who's Who in California* (1948), 66; Stokes, "Elsinore Lacked the Look of Hatred"; Hilltop Community Center Program Bulletin, Lake Elsinore Historical Society Collection, 14; "California Vacation," *Ebony*, May 1948, 21.

60. Overaker, "Elsinore Negro Mayor Retiring"; Stokes, "Elsinore Lacked the Look of Hatred."

61. Site visit by author, accompanied by George Brown, Lake Elsinore Valley and Alberhill resident, Spring 2006.

62. "California Vacation," *Ebony*, May 1948, 19–22.

63. Hudson, *Lake Elsinore Valley*, 86, 89, 91–93, 97, 103; "Historic California Posts—Camp Haan," California State Military Museum; "Cultural Resources Survey, Test, and Evaluation Report for the Meridian Specific Plan Amendment, Riverside, California," submitted by Kimley-Horn & Associates and Tierra Environmental Services, December 2009, http://www.marchjpa.com/docs_forms/meridianappendixj.pdf (accessed November 9, 2014), 12–14, 17–18.
64. Jane Kerina interview, August 21, 2006.
65. Price M. Cobbs, MD, resident of San Francisco CA, telephone interview with author, October 30, 2004; *Negroes Who's Who in California* (1948), 35; official Dexter Gordon website, http://www.dextergordon.com/main.htm (accessed May 8, 2014).
66. Hudson, *Lake Elsinore Valley*, 102–3, 157; 1950 U.S. Census.
67. Hudson, *Lake Elsinore Valley*, 123, 157; The Rutherfords, the Griffiths, and the (David) Williams families of African American heritage built vacation homes in the 1950s at Lake Elsinore, even with the dry lakebed conditions. Thomas Rutherford, interview with the author, August 18, 2006; Liza Griffith Scruggs, Los Angeles resident and Assistant Superintendent-Secondary Instruction for the Los Angeles Unified School District, telephone interview with the author, August 8 and October 7, 2006, Los Angeles, California; Nancy Scruggs Griffith, Los Angeles resident, interview with the author, July 19, 2006, Los Angeles, California; Halvor Miller, Esq., interview, March 12, 2007; "A New Judge in the Largest Court in the World: Griffith Becomes 8th Negro Judge in U.S.," *Sepia USA*, August 1953, n.p., Liza Griffith Scruggs Collection; *Negroes Who's Who in California* (1948), 45, 50; Elaine Woo, "David Williams Dies; Was First Black Federal Judge in West," *LAT*, May 10, 2000, B-1.
68. Foster, "In the Face of 'Jim Crow,'" 131, 136, 143; Gatewood, *Aristocrats of Color*, 202.
69. Foster, "In the Face of 'Jim Crow,'" 136–37. During this period Mexican nationals and Mexican Americans lived in the area. It can be speculated that these residents also used Lake Elsinore around the margins of the Euro-American resort community. "California Vacation," *Ebony*, May 1948, 21.
70. Shirlee Taylor Haizlip, "The Black Resorts," *American Legacy*, Summer 1996, 21.
71. Haizlip, "The Black Resorts," 21; Foster, "In the Face of 'Jim Crow,'" 146; Wolcott, *Race, Riots, and Roller Coasters*, 3, 6; Kahrl, "On the Beach," ix.
72. Hudson, *Lake Elsinore Valley*, 61, 136, 141; Sutton, *Travellers*, 293.
73. Hudson, *Lake Elsinore Valley*, 120–21, 128, 154; Lake Elsinore 2003 State of the City Report, Lake Elsinore Valley Chamber of Commerce, http://www.lakeelsinorechamber.com/ (accessed November 11,2014); City of Lake Elsinore, http://www.lake-elsinore.org/index.aspx?page=1 (accessed November 11, 2014); Lake Elsinore Campground, http://www.rockymountainrec.com/camp/elsinore.htm (accessed November 11, 2014); Lake Elsinore Valley Chamber of Commerce

Community Map (San Diego, California: Map Masters, 2003; Lake Elsinore and San Jacinto Watershed Authority, http://www.mywatersheds.com (accessed November 11, 2014).

74. Hudson, *Lake Elsinore Valley*, 77; Lake Elsinore QuickFacts from the U.S. Census, 2018, https://www.census.gov/quickfacts/fact/table/lakeelsinorecitycalifornia/PST045217 (accessed July 6, 2018); Lake Elsinore Valley Chamber of Commerce Community Map (San Diego, California: Map Masters, 2003); Lake Elsinore Visitors Bureau, http://www.visitlakeelsinore.com/ (accessed November 11, 2014); Lake Elsinore General Plan 2011, 1/1–1/2, http://www.lake-elsinore.org/index.aspx?page=909 (accessed November 11, 2014).

5. EXURBAN ADVENTURES AT THE PARKRIDGE

1. Postscript, "Parkridge, 'Famous Because of its Beauty'" ad, *CE*, August 31, 1928, 2.
2. In an editorial on April 24, 1924, the *Eagle* had supported the idea of country club ownership as means for African American self-determination in leisure and economic development through property control and community determination. The Parkridge project was one of a series of formal and informal Southern California African American attempts to fulfill these goals in the 1910s and 1920s (see chapter 6). "Club Movement Endorsed," April 24, 1924, *CE*, 22; Gaines, *Black Leadership*, 1–5; Mayo, *The American Country Club*, 2–3.
3. "Corona History," Corona Historic Preservation Society, http://www.corona-history.org/corona-lost-treasures.html (accessed December 29, 2014). For information on the Mexican American heritage of Corona, see Alamillo, *Making Lemonade out of Lemons*.
4. Marsh, *Corona*, 102; "Corona History," Corona Historic Preservation Society, http://www.corona-history.org/corona-lost-treasures.html (accessed December 29, 2014); "Brief History of Corona," Corona Public Library, http://www.coronapubliclibrary.org/Heritage-Room-(1)/Heritage-Room/HeritageSubPage.aspx (accessed December 29, 2014).
5. Bowman, *Los Angeles*, 216–18, 224, 227, 247–50.
6. Bowman, *Los Angeles*, 227–63, 285; McWilliams, *Southern California*, 135; 1920 and 1930 U.S. Census.
7. "Chamber of Commerce Endorses Parkridge," *CDI*, April 6, 1925, 1; Alamillo, *Making Lemonade out of Lemons*, 24.
8. Lech, *Resorts of Riverside County*, 7; "Riverside County, 'Empire of Recreation and of Health,'" *CDI*, May 31, 1928, 2.
9. Lech, *Resorts of Riverside County*, 7; Marsh, *Corona*, 10.
10. Charles R. Miller, "Corona Crops Find Good Mart," *LAT*, January 3, 1926; "Large Pool Finished in Parkridge," *LAT*, October 4, 1925; Marsh, *Corona*, 9–10.
11. Marsh, *Corona*, 29, 54–55; Alamillo, *Making Lemonade out of Lemons*, 13–15.
12. Alamillo, *Making Lemonade out of Lemons*, 15; Marsh, *Corona*, 29, 54–55, 80–81.

13. Alamillo, *Making Lemonade out of Lemons*, (quotation) 6, 15, 32.
14. Alamillo asserts that in Corona racial mixing was discouraged and Jim Crow–style conditions were imposed. In Corona, the racially restrictive real estate covenants were probably added to property deeds in the late 1920s. Before that time, property racial restrictions were more likely implemented in Corona by local custom. Alamillo, *Making Lemonade out of Lemons*, 6, 12, 20, 23, 25, 28, 34, 48.
15. Alamillo, *Making Lemonade out of Lemons*, 47. In the 1930 U.S. Census the population of Corona was a little over 4,600, with 23 individuals identified as Negro and almost 2,400 individuals were identified as other. No other racial or ethnic groups were broken out in the town Census that year.
16. Alamillo, *Making Lemonade out of Lemons*, 34–35. My discussion of forms of congregation marginalized groups created when faced with structural limitations of segregation is informed by the work of Earl Lewis. Whites missed the fact that segregation also vested African Americans' and other people in communities of color with the power to redefine their own existence in the battle for empowerment. Lewis, *In Their Own Interests*, 91–92.
17. Marsh, *Corona*, 49, 70–72, 99,102–3, 109.
18. Marsh, *Corona*, 102; Alamillo, *Making Lemonade out of Lemons*, 24.
19. My discussion of country clubs origins is informed by Mayo, *The American Country Club*; and Simon, "Country Clubs."
20. My discussion here of white suburban housing communities and privatized recreational facilities, white privilege and white spatial imaginary, is informed by Wiltse, *Contested Waters*; Sugrue, *Sweet Land of Liberty*; and Lipsitz, *How Racism Takes Place.*
21. "Parkridge Will Open This Fall," *LAT*, September 6, 1925; "Large Pool Finished in Parkridge, Converted Wasteland Is Now Beautiful Country Club Site," *LAT*, October 4, 1925; "Country Club Can't Pay Debts, Fashionable Resort Near Corona May Be Sold To Negro Corporation," *LAT*, August 18, 1927; "Parkridge Country Club, 'The Million Dollar Playground,'" *CE*, May 4, 1928.
22. "Golfers Flock to Join Parkridge Club," *LAT*, January 3, 1925; Marsh, *Corona*, 87.
23. "Parkridge Club Is Hailed as the Best," *LAT*, March 8, 1925; "Commends Parkridge," *LAT*, May 19,1925; "Parkridge Will Open This Fall, Rushing Work on New Club That Offers Diversified Sports for Members," *LAT*, September 6, 1925; "Large Pool Finished In Parkridge, Converted Wasteland Is Now Beautiful Country Club Site," *LAT*, October 4, 1925.
24. "Country Club Can't Pay Debts"; "Parkridge Sale to Negro Syndicate Confirmed," *CC*, August 19, 1927; "L.A. Negroes Buy Club Site, Dan Gilkey Confirms Sale of Parkridge Count[r]y Club to Large Negro Syndicate," *CE*, August 26, 1927; "Parkridge Members Planning Fight on Club Sale at Meeting Tonight Interesting Disclosures Likely," *CDI*, August 19, 1927; "Gilkey Spends Two Sleepless Nights in the Riverside County Jail; Was Arrested at Compton,"*CDI*, August 22, 1927.

25. "Parkridge Members Planning Fight on Club Sale," *CDI*, August 19, 1927; "Parkridge Sale to Negro Syndicate Confirmed."
26. "Parkridge Sale to Negro Syndicate Confirmed"; "Parkridge Members Planning Fight on Club"; Lipsitz, *How Racism Takes Place*, 36–37.
27. Lipsitz, *How Racism Takes Place*, 37.
28. "Keeping Our Record Clean," *CDI*, August 22, 1927.
29. "Keeping Our Record Clean"; Alamillo, *Making Lemonade out of Lemons*, 67.
30. "Parkridge Members Planning Fight on Club"; "Corona's Crisis," *CC*, August 19, 1927; "Parkridge Members Planning Fight on Club Sale"; "Quiet Sunday Is Reported In War Sector Near Club," *CC*, August 26, 1927; "Negro Menace Is Great as Ever," *CDI*, September 3, 1927; "Fiery Cross Burns Near Parkridge," *CDI*, August 19, 1927; "'Mixed Club' Will Never be Possible, Says Corona Citizen," *CC*, November 4, 1927.
31. "Parkridge Members Planning Fight on Club Sale"; "Corona's Crisis"; "Negroes Claim Club, Secretary of Colored Syndicate Pens Letter to Parkridge Members Expressing Much Hope," *CC*, April 20, 1928.
32. "Negroes Claim Club"; "Highlights of Tyler's Talk," *CDI*, August 20, 1927; "Parkridge Sale to Negro Syndicate Confirmed"; "Move Likely to Protect Property of Our Citizens," *CDI*, August 20, 1927; Gilkey, "Bound Over to Superior Court By Corona Justice," *CDI*, August 27, 1927.
33. "Throw Parkridge into Bankruptcy Is Plan," *CDI*, August 20, 1927; "Parkridge Members Planning Fight on Club Sale"; "Dance at Club House Tonight for Members," *CDI*, August 20, 1927; "Parkridge Dance Saturday Night Enjoyable Affair," *CDI*, August 22, 1927; "Parkridge Club Placed In Hands of Receiver," *CC*, August 26, 1927.
34. "Negroes Attempt to Take Club," *CDI*, August 20, 1927; "Club House Is Under Guard," *CDI*, August 20, 1927; "Signs and Men Placed on Road Leading to Club," *CDI*, August 22, 1927.
35. "Parkridge Members Are Dropped; Several Changes Made in By-Laws," *CDI*, August 23, 1927; "Coronans Filed Action against Gilkey, One Big Black Cloud Appears on the Horizon Yesterday," *CDI*, August 24, 1927; "Negro Menace Is Great as Ever," *CDI*, September 3, 1927.
36. "Gilkey's Case to Jury This Afternoon, Attorneys Present Arguments as Testimony Is Completed at Noon," *CDI*, November 9, 1927; "Detectives at Parkridge Today," *CDI*, August 20, 1927.
37. "Fiery Cross Burns Near Parkridge"; "Suggest Norco-Corona United," *CDI*, August 20, 1927; Larralde and del Castillo, "San Diego's Ku Klux Klan 1920–1980"; Engh, "Practically Every Religion Being Represented," 207.
38. "Move Likely to Protect Property of Our Citizens," *CDI*, August 20, 1927; "Corona's Crisis"; Alamillo, *Making Lemonade out of Lemons*, 24, (quotation) 25.

39. "Gilkey, Bound Over to Superior Court by Corona Justice," *CDI*, August 27, 1927.
40. "Negroes Buy Country Club"; "Parkridge Club Receiver Matter Comes Up Monday," *CC*, March 30, 1928; "Parkridge Club Troubles Talked Over in Corona," *CDI*, April 7, 1928; "Negroes Claim Club."
41. "The Largest Country Club in the World Owned and Controlled by Black Americans" was the subtitle on the "Parkridge Country Club, Official Program, Opening Celebration" bulletin, May 30, 1928, Ann Cunningham Smith Collection.
42. "L.A. Negroes Buy Club Site," 1; "Club Can't Pay Debts," *LAT*, August 18, 1927; "Gilkey Freed in Club Trial," *LAT*, November 10, 1927; "Negroes Claim Club"; "Parkridge Country Club to Have Gala Opening, *CE*, May 4, 1928; "Parkridge" ad, *CE*, July 28, 1928.
43. "Parkridge Country Club to Have Gala Opening"; Parkridge Country Club, Official Program, Opening Celebration, May 30, 1928, Ann Cunningham Smith Collection; "Californians Purchase Fine Country Club," *CD*, June 2, 1928; Singh, *Black Is a Country*, 48–49, 68–69; Lipsitz, *How Racism Takes Place*, 51–55.
44. Chandler Owen, "Dr. Eugene Curry Nelson, A Professional and Business Man of a New Type Among Negroes," *TM* 6 (October 6, 1924): 320; "White Stage Star Sticks to Mate: Defies Race Prejudice for Love," *CDI*, December 28, 1929, 1; Eugene C. Nelson, California Death Index, 1940–1997.
45. Chandler Owen, *TM* 6 (October 6, 1924): 320–21; "Former Doctor Freed in Illegal Practice Trial," *LAT*, August 7, 1943, A16; Dr. Eugene C. Nelson, MD, Christmas Greetings paid ad, *CE*, December 17, 1926. Walter L. Gordon Jr., Esq. (retired), interview with the author, April 12, 2011, Los Angeles, California. Nelson's office was at different addresses from the west side and the east side to Hollywood while he practiced medicine in Los Angeles before he moved to the San Diego area sometime in the years following World War II.
46. In 1924 U.S. crude oil was $1.68 per barrel. The average annual U.S. income was between $1,124 and $2,196: Historical U.S. Crude Oil Prices, 1861–present, http://chartsbin.com/view/oau (accessed December 16, 2014); Citizens' Voice, http://citizensvoice.com/arts-living/2.223/wow-the-average-income-in-1924-was-just-2-196-1.819546 (accessed December 16,2014); 1924 Mile Posts, http://local.aaca.org/junior/mileposts/1924.htm (accessed December 16, 2014); Thompson, "These 'Colored' United States, No. 15–California: Horn of Plenty," *TM* 6 (July 24, 1924), 215, 220–21; Chandler Owen, "Dr. Eugene Curry Nelson," *TM* 6 (October 6, 1924): 320; "Long Time Subscriber," *CE*, December 21, 1923, 12; "Eugene C. Nelson MD," *CE*, December 26, 1924, 1; *Negro Who's Who in California* (1948), 59.
47. "Eugene C. Nelson MD," *CE*, December 26, 1924, 1; "Long Time Subscriber," 12; "New Café Opens Doors to Los Angeles Public," *CE*, June 13, 1924, 1, 9; Chandler Owen, *TM* 6 (October 6, 1924): (quotation) 316, 317, 320–21.

48. Helen Lee Worthing, "Hollywood's Most Tragic Marriage," *Ebony*, February 1952, 26–36; Helen Lee Worthing, IMDB, http://www.imdb.com/name/nm0941745/ (accessed December 15, 2014); Bogle, *Bright Boulevards*, 56–59.
49. The story of Journee W. White's military exploits and honors was featured in Beasley, *The Negro Trail Blazers of California*, 286A, 308; and Smith, *The Great Black Way*, 38–39.
50. Smith, *The Great Black Way*, 38–41; W. E. B. Du Bois, "Close Ranks," *Crisis* 16, no. 3 (July 1918): 111; Tolbert, *The UNIA and Black Los Angeles*, 71–72.
51. The Legion Club was also referred to as the Legion Café. "Café Charges Sensational," *LAT*, January 9, 1927, A1; "Ragtime" Billy Tucker, "Coast Dope" column, *CD*, November 1, 1924, 7; Smith, *The Great Black Way*, 41–42; Flamming, *Bound for Freedom*, 275–90. See Hernández, *City of Inmates*, for information on Los Angeles police corruption and the African American community in the 1920s.
52. "Legion Club Management Already to Serve and Entertain Huge Dancing Crowd Saturday and Sunday," *CE*, January 8, 1926, 7; "Café Charges Sensational," *LAT*, January 9, 1927, A1.
53. "Café Charges Sensational"; Smith, *The Great Black Way*, 1–42; Flamming, *Bound for Freedom*, 275–90; Starr, *Material Dreams*, 170–72.
54. 1920, 1930, and 1940 U.S. Census; "Julian Products in New Location at 9th and Central, Journee White To Supervise Operations," *CE*, July 10, 1925, 8; "J. W. White and Clarence Bailey in Jail Over Oil Leases," *CE*, January 18, 1929, 3; "White and Bailey Paroled," 1; "Uncovered Race Bias in Defense Industries," *CD*, November 30, 1940, 7.
55. Gordon interview, April 12, 2011; Beasley, *The Negro Trail Blazers*, 135, 148; "California News," *CD*, August 27, 1927; "Automotive Section, Exhaust Column," *CE*, October 21, 1927, 9; Mamie Cunningham White with her daughter, Emma, and an unidentified woman in Paris during the American Legion convention, 1927, Photograph from Anne Cunningham Smith Collection, Los Angeles, California.
56. The impact of Executive Order 8802 was mostly symbolic, as there was no enforcement capability included. Nonetheless the order was a very important step toward dismantling Jim Crow discrimination in the workplace, as it legitimized a policy of racial equity in hiring, at least in principle, by the federal government due to activist pressure. "Eastside Chamber Confers With Aviation Officials," *CE*, July 25, 1940, 9B; Lawrence F. LaMar, "Conspire to Bar Race From Defense Setup," *CD*, August 3, 1940, 1; Lawrence F. LaMar, "Secret Probe Data Is Given to Gov. Olson," *CD*, September 21, 1940, 7; "Uncovered Race Bias in Defense Industries," *CD*, November 30, 1940, 7; Sides, *L.A. City Limits*, 3; Flamming, *Bound for Freedom*, 361–64; Smith, *The Great Black

Way, 51; Lawrence F. LaMar, "Big Business Trembles During FEP Hearing, Coast Probe Show Bias In Defense Hiring," *CD*, November 1, 1941, 2; "Racial Prejudice Charged in Plants," *LAT*, October 21, 1941, 18.

57. 1900, 1910, and 1920 U.S. Census; Clarence Bailey, Sr., U.S. Social Security Death Index, 1935–2014.
58. "L.A. Colored Man Owns Oil Property in New Field at Long Beach, California," *CE*, September 23, 1927, 6; "J. W. White and Clarence Bailey in Jail Over Oil Leases"; "White and Bailey Paroled"; "Journee White, Secretary of Colored Club Sentenced to Two Years in Jail," *CDI*, January 5, 1929, 1; "Surrender at Jail for Sentences," *LAT*, January 6, 1929, B7.
59. "J.W. White and Clarence Bailey in Jail Over Oil Leases," 3; "White and Bailey Paroled," 1; Rawls and Bean, *California*, 299–300; Bowman, 254–57.
60. Parkridge promotional text, *CE*, July 13, 1928.
61. Flamming, *Bound for Freedom*, 239–42; Gordon Manor promotional text, *CE*, September 10, 1926; Gordon vs. County Supervisors promotional text, *CE*, October 8, 1926; For more on Gordon Manor see note 23, chapter 4, 296; "Alondra Park Bonds Ordered," *LAT*, September 28, 1927; "Park Bond Issue Held to Be Legal," *LAT*, November 27, 1927.
62. Norman O. Houston Park, http://www.laparks.org/dos/parks/facility/houstonNOPk.htm (accessed December 25, 2014); "Parkridge Announcement Extraordinary" ad, *CE*, August 24, 1928, 13.
63. Flamming, *Bound for Freedom*, 5, 44–45, 47. See a discussion of gambling syndicates as an important source of capital for African American businesses in Maryland and Pittsburgh PA at a time when banks denied loans to African Americans in, respectively, Kahrl, *This Land Was Ours*, 178–209; and Ruck, *Sandlot Seasons*.
64. Gregory, *The Southern Diaspora*, 32; Flamming *Bound for Freedom*, 45–47, 227, 231–32; 157; McBroome, "Harvest of Gold"; Wilkerson, *The Warmth of Other Suns*, 233; Rawls and Bean, *California*, 249.
65. DeGraaf and Taylor, "Introduction," in *Seeking El Dorado*, 21–22; Flamming, *Bound for Freedom*, 92–93.
66. Flamming, *Bound for Freedom*, 92–93, 281, 284–89; DeGraaf and Taylor, "Introduction," in *Seeking El Dorado*, 21–22; Vivian, *The Story of the Negro in Los Angeles County 1936*, 35.
67. DeGraaf and Taylor, "Introduction," in *Seeking El Dorado*, 21–22, 26–27; 130–31, 143–44; Flamming, *Bound for Freedom*, 92–93, 128, 289; Deverell and Flamming, "Race, Rhetoric, and Regional Identity," 124–25, 127; "Californians Purchase Fine Country Club," *CD*, 2 June 1928, 7.
68. Oliver and Shapiro, *Black Wealth/White Wealth*, 47–48, (Merah Stuart citation) 49, 50–54. The concept of the "economic detour" appeared in Merah Steven Stuart's book, *An Economic Detour*.

69. "Negroes Claim Club, The Letter of Greetings that the Negro Syndicate Sends to Parkridge Club Members," *CC*, April 20, 1928, 1.
70. "Negroes Claim Club," 1.
71. The newspaper article does not explicitly name the venture in Los Angeles County where land was condemned for a public park, but the correspondent was probably referring to the Gordon Manor development. For more on Gordon Manor see note 23, chapter 4, 296; "Negroes Claim Club," 1.
72. "Parkridge Country Club, 'The Million Dollar Playground,'" *CE*, May 4, 1928; "Parkridge Head Invites Corona Members to Fete," *CDI*, May 29/30, 1928, 1.
73. "Parkridge Beauty Contest" ad, *CE*, May 4, 1928.
74. "The Million Dollar Playground," *CE*, May 4, 1928; "Parkridge Beauty Contest" ad; "Parkridge, 'Famous Because of Its Beauty'" ad, *CE*, August 31, 1928, 2.
75. "Tell Distorted News of Race Riot, Los Angeles Papers Shy from Facts," *CD*, May 31, 1928, 1; "Corona Given Black Eye through United Press Reports Going Back East," *CD*, June 6, 1928, 1, and *CC*, June 8, 1928, 2; "Parkridge Club Pays $15 Fines for Traffic Tickets in Police Court Today," *CC*, June 8, 1928.
76. "Tell Distorted News of Race Riot," 1.
77. "Tell Distorted News of Race Riot," 1; "Corona Given Black Eye Through United Press Reports Going Back East"; "Attorney Charges Plot to Plant Liquor in Colored Club, Before Police Court," *CDI*, June 6, 1928, 1; "Parkridge Club Pays $15 Fines for Traffic Tickets in Police Court Today."
78. No first name for Attorney Donohue was printed in the newspaper accounts. "Attorney Charges Plot to Plant Liquor in Colored Club," 2.
79. "Parkridge Club Pays $15 Fines For Traffic Tickets in Police Court Today."
80. "Attorney Charges Plot to Plant Liquor in Colored Club," 2.
81. "Attorney Charges Plot to Plant Liquor in Colored Club"; "Parkridge Club Pays $15 Fines For Traffic Tickets in Police Court Today."
82. "Los Angeles Papers Shy From Facts," 1; "Corona Given Black Eye Through United Press Reports Going Back East," 2; "Attorney Charges Plot to Plant Liquor in Colored Club," 1; "Parkridge Club Pays $15 Fines For Traffic Tickets in Police Court Today."
83. "Corona 'Race Riot' Story Given Out by Negroes Is Claim of the United Press" and "News and Comment," *CDI*, June 14, 1928, 1–2.
84. "Parkridge Country Club Welcomes the NAACP [National Association for the Advancement of Colored People]," *CE*, June 29, 1928, 8; "Parkridge" ads with Labor Day visit promotion, *CE*, August 10, 1928, 5; "Parkridge, 'Famous Because of Its Beauty'" ad, *CE*, August 31, 1928, 2; "Doings at the Parkridge by the Tattler," *CE*, October 12, 1928, 7; "The Directors of Parkridge Country Club Invite You to a Big Week End," *CE*, November 9, 1928, 10; "Thanksgiving at Parkridge," *CE*, November 23, 1928, 4.
85. "Country Club Value Placed," *LAT*, June 16. 1928, 6; "Negroes Seek to Issue $325,000 in Bonds for Club," *CDI*, June 16, 1928, 1; "Parkridge" ad with information

about the Bond issue, *CE*, July 13, 1928, 10; "Colored Club Is Shy on Cash for Help, Reported," *CC*, September 7, 1928; "Promoter White of Colored Club Facing Trouble," *CC*, October 26, 1928.

86. "Expect Many for Parkridge Meet," *CDI*, July 30, 1929, Parkridge Club File, Special Collections, Corona Public Library; Mayo, *The American Country Club*, 2–3; Simon, "Country Clubs," 193–94.
87. Among his accomplishments, General John J. Pershing led African American troops in segregated regiments in the American West and the Spanish-American War in the Philippines in the late 1800s and in World War I. Pershing always expressed forceful public admiration for the African American troops under his command for their bravery and patriotism. In an attempt to help African American soldiers advance in command in World War I, Pershing placed them under the leadership of the French, who honored 171 of them (including Lieutenant Journee W. White) for their valor in hastening the Armistice that ended the conflict. "Military School Takes Over Old Parkridge," unknown newspaper, January 6, 1931, Parkridge Club File, Special Collections, Corona Public Library; "One-Time Social Center Now Stands Stark, Lonely and Deserted on Hill," Golden Jubilee Edition, *CDI*, April 27, 1936; "General John J. Pershing, Today in History: July 15," American Memory, Library of Congress, http://memory.loc.gov/ammem/today/jul15.html (accessed December 29, 2014).
88. "One-Time Social Center Now Stands Stark"; George Ringwald, "Old Country Club May Recapture Its Days of Glory," *Press Enterprise*, November 29, 1964. In 2017 the total population of Corona was 167,836; African Americans make up 26 percent of the population (43,637); Latinx 43 percent (72,169); and Asian/Pacific Islanders 12 percent (20,140). Corona QuickFacts from the U.S. Census, 2018, https://www.census.gov/quickfacts/fact/table/coronacitycalifornia/PST120217 (accessed July 6, 2018).
89. DeGraaf, "The City of Angels," 348, 349; "Double Crossed," *CE*, June 18, 1926.
90. Hayden, *The Power of Place*, 7–9, 12–13.
91. Shackel, *Memory in Black and White*, 198–99, 209; Trouillot, *Silencing the Past*, 95–107.
92. My discussion here of the distinctive African American business pioneers associated with the 1920s era and the Parkridge project is also generally informed by Richard Bardolph's discussion of African American leadership characteristics from the 1900s to 1936 in *The Negro Vanguard*; see also Foster, "In the Face of 'Jim Crow,'" 146.

6. EUREKA VILLA

1. There were also a few town clubs attempted in Los Angeles, including the Business and Professional Men's Club, *CE*, November 27, 1925, 7, and the Appomattox Club, *CE*, August 1, 1930, 1.

2. For an examination of the evolution of new community promotion around Southern California, see the analysis of Ontario, California, from rural smallhold "colony" to integrated "agriburb" in Sandul, *California Dreaming*; and Wolcott, *Race, Riots, and Roller Coasters*, 18–19.
3. Flamming, *Bound for Freedom*, 193, 231; Baldwin, "Introduction," in *Escape From New York*, 19; Blight, *Race and Reunion*, 390–91; "The Rise and Fall of Jim Crow, A National Struggle," PBS, http://www.pbs.org/wnet/jimcrow/struggle_president2.html (accessed February 21, 2014).
4. Allensworth in Tulare County, California, was a black town project. "In August 1908 Colonel Allen Allensworth, William Payne, Oscar Overr, Josephine Cowes and Alice Hackett with other settlers established a town founded, financed and governed by African Americans. Their dream of developing an abundant and thriving community stemmed directly from a strong belief in programs that allowed blacks to help themselves create better lives. By 1910 Allensworth's success was the focus of many national newspaper articles praising the town and its inhabitants"; Colonel Allensworth State Historic Park, http://www.parks.ca.gov/?page_id=583 (accessed December 10, 2011; Wheeler, *Black California*, 171, 183–84; Flamming, *Bound for Freedom*, 146, 348; McBroome, "Harvest of Gold," 149, 153–54; "Eureka Villa Over the Top," *CE*, September 12, 1924, 1; Wolcott, *Race, Riots, and Roller Coasters*, 18–19. For more on Allensworth, see Royal, Ellinger, and Braley, *Allensworth, The Freedom Colony*. "Negro projects" refers to institutionalized programming that could implicitly sanction, and thereby reinforce, the exclusion and segregation of African Americans' participation in areas including education, employment, housing, and accommodations.
5. "Eureka Villa (EV) Community" ad, *CE*, February 13, 1925, 3; "EV News/Editorial," *CE*, June 19, 1925, 8.
6. "EV Community" ad; "EV News/Editorial."
7. I thought the title of the book about Santa Clarita Valley was an appropriate title for this section, giving context to the formation of the African American resort, "Eureka Villa." Reynolds, *Santa Clarita*.
8. Reynolds, *Santa Clarita*, 44, 94; Boston and the Santa Clarita Valley Historical Society, *Images of America*, 7.
9. Reynolds, *Santa Clarita*, 85–87; McWilliams, *Southern California*, 134.
10. Reynolds, *Santa Clarita*, 21–22, 92; "EV and Community Center" ad, *CE*, June 13, 1924, 4. From old maps of the Ranchos, the area of Eureka Villa appears outside and between Rancho Temescal and Rancho San Francisco.
11. In different accounts the wealthy white woman from Pasadena is referred to with the last name of "Janes" or "James." I verified that the Eureka Tract landowners were Laura C. Janes and Burt N. Janes in the subdivision tract map book from the Los Angeles County Land Records Information, Dept. of Public Works: http://dpw.lacounty.gov/sur/nas/landrecords/tract/MB0102/TR0102-095.pdf

(accessed January 8, 2014). Douglas Flamming cited in a footnote that he obtained his information on the founding of EV/Val Verde (VV) in part from "information as quoted from online Val Verde historical file, Valencia Public Library, Valencia, California"; 423n41. The information noted in his citation is not currently available online or in the Valencia Library. Flamming, *Bound for Freedom*, 348; "Opportunity Knows/Editorials," *CE*, February 6, 1925, 6; "Eureka Villa," *CE*, July 23, 1926, 2; Jocelyn Y. Stewart, "Forgotten Oasis of Freedom VV, the 'Black Palm Springs,'" *LAT*, March 2, 1994, 3; "EV Over the Top."

12. All of the exurban, "clubhouse movement" land development projects described in this book included residential (e.g., cabin-like structures or more substantial tents on platforms) and recreational facilities. These leisure land development projects were sometimes referred to as subdivisions. These sites were in rural areas that would not have been seen in the era as likely to become recreational and residential communities in the 1920s. "Opportunity Knows/Editorials," *CE*, February 6, 1925, 6.
13. "Club House Movement Endorsed/Editorials," *CE*, April 24, 1924, 22.
14. "Editorials," *CE*, May 23, 1924, 14; W. J. Wheaton, "Comments, Residential Segregation," *CE*, October 16, 1925, 1; Wolcott, *Race, Riots, and Roller Coasters*, 19; Flamming, *Bound for Freedom*, 216–18.
15. "Double Crossed/Editorials," *CE*, June 18, 1926, 6; "What a Difference It Makes/Editorials," *CE*, September 26, 1926, 6.
16. "Opportunity Knows/Editorials," *CE*, February 6, 1925, 6; "A Country Club by Our Group Has Been Formed," *CE*, April 18, 1924, 4.
17. "The People to Have Real Country Club," *CE*, April 25, 1924, 1; "Opening Announcement, Peaceful Valley Country Club" ad, *CE*, April 25, 1924, 10; "Peaceful Valley Country Club, Another Winner for Los Angeles" ad, *CE*, May 9, 1924, 10; "The Rush Is On" ad, *CE*, May 2, 1924, 10.
18. "The Rush Is On"; "Peaceful Valley Country Club, A Smashing Success" ad, *CE*, May 2, 1924, 10; "Peaceful Valley Country Club," *CE*, May 9, 1924, 12; "Opening Announcement, Peaceful Valley Country Club" ad, *CE*, April 25, 1924, 10.
19. "The People to Have Real Country Club"; "Peaceful Valley Country Club" ad, *CE*, April 25, 1924, 10; "Eastside Realty Company Promotes Country Club," *CE*, May 9, 1924, 1; "Castaic Country Club in Thousand Canyons District" ad, *CE*, May 9, 1924, 12; "A Pleasant Trip to Castaic Country Club Sub-Division," *CE*, May 23, 1924, 10.
20. "Eastside Realty Company Promotes Country Club"; "Castaic Country Club" ad, *CE*, May 9, 1924, 12.
21. "Eastside Realty Company Promotes Country Club"; "A Pleasant Trip to Castaic Country Club Sub-Division."
22. "Castaic Country Club" ad, *CE*, May 9, 1924, 12.
23. "Eastside Realty Company Promotes Country Club," *CE*, May 9, 1924, 1; "Castaic Country Club" ad; "Letter from Law Office of Afue McDowell," *CE*, May 23, 1924, 4.

24. "The People to Have Real Country Club"; " Eastside Reality Company Promotes Country Club"; "Opening Announcement, Peaceful Valley Country Club" ad, *CE*, April 25, 1924, 10.
25. "Castaic Country Club Subdivision, The Playground of Angelenos" ad, *CE*, June 13, 1924, 7.
26. "What Are We Coming To?: EV News," *CE*, December 18, 1925, 5; "Clubs on the Taboo/Editorials," *CE*, October 8, 1926, 6.
27. "The Sidney P. Dones Co.," *CE*, December 5, 1914, 1; Beasley, *The Negro Trail Blazers of California*, 58, 205; *Negro Who's Who in California* (1948), 127; *L.A. Negro Directory and Who's Who 1930–1931*, "Sidney P. Dones," IMDB, http://www.imdb.com/name/nm0232452/?ref_=nmbio_bio_nm (accessed December 11, 2013; "Wiley College History," http://www.wileyc.edu/history.asp (accessed December 11, 2013); Flamming, *Bound for Freedom*, 120–22; U.S. Census.
28. "The Sidney P. Dones Co."; Beasley, *The Negro Trail Blazers of California*, 205; *Negro Who's Who in California* (1948), 127; Flamming, *Bound for Freedom, 121.*
29. "The Sidney P. Dones Co."; Beasley, *The Negro Trail Blazers of California*, 205; Flamming, *Bound for Freedom*, (*New Age* newspaper quotations as they appear in Flamming text), 121.
30. "Central Avenue and the Eagle," *CE*, April 8, 1916, 4.
31. Beasley, *The Negro Trail Blazers of California*, 205; *Negro Who's Who in California* (1948), 127; Flamming, *Bound for Freedom*, 120–22; *L.A. Negro Directory and Who's Who 1930–1931*, 127.
32. Beasley, *The Negro Trail Blazers of California*, 205; Flamming, "Becoming Democrats," in *Seeking El Dorado*, 392n16; *Negro Who's Who in California* (1948), 127; Flamming, *Bound for Freedom*, 120–22; *L.A. Negro Directory and Who's Who 1930–1931*, 127.
33. "EV and Community Center" ad, *CE*, June 13, 1924, 4; "What's in a Name?," *CE*, June 13, 1924, 8; "EV Community Center and Club" ad, *CE*, June 20, 1924, 4; "California Colored People's Greatest Achievement, EV" ad, *CE*, December 26, 1924, 14.
34. The early published list of board members with their photographs in a December 1924 Eureka Villa advertisement in the *CE* included: Fredrick M. Roberts, California Assembly member and editor of the *New Age* newspaper, was a member of the association's Publicity Committee; J. C. Banks Sr., employed at U.S. Customs, former local head of the NAACP and vice president of the Association; Sidney P. Dones, president of the Association and president of the California Realty Board; Mrs. Ernestine Davidson, secretary of the Association and Eureka Villa Inn owner; Joseph B. Bass, editor of the *California Eagle* and chairman of the publicity committee; Dr. Emily B. Childress (later Portwig), pharmacist and community activist and on the publicity committee; Dr. E. D. Driver, pastor, Saints Home Holiness Church and on the building

committee; Felix Waugh, on the building committee; Elbridge Lee, on the street and park committee; Mrs. Virginia James, on the building committee; Mrs. Eliza Lawrence, on the social committee; Dr. William B. Humphrey, MD, proprietor of the Oklahoma Drug Store (in Los Angeles) and on the health and sanitation committee; W. M. Shelten, manager of the Indiana Realty Company and chairman of the Association's building committee; and George Cushnie, on the water and light committee. "EV" ad, *CE*, June 13, 1924, 4; "EV Community" ad, *CE*, June 20, 1924, 4; "California Colored People's Greatest Achievement, EV" ad, *CE*, December 26, 1924, 14.

35. "We Have Found It! Eureka Villa Community" sales brochure, Aubrey Provost Collection, n.d.
36. "We Have Found It!"; "EV Over the Top"; "EV to Build Community Club," *CE*, September 19, 1924, 3; "This Is Progress/Editorials," *CE*, October 3, 1924, 6.
37. "EV and Community Center" ad, *CE*, June 13, 1924, 4.
38. "A Wonderful Investment!" ad, *CE*, June 27, 1924, 4; "EV Over the Top"; "EV News," *CE*, November 14, 1924, 5, November 21, 1924, 8, and December 12, 1924, 6; "EV News/Geo. A. Cushnie," *CE*, June 26, 1925, 8.
39. "EV to Build Community Club," 3; "EV to Have Good Roads," *CE*, October 3, 1924, 1; "EV News," *CE*, December 19, 1924, 3; Charles Hillinger, "Cattle, Oil Fields, Industries Thrive in Ridge Route Area, Negro Town Among Big Surprises," *LAT*, April 22, 1962, F1; "VV Park, California 1960" bulletin, presented by the Val Verde Chamber of Commerce, Saugus, California, Department of Parks and Recreation Archives, County of Los Angeles, 5; U.S. Census.
40. Several of the early business owners were members of the advisory board. The Eureka Inn and Cafe, La Casa del Sol, the Hummingbird Inn, Mosley's Oriental Lunch Room and Inn, and Mrs. Ethel Davis's establishment offered refreshments, meals, and a few rooms for overnight stays. In addition to selling refreshments to visitors, Three Buddies establishment partner Arthur L. Provost also would take visitors around to show and sell them lots. "EV Townsite, The Week, Race Progress," *CE*, April 3, 1925, 8; "EV," *CE*, April 24, 1925, 5; "EV News" page, *CE*, June 26, 1925, 8; "EV News/Mrs. Ethel Davis Drills Well in the First Unit," *CE*, December 4, 1925, 5.
41. This author has not found evidence the newsreels were produced at this date. "Eureka Villa News," *CE*, December 19, 1924, 3: "Sidney P. Dones," *CE*, September 4, 1925, 1.
42. The pursuit of U.S. Army soldiers was also part of the Allenworth's lot sales effort. "Eureka Villa News/ Mrs. Mary Carter/ Eureka Villa Invades U.S. Army," *CE*, September 11, 1925, 8; "Eureka Villa News/ Warrant Officers Wade O. Hammond and V.H. Marchbank," *CE*, September 28, 1925, 8.
43. "Beach Resort a Reality," *CE*, February 20, 1925, 1; "Pacific Beach Club Announces Grand Opening and Ground Breaking Sunday, March 22, 1925," *CE*, March 20,

1925, 1; "Only One Way/Editorials," *CE*, September 11, 1925, 6; "Pacific Beach Club Opening on March 22 Huge Success," *CE*, April 3, 1925, 1; "Opportunity No. 1 Passes Monday Morning, April 6" ad, *CE*, April 3, 1925, 2.

44. "Fortunate Indeed/Editorials," April 3, 1925, *CE*, 6; "10 Things To Remember" Pacific Beach Club ad, *CE*, September 18, 1925, 4.
45. "Fortunate Indeed/Editorials"; "10 Things To Remember" Pacific Beach Club ad; "Prominent Men Endorse Pacific Beach Club," *CE*, January 15, 1926, 6; Beasley, *The Negro Trail Blazers of California*, 192–94, 200.
46. "Beach Club Is Proposed by Negroes," *LAT*, April 2, 1925, 19: "Beach Resort a Reality"; "Beach Lost to Race for $35,000 to House $1,000,000 White Club House," *TPD*, April 1, 1927, 4.
47. "Beach Club Is Proposed by Negroes," 19.
48. "Beach Resort a Reality"; George Perry, "$100,000 Race Beach Resort Faces Foreclosure," *Topeka Plain Dealer*, October 29, 1926, 2; "Refuse Permission to Extend Service," *LAT*, October 12, 1925, 6; "Pacific Coast Resort Butted By Fire; White Who Made Threats Are Blamed," *CD*, January 30, 1926, 1.
49. Other Pacific Beach Club board members included Dr. (Georgia K.) Boone C. Offut (Chiropodist), Dr. William R. Carter, Dr. J. T. Smith, and Dr. Batie Robinson. Other African American citizens involved with the Pacific Beach Club included Dr. R.S. Whittaker, Dr. Charles S. Diggs, Dr. H. Claude Hudson, Dr. J. T. Smith, Clarence A. Jones, Esq., and Mamie V. White (employment agency owner). "Pacific Beach Club Pays Off to All Members," *CE*, January 28, 1927, 1; "Prominent Men Endorse Pacific Beach Club," *CE*, January 15, 1926, 6; "Beach Resort a Reality"; "No. 1, A Series of Ten Talks About Pacific Beach Club" ad, *CE*, October 9, 1925, 6; "Baumann, Albert-Pharmacist," in *L.A. Negro Directory and Who's Who 1930–1931*, n.p.
50. "An Invitation to a Limited Number of Colored People in Southern California to Become Members" ad, *CE*, March 13, 1925, 3; "Draw Up Nearer Folks" ad, *CE*, March 27, 1925, 4.
51. African American vacation leisure did occur unabated at Orange County's Huntington Beach as mentioned in different social items in the *California Eagle* in 1925 about the Scott family and friends, and the Brooks family. More social news ("At Huntington Beach") appeared in the same July 10 issue. Charlotta Bass, managing editor of the *Eagle*, was described as "the weekend guest of Mrs. Ella Cassells . . . at beautiful Huntington Beach," where the two took a Sunday afternoon sightseeing trip to Newport and Balboa Beaches, hosted by Mrs. Lois Best. It was noted that Mrs. Cassells had made her "permanent home" in the community since its founding in 1909. The item went on to say she was the owner of "some of the most valuable property there, and [was] one of the most highly respected citizens in that city." The 1910 U.S. Census lists Mrs. Ella L. Cassells and her two brothers (William and Henry) as the only "Mulattoes" living on Alhambra Avenue in the

Orange County beach city. Before the oil boom in the 1920s and after the dream of Huntington Beach's development into the Pacific Coast version of Atlantic City had passed, Cassells and her relatives would have been some of the few recognized African American property owners living in this south coast Orange County area in the first decades of the twentieth century. "At Huntington Beach," Social Intelligence, Heard or Seen In Passing Column, *CE*, July 10, 1925, 5. 1910 and 1920 U.S. Census Enumeration Sheet each list the Cassells family members' race as "Mulatto." In the 1930 U.S. Census Enumeration Sheet, Cassells's race is listed as a "Negro." "City of Huntington Beach History," http://www.huntingtonbeachca.gov/about/history/ (accessed June 30, 2014). In 2010 the demographics had not changed. African Americans were less than 1 percent of the Huntington Beach population. The 2017 U.S. Census reported that African Americans only made up about 2 percent of Orange County's population (3,090,132). Orange County QuickFacts from the U.S. Census Bureau, https://www.census.gov/quickfacts/fact/table/orangecountycalifornia/PST045217 (accessed July 6, 2017).

52. "Beach Club Is Proposed by Negroes," 19: "Beach Resort a Reality"; "A Series of Ten Talks About Pacific Beach Club, Talk No. 4" ad, *CE*, November 6, 1925, 7; "Draw Up Nearer Folks," *CE*, March 27, 1925, 4.
53. "A Series of Ten Talks About Pacific Beach Club, Talk No. 4" ad, *CE*, November 6, 1925, 7; "A Series of Ten Talks About Pacific Beach Club, Talk No. 5" ad, *CE*, November 13, 1925, 7; "Beach Resort a Reality"; "Draw Up Nearer Folks"; "No. 1, A Series of Ten Talks About Pacific Beach Club" ad, *CE*, October 9, 1926, 6; "Bathing Beauties Attract Many Thousand Spectators to New Pacific Beach Club," *CE*, September 11, 1925, 7.
54. "Bathing Beauties Attract Many Thousand Spectators to New Pacific Beach Club"; "Great Day, Dese Heah Colo'd Folk Suh Do Put On Some Bathing Parade," *Santa Ana Register*, September 8, 1925.
55. My discussion about the significance of the representations and preservation of cultural memories in film and photography is informed by my reading of Willis's *Posing Beauty*. Images of the Pacific Beach Bathing Girl and Children Contest and Beauty Parade from September 7, 1925, can be viewed in Willis's book on pages 122–23. At the time of this writing, the author of this text, also has uncovered and collected photographs from the September 7, 1925, Pacific Beach Club event in Los Angeles. It is mostly professional historians documenting the Pacific Beach Club who are aware of the rich, although limited visual and written archives of the Club. There is scant popular memory of the 1920s event or the site.
56. "EV News/EV Mountains Are Calling You" ad and "Big Celebration Sat. and Sun. at EV," *CE*, June 26, 1925, 8; "EV News/Fourth of July Will be Big Day at Eureka," *CE*, July 3, 1925, 8; "EV News/Free Barbecue at EV Labor Day" ad, *CE*, September 4, 1925, 8. For information on the extremely popular 1920s-era Sunnyland Jazz band, see DjeDje and Meadows, *California Soul*.

57. "Pacific Beach In Ashes," *CE*, January 22, 1926, 1; "Pacific Coast Resort Gutted by Fire: Whites Who Made Threats are Blamed," *CD*, January 30, 1926, 1; "Inquiry Begun in Club Blaze," *LAT*, January 22, 1926, A20; "Arson Arrests Expected," *LAT*, January 23, 1926, A8; "Arsonist Burn Negro Beach Club," *Santa Ana Register*, January 21, 1926, 1.
58. "Pacific Beach Club Pays Off to All Members," *CE*, January 28, 1927, 1–2; "Beach Lost to Race for $35,000 to House $1,000,000 White Club House," *TPD*, April 1, 1927, 4.
59. "EV" ad, *CE*, July 23, 1926, 2; "EV" ad, *CE*, September 17, 1926, 2; "Sidney Preston Dones/EV—X-Mas Present" ad, *CE*, November 18, 1927, 2; "Sidney P. Dones/Associated Loan Company" ad, *CE*, January 27, 1928, 5.
60. "Val Verde Park—Historical Information," Val Verde Park File, Department of Parks and Recreation, County of Los Angeles (VVPFCLA); "Free—Barbecue Picnic—Free" ad, *CE*, June 29, 1928, 3; "Supervisor Jack H. Bean, Los Angeles County Board of Supervisors," http://file.lacounty.gov/lac/jbean.pdf (accessed February 20, 2014).
61. "Free—Barbecue Picnic—Free" ad.
62. "Thousands are Coming to Worship at the Easter Sunrise Service on Sunrise Hill VV" ad, *CE*, March 19, 1929, 5; "Thousands of Dollars Are Being Spent at Val Verde" ad, *CE*, 2; "VV News," *CE*, March 13, 1931, 6; Flamming, *Bound for Freedom*, 348–49.
63. See "EV News" articles in the *California Eagle* from 1930 to 1940 for site improvements and social and cultural news and events; Flamming, *Bound for Freedom*, 348–49.
64. Lipsitz, *How Racism Takes Place*, 51, (quotation) 52, 53–56.
65. "VV to Be Improved," *LAS*, July 2, 1936, 1; "Swimming Pool at VV Near Finish," *LAS*, February 1, 1940, 1; Flamming, *Bound for Freedom*, 349.
66. "Happy Throngs See Cornerstone Laid at VV," *CE*, April 20, 1939, 1, 5A; Flamming, *Bound for Freedom*, 349.
67. "Item Number 76c: Letter from Gordon L. McDonough, Supervisor 2nd District, Los Angeles County," Val Verde Time Capsule, Department of Parks and Recreation Archives, County of Los Angeles (VVPFCLA), 1939; Flamming, *Bound for Freedom*, 349; Sitkoff, *A New Deal for Blacks*, ix, 330–31; Singh, *Black Is a Country*, 68–69; Badger, *The New Deal*, 253–55.
68. "Happy Throngs See Cornerstone Laid at VV," (Jackson quotation) 1–5A; "Swimming Pool at VV Near Finish," *LAS*, February 1, 1940, (Waterman quotation) 1; "Spend Your Week-Ends in VV" ad, *LAS*, February 8, 1940, 6; Naro, *Westways*, February 1995, 71; Jill Nelson, Nanine Alexander, and Pamela Douglas, "A Summer Place: Black Resorts Are Havens, Communities of Neighbors and Real Property," *Black Enterprise*, August 1981, 59; "Item Number 15: Possible Speech of Emily Brown Childress Portwig," (Portwig quotation) Val Verde Time Capsule,

VVPFCLA, 1939. Whether Sidney P. Dones was at the event is not clear. He was not listed as being present at the program in any of the newspaper accounts or time capsule contents of the day available for review by the author. Dr. Portwig was one of the first lot buyers at Eureka Villa in 1924. In the mid-1990s, as a result of damage from the Northridge earthquake the Val Verde Park, 1939 swimming pool was rebuilt, the original bathhouse was torn down, and a new building was constructed. At the time of this writing the cornerstone and time capsule from the original bathhouse had been removed and stored in the Department of Parks and Recreation Archives, County of Los Angeles.

69. Gregory, *The Southern Diaspora*, 23–41; Sides, *L.A. City Limits*, 3–4, 37–43.
70. Gregory, *The Southern Diaspora*, 23–41; Sides, *L.A. City Limits*, 9, 47; 1900, 1940 and 1950 U.S. Census.
71. "Go West, The VV Way!," VV Properties ad, *CE*, May 16, 1940, 4A.
72. "Go West."
73. "Go West."
74. "Where to Go Vacationing," *Ebony*, July 1947, 14.
75. "VV Park, California 1960" bulletin, presented by the VV Chamber of Commerce, Saugus, California, 18; "Perdue Retires as VV Recreation Head," ca. 1964, unidentified newspaper, Frank D. Godden Collection of the Salaam Mohammad Collection; "Hobby Show Is Big Success," *VV News*, August 1982, Frank D. Godden/Salaam Mohammad Collections, 3.
76. "Display Ad 16–No Title," *LAS*, June 27, 1940, 4; "Display Ad 48–No Title," *LAS*, June 27, 1946, 23; "Go West"; "VV Park, California 1960" bulletin, 29–30; "Dedication Slated," *LAS*, June 21, 1956, B2; "Where the Future Is More Golden Than the Past," *VV* News section, *LAS*, August 6, 1964, C10; Kathleen Hendrix, "Moving Toward Progress," *LAT*, September 3, 1980, V-1.
77. "Ceramists Exhibit to Be Held," *LAT*, August 21, 1948, B6; "Dedication Slated," *LAS*, June 21, 1956, B2; Marguerite Carr, "VV," July 21, 1960, *LAS*, C6; "Hobby Show is Big Success," *VV News*, August 1962, 3; "Where the Future Is More Golden Than the Past"; "21st Annual Alice T. Gafford Art & Hobby Show, June 22–23, 1968" flier, Frank D. Godden/Salaam Mohammad Collection; "Annual Arts And Hobby Show Set," *LAS*, June 19, 1975, C14; "Annual Alice T. Gafford Art and Hobby Show," *LAT*, June 24, 1977, L32; Lewis and Waddy, *Black Artists on Art*, 84.
78. Collections that include Gafford's paintings are those of Dr. Hans Schwepke (Germany); Howard University (Washington DC); the Bowers Museum (Santa Ana, California); the Long Beach Museum of Art; the Los Angeles County Art Museum; the Golden State Mutual Life Insurance Company (Los Angeles); and others. This author inherited an Alice Taylor Gafford painting in 1995 from the estate of Marcelyn Cobbs Jefferson. The author remembers her mother, Marcelyn, sharing a short discussion about the artist's life when this still-life painting

was purchased and first displayed at the family home in the mid-1970s; Lewis and Waddy, *Black Artists on Art*, 136; "Memorial Service Held for Artist," *LAS*, November 12, 1981, C15; "Life Begins at Eighty for Gracious Artist," *LAS*, July 13, 1967, A5; Lipsitz, 60.

79. Stewart, "Forgotten Oasis VV," *LAT*, March 2, 1994, (Godden quotations) 1; Jocelyn Y. Stewart, "Godden Obituary," *LAS*, September 6, 2012, A4; "Mr. Frank D. Godden, VV Park's Distinguished Citizen, History," May 18, 1962, testimonial dinner for Frank D. Godden bulletin, Frank D. Godden/Salaam Mohammad Collection, 3; "VV Attracts," *CD*, October 4, 1947, 2.
80. Stewart, "Godden Obituary"; "Mr. Frank D. Godden," May 18, 1962, Testimonial Dinner bulletin; "Dedication Slated," *LAS*, June 21, 1956, B2; Valerie J. Nelson, "Frank Godden Dies at 101; Helped Develop African American Resort," Obituaries, *LAT*, April 19, 2012. Hattie S. Baldwin was a former president and an effective member of the leadership of the Val Verde Improvement Association and community builder, particularly in the 1930s.
81. Stewart, "Forgotten Oasis."
82. Alma Hill, Pasadena resident and retired grade schoolteacher, telephone interview with the author, November 16, 2004, and May 8, 2014, Los Angeles.
83. Hill interview.
84. Hill interview.
85. Marilyn Hudson interview, October 27, 2004; Hugh MacBeth Jr., San Francisco resident and retired attorney, telephone interview with the author, October 27, 2004, Los Angeles.
86. Photo Standalone 10, no title (includes Florence LaRue and Bradley Polk when they were crowned Miss and Mr. Val Verde and Muscle Man, respectively), *LAS*, September 23, 1965, A8; Stewart, "Forgotten Oasis."
87. Marie Rogers, grade-school teacher and sportswoman, interview with the author, May 22, 2014, Rolling Hills, California.
88. Rogers interview.
89. "Where the Future Is More Golden Than the Past"; Mike Goodman, "Whites in All-Black Hamlet Accorded Peaceful Acceptance," *LAT*, August 17, 1972, SF1; Mike Goodman, "NAACP Gets VV Complaints: Black Community Charges Bias," *LAT*, February 2, 1973, SF6; Mike Goodman, "Could Be Growing Pains: VV Complains Expansion Stifled," *LAT*, February 5, 1973, S6; Stewart, "Forgotten Oasis."
90. Martha L. Willman, "Influx of Latinos Felt in Santa Clarita Valley; Housing Squeeze Cited," *LAT*, June 15, 1980, V1; Sharon L. Warzocha, "Rural Retreat Wants to Stay That Way, VV: Once a 'Kind of black Palm Springs,'" *LAT*, August 5, 1990, 2.
91. Goodman, "Could Be Growing Pains," *LAT*, February 5. 1973, S6.
92. Carmen Ramos Chandler, "Changes in Store for VV," *DNLA*, February 7, 1988, N1; Kimberly Heinrichs, "Revived VV Enters '90s—Community Drawing Newcomers" *DNLA*, January 2, 1990, SAC1.

93. Elizabeth Campos Rajs, "In the News—Civic Leader Maps Out Future for VV," *DNLA*, November 28, 1988, N3; Patricia Farrell Aidem, "VV Battles to Remain Rural," *DNLA*, June 5, 1989, N3; Kimberly Heinrichs, "Changing Face of VV—Building Boom Transforms Town," *DNLA*, January 6, 1990, SAC1; Eureka Tract Numbers: 860, 8672 and 8673 (owners Laura C. Janes and Burt N. Janes) in the subdivision track map book from Los Angeles County Land Records Information, Department of Public Works, http://dpw.lacounty.gov/sur/nas/landrecords/tract/MB0102/TR0102-095.pdf (accessed January 8, 2014); VV Tract Numbers 5317 and 8676 (owner Harry M. Waterman) in the subdivision tract map book from Los Angeles County Land Records Information, Department of Public Works, http://dpw.lacounty.gov/sur/nas/landrecords/tract/MB0108/TR0108-001.pdf and http://dpw.lacounty.gov/sur/nas/landrecords/tract/MB0113/TR0113-022.pdf (accessed January 8, 2014).
94. Dion Lefler, "Integrated Town Faces Trash Apartheid," *DNLA*, October 6, 1994, N13. Environmental racism and "not in my backyard" (NIMBY) are beyond the scope of this author's present study, but this set of issues opens up opportunities for future study around the history of public policies implementation involving the Val Verde community.
95. Elijah Canty, Val Verde resident and retired administrator, telephone interview with the author, October 30, 2004, Los Angeles; Heinrichs, "Changing Face of VV," *DNLA*, January 2, 1990, SAC1.
96. VV, California data, 2010, www.city-data.com/city/Val-Verde-California.html (accessed February 22, 2014).
97. A short segment on the history of VV in a 1996 television program, "More Things That Aren't Here Anymore with Ralph Story," still airs on the local public television station KCET occasionally. This segment on the history of VV features retired California State Senator Diane Watson, businessman Celes King (1924–2003), singer Florence LaRue, and others. At the time of this writing, it can be viewed on the Santa Clarita Valley History TV web portal: http://www.scvtv.com/html/valverde1996kcet.html (accessed November 30, 2015). There is also supposed to be a film on Val Verde that KCET-TV commissioned independent filmmaker St. Clair Bourne (1943–2007) to produce that the author has not been able to locate to date. "Progress Presses in on Black Village," *Los Angeles Herald Examiner*, August 22, 1978.
98. My interpretation here of public memory is informed by Pierre Nora's *lieux de memoire*, or "sites of memory," and David Glassberg's ideas about the collective memory of communities. Nora, "From *Lieux de memoire* to Realms of Memory," xv, xvi, xvii; and Glassberg, *Sense of History*, 122–26. As VV has become a community of many Spanish speakers for whom English is a second language, understanding their engagement with the public memory of the historical African American leisure escape seekers could be another possible research study.

1. Cobbs's memoir is titled *My American Life.*
2. Nora, "From *Lieux de memoire* to Realms of Memory," xv, xvi, xvii.
3. Rymer, *American Beach*, 157; Trouillot, *Silencing the Past*, 26–27, (quotation) 48; Schrank, *Art and the City*, 2.
4. Christine E. Sleeter, "The Academic and Social Value of Ethnic Studies, A Research Review," National Education Association, 2011, 2, 5, 16–17, https://www.nea.org/assets/docs/NBI-2010-3-value-of-ethnic-studies.pdf (accessed April 7, 2015).
5. Sleeter, "The Academic and Social Value of Ethnic Studies"; Noah Remnick, "Why Ethnic Studies: In California Especially, Understanding Race and Ethnicity Isn't a Luxury, It's a Necessity," *LAT*, July 3, 2014, A-19.
6. Sleeter, "The Academic and Social Value of Ethnic Studies," viii, 5–6.
7. Pupil Instruction: Prohibition of Discriminatory Content, Senate Bill 48/Ch. 81, California Legislature, March 18, 2015, http://leginfo.legislature.ca.gov/faces/billAnalysisClient.xhtml (accessed April 6, 2015).
8. The American Historical Association (AHA) is the largest professional organization in the United States devoted to the study and promotion of history and historical thinking: https://www.historians.org/about-aha-and-membership (accessed April 7, 2015). "AHA Supports FAIR Act in California K–12 History Education," *AHA* Today, http://blog.historians.org/2014/11/aha-submits-letter-support-fair-act-revisions/ (accessed April 7, 2015); History—Social Science Framework for California Public Schools adopted July 14, 2016, California Department of Education, https://www.cde.ca.gov/ci/hs/cf/sbedrafthssfw.asp (accessed November 24, 2017).
9. Pupil instruction: Prohibition of Discriminatory Content , California Legislature, March 18, 2015, (accessed April 6, 2015); Remnick, "Why Ethnic Studies," *LAT*, July 3, 2014, A-19; Stephen Ceasar, "El Rancho Schools Don't Wait on State, Adopt Ethnic-studies Curriculum," *LAT*, July 7, 2014; Stephen Ceasar, "L.A. Unified to Require Ethnic Studies for High School Graduation," *LAT*, December 8, 2014; Cynthia Liu, "The Case for Requiring Ethnic Studies in High School," *Washington Post*, December 8, 2014; Sleeter, "The Academic and Social Value of Ethnic Studies"; Stephen Ceasar, "Governor Vetoes Ethnic Studies Bill," *LAT*, October 13, 2015. In the Los Angeles Unified School District (LAUSD), even some elementary schools are beginning to incorporate ethnic studies with visual arts in innovative curricula. A program partnership between LAUSD and Loyola Marymount University's (LMU) Family of Schools was awarded in 2015 a four-year grant of more than $1.65 million from the U.S. Department of Education to help teachers integrate arts education and ethnic studies to increase student achievement and engagement. LMU's faculty in Chicano and Latino studies and African American studies will present history, culture, and context, and local artists and arts instructors will help teachers develop the skills and the process

of creating art in the context of cultural history instruction. Mary Plummer, "LAUSD Teachers to Learn Visual Arts and Cultural History Integration," 89.3 KPCC, http://www.scpr.org/blogs/education/2015/02/13/17915/lausd-teachers-to-learn-visual-arts-and-cultural-h/ (accessed April 7, 2015); and "Arts Education Wins Federal Funding," Loyola Marymount University Newsroom, February 20, 2015, https://newsroom.lmu.edu/2015/02/20/family-of-schools-receives-1-million-arts-education-grant/ (assessed June 6, 2019).

10. Hayden, *The Power of Place*, 8–9; Kaufman, *Place, Race, and Story*, 307; Stephanie Meeks, "Sustaining the Future," Remarks at the California Preservation Foundation Conference: Preservation on the Edge, Santa Monica, California, May 16, 2011, 2, 4; Donna Graves, "The Legacy of California's Landmarks: A Report for the California Cultural and Historical Endowment," September 2012, 36–37, http://resources.ca.gov/docs/cche/TheLegacy_of_CaliforniasLandmarks.pdf (accessed April 7, 2015).
11. Meeks, "Sustaining the Future," 5–7; Kaufman, *Place, Race, and Story*, 2–5, 12–13, 326; Hayden, *The Power of Place*, 7–13, 15, 22, 46–48, 54; Kaufman, "Putting Intangible Heritage in its Place[s]," 21.

BIBLIOGRAPHY

MANUSCRIPTS AND ARCHIVES

Bay Cities Directories. Santa Monica Public Library Special Collections.

Bradford Luke, Anne, Personal Collection, Los Angeles, California

Bundles, A'Lelia, Personal Collection, Washington DC

California African American Museum

California State Archives

California State University, Fullerton, Center for Oral History

City of Lake Elsinore

- 2003 State of the City Report
- Cemetery Records
- Civic Center Session Study, February 22, 2007
- City Directories, Lake Elsinore Public Library Special Collections
- Public Library Local File, Riverside County, California

City of Santa Monica

- City Directories, Santa Monica Public Library
- Historic Resources Inventory Sheet for Phillips Chapel. Prepared by Leslie Heumann of the City of Santa Monica Landmarks Commission, 1992
- Historic District Application for Third Street Neighborhood in Ocean Park, vols. 1 and 3. Prepared by the Third Street Neighbors for the City of Santa Planning Department, 1990

Clayton, Mayme A., Library and Museum Collection

Corona Historical Society

Corona Public Library

Cosmos Club Archives, Los Angeles, California

County of Los Angeles, Assessor's Parcel Map

Cunningham Smith, Ann, Personal Collection, Los Angeles, California

Department of Parks and Recreation Archives, County of Los Angeles

Dennis, Jan, Personal Collection, Manhattan Beach, California

Elsinore Valley Municipal Water District. "Celebrating 50 Years of Water History." Prepared by Mary Brown, 2000.

Godden, Frank D., Collection of the Salaam Mohammad, Los Angeles, California

Gordon, Walter L., Jr., Personal Collection of the William Beverly Jr. Collections, Los Angeles

Grenier, Judson. *Manhattan Beach: Yesterdays*. Manhattan Beach Historical Series. No. 3. Manhattan Beach CA: City of Manhattan Beach Historical Committee, 1976.

Huntington Library Collection

Jackson, Fay M., Memorial Collection of Dale Lya Pierson, Los Angeles, California

Jefferson, Alison Rose, Personal Collection, Los Angeles, California

Lake Elsinore Historical Society. "History of Lake Elsinore." Compiled from newspaper stories by Altha Merrifield Cauch, 1956.

Lake Elsinore Valley Chamber of Commerce Community Map. Map Masters, San Diego, California, 2003.

Lake Shore Beach Company. Board of Directors meeting notes. Arthur L. Reese Family Archives, Los Angeles, California.

Lawson, Cristyne, Personal Collection, Santa Monica, California

Leake, Robert L. "The History of Calvary Baptist Church" pamphlet. Prepared for Calvary Baptist Church Men and Women's Day Program. Santa Monica, California, October 28, 2001.

Lewis, Arthur and Elizabeth, Personal Collections, Los Angeles, California

Los Angeles City Directories. Los Angeles Central Library.

Los Angeles County Archives

Los Angeles County Courthouse Records

Los Angeles Public Library Digital Photography Collections

Manhattan Beach: Yesterdays. Manhattan Beach Historical Series. No. 4. Compiled by Frances Dow and Jud Grenier. Manhattan Beach CA: City of Manhattan Beach Historical Committee, 1976.

Manhattan Beach City Council Archives

Manhattan Beach Historical Society Archives

Manhattan Beach Public Library, Historical Document Files

McCallister, Linda Chilton. *The Waterfront of Manhattan Beach*. Manhattan Beach Historical Series. No. 6. Manhattan Beach CA: City of Manhattan Beach Historical Committee, n.d.

Miller, Halvor, Personal Collection, Los Angeles, California

Peace, Harold, Jr., Personal Collection, Los Angeles, California

Phillips Chapel Christian Methodist Episcopal Church Files

Provost, Aubrey, Personal Collection, Los Angeles, California

Reese, Arthur L., Family Archives, Los Angeles, California

Ringelstein, Austin. "The African Heritage of the Santa Monica Mountains." Unpublished paper, prepared for the Santa Monica Mountains National Recreation Area, National Park Service, September 16, 2018.

Riverside County Courthouse Records. Riverside, California.

Sanborn Fire Insurance Maps. Library of Congress, https://www.loc.gov/collections/sanborn-maps (accessed June 17, 2019).

San Diego Historical Society

Santa Monica City Archives

Santa Monica Historical Society renamed the Santa Monica History Museum

Santa Monica Public Library

Schomburg Center for Research in Black Culture, Manuscripts, Archives, and Rare Books Division, New York Public Library and Digital Collections

Seaver Center for Western History Research, Natural History Museum of Los Angeles County

Seville-Jones, Sandra, Personal Papers, the Leadership Manhattan Beach Class of 2003 Project

Site visits by author to Bruce's Beach, Bay Street Beach, Val Verde, Corona, and Lake Elsinore, California.

Social Security Index. http:www.ancestry.com (accessed June 19, 2019).

Southern California Library for Social Studies and Research

United States Census. http:www.ancestry.com (accessed June 19, 2019).

University of California, Berkeley, Library Special Collections

University of California, Los Angeles Library Special Collections

University of Southern California Special Collections

Val Verde Chamber of Commerce. "Val Verde Park, California 1960" bulletin. Department of Parks and Recreation Archives, County of Los Angeles, Saugus, California.

Williams, Verna. "Shades of L.A." Oral History Project interview, Los Angeles Public Library, 1996.

PUBLISHED WORKS

"About H. M. Newhall." Henry Mayo Newhall Foundation, www.newhallfoundation.org (accessed January 17, 2014).

Adams, Luther. "My Old Kentucky Home: Black History in the Bluegrass State." *Register of Kentucky Historical Society* 113, nos. 2–3 (Spring/Summer 2015): 385–419.

Alamillo, Jose M. *Making Lemonade out of Lemons: Mexican American Labor and Leisure in a California Town 1880–1960*. Urbana: University of Illinois Press, 2006.

Alexander, Carolyn Elayne. *Abbot Kinney's Venice-of-America, the Golden Years: 1905–1920*. Vol. 1. Los Angeles: Westside Genealogical Society, 1991.

Allen, James P., and Eugene Turner. *The Ethnic Quilt: Population Diversity in Southern California*. Northridge CA: Center for Graphic Studies, 1997.

Allmendinger, Blake. *Imagining the African American West*. Lincoln: University of Nebraska Press, 2008.

Almaguer, Tomás. *Racial Fault Lines: The Historical Origins of White Supremacy in California*. Berkeley: University of California Press, [1994] 2009.

Alvarez, Luis. *The Power of the Zoot: Youth Culture and Resistance During World War II*. Berkeley: University of California Press, 2008.

Amory, Cleveland. *The Last Resorts*. New York: Harper & Brothers, 1952.

Anderson, Ernest Frederick. "The Development of Leadership and Organization Building in the Black Community of Los Angeles from 1900 Through World War II." PhD diss., University of Southern California, 1976.

Armstead, Myra B. Young. *Lord, Please Don't Take Me in August: African Americans in Newport and Saratoga Springs, 1870–1930*. Urbana: University of Illinois Press, 1999.

Aron, Cindy Sondik. *Working at Play: A History of Vacations in the United States*. New York: Oxford University Press, 1999.

Austen, Ruth. *Riverside: The Heritage, the People, the Vision*. Montgomery AL: Community Communications, 1996.

Avila, Eric. *Popular Culture in the Age of White Flight: Fear and Fantasy in Suburban Los Angeles*. Berkeley: University of California Press, 2006.

Badger, Anthony. *The New Deal: The Depression Years, 1933–1940*. Chicago: Ivan R. Dee, 1989.

Baldwin, Davarian. *Chicago's New Negroes: Modernity for Great Migration, and Black Urban Life*. Chapel Hill: University of North Carolina Press, 2007.

——, and Minkah Makalani, ed. *Escape from New York: The New Negro Renaissance beyond Harlem*. Minneapolis: University of Minnesota Press, 2013.

Bardolph, Richard. *The Negro Vanguard*. New York: Rinehart, 1959.

Bass, Charlotta A. *Forty Years: Memoirs from the Pages of a Newspaper*. Unpublished manuscript, 1960.

Basten, Fred E. With an introduction by Carolyn See. *Paradise by the Sea, Santa Monica Bay: A Pictorial History of Santa Monica Venice, Marina del Rey, Ocean Park, Pacific Palisades, Topanga, and Malibu*. Santa Monica CA: Hennessey & Ingalls, 1997.

Beasley, Delilah. *The Negro Trail Blazers of California*. Vacaville CA: James Stevenson, 2004.

Bederman, Gail. *Manliness and Civilization: A Cultural History of Gender and Race in the United States, 1880–1917*. Chicago: University of Chicago Press, 1995.

Blight, David W. *Race and Reunion: The Civil War in American Memory*. Cambridge MA: Harvard University Press, 2001.

Bogle, Donald. *Bright Boulevards: The Story of Black Hollywood*. New York: One World/Ballantine Books, 2005.

Bond, J. Max. "The Negro in Los Angeles." PhD diss., University of Southern California, 1936.

Boston, John, and the Santa Clarita Valley Historical Society. *Images of America: Santa Clarita Valley*. San Francisco: Arcadia, 2009.

Bowman, Lynn. *Los Angeles: Epic of a City*. Berkeley CA: Howell-North Books, 1974.

Brigham, Robert L. *Landownership and Occupancy by Negroes in Manhattan Beach*. Master's thesis, Fresno State University, 1956.

Brilliant, Mark. *The Color of America Has Changed: How Racial Diversity Shaped Civil Rights Reform in California, 1941–1976*. New York: Oxford University Press, 2010.

Broussard, Albert S. "African Americans in the West: Introduction." *Journal of the West* 44, no. 2 (Spring 2005): 5–7.

———. *Black San Francisco: The Struggle for Racial Equality in the West, 1900–1954*. Lawrence: University of Kansas Press, 1993.

Bryant, Clora, Buddy Collette, William Green, Steve Isoardi, and Marl Young. *Central Avenue Sounds: Jazz in Los Angeles*. Berkeley: University of California Press, 1999.

Bundles, A'Lelia. *On Her Own Ground: The Life and Times of Madam C. J. Walker*. New York: Washington Square/Pocket Books, 2001.

Bush, Gregory W. *White Sand Black Beach: Civil Rights, Public Space, and Miami's Virginia Key*. Gainesville: University Press of Florida, 2016.

Cady, Daniel. "'Southern California': White Southern Migrants in Greater Los Angeles, 1920–1930." PhD diss., Claremont University, 2005.

California Death Index.

California Eagle Publishing Company. *Los Angeles Negro Directory and Who's Who, 1930–1931*. Los Angeles, California.

———. *Who's Who in California: California Negro Directory, 1942–1943*. Los Angeles, California.

California Voter Registration List. http:www.ancestry.com (accessed June 17, 2019).

Campbell, Marne L. *Making Black Los Angeles: Class, Gender, and Community, 1850–1917*. Chapel Hill: University of North Carolina Press, 2016.

Cartwright, Marguerite. "James Garrott, California Architect." *Negro History Bulletin* (April 1955): 155–53.

Chan, Sucheng, Douglas H. Daniels, Mario T. García, and Terry P. Wilson, ed. *People of Color in the American West*. Lexington MA: D. C. Heath, 1994.

Cheng, Wendy. *The Changs Next Door to the Diazes: Remapping Race in Suburban California*. Minneapolis: University of Minnesota Press, 2013.

Cobbs, Price M. *My American Life: From Rage to Entitlement*. New York: Atria Books/Simon & Schuster, 2005.

Connerton, Paul. *How Societies Remember*. New York: Cambridge University Press, 1989.

Corbett, Theodore. *The Making of American Resorts: Saratoga Springs, Ballston Spa, Lake George*. New Brunswick NJ: Rutgers University Press, 2001.

Couvares, Francis G., Martha Saxon, Gerald N. Grob, and George Athan Billias, ed. *Interpretations of American History, Volume Two: From Reconstruction*. Boston: Bedford/St. Martin's, 2009.

Cox, Bette Yarbrough. *Central Avenue—Its Rise and Fall (1890–c. 1955), Including the Musical Renaissance of Black Los Angeles*. Los Angeles: BEEM, [1993] 1996.

Culver, Lawrence. *The Frontier of Leisure: Southern California, and the Shaping of Modern America*. Oxford: Oxford University Press, 2010.

Culver, Milton Lawrence. *Island, the Oasis, and the City: Santa Catalina, Palm Springs, Los Angeles, and Southern California's Shaping of American Life and Leisure*. PhD diss., University of California, Los Angeles, 2004.

Daniels, Douglas Henry. *Lester Leaps In: The Life and Times of Lester "Pres" Young*. Boston: Beacon, 2002.

———, with a foreword by Nathan Irvin Huggins. *Pioneer Urbanites: A Social and Cultural History of Black San Francisco*. Berkeley: University of California Press, [1980] 1990.

DeGraaf, Lawrence. "The City of Angels: The Emergence of the Los Angeles Ghetto, 1890–1930." *Pacific Historical Review* 39, no. 3 (1970): 323–52.

———. "Recognition, Racism, and Reflections on the Writing of Western Black History." *Pacific Historical Review* 44, no. 1 (1975): 22–51.

———, Kevin Mulroy, and Quintard Taylor, ed. *Seeking El Dorado: African American Experiences in California*. Seattle: Autry Museum of Western Heritage/University of Washington Press, 2001.

Dennis, Jan. *Manhattan Beach, California*. San Francisco: Arcadia, 2001.

———. *A Walk Beside the Sea: A History of Manhattan Beach*. Manhattan Beach CA: Janstan Studio, 1987.

Deverell, William. *Whitewashed Adobe: The Rise of Los Angeles and the Remaking of its Mexican Past*. Berkeley: University of California Press, 2004.

———, and Douglas Flamming. "Race, Rhetoric, and Regional Identity, Boosting Los Angeles, 1880–1930." In *Power and Place in the North American West*, ed. Richard White and John M. Findlay, 117–43. Seattle: Center for the Study of the Pacific Northwest/University of Washington Press, 1999.

DiAngelo, Robin. "White Fragility." *International Journal of Critical Pedagogy* 3, no. 3 (2011): 54–74.

DjeDje, Jacqueline Cogdell, and Eddie S. Meadows. *California Soul: Music of African Americans in the West*. Berkeley: University of California Press, 1998.

Dowden-White, Priscilla A. *Groping toward Democracy: African American Social Welfare Reform in St. Louis, 1910–1945*. Columbia: University of Missouri Press, 2011.

Engh, Michael E. "Practically Every Religion Being Represented." In *Metropolis in the Making: Los Angeles in the 1920s*, ed. Tom Sitton and William Deverell, 201–19. Berkeley: University of California Press, 2001.

Esparza, Richard R., and H. Vincent Moses. *Westward to Canaan: African American Heritage in Riverside, 1890 to 1950*. Riverside, CA: Riverside Municipal Museum, 1996.

Estrada, William David, with a foreword by Devra Weber. *The Los Angeles Plaza: Sacred and Contested Space*. Austin: University of Texas Press, 2008.

Flamming, Douglas. *African Americans in the West*. Santa Barbara CA: ABC-CLIO, 2009.

——. *Bound for Freedom: Black Los Angeles in Jim Crow America*. Berkeley: University of California Press, 2005.

Feifer, Maxine. *Tourism in History: From Imperial Rome to the Present*. New York: Stein & Day, 1985.

Fisher, James Adolphus. "A History of the Political and Social Development of the Black Community in California, 1850–1950." PhD diss., State University of New York at Stony Brook, 1971.

Fogelson, Robert M. *The Fragmented Metropolis: Los Angeles, 1850–1930*. Berkeley: University of California Press, 1967.

Foster, S. Mark. "In the Face of 'Jim Crow': Prosperous Blacks and Vacations, Travel, and Outdoor Leisure, 1890–1945." *Journal of Negro History* 84, no. 2 (Spring 1999): 130–39.

Fredrickson, George M. *White Supremacy: A Comparative Study in American and South African History*. New York: Oxford University Press, 1981.

Fresco, Nina. "Ocean Park in Santa Monica . . . and that other Ocean Park (Venice, California)." Unpublished paper, March 10, 2018.

Gaines, Kevin Kelly. *Black Leadership, Politics, and Culture in the Twentieth Century*. Chapel Hill: University of North Carolina Press, 1996.

——. *Uplifting the Race: Black Leadership, Politics, and Culture in the Twentieth Century*. Chapel Hill: University of North Carolina Press, 1996.

Gatewood, Willard B. *Aristocrats of Color: The Black Elite, 1880–1920*. Bloomington: Indiana University Press, 1990.

Glasrud, Bruce A., and Cary D. Wintz. *The Harlem Renaissance in the American West: The New Negro's Western Experience*. New York: Routledge, 2012.

——, and Michael N. Searles. *Buffalo Soldiers in the West: A Black Soldiers Anthology*. College Station: Texas A&M University Press, 2007.

Glassberg, David. *Sense of History: The Places of the Past in American Life*. Amherst: University of Massachusetts Press, 2001.

Gleaves, Milnor E. "Civil Rights: Extent of California Statute and Remedies Available for Its Enforcement." *California Law Review* 30, no. 5 (1942): 563–68.

Greene, Edythe J., Elizabeth Hepler, and Mary Louise Rowden. *Images of America: Lake Elsinore*. San Francisco: Arcadia, 2005.

Gregory, James. *The Southern Diaspora: How the Great Migrations of Black and White Southerners Transformed America*. Chapel Hill: University of North Carolina Press, 2005.

Gregory, Steven. *Black Corona: Race and the Politics of Place in an Urban Community*. Princeton NJ: Princeton University Press, 1998.

Hall, Jacquelyn Dowd. "The Long Civil Rights Movement and the Political Uses of the Past," *Journal of American History* 91, no. 4 (2005): 1–28.

Harris, Cheryl. "Whiteness as Property." In *Critical Race Theory: The Key Writings that Formed the Movement*, ed. Kimberlé Crenshaw, Neil Gotanda, Gary Peller, and Kendall Thomas, with a foreword by Cornel West, 276–91. New York: New Press, 1995.

Hassan, Amina. *Loren Miller: Civil Rights Attorney and Journalist*. Norman: University of Oklahoma Press, 2015.

Hayden, Delores. *The Power of Place: Urban Landscapes as Public History*. Cambridge MA: MIT Press, 1995.

Hernández, Kelly Lytle. *City of Inmates: Conquest, Rebellion, and the Rise of Human Caging in Los Angeles, 1771–1965*. Chapel Hill: University of North Carolina Press, 2017.

Horne, Gerald. *Fire This Time: The Watts Uprising and the 1960s*. Charlottesville: University of Virginia Press, 1995.

Horton, James Oliver, and Lois E. Horton, ed. *Slavery and Public History: The Tough Stuff of American Memory*. Chapel Hill: University of North Carolina Press, 2006.

Hudson, Karen E., with a foreword by David Gebhard. *Paul R. Williams, Architect: A Legacy of Style*. New York: Rizzoli International, 1993.

Hudson, Tom. *Lake Elsinore Valley: Its Story, 1776–1977*. Lake Elsinore CA: Mayhall Print Shop, 2001.

Hunt, Darnell, and Ana-Christina Ramon. *Black Los Angeles: American Dreams and Racial Realities*. New York: New York University Press, 2010.

Ingersoll, Luther A. *Ingersoll's Century History: Santa Monica Bay Cities, 1542 to 1908*. Los Angeles: L.A. Ingersoll, 1908.

Jackson, Kenneth T. *The Ku Klux Klan in the City, 1915–1930*. New York: Oxford University Press, 1967.

Jacobson, Matthew Frye. *Whiteness of a Different Color: European Immigrants and the Alchemy of Race*. Cambridge MA: Harvard University Press, 1998.

Jefferson, Alison Rose. "Lake Elsinore: A Southern California African American Resort Area During the Jim Crow Era, 1920s–1960s, and the Challenges of Historic Preservation Commemoration." Master's thesis, University of Southern California, 2007.

———. "Leisure's Race, Power, and Place: The Recreation and Remembrance of African Americans in the California Dream." PhD diss., University of California, Santa Barbara, 2015.

Jeffries, Hasan Kwame. *Bloody Lowndes: Civil Rights and Black Power in Alabama's Black Belt*. New York: New York University Press, 2009.

Johnson, Charles. "Industrial Survey of the Negro population of Los Angeles, California, Made by the Department of Research and investigations of the National Urban League." Los Angeles: Urban League, 1926.

———. "Negro Workers in Los Angeles Industries." *Opportunity*, August 1928, 234–40.

Johnson, Gaye Theresa. *Spaces of Conflict, Sounds of Solidarity: Music, Race, and Spatial Entitlement in Los Angeles*. Berkeley: University of California Press, 2013.

Jones, Kellie. *South of Pico: African American Artists in Los Angeles*. Durham NC: Duke University Press, 2017.

Kahrl, Andrew W. *The Land Was Ours: African American Beaches from Jim Crow to the Sunbelt South*. Cambridge MA: Harvard University Press, 2012.

———. "On the Beach: Race and Leisure in the Jim Crow South." PhD diss., Indiana University, 2008.

———. "The Slightest Semblance of Unruliness: Steamboat Excursions, Pleasure Resorts, and the Emergence of Segregation Culture on the Potomac River." *Journal of American History* 94, no. 4 (March 2008): 1–40.

Kanfer, Stefan. *A Summer World: The Attempt to Build a Jewish Eden in the Catskills, from the Days of the Ghetto to the Rise and Decline of the Borscht Belt*. New York: Farrar, Straus & Giroux, 1989.

Katz, William Loren. *The Black West: A Documentary and Pictorial History of the African American Role in the Westward Expansion of the United States*. New York: Simon & Schuster, [1987] 1996.

Kaufman, Ned. *Place, Race, and Story: Essays on the Past and Future of Historic Preservation*. New York: Routledge, 2009.

———. "Putting Intangible Heritage in its Place[s]: Proposals for Policy and Practice." *International Journal of Intangible Heritage* 8 (2013): 20–36.

Klein, Ronald P. "The California Equal Rights Statutes in Practice." *Stanford Law Review* 10, no. 2 (1958): 253–73.

Kurashige, Scott. *The Shifting Grounds of Race: Black and Japanese Americans in the Making of Multiethnic Los Angeles*. Princeton NJ: Princeton University Press, 2008.

Lakey, Othal Hawthrone. *The History of the CME Church*. Memphis TN: CME, 1985.

Lapp, Rudolph M. *Blacks in Gold Rush California*. New Haven CT: Yale University Press, 1977.

Larralde, Carlos M., and Richard Griswold del Castillo. "San Diego's Ku Klux Klan 1920–1980." *Journal of San Diego History* 46, nos. 2–3 (Spring/Summer 2000): https://sandiegohistory.org/journal/2000/april/klan/ (accessed June 17, 2019).

Laslett, John H. M. *Sunshine Was Never Enough: Los Angeles Workers, 1880–2010*. Berkeley: University of California Press, 2012.

Lech, Steve. *Resorts of Riverside County*. San Francisco: Arcadia, 2005.

LeFebvre, Henri. *The Production of Space*. Translated by Donald Nicholson-Smith. Oxford: Blackwell, 1991.

Lemke-Santangelo, Gretchen. *Abiding Courage: African American Migrant Women and the East Bay Community*. Chapel Hill: University of North Carolina Press, 1996.

Lewis, Earl. *In Their Own Interests: Race, Class, and Power in Twentieth-Century Norfolk, Virginia*. Berkeley: University of California Press, 1991.

Lewis, Samella S., and Ruth G. Waddy. *Black Artists on Art*. Los Angeles: Contemporary Crafts, 1971.

Lewis Publishing Company. *An Illustrated History of Southern California*. Chicago: Lewis, 1890.

Limerick, Patricia Nelson. *The Legacy of Conquest: The Unbroken Past of the American West*. New York: W. W. Norton, 1987.

Lipsitz, George. *How Racism Takes Place*. Philadelphia: Temple University Press, 2011.

———. *Midnight at the Barrelhouse: The Johnny Otis Story*. Minneapolis: University of Minnesota Press, 2010.

Locke, Alain, ed., with a foreword by Arnold Rampersad. *The New Negro Voices of the Harlem Renaissance*. New York: Simon & Schuster, 1925.

Lofgrun, Orvar. *On Holiday: The History of Vacationing*. Berkeley: University of California Press, 1999.

Los Angeles Classified Buyers' Guide, 1942–1943. Southern California Library for Social Research Collection, Los Angeles, California.

Lungsford, James W. *Looking at Santa Monica: The Ocean, the Sunset, the Hills, and the Clouds*. Santa Monica: James W. Lungsford, 1993.

Lupoma, Jewll. *Arthur L. Reese, "The Wizard of Venice."* Marina del Rey CA: JTI DEMC, 2006.

Malibu CA (television show). http://www.tv.com/malibu-ca/show/1661/summary.html (accessed May 18, 2008).

Marquez, Ernest. *Santa Monica Beach: A Collector's Pictorial History*. Santa Monica CA: Angel City, 2004.

Marsh, Diann. *Corona, the Circle City: An Illustrated History of Corona*. Corona CA: Heritage Media, 1998.

Mayo, James M. *The American Country Club: Its Origins and Development*. New Brunswick NJ: Rutgers University Press, 1998.

McBroome, Delores N. *Parallel Communities: African Americans in California's East Bay, 1850–1963*. New York: Garland, 1993.

McWilliams, Carey. *Southern California: An Island on the Land*. Layton UT: Gibbs Smith, [1946] 1973.

Meeks, Stephanie. "Sustaining the Future." Remarks at Preservation on the Edge, California Preservation Foundation Conference. Santa Monica, California, May 16, 2011.

Moore, Shirley Ann Wilson. *To Place Our Deeds: The African American Community in Richmond, California, 1919–1963*. Berkeley: University of California Press, 2000.

National Park Service. The National Park Service and Civic Engagement Report, 2001, https://www.nps.gov/civic/about/civic.pdf (accessed June 6, 2019).

Nelson, Jack E., Raymond L. Langston, and Margo Dean Pinson. *Highland Beach on the Chesapeake Bay: Maryland's First African American Incorporated Town.* Virginia Beach VA: Donning, 2008.

Nelson, Jill. *Finding Martha's Vineyard: African Americans At Home on an Island.* New York: Doubleday, 2005.

Nicolaides, Becky M. *My Blue Heaven: Life and Politics in the Working-Class Suburbs of Los Angeles, 1920–1965.* Chicago: University of Chicago Press, 2002.

1924 Mile Posts. http://local.aaca.org/junior/mileposts/1924.htm (accessed December 16, 2014).

Novick, Peter. *That Noble Dream: The "Objectivity Question" and the American Historical Profession.* Cambridge: Cambridge University Press, 1988.

Nugent, Walter. *Into The West: The Story of Its People.* New York: Alfred A. Knopf, 1999.

The O.C. (television show). http://www.tv.com/o-c/show/16960/summary.html (accessed May 18, 2008).

Oliver, Melvin L., and Thomas M. Shapiro. *Black Wealth/White Wealth: A New Perspective on Racial Inequality.* New York: Routledge, 2006.

Peace Through People: 50 Years of Global Citizenship. Louisville KY: Sister City International/Butler Books, 2006.

Perkins, Maggi. *Images of America: Newhall.* San Francisco: Arcadia, 2010.

Phelts, Marsha Dean. *An American Beach for African Americans.* Gainesville: University Press of Florida, 1997.

Pulido, Laura. "Rethinking Environmental Racism: White Privilege and Urban Development in Southern California." *Annals of the Association of American Geographers* 90, no. 3 (2000): 12–40.

Quintard, Taylor. *In Search of the Racial Frontier: African Americans in the American West, 1528–1990.* New York: W. W. Norton, 1998.

———, with a foreword by Norman Rice. *Forging of a Black Community: Seattle's Central District from 1900 through the Civil Rights Era.* Seattle: University of Washington Press, 1994.

Railton, Arthur, ed. *African Americans on Martha's Vineyard: A Special Edition of the Dukes County Intelligencer.* Martha's Vineyard MA: Martha's Vineyard Historical Society, 1997.

Rawls, James J., and Walton Bean. *California: An Interpretive History.* Boston: McGraw Hill Higher Education, 1968/2003.

Reynolds, Jerry. *Santa Clarita: Valley of the Golden Dream.* Granada Hills CA: World of Communications, 1997.

Riverside African American Historical Society. *The African American Presence in Riverside: Preserving the Past—Capturing the Present,* 2004.

Riverside Municipal Museum. *Our Families, Our Stories: From the African American Community, Riverside, California, 1870–1960*. Riverside, CA: Riverside Municipal Museum, 1997.

Robinson, Florence Keeney. *Problems in Training Adult Negroes in Los Angeles*. Master's thesis, University of Southern California, 1929.

Robinson, William Wilcox. *The Story of Riverside County*. Los Angeles: Title Insurance, 1957.

Rosenzweig, Roy. *Eight Hours for What We Will: Workers and Leisure in an Industrial City*. Cambridge: Cambridge University Press, 1983.

Royal, Alice C., Mickey Ellinger, and Scott Braley. *Allensworth, the Freedom Colony: A California African American Township*. Berkeley CA: Heyday, 2008.

Reed, Tom. *The Black Music History of Los Angeles—Its Roots*. Los Angeles: Black Accent LA, [1987] 2000.

Ruck, Rob. *Sandlot Seasons: Sports in Black Pittsburgh*. Urbana: University of Illinois Press, 1987.

Ruffin, Herbert G., II, and Dwayne A. Mack, ed., with a foreword by Quintard Taylor. *Freedom's Racial Frontier: African Americans in the Twentieth-Century West*. Norman: University of Oklahoma Press, 2018.

Rymer, Russ. *American Beach: How "Progress" Robbed a Black Town—and Nation—of History, Wealth, and Power*. New York: HarperPerennial, 2009.

Salvini, Emil R. *The Summer City by the Sea: Cape May, New Jersey, an Illustrated History*. New Brunswick NJ: Rutgers University Press, 1995.

Sanchez, George J. *Becoming Mexican American: Ethnicity, Culture and Identity in Chicano Los Angeles, 1900–1945*. New York: Oxford University Press, 1993.

Sandul, Paul. *California Dreaming: Boosterism, Memory, and Rural Suburbs in the Golden State*. Morgantown: West Virginia University Press, 2014.

Savage, W. Sherman. *Blacks in the West*. Westport CN: Greenwood, 1976.

Schrank, Sarah. *Art and the City: Civic Imagination and Cultural Authority in Los Angeles*. Philadelphia: University of Pennsylvania Press, 2009.

Scott, Paula. *Santa Monica: A History on the Edge*. Charleston SC: Arcadia, 2004.

Self, Robert O. *American Babylon: Race and the Struggle for Postwar Oakland*. Berkeley: University of California Press, 2003.

Shackel, Paul A. *Memory in Black and White: Race, Commemoration, and the Post-Bellum Landscape*. Walnut Creek CA: Altamira, 2003.

Shuck, Oscar T., ed. *History of the Bench and Bar of California: Being Biographies of Many Remarkable Men, A Store of Humorous and Pathetic Recollections, Accounts of Important Legislation and Extraordinary Cases Comprehending the Judicial History of the State*. Los Angeles: Commercial Printing House, 1901.

Sides, Josh. *L.A. City Limits: African American Los Angeles from the Great Depression to the Present*. Berkeley: University of California Press, 2003.

Simon, Roger D. "Country Clubs." In *The Encyclopedia of American Urban History*, edited by David R. Goldfield, 192–93. Thousand Oaks CA: SAGE, 2006.

Singh, Nikhil Pal. *Black Is a Country: Race and the Unfinished Struggle for Democracy*. Cambridge MA: Harvard University Press, 2004.

Sitkoff, Harvard. *A New Deal for Blacks: The Emergence of Civil Rights as a National Issue*. New York: Oxford University Press, 1978.

Sitton, Tom, and William Deverell. *Metropolis in the Making: Los Angeles in the 1920s*. Berkeley: Univeristy of California Press, 2001.

Slaton, Deborah, Chad Randl, and Lauren Van Demme, ed. *Preserve and Play: Preserving Historic Recreation and Entertainment Sites, Conference Proceedings*. Washington DC: Historic Preservation Education Foundation, 2006.

Smith, J. Clay, Jr. With a foreword by Thurgood Marshall. *Emancipation: The Making of the Black Lawyer, 1844–1944*. Philadelphia: University of Pennsylvania Press, 1993.

Smith, R. J. *The Great Black Way: L.A. in the 1940s and the Lost African American Renaissance*. New York: Public Affairs/Perseus, 2006.

Sorin, Gretchen Sullivan, and Jane W. Rehl. *Honorable Work: African Americans in the Resort Community of Saratoga Springs, 1870–1970*. Saratoga Springs NY: Historical Society of Saratoga Springs, 1992.

Starr, Kevin. *California: A History*. New York: Modern Library/Random House, [2005] 2007.

———. *The Dream Endures: California Enters the 1940s*. New York: Oxford University Press, 1997.

———. *Inventing the Dream: California through the Progressive Era*. New York: Oxford University Press, 1985.

———. *Material Dreams: Southern California Through the 1920s*. New York: Oxford University Press, 1990.

Stephens, Ronald J. *Idlewild: The Rise, Decline, and Rebirth of a Unique African American Resort Town*. Ann Arbor: University of Michigan Press, 2013.

Stevenson, Brenda E. *The Contested Murder of Latasha Harlins: Justice, Gender, and the Origins of the L.A. Riots*. New York: Oxford University Press, 2013.

Stuart, Merah Steven. *An Economic Detour: A History of Insurance in the Lives of American Negroes*. New York: Wendell Malliet, 1940.

Sturken, Marita. *Tangled Memories: The Vietnam War, the AIDS Epidemic, and the Politics of Remembering*. Berkeley: University of California Press, 1997.

Sugrue, Thomas J. *Sweet Land of Liberty: The Forgotten Struggle for Civil Rights in the North*. New York: Random House, 2008.

Sutton, Horace. *Travellers: The American Tourist from Stagecoach to Space Shuttle*. New York: William Morrow, 1980.

Talesky, Nick. *Rock Obituaries: Knocking on Heaven's Door*. London: Onmibus, 2010.

Thelen, David, ed. *Memory and American History*. Bloomington: Indiana University Press, 1990.

Tolbert, Emory J. *The UNIA and Black Los Angeles: Ideology and Community in the American Garvey Movement*. Los Angeles: CAAS, 1980.

Trouillot, Michel-Rolph. *Silencing the Past: Power and the Production of History.* Boston: Beacon, 1995.

Turner, Frederick Jackson, "The Significance of the Frontier in American History" (1893). In *The Early Writings of Fredrick Jackson Turner*, ed. Everett E. Edwards, 183–229. Madison: University of Wisconsin Press, 1938.

Vickers, Lu, and Cynthia Wilson-Graham. *Remembering Paradise Park, Tourism and Segregation at Silver Springs.* Gainesville: University Press of Florida, 2015.

Vivian, Octavia B. *The Story of the Negro in Los Angeles County.* Washington DC: Federal Writers' Project of the Works Progress Administration, 1936.

Von Blum, Paul. "African American Visual Representation: From Repression to Resistance." *Journal of Pan African Studies* 5, no. 8 (2012): 41–51.

Walker, Lewis, and Ben C. Wilson. *Black Eden: The Idlewild Community.* East Lansing: Michigan State University Press, 2002.

Webb, Walter Prescott. "The American West: Perpetual Mirage." *Harper's*, May 1957, 25–31.

Weyeneth, Robert. "History, Memory, and Apology: The Power of Apology and the Process of Historical Reconciliation." *Public Historian* 23, no. 3 (Summer 2001): 9–38.

Wheeler, B. Gordon. *Black California: The History of African-Americans in the Golden State.* New York: Hippocrene, 1993.

White, Richard. *It's Your Misfortune and None of My Own: A History of the American West.* Norman: University of Oklahoma Press, 1991.

Widener, Daniel. *Black Arts West: Culture and Struggle in Postwar Los Angeles.* Durham NC: Duke University Press, 2010.

Wild, Mark. *Street Meetings: Multiethnic Neighborhoods in Early Twentieth-Century Los Angeles.* Berkeley: University of California Press, 2005.

Wilkerson, Isabel. *The Warmth of Other Suns: The Epic Story of America's Great Migration.* New York: Random House, 2010.

Willis, Deborah. *Posing Beauty: African American Images from the 1890s to Present.* New York: W. W. Norton, 2009.

Wiltse, Jeff. *Contested Waters: A Social History of Swimming Pools in America.* Chapel Hill: University of North Carolina Press, 2007.

Wolcott, Victoria W. *Race, Riots, and Roller Coasters: The Struggle over Segregated Recreation in America.* Philadelphia PA: University of Pennsylvania Press, 2013.

Wolf, Marvin J., and Katherine Mader. *Santa Monica: Jewel of the Sunset Bay.* Chatsworth CA: Windsor, 1989.

Youngken, Richard C. *African Americans in Newport: An Introduction to the Heritage of African Americans In Newport, Rhode Island, 1700–1945.* Newport RI: Rhode Island Historical Preservation and Heritage Commission and the Newport Historical Society, 1998.

Zimmerman, Dorothy Georgia. *The History of the Elsinore Region, Riverside County, California.* Master's thesis, University of Southern California, 1934.

INDEX

Illustrations are indicated by F *with a numeral*

CPSIA information can be obtained
at www.ICGtesting.com
Printed in the USA
LVHW110733170322
713683LV00002B/76